VISUAL QUICKSTART GUIDE

WINDOWS XP

Chris Fehily

 **Peachpit Press**

Visual QuickStart Guide
Windows XP
Chris Fehily

Peachpit Press
1249 Eighth Street
Berkeley, CA 94710
510/524-2178
800/283-9444
510/524-2221 (fax)
Find us on the World Wide Web at: http://www.peachpit.com
To report errors, please send a note to errata@peachpit.com
Peachpit Press is a division of Pearson Education

Copyright © 2003 by Chris Fehily
Editor: Kip Crosby
Production Coordinator: Hilal Sala
Copyeditor: Kathy Simpson
Compositor: Jerry Ballew
Illustrator: Jeff Tolbert
Indexer: Cheryl Lenser
Cover Production: Nathalie Valette
Cover Design: The Visual Group

ISBN 0-321-17407-0
9 8 7 6 5 4 3

Printed and bound in the United States of America

Dedication

For my brother, Peter.

Special thanks to...

Kip Crosby for his selective vigilance

Marjorie Baer, the Suggestionator

Kathy Simpson for her sense of restraint

Hilal Sala for using both columns

Nancy Aldrich-Ruenzel for valor

Liz and Don Field, image makers

Diane Yee for enduring

TABLE OF CONTENTS

Chapter 4   **Personalizing
Your Work Environment**   **83**

Chapter 5   **Organizing Files and Folders**   **139**

INTRODUCTION

Windows XP—for eXPerience—is the latest
Microsoft operating system for personal computers and the biggest overhaul of Windows
since Windows 95. Building on the solid
core of Microsoft's corporate operating system, Windows 2000, XP is meant for both
business and personal users. Compared with
earlier versions, it simplifies the Windows
environment, makes routine tasks quicker
and easier, and sports a host of new features.

What Windows XP Does

Windows XP—like every operating system, Microsoft or otherwise—is software that controls:

◆ **The user interface.** Windows manages the appearance, behavior, and interaction of the icons, folders, menus, and other visual elements on your computer screen, either directly or indirectly through another program.

◆ **Storage.** Windows allocates space for and gives access to files—programs and documents—stored on disk or in memory.

◆ **Other software.** Windows is a launching platform for applications. When you run a "Windows program" such as Microsoft Word or Adobe Photoshop, that program relies on the services and building blocks that Windows provides for basic operations such as drawing a user interface and saving files.

◆ **Peripheral devices.** Windows controls peripheral hardware, such as your mouse, keyboard, monitor, printer, and digital camera.

◆ **Networks and security.** Windows controls the interaction of a group of computers (and peripheral devices) connected by a communications link. Windows also protects your system and data from harm or loss.

◆ **System resources.** Windows handles the allocation and use of your computer's low-level hardware resources, such as memory and central processing unit (CPU) time.

◆ **Task scheduling.** Windows acts like a traffic cop, setting priorities and allocating time slices to the processes running on your PC.

The Two Versions of Windows XP

There are two main versions of Windows XP: *Home,* meant for individual, home, and home-office use; and *Professional,* which costs more but has extra features that make life easier for power users and network administrators (**Table i.1**). This book covers both. In general, they look and work alike, so most discussions apply to both editions equally.

- If you're interested in system administration and troubleshooting, consult an advanced text such as *Microsoft Windows XP Resource Kit Documentation* (Microsoft Press).

- Windows XP also has Server editions. These editions are intended to be used on high-end server platforms rather than on the desktops of end users, so they're not covered in this book.

✔ Tips

- **PRO** You'll see this symbol wherever I discuss a feature offered in Windows XP Professional edition but not in Home edition.

- To find out which edition of Windows XP you're running, choose Start > Control Panel > Performance and Maintenance > System > General tab.

Table i.1

Features Unique to XP Pro	
PRO FEATURE	**LETS YOU DO THIS**
Domain membership	Join a large group of networked computers that is administered as a unit.
Dynamic disks	Treat multiple hard disks as a single large disk.
Encrypting file system	Encrypt files and folders to keep them safe from intruders.
Internet Information Services	Host and manage simple Web sites.
Multilanguage support	Dynamically change the language used for input, spell checking, help files, user-interface elements, and other text.
Multiprocessor support	Automatically recognize and exploit systems with two processors.
Offline files	Make network files available offline by storing shared files on your laptop so that they're accessible when you're not connected to the network. Reconnecting to the network updates your changes to the network files.
Remote Desktop	Control a remote computer when you're at another computer—use your home computer to control your computer at work, for example.
Roaming user profiles	Have your personal settings and desktop appear on any networked computer you log on to (not just your personal PC).
User management	Define and enforce full disk-, folder-, and file-level security policies by user. (The Home edition has only two security levels and allows *all* users to use shared data.)

What's New in Windows XP

Windows XP sports a revamped, streamlined user interface that includes a redesigned Start menu and Control Panel, as well as many visual enhancements. If you're familiar with earlier versions of Windows, these are the aspects of Windows XP that you might find most notable.

Interface

Cleaner desktop. The default desktop (**Figure i.1**) is austere, with only one icon: Recycle Bin. You can add any other icons that you find useful or run the Desktop Cleanup Wizard to remove icons that you rarely use.

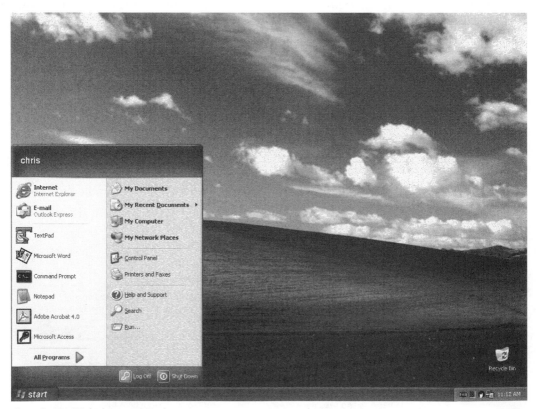

Figure i.1 The XP desktop and Start menu.

WHAT'S NEW IN WINDOWS XP

Figure i.2 The new Start menu centralizes command and control in two columns, not one.

Figure i.3 Control Panel's new Category view groups items by function.

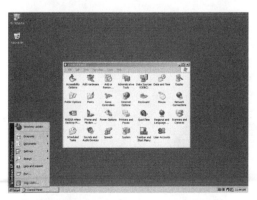

Figure i.4 Feeling nostalgic? Revert to the classic Windows interface.

Redesigned Start menu. The new Start menu (**Figure i.2**) has two columns: programs on the left, and features such as Help and Support, My Documents, and Control Panel on the right. You can let it manage itself or customize it to your liking.

Uncluttered taskbar. The Windows XP taskbar is dynamic. If buttons for open programs overflow the space, it redistributes them to hidden rows, which can be scrolled. If you have several documents open in the same program, button grouping lets you control all the documents with one button. Icons in the *notification area* (which used to be called the system tray and got awfully crowded) duck out of sight if you haven't used them recently.

Simplified theme selection. You can customize Windows XP's look by using *themes*— style-coordinated groups of controls and backgrounds. As before, you can change individual elements, such as colors, and save the edited theme under a new name.

Categorized Control Panel. Control Panel presents a new Category view (**Figure i.3**) that groups control applets by what they do. This view reduces clutter but makes you click through an extra layer to get where you're going. Veterans can choose Classic view to display all the applets individually.

Visual effects. Windows XP's graphical user interface adds animation, shadows, fades, slides, translucence, and other effects. You can turn these effects off if they distract you or make an older computer too slow.

Relive the past. Windows XP has vivid, softened 3D icons, windows, buttons, and colors, but you can restore the flat-faced, square-cornered look of Windows 2000/98/ Me (**Figure i.4**).

Files and folders

Windows XP lets you work with your files and folders more efficiently and makes it easier to organize your stuff—with a little practice.

Task pane. The new task pane (**Figure i.5**) provides shortcuts to related folders and locations; lets you perform common tasks easily; and displays details about the selection.

Compressed folders. Windows XP has built-in support for compressing folders in Zip and other formats, conserving disk space. Windows Explorer displays the contents of zipped folders just as it does normal folders.

PRO Offline files. You can store copies of your network files on your laptop's local disk and continue to work with them when you're disconnected from the network.

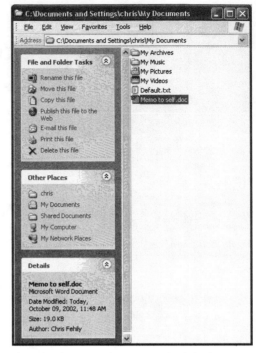

Figure i.5 The new task pane provides links that are relevant to the selection or current folder's contents.

Figure i.6 The new Windows Media Player plays and manages your digital music.

Figure i.7 Windows Messenger lets you chat online.

Digital media

Music, photos, and movies. A greatly improved Windows Media Player (**Figure i.6**) plays CDs and DVDs, copies files to portable music players, receives Internet radio, and helps you organize media files (see Chapter 10). The Scanner and Camera Wizard links your scanner or digital camera to your PC and its hard drive. Windows Movie Maker lets you transfer and edit recorded video from your analog camcorder or digital video camera.

CD burning. Windows Explorer and Windows Media Player now include the seamless capability to compile and create (*burn*) recordable CDs.

Internet and communications

Web and mail. The newest versions of Internet Explorer and Outlook Express are beefed up, with more attention to privacy and security.

Internet management. Windows XP's Internet Connection Firewall establishes a barrier between your machine or network and the outside world, with no need for third-party software. If you've set up a home or small-office network, you can use Internet Connection Sharing to let all the computers in that network share one connection.

Windows Messenger. Use Windows Messenger (**Figure i.7**) to see who's online, chat with instant messages, play games, send and receive files, and eat time like popcorn. See Chapter 15.

WHAT'S NEW IN WINDOWS XP

Stability

Protected memory. Windows XP prevents poorly written programs from invading or overwriting memory. An errant program may crash, but it won't bring down other programs or freeze your computer, as Windows 95/98/Me routinely would.

Windows File Protection. Windows File Protection keeps crucial system files safe from being overwritten by outdated or unstable versions. This feature is familiar to users of Windows 2000/NT but a vast improvement over the internal recklessness of 95/98/Me.

System Restore. System Restore (**Figure i.8**) records the state of your system both periodically and when you make changes such as installing programs or changing device drivers. If a change causes a severe system problem (such as inability to boot your computer), you can roll back to a previous state without losing your personal data. The Windows 2000 version of this feature, called Last Known Good, was hard to use correctly; System Restore is easier.

Networking and user accounts

Automated network configuration. Windows XP makes it easy—much easier than in previous versions—to set up your own network or join an existing one. The Network Setup Wizard walks you through a series of steps that automates the configuration of your Internet connection and local network settings. See Chapter 17.

Welcome screen. The Welcome screen lists the account of each authorized user. Each user can click his or her name, enter a password, and start a session with a personalized desktop and access to private files.

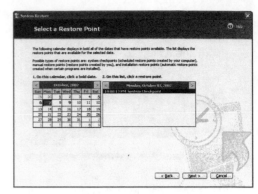

Figure i.8 System Restore restores your computer to a previous state without losing your personal files.

Fast User Switching. You can switch to another user account without actually logging off yourself—to, say, let someone check email—and then get back on quickly.

Security features. Windows XP is a secure multiuser OS. Password-protected user accounts and file and folder permissions let you share your computer while you protect your personal files and prevent unwelcome software installation or virus infection. (And you can't bypass logging on by pressing Esc, the way you could in Windows 9*x*.).

PRO **Remote Desktop.** Use your home computer to control your office computer (or vice versa) over a network or the Internet. You can control the remote computer as though you were sitting at it (**Figure i.9**). See Chapter 18.

Forgotten-password recovery. Use the Forgotten Password Wizard to recover (or change) a forgotten password and create a password reset disk. See "Setting up User Accounts" in Chapter 16.

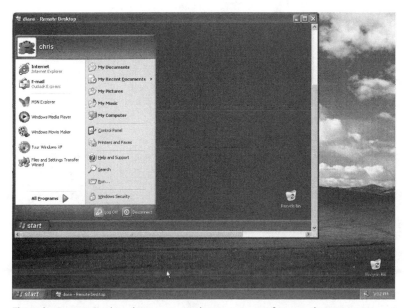

Figure i.9 Remote Desktop lets you control your computer from another computer.

Installation and update

Several new features make Windows XP easier to install and keep up to date, but some of them bind your computer more closely to Microsoft.

Product activation. Windows XP includes an invasive copy-protection scheme that prevents you from installing one copy of the OS on more than one machine at a time (**Figure i.10**). Bulk-purchased corporate copies of Windows XP are exempt from activation, and many new PCs come with a pre-activated copy. See "Activating Windows XP" in Appendix A.

Files and Settings Transfer Wizard. This wizard moves selected files and personal settings from your old PC to your new one, to streamline the process of configuring the new one. See "Transferring Existing Files and Settings" in Appendix A.

Device-driver library. The vast collection of drivers built into Windows XP increases the chance that a new Plug and Play device—say, a printer, scanner, or camera—will work out of the box.

Automatic updating. Windows Update uses your Internet connection periodically to deliver and install the latest Windows XP bug fixes, device drivers, and enhancements that are stored on Microsoft's Web site. You have some control over this process. See "Updating Windows XP" in Chapter 19.

Uninstall Windows XP. If you decide to scrap Windows XP after installation, you can revert to your previous Windows 98/Me installation. You *can't* roll back to a Windows NT/2000 installation, however. See "Uninstalling Windows XP" in Appendix A.

No more DOS. Windows XP, unlike Windows 95/98/Me, isn't stacked on top of rickety DOS. You can't boot into DOS directly, even by using a DOS boot floppy.

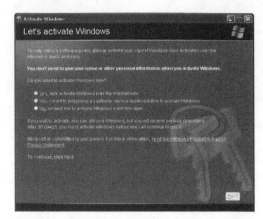

Figure i.10 Windows product activation is a controversial new "feature" designed to enforce Microsoft's licensing policies and forestall piracy.

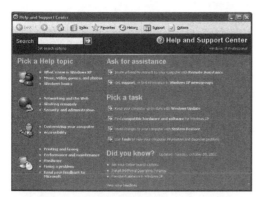

Figure i.11 Help and Support Center is a comprehensive source of local and online information about Windows XP.

Help and support

Windows XP offers more help—and more types of help—than its predecessors. You can use the expanded help system to search the help files stored on your disk or use it as a gateway to find help online.

Help and Support Center. Use online tutorials, tours, and troubleshooting guides to learn about Windows XP (**Figure i.11**). Use your Internet connection to search Microsoft's support Web site or participate in Windows newsgroups.

Remote Assistance. Get live help from a friend or colleague who can view your screen or even take control of your computer (**Figure i.12**).

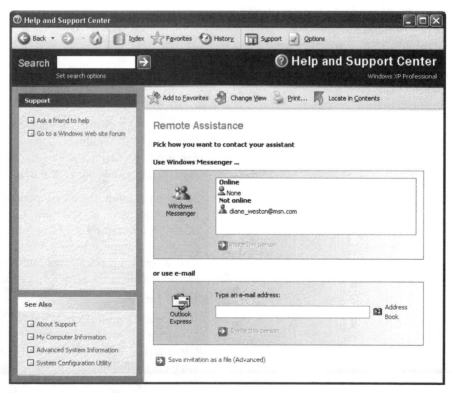

Figure i.12 Remote Assistance lets you invite someone you trust to view your screen or even work on your computer.

If You're Upgrading to Windows XP

If you're jumping to Windows XP from Windows 98/Me, the improvement you'll probably appreciate most is increased stability; the dreaded blue screens will be few and far between. There's more to like about Windows XP than simply crashing less often, however. To Windows 2000 users, Windows XP will appear to be only an incremental upgrade, but you'll still find plenty of new stuff.

As usual with Windows, the version upgrade is significantly less expensive than the full version. Therefore, it pays to know which versions of Windows entitle you to the upgrade (**Table i.2**).

You *may not* upgrade to XP from Windows 95 (see sidebar), Windows 3.1, Windows NT 3.51, *any* evaluation version, or *any* server version. If you want to upgrade from a server version, Microsoft says, you should be looking into Windows 2003 Server.

Table i.2

Upgrading from Earlier Windows Versions		
CURRENT VERSION	TO XP HOME	TO XP PRO
Windows 98/Windows 98 SE	✓	✓
Windows Me	✓	✓
Windows NT Workstation 4.0	✗	✓
Windows 2000 Professional	✗	✓
Windows XP Home Edition		✓
Windows XP Professional	✗	

A Note on Windows 95

Much as you might like to upgrade from Windows 95 to Windows XP, it's rarely realistic to do so. First of all, Microsoft says you're not eligible for the upgrade.

More to the point, the recommended system requirements for Windows XP are a 300 MHz processor, 128 MB of RAM, and 1.5 GB of disk space. Does your Windows 95 box—which probably was built in the spring of 1998 at the latest—have that to spare? Doubtful.

If you *must* upgrade from Windows 95 to Windows XP, you can do it by applying the upgrade to 98 or Me first and then applying the XP upgrade to that. Are you sure that you wouldn't just like to get a new computer?

Table i.3

Switching from Mac OS 8/9?	
MAC FEATURE	XP EQUIVALENT
Alias	Shortcut
Apple menu	Start menu
Application menu	Taskbar (or Alt+Tab)
Chooser (Network)	Start > My Computer > My Network Places
Chooser (Printers)	Start > Control Panel > Printers and Faxes
Command key	Ctrl key (usually)
Control Panel	Start > Control Panel
Drive (HD) icons	Start > My Computer
Eject Disk	Pushbutton on drive
Find	Start > Search
Finder	Desktop/Windows Explorer
Folders	Folders or directories
Force Quit (Command+Option+Esc)	Task Manager (Ctrl+Alt+Del)
Get Info	Right-click icon > Properties
Key Caps	Character Map
One-button mouse	Two-button mouse (left button for normal clicks, right button for a shortcut menu)
Option key	Alt key (usually)
Quit (Command+Q)	File > Exit (Alt+F4)
Restart	Start > Turn Off Computer
Sherlock	Start > Search
Shut Down	Start > Turn Off Computer
SimpleText	Notepad (or WordPad)
Trash	Recycle Bin

If You're Switching Over from a Macintosh

If you're a Mac user moving to Windows, don't worry—the disorientation won't last long. Many of the differences between Windows and Mac OS are superficial. To get started, look at **Table i.3** for a list of some analogous features between Mac OS 8/9 and Windows XP, based on the most common "Where is it?" questions from people who've made the switch. Some features aren't completely equivalent but are XP's closest approximations.

About This Book

I hope you'll find this book useful if you're new to Windows, if you're upgrading to XP from a previous version of Windows, or if you like having a quick reference at hand. It's meant primarily for beginning and intermediate users of Windows XP and gives abundant introductory information for those who are purchasing XP along with their first computers. Veteran Windows users can look up specific tasks quickly and will find plenty of tricks, shortcuts, and secret lore. Wherever possible, I give step-by-step instructions for using Windows XP features and programs.

If you're new to Windows, start with Chapters 1 and 2 to learn the basics of logging on, looking around, and making it work. (Upgraders will find useful information here too.) After that, I cover the material task by task, with plenty of screen shots.

✔ Tip

- Many of the tasks in this book require that you have an Administrator user account. If you're the only user, or if you installed Windows or maintain it, you're an administrator. Otherwise, see "Setting up User Accounts" in Chapter 16.

Conventions used in this book

Taking actions. I use a concise symbolic method to describe how to open a particular folder, program, or icon, rather than list the steps separately. Here's an example sequence for opening a nested folder:

◆ Choose Start > My Computer > Local Disk (C:) > Documents and Settings > All Users.

This step means: Click the Start menu (on the taskbar, in the bottom-left corner of the desktop); then click My Computer. Inside the window titled My Computer, double-click the icon labeled Local Disk (C:) to open it. Inside that window, double-click the icon Documents and Settings to open it. Inside *that* window, double-click the icon All Users to open it.

Each shorthand element (between the > symbols) refers to an icon, window, menu, button, dialog box, or some other user-interface component; just look for the component whose label matches the element name. Whenever a particular step is unclear or ambiguous, I spell it out rather than use shorthand.

Here's an example sequence for launching a program:

◆ Choose Start > Programs > Accessories > Notepad.

(continues on next page)

Using keys. Windows makes heavy use of the so-called *modifier keys,* which occupy the bottom corners of the keyboard's main section. These keys, Shift, Ctrl (Control), and Alt (Alternate), can be pressed together with other keys to modify the signal that they send to the computer. The C key pressed by itself produces a lowercase c; pressed along with the Shift key, it produces an uppercase C; and pressed along with the Ctrl key, it produces the Windows Copy command.

When I join a modifier to a key with a plus sign, as in Ctrl+C, it means "push down the Ctrl key, hold it down while you push down the C key, and then release both keys."

Windows has a few three-key combinations, such as Ctrl+Alt+Esc and Alt+Shift+Tab. In these cases, hold down the first *two* keys while you press the third one; then release all three. The modifiers are always listed before the key that performs the action.

The newer *Windows logo key,* between the Ctrl and Alt keys on some keyboards, pulls up the Start menu when used by itself; but it can also be used as a modifier, so that, for example, Windows logo key+D minimizes all running programs. When I give a Windows-logo-key shortcut, I usually add "(if your keyboard supports it)," because not all keyboards have such keys.

Corrections and comments

I welcome email to fehily@pacbell.net with questions, suggestions, corrections, and gripes related to this book.

GETTING STARTED WITH WINDOWS XP

When you first meet it, you might think that Windows XP is quite complicated—and you'd be right. But its interface is designed to let you unlock a lot of Windows' power with a relatively small amount of learning. The secret is to understand the underlying consistency of the ways that Windows works. As you use Windows XP, techniques like switching programs, sizing windows, drag-and-drop, and cut-and-paste will become as familiar to you as typing your own name.

This chapter and the next one get you up and running and introduce you to the fundamentals of Windows. Chapter 3 tells you how to get help with learning and configuring Windows, on or off the Internet. After that, you're on your way to making Windows your tireless servant and becoming an XP power user.

Logging on and Logging off Windows XP

Logging on is the process of starting a session in Windows XP—the first thing you do after turning on your computer. After your computer powers up—or *boots*—you'll see a screen in which you enter your user name and (optional) password. Windows XP creates *user accounts* to identify who has permission to use a particular computer (or network). User accounts are covered in Chapter 16, but for now, you need to know only your user name and password, which depend on your installation:

- If you upgraded to Windows XP from Windows 98/Me without a user profile, there is no password.

- If you did a clean install of Windows XP, you set up at least one account during installation. Enter the user name and password you set for that account.

- If your PC came with Windows XP preinstalled, the Welcome screen that appears after booting lists account names. Follow the manufacturer's instructions for logging on.

- If you upgraded to Windows XP from Windows 2000 or NT 4.0, or from Windows 98/Me with user profiles enabled, your existing accounts migrated to the new installation. See "Setting up User Accounts" in Chapter 16.

- If you're on a large network, ask your network administrator.

✔ Tip

- If you're the only user set up on your computer *and* you specified a blank password during setup, Windows bypasses the logon screen and boots to the desktop directly (see "Exploring the Windows Interface" later in this chapter).

Figure 1.1 The Welcome screen is the easiest way to log on to a computer that only a few people use.

Figure 1.2 The classic logon prompt usually displays the name of the previous user who logged on.

Figure 1.3 If you've set a password hint (see "Setting up User Accounts" in Chapter 16), you can click the ? button to display it.

Logging on

Logging on to a computer identifies you so that Windows XP can load your personal settings and grant you certain permissions. You have two ways to log on: the Welcome screen (**Figure 1.1**) and the classic logon prompt (**Figure 1.2**). If you're a home or small-business user, you'll probably log on via the Welcome screen. If you're on a large workplace network or using the classic prompt, see "Logging on to a Domain" in Chapters 16.

To use the Welcome screen:

1. Click your user name or picture.

2. If your account is password-protected, type your password in the Type Your Password box (**Figure 1.3**).

3. Press Enter or click the arrow button. Your personalized Windows desktop appears.

Switching users

Unlike previous versions of Windows, Windows XP lets more than one user be logged on at the same time, via *Fast User Switching*. If you step away from your computer for a short time, you can leave your programs running *and* let another user log on to, say, check email. When you log back on, Windows resumes your session where you left off.

Only one user at a time—the *active user*—actually can *use* the computer. Users who are logged on but not active—*disconnected users*—can keep their programs running and files open in the background. To switch users, Fast User Switching must be turned on (and it won't work in a few situations). See "Controlling the Logon Process" in Chapter 16.

LOGGING ON AND LOGGING OFF WINDOWS XP

To switch users without logging off:

1. Choose Start > Logoff.

2. Click Switch User (**Figure 1.4**).

3. In the Welcome screen, click another account name or picture; then log on normally.

To find out who else is logged on to your computer:

1. Right-click an empty space on the taskbar; then click Task Manager.

   or

   Press Ctrl+Shift+Esc.

2. Click the Users tab to view users and their status (**Figure 1.5**).

If your computer is running slowly, use Task Manager to see the programs that other logged-in users are running and how much memory they're chewing up. Task Manager lists filenames rather than program names; *winword.exe* appears instead of *Microsoft Word,* for example.

To find out which programs other users are running:

1. Right-click an empty space on the taskbar; then click Task Manager.

   or

   Press Ctrl+Shift+Esc.

2. Click the Processes tab.

3. Check Show Processes from All Users (**Figure 1.6**).

✔ Tips

- To identify the active user quickly, click Start and read the account name at the top of the Start menu.

- To log another user off, see "Logging off" later in this section.

Figure 1.4 Choose Switch User to keep all your work running in background memory while someone else uses the computer.

Figure 1.5 The Users tab is displayed only if Fast User Switching is enabled.

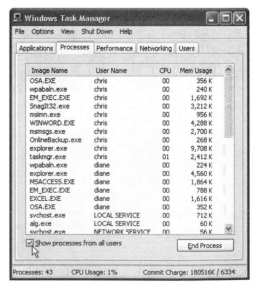

Figure 1.6 This list is sorted by user name. Click any column heading to sort by that column.

Figure 1.7 You get this limited dialog box if you choose Start > Log Off when Fast User Switching is turned off.

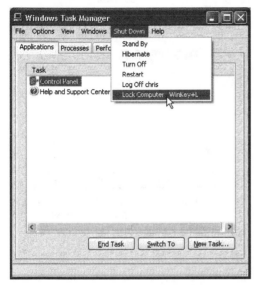

Figure 1.8 Your programs continue to run while your computer is locked.

- A faster way to switch users is to right-click a user name in the Task Manager Users tab and then choose Connect or Disconnect from the shortcut menu.

- If Fast User Switching is turned off, **Figure 1.7** appears instead of Figure 1.4.

- If Fast User Switching is turned on, press Windows logo key+L (if your keyboard supports it) to switch users.

Locking your computer

You can *lock* your computer—that is, set it so that the keyboard and mouse won't change anything—to protect your programs and personal information while you're away from your computer. Locking prevents everyone except you (or an administrator) from unlocking your system and viewing your files or programs.

To lock your computer:

◆ If the Welcome screen is turned on, press Ctrl+Shift+Esc; then choose Shut Down > Lock Computer (**Figure 1.8**).

or

If the Welcome screen is turned off, press Ctrl+Alt+Delete; then click Lock Computer.

Windows will display the Unlock Computer dialog box until you return.

To unlock your computer:

◆ In the Unlock Computer dialog box, type your password; then click OK.

✔ Tips

- If you have more than one user defined and Fast User Switching enabled, you can't lock the computer.

- If the Welcome screen is turned off, press Windows logo key+L (if your keyboard supports it) to lock your computer.

Logging off

Logging off ends your session in Windows XP. When you log off of your user account:

♦ Windows closes all your open programs and files. (Each program prompts you to save any unsaved work.)

♦ Windows terminates your dial-up connections.

♦ You prevent curious or malicious passersby from using your user account to access your files or network.

♦ Your computer remains turned on.

♦ Windows displays a screen to let the next person log on.

To log off:

1. Choose Start > Log Off (**Figure 1.9**).

2. Click Log Off.

If Fast User Switching is turned on, and other users are logged on to your machine, you can use Task Manager to log them off.

To log someone else off your computer:

1. Right-click an empty space on the taskbar; then click Task Manager.

   or

   Press Ctrl+Shift+Esc.

2. Click the Users tab to view users.

3. Select a user; then click Logoff.

   or

   Right-click a user; then choose Log Off from the shortcut menu (**Figure 1.10**).

4. Click Yes to end the user's session.

Figure 1.9 Logging off is an option in the Start menu.

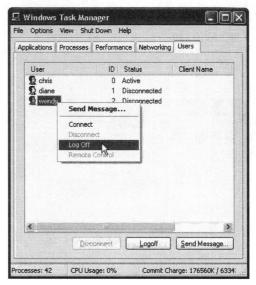

Figure 1.10 Logging other users off without warning is impolite, as it kills their programs without saving their unsaved work.

Figure 1.11 The Turn Off Computer screen contains four choices. The fourth one, Hibernate, is hidden until...

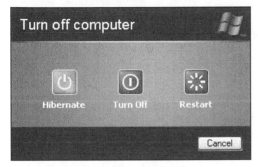

Figure 1.12 ...you hold down the Shift key to see it.

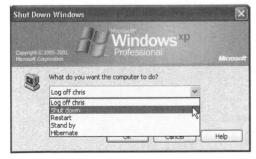

Figure 1.13 If the Welcome screen is turned off or you're a domain member, you'll see this screen instead of the one shown in Figure 1.11.

Turning off your computer

Turning off your computer requires more than flipping the power switch absently. Windows needs to prepare itself for shutdown; it saves session and system information, and disconnects external connections. If it can't go through this shutdown procedure, Windows may corrupt some of your files.

To turn off your computer:

1. Choose Start > Turn Off Computer.

2. In the Turn Off Computer dialog box (**Figures 1.11** through **1.13**), choose one of the options listed in **Table 1.1** (on next page).

✔ Tips

- To learn more about hibernate and standby, see "Conserving Power" in Chapter 4.

- Always save your work before putting your computer on standby. Standby saves your session in RAM (not on hard disk), so a power interruption will trash your session.

- Hibernate saves everything in memory on your hard disk. If you have a lot of RAM, you need a lot of free disk space to put your computer into hibernation.

- Hibernate's faster startup speed might tempt you to use it instead of Turn Off *all* the time. But use Turn Off occasionally to allow Windows to perform its background maintenance operations that require a clean startup. Also, Windows often needs a clean startup to detect newly installed hardware.

(continues on next page)

- If the desktop is active, you can press Alt+F4 to display the Turn Off Computer dialog box.

- If the Welcome screen is enabled, you can click Turn Off Computer in the bottom-left corner of the Welcome screen itself, or, if you're logged on, use Task Manager: Press Ctrl+Shift+Esc; then choose a command from the Shut Down menu.

Table 1.1

Shutdown Options	
OPTION	WHAT IT DOES
Turn Off	Ends your session and shuts down Windows so that you can turn off the power safely. Many computers turn off the power automatically; if yours doesn't, push the power button after the "It's safe" message appears. This option quits your programs, prompting you to save any unsaved work. Use Turn Off when you're done for the day or when you need to muck around inside your computer.
Restart	Ends your session, shuts down Windows, and starts Windows again automatically. This option quits your programs, prompting you to save any unsaved work. Use Restart if you've installed hardware or software that requires a restart, or if Windows is acting erratically or sluggishly.
Stand By	Turns off hard disks, fans, the CPU, and other hardware but draws just enough power to maintain your session (your open programs and any work that you're doing in them) in memory. Use Stand By to stop using your computer for a short time and save power (especially useful for laptops). In standby mode, your computer springs to life quickly—with your desktop exactly as you left it—when you use your mouse or keyboard, or press Ctrl+Alt+Delete.
Hibernate	Combines the safety of Turn Off with the convenience of Stand By. Hibernate saves your session to a file on your hard disk before turning off the power. When you restart the computer, your desktop is restored quickly and exactly as you left it. Older computers may not support this option.

Exploring the Windows Interface

Figure 1.14 shows the basic elements that you'll find on the Windows XP desktop. Microsoft modeled Windows on a real-world office environment: You have a desktop, on which you work and use tools, and folders, in which you organize files.

◆ **Desktop.** After you log on to Windows, the *desktop*—a work area that uses menus, icons, and windows to simulate the top of a desk—appears automatically.

◆ **Start menu.** The *Start menu* is the central menu that lets you access the most useful folders, programs, and commands on your computer. I cover the Start menu in Chapter 2.

(continues on next page)

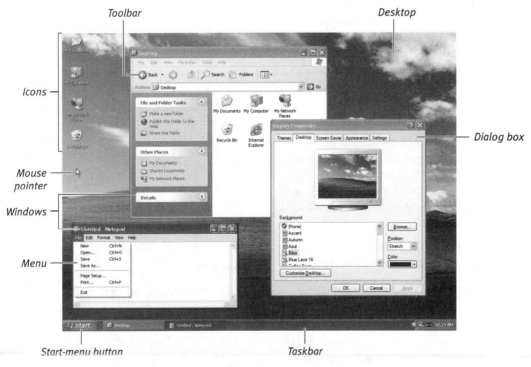

Toolbar   Desktop

Icons

Mouse pointer

Windows

Menu

Start-menu button   Taskbar

Dialog box

Figure 1.14 Basic elements of the Windows XP desktop. The desktop makes it easier to use the computer by letting you move items and manage your tasks in much the same way that you would on a physical desktop.

◆ **Taskbar.** The *taskbar* lets you switch between open programs and documents. It also lets you launch programs and alerts you to certain events, such as appointment reminders or incoming email. I cover the taskbar in Chapter 2.

◆ **Mouse pointer.** By using your mouse or a similar input device, such as a trackball or touchpad, you move the *mouse pointer* to select items or choose commands onscreen.

◆ **Menus.** A *menu* is a list of related commands. Most programs use menus to provide an easy-to-learn, easy-to-use alternative to memorizing instructions.

◆ **Toolbars.** A *toolbar* is a row, column, or block of buttons or icons. When you click one of these buttons or icons, the program carries out a command or task.

◆ **Icons.** An *icon* is a small image that represents an item ready to be opened (such as a file or folder) or launched (such as a program). An icon's picture is a visual cue designed to help you recall what the icon represents.

◆ **Windows.** A *window* is a rectangular portion of your screen where a program runs. You can open several windows at the same time. Windows can be resized, moved, closed, maximized to occupy the entire screen, or minimized to a button on the taskbar.

◆ **Dialog boxes.** A special type of window called a *dialog box* contains buttons, tabs, scrolling lists, or drop-down lists that let you set preferences or run commands. Some dialog boxes—such as Open, Save As, and Print—are much the same in every Windows program. Others, such as the Properties dialog box shown in Figure 1.14, depend on the program or context.

The User Interface

You work with Windows XP through its *graphical user interface,* which offers pictures along with words to help you perform tasks. To make learning easier, Windows displays visual clues about how things work. Often, these clues are analogous to those you'll see in the real world. If a door has a flat plate rather than a handle to grasp, it's a clue to push that door, not pull it. The 3D look of buttons on your screen implies that you're supposed to push them (click them). You'll recognize similar hints throughout the user interface.

This chapter and the next introduce you to the standard elements that you'll see when you use Windows and explain why you need to know about them. (Experienced Windows users, feel free to skip or skim these chapters; you won't find much new here.)

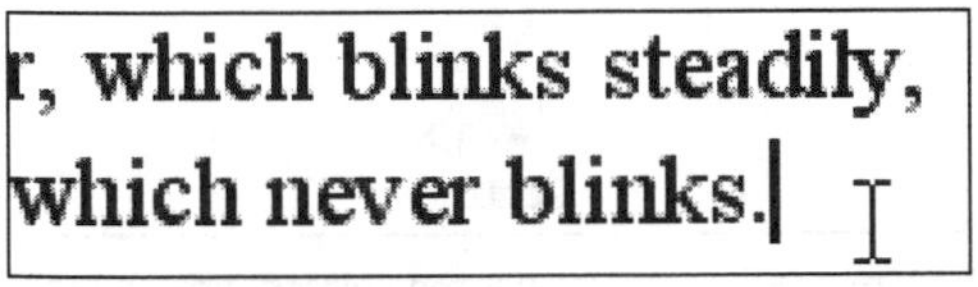

r, which blinks steadily,
which never blinks.|

Figure 1.15 The cursor—the vertical bar at the end of the text—marks the insertion point for newly typed text. To move the insertion point, click the mouse pointer—the I-beam on the right—at a new insertion point, or use the arrow keys.

Table 1.2

Mouse Pointers

SHAPE	WHEN IT APPEARS
⍩	The normal pointer. Click the area or item that you want to work with.
⍩?	Appears when you click the question mark (?) in the top-right corner of a dialog box. Click any dialog-box item to get "What's This?" help.
⍩⌛	Windows XP is doing something in the background—opening or saving a temporary file, for example. You can keep doing your own work, but XP's response time may be longer than usual.
⌛	Windows is busy with a task and will ignore you until it finishes. (Typically, this pointer will appear in only one program at a time; if it appears everywhere, your computer is *really* busy.)
 ↕ ↔ ↖	Appears when you point to a window's border (side or corner). Drag the border to resize the window. See "Windows" later in this chapter.
⍟	Appears when you point to a word or image linked to a help text, command, or Web site. Click the link to jump to a related destination or display pop-up information.
⊘	The action that you're trying to perform is forbidden, or the item that you're pointing at is unavailable.
I	The *I-beam* or *I-bar* appears where you can select or edit text. Click to set the insertion point, or click and hold to select (or *highlight*) text.
+	Helps you move an item precisely. This pointer appears primarily in drawing programs.
⊕	Appears when you choose Move or Size from a window's control menu. While it does, use the arrow keys to move or resize the window and then press Enter, or press Esc to cancel. See "Windows" later in this chapter.

The Mouse

The mouse is one of two primary input devices in Windows—the other, of course, being the keyboard. Moving the mouse on your physical desk controls the motion of the mouse pointer on your screen. By moving the mouse pointer over an icon, control, or option and then clicking, you can select an item, open or move a file, run a program, or throw something away, for example.

A mouse has a left and a right button. You'll use the left button for most actions, but skillful use of the right button is a key to working quickly.

✔ Tips

- Some mice have more than two buttons or a scroll wheel (a small wheel between the two main buttons) that you can program by following the instructions that came with the mouse.

- Instead of a mouse, you may have a touchpad (used on many laptops), trackball, or stylus.

- Lefties can swap the functions of the left and right mouse buttons. See "Configuring the Mouse" in Chapter 4.

- The pointer's shape changes depending on what it's pointing to. **Table 1.2** shows the default pointers that you'll encounter in Windows XP. To change the shapes, see "Configuring the Mouse" in Chapter 4.

- Don't confuse the cursor, which blinks steadily, with the mouse pointer, which never blinks. The *cursor* (also called the *insertion point*) indicates where text will be inserted when you type (**Figure 1.15**).

To point:

◆ Move the tip of the pointer over the item to which you want to point (**Figure 1.16**).

To click:

◆ Point to an item; then press and release the left mouse button without moving the mouse (**Figures 1.17** and **1.18**).

To double-click:

◆ Point to an item, and click the left mouse button twice in rapid succession without moving the mouse.

✔ Tip

■ If you double-click too slowly, Windows interprets your action as two single clicks, which isn't the same thing. To change the speed of what Windows recognizes as a double-click, see "Configuring the Mouse" in Chapter 4.

To right-click:

◆ Point to an item; then click the *right* mouse button without moving the mouse (**Figure 1.19**).

To drag:

◆ Point to an item; press *and hold* the left mouse button while you move the pointer to a new location; then release the button. (**Figure 1.20**)

✔ Tips

■ Drag an object with the *right* mouse button to display a shortcut menu when you reach the new location.

■ Press Esc during a drag to cancel it.

■ Drag in a folder window or on the desktop to draw a rectangular *marquee* around icons. Releasing the mouse button selects, or *highlights,* the enclosed icons.

■ To highlight text, drag through the text. You can highlight from the beginning to the end of the text or vice versa.

Figure 1.16 One tiny pixel is the pointer's hot spot that you use to point precisely. For an arrow pointer, it's the tip of the arrow. In some of Microsoft's wilder alternative pointer schemes, finding the hot spot may take a little work.

Figure 1.17 Click to select an icon...

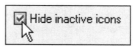

Figure 1.18 ...or activate a dialog-box item.

Figure 1.19 Right-click an item to display its shortcut menu.

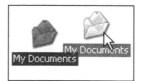

Figure 1.20 Drag to move items such as icons and folders. What this action actually accomplishes depends slightly on context.

Table 1.3

Modifier Keys

KEY	PRESS TO
Shift	Type symbols or uppercase letters, or extend the selection when used with the mouse.
Ctrl	Modify the function of other keys. (Ctrl stands for Control.)
Alt	Access menus or modify the function of other keys. (Alt stands for Alternate.)

Table 1.4

Navigation Keys

KEY	PRESS TO
Home	Scroll to the beginning.
End	Scroll to the end.
Page Up	Scroll up one page.
Page Down	Scroll down one page.
Arrow keys	Scroll in that direction or change the insertion point.

The Keyboard

The keyboard isn't just for typing text. Many experienced Windows users use the keyboard instead of the mouse to issue commands. Windows provides hundreds of *keyboard shortcuts* that replicate almost every common mouse maneuver. You can use keyboard shortcuts to open, close, and navigate the Start menu, desktop, menus, windows, dialog boxes, and Web pages.

In addition to keys for letters, numbers, and symbols, your keyboard has other types of keys:

◆ **Modifier keys** alter the meaning of the other key(s) being pressed (**Table 1.3**).

◆ **Function keys** are the keys along the keyboard's top or left side labeled F1, F2, and so on. Their function depends on the program that you're using.

◆ **Navigation keys** scroll windows and move things around (**Table 1.4**).

To use a keyboard shortcut:

1. Hold down the modifier key(s) Shift, Ctrl, or Alt.

2. Press the given letter, number, symbol, or function key.

3. Release all the keys.

✔ Tips

■ Typing a keyboard shortcut often is much faster than moving the mouse to do the same thing.

■ For a complete list of Windows XP keyboard shortcuts, search for *keyboard shortcuts* in Help and Support Center. See Chapter 3.

(continues on next page)

THE KEYBOARD

- Alt behaves a little differently from Shift and Ctrl. Shift or Ctrl does nothing when pressed by itself, but Alt pressed by itself activates the menu bar. (If you press Alt accidentally, press Alt again to get back to normal.)

- Newer keyboards contain extra Windows keys on either side of the spacebar: the Windows logo key and the Application key, which looks like a tiny menu with an arrow pointing to it. Press the Application key to display the shortcut (or right-click) menu for the selected item. The Windows logo key can be used alone to open the Start menu or combined with letters to provide shortcuts, which I discuss where they're most appropriate.

- Some keyboard shortcuts are consistent across all programs (F1 for help and Ctrl+C to copy, for example), but programs can define custom keyboard shortcuts.

- Some keyboard shortcuts may not work if StickyKeys is turned on in Accessibility Options. See "Accommodating Disabled Users" in Chapter 4.

To Shift-click:

♦ Hold down Shift; then click before releasing the key.

To Shift-drag:

♦ Hold down Shift; then drag-and-drop before releasing the key.

✔ Tip

- There are also *Ctrl-click, Alt-click, Ctrl-drag,* and *Alt-drag* commands in Windows, especially for file operations.

The Esc Key

The Esc (for *Escape*) key in the top-left corner of your keyboard may become one of your favorites. In most cases, it means either *never mind* or *stop what you're doing*. Press it to cancel commands, interrupt long processes, cancel dialog boxes, close menus, and dismiss message boxes. Sometimes, Esc does nothing; its exact function depends on the context and the active program.

Menus

Windows uses menus to list commands in groups (**Figure 1.21**). Menus are particularly convenient when you're new to a program, because they show you what commands are available and make experimenting easy.

Experienced users prefer to use keys instead of the mouse to choose menu commands. Programs often provide a keyboard shortcut for a frequently used command, which will appear to the right of the command on its menu line. To choose Copy, for example, press Ctrl+C. If no shortcut key is listed for the command, you can use Alt+ the menu's underlined letters instead.

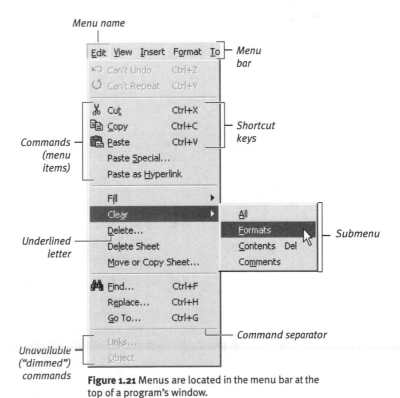

Figure 1.21 Menus are located in the menu bar at the top of a program's window.

✔ Tips

- Commands with a triangular arrowhead next to them have additional choices listed in a *submenu*. To open a submenu, click or point to the command.

- Checked commands (**Figure 1.22**) represent on/off options or mutually exclusive choices.

- Dimmed commands are unavailable in the current context.

- Within individual menus, commands are grouped logically by horizontal lines called *command separators*.

- Some menus are consistent across programs. The File menu almost always includes the New, Open, Save, Print, and Exit commands; the Edit menu has the Undo, Cut, Copy, and Paste commands.

Figure 1.22 A checked command indicates an option that is turned on or selected.

To choose a menu command:

1. Click the menu name. The menu appears, displaying its commands.

2. Point to the desired menu command.

3. Click to choose the command. The menu disappears.

To choose a menu command with the keyboard:

1. Hold down Alt; press the underlined letter in the menu name; then release both keys.

2. On the keyboard, press the underlined letter of a menu command.

✔ Tips

- Another way to use the keyboard: Press F10 or Alt (by itself) to activate the menu bar; use the arrow keys to navigate to a command; then press Enter.

- To close a menu without choosing a command, press Esc twice (or click outside the menu).

- Menu letters may not be underlined until you hold down Alt. To change this setting, choose Start > Control Panel > Appearance and Themes > Display > Appearance tab > Effects button > Hide Underlined Letters check box.

Figure 1.23 The right mouse button's shortcut menus offer common commands quickly. Here are the shortcut menus of Explorer, the Recycle Bin, and My Computer.

Shortcut menus

A *shortcut menu* is a context-sensitive menu that appears when you right-click an item (**Figure 1.23**). Windows provides shortcut menus for nearly all interface elements: files, folders, disks, the taskbar, the Start button, the Recycle Bin, and so on. Try right-clicking any item to see whether a shortcut menu pops up.

You can use the keyboard to choose a command from a shortcut menu as you do from a normal menu.

✔ Tips

- Shortcut-menu commands apply only to the item (or group of items) to which you point.

- Applications provide special shortcut menus for contexts. Right-click a link in Internet Explorer or selected text in Notepad, for example.

- Right-clicking a taskbar button or a title bar displays the control menu (sizing menu) for that program's window. See "Windows" later in this chapter.

MENUS

To choose a shortcut-menu command:

1. Right-click an item.

The shortcut menu appears, displaying its commands.

2. Point to the desired menu command.

3. Click to choose the command.

The menu disappears.

To choose a shortcut-menu command with the keyboard:

1. Select (highlight) an item.

2. Hold down Shift; press F10; then release both keys.

3. Press the underlined letter of a menu command.

✔ Tips

■ If you have a special Windows keyboard, press the Application key (which looks like a tiny menu with an arrow pointing to it) to display the shortcut menu for the selected item.

■ To close a shortcut menu without choosing a command, press Esc or left-click outside the menu. (Right-clicking outside the menu makes the menu jump to the pointer.)

MENUS

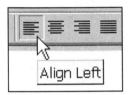

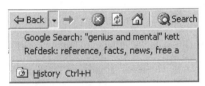

Figure 1.24 Toolbars from Windows Explorer (top) and WordPad (middle). The bottom toolbar shows Microsoft's standard icons, which many programs adopt for consistency. Left to right: New, Open, Save, Print, Print Preview, Spell Check, Cut, Copy, Paste, Copy Format, Undo, and Redo.

Figure 1.25 A typical word processing tool tip.

Figure 1.26 Internet Explorer's toolbar drop menu gives you quick access to sites you've visited recently.

Figure 1.27 Toggle buttons stay pressed—like these buttons for Italic and Left Align—until clicked a second time.

Toolbars

A *toolbar* is a row, column, or block of buttons with icons that you click to perform some action, choose a tool, or change a setting (**Figure 1.24**). Toolbar buttons often duplicate functions that are accessible through menus, but they're convenient because they're always visible—generally, at one edge of the work area. Programs typically have several toolbars, each responsible for a group of tasks. In a word processor, for example, there's a toolbar for formatting text and paragraphs and another for performing file operations.

✔ Tips

- Many programs display *tool tips*—short descriptions of toolbar buttons and icons when the mouse pointer pauses on them (**Figure 1.25**).

- A toolbar button with a small triangular arrow pointing to the right or down will reveal its own small, self-contained menu when clicked (**Figure 1.26**).

- Often, you can customize toolbars, create new ones, and move them around on the screen to suit your preferences. Experiment. Right-click a toolbar to see whether a shortcut menu appears. Click an empty area of a toolbar (usually, the left end of it); then try dragging to dock it at an edge of the window, or just let it float in the middle.

- Some toolbars have *toggle buttons* that push in (turn on) with one click and pop out (turn off) with the next. They set conditions for a highlighted section of what you're working on, such as character formatting in a word processor (**Figure 1.27**).

- Toolbars may appear and disappear automatically, depending on what you're doing in the program.

TOOLBARS

Icons

An *icon* is a small picture that represents an item you can manipulate. Windows uses icons on the desktop and in Windows Explorer to represent folders, files, disks, programs, the Recycle Bin, and hardware devices (**Figure 1.28**).

You select (highlight) an icon or group of icons to perform an action on it. Left-click to select; right-click to open the (very useful) shortcut menu.

What happens when you open an icon depends on the icon's type. A *folder* or *disk* icon opens in Windows Explorer. A *document* or *image* icon opens in its associated program, launching that program if it's not already open. A *program* icon launches the program. The *Recycle Bin* icon displays the items to be deleted when you empty the bin.

To select an icon:

◆ Click it (**Figure 1.29**).

or

Press the arrow keys until the icon is selected.

or

Press the first letter of the icon's name. If more than one icon has the same initial, press the letter again until you select the right icon.

✔ Tips

■ Selecting an icon deselects any other selected icons.

■ You can configure Windows to select an icon just by pointing at it. See "Using Alternative Mouse Behavior" in Chapter 4.

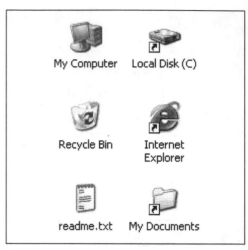

Figure 1.28 An icon's image depends on what it represents. System objects, such as the Recycle Bin and My Computer, have default images. All documents of the same type—.txt files, for example—have the same icon. Programs (.exe files), such as Internet Explorer, have icons created for and incorporated into the program.

Figure 1.29 Click an icon to select it.

Figure 1.30 Ctrl-click to select multiple (nonconsecutive) icons. This window shows icons in Details view.

Figure 1.31 You can drag across icons diagonally (rubberband) to create a marquee selection. Icons within the rectangle darken to confirm that they're selected.

To select multiple icons:

◆ Ctrl-click each icon that you want to select (**Figure 1.30**).

or

Drag a selection rectangle (rubberband) around the icons (**Figure 1.31**). It's always a rectangle; you can't surround an odd-shaped area.

or

Click the first icon that you want to select; then Shift-click the last icon. All icons in between are selected automatically—at least by Windows' definition of "in between."

✔ Tip

■ In Windows Explorer, it's easiest to work with multiple icons in Details view, in which all icons appear in a single column. To use Details view, choose View > Details. See "Viewing Files and Folders in Different Ways" in Chapter 5.

To select all icons in a window:

◆ Choose Edit > Select All.

or

Press Ctrl+A.

To deselect an icon:

◆ If the icon is the only one selected, click anywhere in the window or desktop other than the selected icon.

or

If the icon is part of a multiple selection, Ctrl-click it to remove it from the selection.

✔ Tips

■ To select *almost* all the icons in a window, press Ctrl+A; then Ctrl-click the icons you *don't* want.

■ Choose Edit > Invert Selection to reverse which icons are selected and which are not.

ICONS

To move an icon:

◆ Drag it to a new position (**Figures 1.32** and **1.33**).

✔ Tips

■ Icon position within a window is controlled by settings in View > Arrange Icons By.

■ You can drag icons to new positions within windows set to Thumbnails, Tiles, or Icons view but not within windows set to List or Details view.

■ You can move multiple icons at the same time.

To open an icon:

◆ Double-click it.

or

Select it; then press Enter or choose File > Open.

✔ Tips

■ To open *multiple* icons at the same time, select the icons; then press Enter or choose File > Open.

■ To open a document or image with anything besides the associated (default) program, right-click its icon; then choose File > Open With > Choose Program.

■ You can configure Windows to open an icon with a single click. See "Using Alternative Mouse Behavior" in Chapter 4.

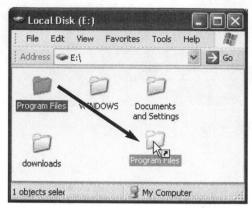

Figure 1.32 Drag-and-drop an icon to move it to...

Figure 1.33 ...a new position in the window (or on the desktop).

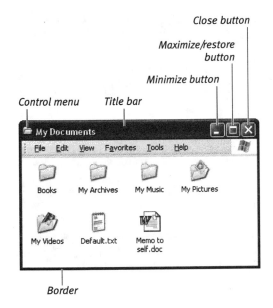

Close button

Maximize/restore button

Minimize button

Control menu   Title bar

Border

Figure 1.34 Your basic window.

Windows

The Windows interface takes its trademark name from the rectangles on your screen—the windows—in which you work. **Figure 1.34** shows a typical window with its parts labeled. When you work with Windows XP, you'll probably have multiple (overlapping) windows open at the same time so that you can, say, alternate working with a word processor, email program, and Web browser.

You can identify a window by its *title bar*, which lists the name of the program, file, or folder. Each window has its own boundaries and can present a different view of a folder, document, or program. To manage multiple windows, you need to learn a few basic skills.

✔ Tips

■ The windows that you actually work with often are crowded with other items, such as menus, toolbars, status bars, and task panes. You can close or turn off these options when you don't need them.

■ Windows don't *have* to be rectangular. See "Windows Media Player" in Chapter 10.

Activating a window

If you have multiple windows open, only one window is active at any time. The *active window* is the one that receives your keystrokes (text entry, navigational movements, or commands). You can identify the active window by its dark-blue title bar; inactive window title bars are a washed-out blue (**Figure 1.35**). (To change these colors, see "Choosing a Desktop Theme" in Chapter 4.) An inactive window can be hidden partially or entirely behind another window, where it remains inactive until you bring it to the foreground.

To activate a window:

◆ Click anywhere on the window (but don't click a button or menu, lest you activate it accidentally).

or

Click the window's taskbar icon.

or

While holding down Alt, press Esc repeatedly until the desired window appears; then release both keys.

or

While holding down Alt, press Tab repeatedly until the desired program icon is highlighted in the pop-up selection bar; then release both keys.

✔ Tips

■ Programs whose windows are inactive can still carry out tasks—called *background tasks*—such as downloading files or printing documents. *Inactive* means that *you* are ignoring the window, but Windows XP still gives it the resources to do its job.

Figure 1.35 You can tell which window is active by looking for the darker color of the title bar—the center one, in this case.

■ Generally, the active window is in front of all other windows. But some windows, such as Task Manager and Help, can be set to stay on top—in the foreground—even when inactive.

■ Alt+Esc and Alt+Tab don't produce identical results. For details, see "Switching Programs" in Chapter 6.

Figure 1.36 A maximized window reduces the need for scrolling but hides other windows. When a window is maximized, its Maximize button changes to the Restore button.

Figure 1.37 A minimized window reduces screen clutter and reveals other windows lurking in the background.

Figure 1.38 You can resize or move a restored window to work with multiple windows conveniently. When a window is restored, its Restore button changes to the Maximize button.

Figure 1.39 Right-clicking a taskbar icon displays its control menu.

Resizing, moving, and closing windows

You can *maximize* a window to the size of your whole screen (**Figure 1.36**), *minimize* a window to a button on the taskbar (**Figure 1.37**), or *restore* a window to a free-floating rectangle on your screen (**Figure 1.38**). To adjust the size of a restored window, drag its corners or edges.

To resize a window:

◆ Drag any window border (side or corner). The pointer changes to a double-headed arrow when it's moved over a border. See "The Mouse" earlier in this chapter.

or

Press Alt+spacebar; press S; use the arrow keys to resize the window; then press Enter.

To maximize a window:

◆ If the window is minimized, right-click its taskbar button; then choose Maximize (**Figure 1.39**).

or

If the window is restored, click its Maximize button (▢) or double-click its title bar.

or

If the window is restored, press Alt+spacebar; then press X.

To minimize a window:

◆ Click its Minimize button (▬).

or

Press Alt+spacebar; then press N.

To restore a window:

◆ Right-click its taskbar button; then choose Restore.

or

If the window is maximized, click its Restore button () or double-click its title bar.

or

If the window is maximized, press Alt+spacebar; then press R.

Figure 1.40 The title bar provides convenient ways to move and resize a window: Drag it to move the window, or double-click it to alternate between restored and maximized states.

✔ Tips

■ If you use Alt+spacebar+(letter) to maximize or restore a window, that window remains selected; if you minimize it, it doesn't.

■ You can resize only restored windows, not maximized or minimized windows.

■ Many windows have resize handles in the bottom-right corner; these handles are ridged and easy to grab.

■ To arrange multiple (restored) windows neatly on your desktop, see "Managing Windows with the Taskbar" in Chapter 2.

■ Some utility programs, such as Calculator, can't be maximized or resized.

To move a window:

◆ Drag its title bar (**Figure 1.40**).

or

Press Alt+spacebar; press M; use the arrow keys to move the window; then press Enter.

✔ Tips

■ You can move only restored windows, not maximized or minimized windows.

■ You can move a window so that a portion of it lies off the screen's edge.

WINDOWS

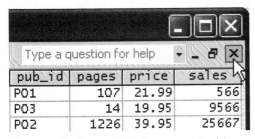

pub_id	pages	price	sales
PO1	107	21.99	566
PO3	14	19.95	9566
PO2	1226	39.95	25667

Figure 1.41 If a document window is maximized, its window controls appear directly below the program's window controls.

To close a window:

◆ Click its Close button ( ).

or

Right-click its taskbar button; then click Close.

or

Double-click the icon at the far-left end of the title bar.

or

Press Alt+F4.

or

Press Alt+spacebar; then press C.

or

Choose File > Close to close the file or File > Exit to leave the application, whichever is appropriate. (This distinction between Close and Exit isn't consistent across all programs, unfortunately.)

If you choose Close or Exit and haven't saved your work, you'll be reminded to save the file.

✔ Tips

■ In Windows Explorer, Internet Explorer, and some other programs, closing a window quits the program entirely.

■ The desktop itself is a window open under all other windows; you "close" it by logging off or shutting down.

■ Many applications, such as Word or Excel, let you have more than one file window open at the same time. Each file window has a title bar and dedicated controls, letting you work in it without affecting other windows (**Figure 1.41**).

WINDOWS

Scrolling

If a window is too small to display all its contents, scroll bars appear. A *scroll bar* is a vertical or horizontal bar at the side or bottom of a window that you can move with the mouse to slide that window's contents around.

A scroll bar has four active areas: *scroll arrows* at its ends for moving incrementally, a sliding *scroll box* for moving to an arbitrary location, and the scroll-bar *background* for jumping by one windowful at a time (**Figure 1.42**).

To scroll a window's contents:

◆ To scroll up or down line by line, click the up or down scroll arrow.

or

To scroll left or right incrementally, click the left or right scroll arrow.

or

To scroll left or right by a windowful, click the gray area to the left or right of the horizontal scroll box.

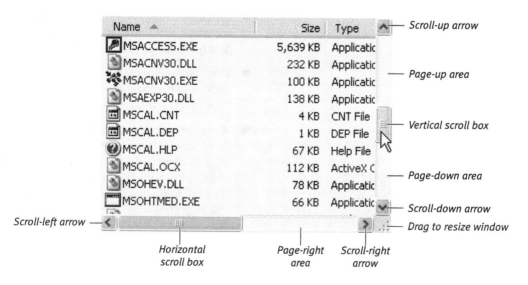

Figure 1.42 The size of a scroll box is proportional to fraction of the file's total area displayed, so the scroll box indicates visually how much you *can't* see, as well as showing you where you are.

or

To scroll up or down incrementally, press an arrow key. (But if you scroll by leaning on an arrow key for more than a few seconds, Windows can lose track of video memory, and lines of text can be doubled or sliced in half. Recover by pressing Page Up or Page Down.)

or

To scroll up or down by screenfuls (or sometimes less), click the gray area above or below the vertical scroll box, or press Page Up or Page Down.

or

To move to an arbitrary location, drag a scroll box to the place you want. (This makes the most sense if the program is smart enough to show the scrolling text while you drag, so you know when to stop. Older programs don't refresh the text box till you stop dragging, which makes you fly blind.)

✔ Tips

- If your mouse has a little rubber tire between its buttons, called a *scroll wheel,* you can often scroll up or down by turning it.

- In many programs, you can press Ctrl+Home and Ctrl+End to go to a document's beginning or end. If yours won't, the fastest way to scroll is to drag the scroll box to the top or bottom of the scroll bar.

Dialog Boxes

Dialog boxes are Windows' primary way of letting you enter new information or view or change settings. A dialog box is a small temporary window that a program displays to respond to a command or event (**Figure 1.43**).

OK, Cancel, Apply

In dialog boxes, the OK, Cancel, and Apply buttons work this way:

OK. Saves your changes and closes the dialog box (often equivalent to pressing Enter).

Cancel. Discards changes and closes the dialog box (equivalent to pressing Esc).

Apply. Saves your changes and leaves the dialog box open; handy if you want to try a change to your system and possibly change it right back.

If you click Apply and then click Cancel, changes made *before* you click Apply are saved, but changes made *after* you click Apply are lost—usually, that is. Some programs behave differently.

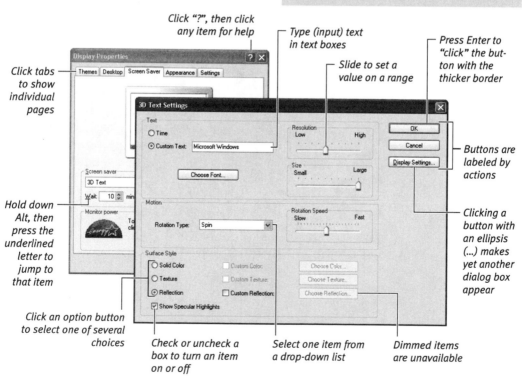

Figure 1.43 Dialog boxes let you change settings by using buttons, check boxes, text boxes, and other controls.

DIALOG BOXES

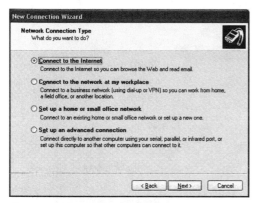

Figure 1.44 Use the Back and Next buttons to step through a wizard. You can always cancel out of a wizard if you want to make your settings manually.

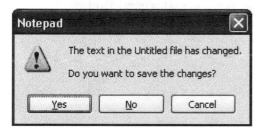

Figure 1.45 Message boxes bring your program to a halt. You must respond before the program can do anything further.

There are a few differences between dialog boxes and normal windows:

◆ File Open and File Save dialog boxes usually are resizable, to let you vary the number of files that they display. Most other dialog boxes aren't resizable.

◆ Some open dialog boxes won't let you keep working in their program until you close them. You can still use other programs, although you may need to switch to them with a keystroke, such as Alt+Tab.

◆ While you edit text in a dialog box, you can't use the Edit menu to cut, copy, and paste, but you can use keyboard shortcuts (Ctrl+X, Ctrl+C, and Ctrl+V) or right-click to use a shortcut menu.

◆ Using keyboard shortcuts to navigate dialog boxes is often faster than using the mouse (**Table 1.5**).

◆ A *wizard* is a series of interactive dialog boxes that guides you through the steps of a complex task to speed it up (**Figure 1.44**).

◆ Windows uses a *message box* to notify you of events or ask for a decision (**Figure 1.45**).

Table 1.5

Dialog-Box Keyboard Shortcuts	
PRESS	TO
Tab	Select (highlight) the next item.
Shift+Tab	Select (highlight) the previous item.
Alt+underlined letter	Jump to (highlight) the corresponding item.
Spacebar	Click a button, toggle a check box, or select an option button (if that item is highlighted).
Enter	Click the selected button (with the dotted outline) or the default button (with the shadow).
Esc	Click the Cancel button.

DIALOG BOXES

Properties

Almost every object in Windows has a Properties dialog box—usually accessed via its shortcut menu—full of compact, dense information about its contents and settings. Items or groups with properties include files, folders, disks, programs, hardware devices, the taskbar, the Start menu, and My Computer.

To display an item's properties:

◆ Right-click the item; then choose Properties (**Figure 1.46**).

   or

   Select (highlight) the item; then press Alt+Enter.

   or

   Hold down Alt; then double-click the item.

Figure 1.47 shows Properties dialog boxes for a Word file and a hard disk. Windows lets you change some properties; you can rename the file or compress the hard disk. Many properties, however, are *read-only,* meaning that Windows sets them, and you can't modify them. You can inspect—but not change—a hard disk's capacity or a file's creation date, for example.

Figure 1.46 You can choose an item's properties from its shortcut (right-click) menu.

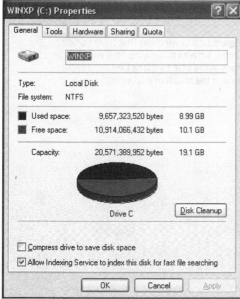

Figure 1.47 The properties information you see is appropriate to the item you select. Here are properties for a Word document (top) and a hard disk (bottom).

✔ Tips

■ Read-only properties usually are shown as black text on a colored background; modifiable properties are set in a rectangular white field. If it's not obvious whether you can change a property, try to click it or tab to it.

■ Some dialog boxes have a button labeled Restore, Restore Defaults, Defaults, or Reset. Clicking this button changes your current settings back to Windows XP's factory-installed settings. Be careful, because you (or the programs you've installed) have probably made more changes than you remember—or even know about.

■ Some programs let you add file properties, such as comments. In the Properties dialog box of a Microsoft Word file, for example, click the Custom tab (or choose File > Properties inside Word itself).

■ To see how much disk space a group of files or folders occupies, select their icons; then display the properties for the selected group.

PROPERTIES

Cutting, Copying, and Pasting

Windows' cut-and-paste and copy-and-paste operations are useful for organizing a document, folder, or disk.

Cut-and-paste removes (cuts) information and places it in memory temporarily so that it can be moved (pasted) elsewhere. Cutting deletes the data from the original location.

Copy-and-paste copies information and places it in memory temporarily so that it can be duplicated (pasted) elsewhere. Copying leaves your original data intact.

You'll find Cut, Copy, and Paste commands in a program's Edit menu (**Figure 1.48**), but each program may handle these operations differently. In Windows Explorer, for example, you can copy or move files and folders from one disk or folder to another. In Microsoft Word, you can copy or move text or graphics to another part of a document or to a different document. Microsoft Office applications can hold several cut or copied items in a stack.

To cut:

◆ Select (highlight) what you'd like to remove and then choose Edit > Cut (Ctrl+X).

To copy:

◆ Select (highlight) what you'd like to copy; then choose Edit > Copy (Ctrl+C).

To paste:

◆ Click the mouse (or move the cursor) to where you want to the information to appear; then choose Edit > Paste (Ctrl+V).

To undo a cut or paste:

◆ Immediately after you cut or paste, choose Edit > Undo (Ctrl+Z).

The keyboard shortcuts save time, but they're especially useful when the Edit menu is unavailable (**Figure 1.49**).

Edit	View	Favorites	Tools
Cut			Ctrl+X
Copy			Ctrl+C
Paste			Ctrl+V
Select All			Ctrl+A
Find (on This Page)...			Ctrl+F

Figure 1.48 If nothing is selected, the Cut and Copy commands are unavailable—also called *dimmed*.

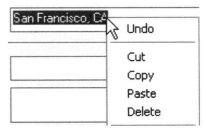

Figure 1.49 In windows that have no Edit menu, such as this dialog box, you can cut, copy, and paste by using keyboard shortcuts or the shortcut (right-click) menu.

✔ Tips

- The area of memory where Windows stores cut or copied information is called the *clipboard*. Whatever you put on it remains there until you cut or copy another piece of information. This scheme lets you paste the same information multiple times in different places.

- If you mean to copy (Ctrl+C) something and accidentally cut (Ctrl+X) it instead, you can recover the item by pasting it back where it came from.

- The clipboard allows information to be transferred from one program to another, provided that the second program can read data generated by the first.

- Use ClipBook Viewer to see what's in the clipboard: Choose Start > Run; type `clipbrd`; then click OK.

- You can't paste something that you've *deleted* or *cleared* (as opposed to cut), because Windows doesn't place that something on the clipboard.

- If you drag highlighted text to your the desktop, you create a persistent *scrap*, which remains there for future pasting.

THE START MENU AND TASKBAR

After you log on, Windows displays the desktop and its components (**Figure 2.1**). The *desktop* sets the backdrop for your working environment and lets you organize the resources on your computer. The *Start menu* is the central location that lists the most useful folders, programs, and commands. The *taskbar* lets you know what programs are running on your computer and allows you to activate or close them.

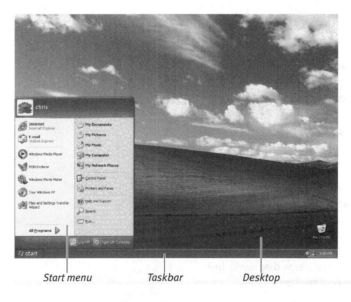

Start menu   Taskbar   Desktop

FIGURE 2.1 Basic desktop elements. Your desktop may look a little different if you've upgraded from a previous version of Windows or if your PC's manufacturer added custom icons.

Exploring the Start Menu

The Start menu lets you access useful software and services, including programs, documents, folders, and commands, while the majority of Windows XP's files run in the background to support Windows itself and other programs.

If you've used a previous version of Windows, you'll notice that the redesigned Start menu has two columns instead of one. The left side shows a list of programs, and the right side shows links to common Windows components and system folders.

To open the Start menu:

◆ Click Start, at the left end of the taskbar (or press Ctrl+Esc).

or

Press and release the Windows logo key (if your keyboard has one).

Start menu left column

The left column of the Start menu has three parts, separated by horizontal lines (**Figure 2.2**):

Pinned Items list. Items in the top section of this column remain there, available to start. You can select programs to appear here, as well as their order. Internet Explorer and Outlook Express are two appropriate choices, especially if you have a full-time (broadband) Internet connection.

Most Frequently Used Programs list. Windows maintains this list by appending programs as you use them. Each added program replaces one that you haven't used recently. You can delete items from this list and set the number of items displayed, but you can't reorder or add items.

All Programs menu. The All Programs menu displays all the programs that you've installed or that Windows Setup has installed. Click the right-pointing arrow (Alt+P) to see it; it's not displayed by default, because it's huge.

Start menu right column

The right column of the Start menu also is divided into three sections.

Files, Drives, and Network: My Documents, My Recent Documents, My Pictures, My Music, My Computer, My Network Places. This part of the Start menu lets you open your personal documents and other files, open Windows Explorer for all the drives in your computer, and reach places on your network (if you're on a network).

(continues on next page)

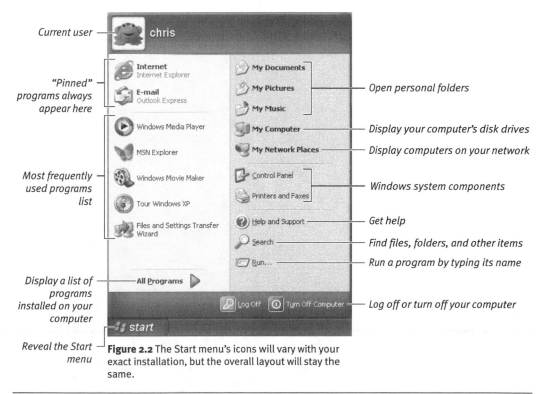

Current user

"Pinned" programs always appear here

Most frequently used programs list

Display a list of programs installed on your computer

Reveal the Start menu

Open personal folders

Display your computer's disk drives

Display computers on your network

Windows system components

Get help

Find files, folders, and other items

Run a program by typing its name

Log off or turn off your computer

Figure 2.2 The Start menu's icons will vary with your exact installation, but the overall layout will stay the same.

EXPLORING THE START MENU

Device Management: Control Panel, Printers and Faxes. Control Panel lets you change the settings of the hardware—such as your monitor, modem, or sound card—in your computer or on the network. Printers and Faxes lets you change print settings such as page orientation, fineness (resolution) of printed copies, whether to print in color, and whether your fax call should pick up automatically or wait for you to do it.

Everything else: Help and Support, Search, Run. Help and Support, a vast improvement over Windows Help, is connected to the Internet whenever you are and displays everything that could help you with Windows—from the smallest help file to the vast Microsoft Knowledge Base. Search lets you find files, folders, objects, and text strings on any drive that you're permitted to access. Run lets you run a program by typing its name.

To close the Start menu:

◆ Press and release the Windows logo key (if your keyboard has one), or press Esc.

or

Click anywhere off the menu (on the desktop, for example).

Using the Start Menu

As in previous Windows versions, choosing a Start menu command is a click away. If you don't like the Start menu's default layout and behavior, you'll be happy to know that it's susceptible to behavior modification therapy.

To choose a Start-menu item:

◆ Click the item.

or

Use the arrow keys to navigate to the item; then press Enter.

or

Press the key of the item's first letter.

✔ Tips

■ If items share the same first letter, press that letter repeatedly until the desired item is highlighted; then press Enter.

■ A menu item with a right-pointing arrow (such as All Programs in Figure 2.2) opens a submenu when you click or point to it.

■ If you prefer to use the previous Start-menu style, called the classic Start menu, see "Restoring the Look of Previous Windows Versions" in Chapter 4.

Adding items to the Start menu

Icons in the Start menu are *shortcuts*—links to items on your computer or network, such as programs, files, folders, disks, Web pages, printers, devices, or other computers. You can add any item or object to the Start menu by dragging and dropping or pinning. You can also remove an item or shuffle items.

✔ Tip

■ Changing or deleting a shortcut has no effect on the item it links to; removing a program's shortcut won't uninstall the actual program.

USING THE START MENU

To pin an item to the Start menu:

1. Locate the item (icon) that you want to display at the top of the menu.

2. Right-click the icon; then choose Pin to Start Menu (**Figure 2.3**).

   or

   Drag the item to the Start button (**Figures 2.4** and **2.5**).

✔ Tips

- If you don't know the item's location, use the Search command in Windows Explorer to find it; then right-click it or drag it from the Search Results window.

- If you can't drag icons onto the Start menu, or if right-clicking Start-menu items has no effect, turn on Start-menu dragging and dropping. See "Customizing the Start Menu" later in this chapter.

- You can't pin items to the old-style (classic) Start menu.

Figure 2.3 You can right-click an item in the Start menu, in Windows Explorer, in My Computer, or on the desktop.

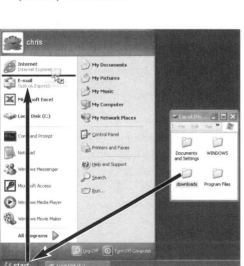

Figure 2.5 The Start menu pops open if you pause on the Start button while dragging, letting you drop the item in the desired position.

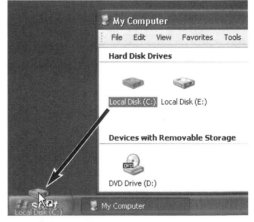

Figure 2.4 You can pin a program, folder, file, or even a disk to the Start menu by dropping it on the Start button.

USING THE START MENU

Figure 2.6 The horizontal black line shows where the item will land when it's dropped.

Figure 2.7 This technique works in both the Pinned Items and the Most Frequently Used Programs lists. In the Pinned Items list, you also can choose Unpin from Start Menu.

To move a pinned item:

◆ Drag the item to a new position (**Figure 2.6**).

To remove an item:

◆ Right-click the item; then choose Remove from This List (**Figure 2.7**).

To configure the program lists:

1. Right-click the Start button, then choose Properties (**Figure 2.8**).

2. Make sure that Start Menu (not Classic Start Menu) is selected; then click Customize (**Figure 2.9**).

3. Select an icon size for programs. Choose Small Icons to make the Start menu's left column less cluttered or Large Icons to make the menu easier to read.

(continues on next page)

Figure 2.9 The General tab of the Customize Start Menu dialog box affects what you see in the menu's left column, where programs are listed.

Figure 2.8 Besides letting you configure the Start menu, this dialog box lets you choose the old-style, one-column Start menu.

USING THE START MENU

4. In the Programs section, type the number of programs to display in the bottom-left section.

Having more programs here gives you quicker access but makes the menu take up more space.

5. Click Clear List to remove your most recently used programs from the bottom-left section, if you don't want someone else to know what you've been running. Windows will repopulate the list.

6. In the Show on Start Menu section, check the boxes if you want your Web browser and email program pinned in the top-left section.

7. Use the drop-down lists to choose the programs.

8. Click OK.

✔ Tips

■ You can't choose Large Icons for the right column or for All Programs; that setting is always Small.

■ Changes you make to the Start menu apply only to you, the logged-on user.

■ You can inspect Start-menu properties in Control Panel: Choose Start > Control Panel > Appearance and Themes > Taskbar and Start Menu > Start Menu tab.

Modifying the All Programs menu

The All Programs menu, which appears when you click or point to All Programs in the Start menu (**Figure 2.10**), displays all the programs that you've installed on your computer. A program's installer generally adds that program's icon to the All Programs menu, but you can add, delete, or reorder these items. The menu accepts not only program icons, but also document, folder, and disk icons.

Figure 2.10 The All Programs menu superimposes itself over the right side of the Start menu.

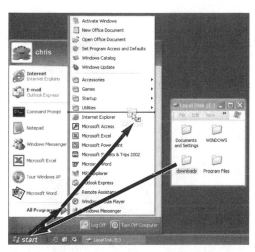

Figure 2.11 Dragging an item to the All Programs menu requires patience.

Figure 2.12 If your desktop is clear, you also can drag an item off the menu and drop it into the Recycle Bin to delete it.

To add an item to the All Programs menu:

1. Locate the item (icon) that you want to add.

2. Drag the icon over the Start button, and pause until the Start menu opens.

3. Continue to drag, and pause over All Programs until the submenu opens.

   The black horizontal line shows where the icon will appear when it's dropped (**Figure 2.11**).

4. Drop the icon on the submenu.

✔ Tips

- Adding a folder to the All Programs menu creates a submenu that lists its contents.

- The default name for an item's shortcut starts with Shortcut To (Shortcut to Outlook Express, for example). To change the name, right-click the item; then choose Rename from the shortcut menu.

- If you can't drag icons to the All Programs menu, or if right-clicking icons has no effect, enable Start-menu dragging and dropping. See "Customizing the Start Menu" later in this chapter.

- If you're using the classic Start menu, you can manage icons with the Customize Classic Start Menu dialog box. Right-click Start; choose Properties; then click Customize.

To delete an item:

1. Right-click the item; then choose Delete (**Figure 2.12**).

2. If a confirmation dialog box appears, click Yes or Delete Shortcut.

✔ Tip

■ To undelete an item from the Recycle Bin, see "Deleting Files and Folders" in Chapter 5.

To move an item:

◆ Drag the item to a new position.

This technique works as shown in Figure 2.6.

To sort items alphabetically:

◆ Right-click any menu item; then choose Sort by Name.

Windows sorts folders in alphabetical order at the top, followed by other menu items in alphabetical order.

✔ Tip

■ You can sort any submenu this way, not just All Programs.

Managing All Programs items with folders

To keep your All Programs menu from becoming wildly long, you can consolidate menu items into submenus (**Figure 2.13**). You add submenus by creating more folders.

Every item that appears on the Start menu is contained in one of two folders: \Documents and Settings\<*your user name*>\Start Menu, and \Documents and Settings\All Users\Start Menu. Items in the <*your user name*> folder are accessible only to you as the logged-on user; I cover those here. Items in the All Users folder are accessible to everyone who has a user account; I cover those in Chapter 16, "User Accounts."

To add or delete All Programs items:

1. Right-click the Start button; then choose Explore (**Figure 2.14**).

Figure 2.13 The Games submenu lists all the games that come with Windows.

Figure 2.14 You can add or delete items that are visible only to you (as shown here) or to all users.

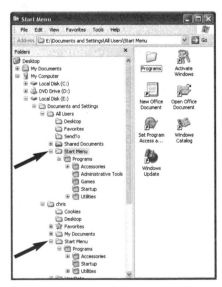

Figure 2.15 The arrows indicate two Start Menu folders: one for all users (top arrow) and one for only you (bottom arrow). Click the plus sign (+) next to a folder to reveal its nested folders.

Figure 2.16 Icons placed inside the Start Menu folder itself appear above the horizontal line in the All Programs menu. (Note where the icons in the right pane of Figure 2.15 appear here.) Icons placed inside the Programs folder appear below the line. Subfolders inside the Programs folder appear as submenus.

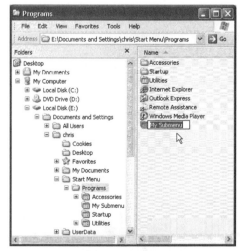

Figure 2.17 A subfolder within the Programs folder appears as a submenu in the All Programs menu.

2. To add (or delete) menu items, drag icons into (or delete icons from) the Start Menu\Programs folder or any folder nested in the Programs folder (**Figures 2.15** and **2.16**).

To add a submenu:

1. Right-click the Start button; then choose Explore (refer to Figure 2.14).

2. Click the Start Menu\Programs folder in the window's left pane (refer to Figure 2.15, top arrow).

3. Choose File > New > Folder.

or

Right-click blank space in the right pane; then choose New > Folder.

4. Type the name of the folder; then press Enter.

You create an empty folder, which is an empty submenu (**Figure 2.17**).

5. To make a particular icon appear in the new submenu, drop it on the new folder; then close the Explorer window.

6. Choose Start > All Programs to see the new submenu (**Figure 2.18**).

✔ Tip

■ To create a nested submenu, follow the same instructions, but in step 2, click the plus sign next to Programs; click the first folder you added; then continue with step 3.

Figure 2.18 The new folder appears as an empty submenu at the bottom of the All Programs menu. You can drag the folder up or down the menu to reposition it.

Customizing the Start Menu

The Start menu's Windows components and its overall behavior are as easy to customize as the Programs lists. You can, for example, substitute any other name for My Computer. You can decide what your Start menu displays or doesn't, choose highlighting for recently installed programs, and generally make your computer PC (Personal and Convenient).

To rename a Start-menu item:

1. Right-click any menu item; then choose Rename.

2. Type a new name or edit the existing one; then press Enter (**Figure 2.19**).

✔ Tips

- It's okay to rename any folder in the Start menu, even My Documents; but *don't* rename the Startup folder. If you do, Windows won't launch programs automatically when the computer boots.

- The keyboard shortcuts for Cut, Copy, and Paste (Ctrl+X, Ctrl+C, Ctrl+V) work in the edit box.

- To cancel renaming an item, press Esc while editing.

To configure the Start menu:

1. Right-click Start; then choose Properties.

2. Make sure that Start Menu (not Classic Start Menu) is selected; then click Customize.

3. Click the Advanced tab (**Figure 2.20**).

4. Follow any desired directions in **Table 2.1**.

5. Click OK.

6. On the Start Menu tab, click OK (or Apply).

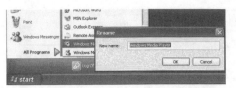

Figure 2.19 If you rename a top-level menu item, you edit in the Start menu directly. If you rename a submenu item, you edit in a dialog box.

Figure 2.20 The Advanced tab (which isn't that advanced) of the Customize Start Menu dialog box affects overall Start-menu behavior, including what you see in the menu's right column, where Windows components are listed.

Figure 2.21 Display As a Menu makes a Start-menu folder expand as a submenu that displays its contents (rather than open as a window).

Table 2.1

Start-Menu Advanced Tab Settings	
OPTION/SETTING	DESCRIPTION
Open Submenus When I Pause on Them With My Mouse	Checked: Display a submenu when you *point* to it. Unchecked: Display a submenu when you *click* it.
Highlight Newly Installed Programs	Checked: Highlight new programs in orange for a few days. Unchecked: Don't distinguish new programs.
Control Panel, My Computer, My Documents, My Music, My Pictures, Network Connections	Display As a Link: Display a shortcut that opens that folder. Display As a Menu: Open a submenu (**Figure 2.21**). Don't Display This Item: Remove that folder from the Start menu.
Enable Dragging and Dropping	Checked: Lets you drag icons on, off, and within the Start menu and display their shortcut (right-click) menus. Unchecked: Lock Start-menu items in place.
Favorites Menu	Checked: Add a link to your Favorites folder, which contains your book-marked Web pages. Unchecked: Favorites menu doesn't appear.
Help and Support, Run, Search	Checked: Item appears in bottom-right section of Start menu. Unchecked: Item doesn't appear on Start menu (If you use these commands rarely or invoke them with keystrokes, uncheck them to save space.)
My Network Places	Checked: Show a link to shared resources on your network. Unchecked: Show this computer and its peripherals only.
Printers and Faxes	Checked: Add a link to the Printers and Faxes folder. Unchecked: Printers and Faxes appears in only Control Panel.
Scroll Programs	Checked: Items in the All Programs menu appear as one long list with scroll arrows. Unchecked: Items appear in columns in a giant submenu, classic-Windows style.
System Administration Tools	Display On the All Programs Menu: Tools appear in All Programs menu and in Control Panel. Display On the All Programs Menu And the Start Menu: Tools appear in All Programs menu, Start menu, and Control Panel. Don't Display This Item: Tools appear in only Control Panel.
List My Most Recently Opened Document	Checked: Display shortcuts to your 15 most recently used documents as My Recent Documents in Start menu; reopen any document by clicking its name. Unchecked: Hide list. Click Clear List to empty the list without deleting the documents.

✔ Tips

- You still can open a folder for which you have chosen Display As a Menu, even though a left-click will just open or close the submenu. Instead, *right-click* the folder; then choose Open.

- Right-click an individual document to delete it from the My Recent Documents list. The list will still contain 15 items.

- In the classic Start menu, My Recent Documents is named Documents.

Exploring the Taskbar

The taskbar provides quick access to programs and the status of background processes. It appears by default at the bottom of your screen and is divided into segments with distinct functions (**Figure 2.22**):

Start button. Click this button to open the Start menu.

Quick Launch bar. A customizable toolbar that lets you display the desktop or launch a program with a single click. The taskbar has a few other handy toolbars that you can hide or show.

Taskbar buttons. Nearly every running program is represented by a button on the taskbar. You can use these buttons to resize, switch between, or close programs.

Notification area. This area displays the clock and shows the status of programs and activities.

Empty area. The taskbar has its own shortcut menu, which you reach by right-clicking an empty spot. If your taskbar is crowded, right-click just to the right of the Start button, where there's always an unoccupied sliver.

✔ Tip

■ Point to any icon on the taskbar to display a helpful tool tip.

Start-menu button | Quick Launch toolbar | Taskbar buttons | Empty area | Notification area

Figure 2.22 The elements of the taskbar.

EXPLORING THE TASKBAR

Managing Windows with the Taskbar

The windows of multiple open programs tend to overlap or hide one another, making them hard to tell apart or find. When you launch a program, its button appears on the taskbar; you can use the taskbar to manage open programs and switch among windows easily.

To view several windows at the same time, you can drag and resize them, or use taskbar controls to tile them on your desktop. To clear your desktop, you can minimize all windows to taskbar buttons.

To activate a window:

◆ Click the taskbar button representing that window (**Figure 2.23**).

✔ Tip

■ The active window's taskbar button appears pushed in; others appear normal.

■ If a window is active, clicking its taskbar button minimizes (hides) it.

■ An inactive program's taskbar button appears normal (popped out), whether its window is minimized, restored, or maximized.

■ If a program is busy, clicking its taskbar button may not activate the window.

■ Right-click a taskbar button to access the window's control (resizing) menu (**Figure 2.24**).

■ To switch windows without using the taskbar, press Alt+Tab, or see "Switching Programs" in Chapter 6.

■ Some programs—usually, programs that run all the time—have notification-area icons (covered later in this chapter) instead of taskbar buttons.

Figure 2.23 Clicking a window's toolbar button brings the window to the top of the pile, if it happens to be hidden by other windows.

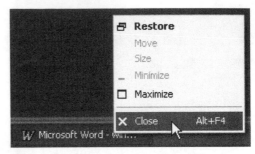

Figure 2.24 Among other things, the control menu lets you close a window without first restoring it.

Figure 2.25 Showing the desktop even minimizes dialog boxes (which don't appear as taskbar buttons).

Figure 2.26 Here, I chose Tile Windows Horizontally.

■ To press taskbar buttons with the keyboard: Press Ctrl+Esc to open the Start menu; press Esc to close it; then tab to the first taskbar button. Next, use the arrow keys to highlight the desired button; then press the spacebar to activate the window or Shift+F10 to display its control menu.

To minimize all windows:

◆ Right-click blank space on the taskbar; then choose Show the Desktop.

or

If the Quick Launch toolbar is displayed, click the desktop icon (**Figure 2.25**).

or

Press Windows logo key+D or Windows logo key+M (if available).

To restore minimized windows:

◆ Right-click blank space on the taskbar; then choose Undo Minimize All.

or

Click the desktop icon on the Quick Launch toolbar.

or

Press Windows logo key+D or Windows logo key+Shift+M (if available).

To arrange windows on your desktop:

1. Minimize the windows that you *don't* want arranged on the desktop.

2. Right-click blank space on the taskbar; then choose Cascade Windows, Tile Windows Horizontally, or Tile Windows Vertically (**Figure 2.26**).

✔ Tips

■ To reverse this arrangement, right-click blank space on the taskbar; then choose Undo Cascade or Undo Tile.

■ To display the Quick Launch toolbar, right-click blank space on the taskbar; then choose Toolbars > Quick Launch.

Configuring the Taskbar

You can change many aspects of the taskbar. A space-saving feature in Windows XP groups similar windows in one menulike taskbar button, rather than associating a truncated taskbar button with each program.

To configure the taskbar:

1. Right-click blank space on the taskbar; then choose Properties (**Figure 2.27**).

2. Check Lock the Taskbar to keep the taskbar at its current size and position.

    Uncheck this box if you want to resize or move the taskbar or any of its toolbars.

3. Check Auto-Hide the Taskbar to hide the taskbar when you don't need it.

    The taskbar disappears until you point to the edge of the screen where it's located.

4. Check Keep the Taskbar on Top of Other Windows to prevent other windows— even maximized windows—from covering the taskbar.

5. Check Group Similar Taskbar Buttons to reduce taskbar clutter.

    Windows rearranges taskbar buttons for each program—say, Internet Explorer— so that all of them are adjacent. If the taskbar becomes so crowded that button text is truncated, buttons for the same program are consolidated into one button displaying the number of program sessions (**Figure 2.28**).

6. Check Show Quick Launch to display the Quick Launch toolbar as part of the taskbar.

    Use it to display the desktop or launch a program with a single click. See "Adding Toolbars to the Taskbar" later in this chapter.

7. Click OK (or Apply).

Figure 2.27 The Taskbar and Start Menu Properties dialog box lets you change the taskbar's appearance and behavior.

Figure 2.28 A group button displays a small arrow and the number of open documents for the program. Click the button to access the document you want.

Figure 2.29 A group button's shortcut menu lets you arrange all windows in the group (without affecting other windows), minimize all windows in the group, or close all windows in the group.

Figure 2.30 These scroll buttons let you access hidden buttons on a jam-packed taskbar.

Figure 2.31 The taskbar widens automatically when you drag it to the left or right edge. Open windows self-adjust to accommodate the taskbar's new location.

✔ Tips

- To pop up an auto-hidden taskbar with the keyboard, press Ctrl+Esc or the Windows logo key (if your keyboard has one).

- To lock or unlock the taskbar quickly, right-click blank space on it; then choose Lock the Taskbar. A check mark will appear. Repeating this process toggles the lock on or off.

- You can also display taskbar properties through Control Panel: Appearance and Themes > Taskbar and Start Menu > Taskbar tab.

- Right-click a group button to manage multiple windows as a group (**Figure 2.29**).

- If the taskbar becomes *too* crowded, Windows hides some taskbar buttons and displays scroll buttons (**Figure 2.30**).

- The taskbar won't group a program's windows into one button if there's enough room for a separate button for each window.

To move the taskbar:

1. If the taskbar is locked, unlock it (right-click blank space on the taskbar; then uncheck Lock the Taskbar).

2. Click blank space on the taskbar; then drag it to any edge of your screen.

✔ Tip

- Try attaching the taskbar to the screen's left edge (**Figure 2.31**). It may feel awkward at first, but it reduces the amount of mousing required for routine tasks.

CONFIGURING THE TASKBAR

To resize the taskbar:

1. If the taskbar is locked, unlock it.

2. Point to the inside edge of the taskbar (the pointer becomes a double-headed arrow); then drag it toward the desktop for a larger taskbar or toward the screen edge for a smaller one (**Figure 2.32**).

✔ Tips

■ If you make your taskbar more than one line deep, truncated buttons and toolbars will expand.

■ If you shrink the taskbar until it disappears off an edge, drag the thin blue line at that edge to get it back. If you can't grab the blue line: Press Ctrl+Esc, Esc, Alt+spacebar, and S; use the arrow keys to resize the taskbar; then press Enter.

Figure 2.32 Taskbars at the screen's top or bottom resize in button-height increments. Taskbars to the left or right resize without constraints.

Taskbar Recommendations

As the uniform command center for all your running programs, the taskbar is one of the most powerful features of Windows and among the ones you'll use most often. Efficient taskbar settings can make using your computer much more pleasant. Here are my recommendations for taskbar Properties settings:

Lock the Taskbar: On.

Auto-Hide the Taskbar: Off, unless you're working with a small screen or want to devote every pixel to a particular window.

Keep the Taskbar on Top of Other Windows: On.

Group Similar Taskbar Buttons: On, unless you work regularly with few open windows.

Show Quick Launch: On.

CONFIGURING THE TASKBAR

Figure 2.33 Notification-area icons give the status of background programs, tasks, and services. A clean installation of Windows XP has few, if any, status icons initially.

Figure 2.34 The tool tip for this icon tells me how much time I have left to activate my copy of Windows XP.

Figure 2.35 The Taskbar and Start Menu Properties dialog box lets you change the notification area's appearance and behavior.

Using the Notification Area

Windows XP changes the name of the *system tray* (or just *tray*) to the *notification area*, which lives at the right end of the taskbar, holding the clock and small icons that monitor activities on your computer or network (**Figure 2.33**).

Windows and other programs use icons here to let you know things—that you've received new email, for example. Some icons flash to get your attention, whereas others appear for the duration of an event (such as printing a document). Hover the pointer over an icon to find out what it represents (**Figure 2.34**).

These icons have no standard controls. Some, you click; others, you double- or right-click; and some ignore clicks.

✔ Tips

- Programs can display what they please in the notification area (and some abuse the privilege). You can dismiss some icons with a right-click, whereas others cling like barnacles. A program's options or preferences may let you control notification-area settings.

- If you hide the clock, you have more room for icons.

To show or hide the clock:

1. Right-click blank space on the taskbar or notification area; then choose Properties (**Figure 2.35**).

2. Check Show the Clock to display the time, or uncheck this option to hide it.

3. Click OK (or Apply).

✔ Tips

- Hover the pointer over the time to display the day and date.

- A taskbar on the left or right screen edge (or a tall one at the top or bottom) displays the day and date automatically (**Figure 2.36**).

- Double-click the clock to display the Date and Time Properties dialog box. See "Changing the Date and Time" in Chapter 4.

Windows manages the notification area by watching you work. If an icon isn't used regularly, Windows calls it inactive and hides it. Windows XP lets you control icon display rather than accept a default (**Figure 2.37**).

To control icon display in the notification area:

1. Right-click blank space on the taskbar or notification area; then choose Properties.

2. To display all icons, uncheck Hide Inactive Icons; click OK twice; then skip the remaining steps.

3. To customize the behavior of icons, click Customize.

   The Name column shows the programs (**Figure 2.38**).

4. In the Behavior column, click each program that you want to customize; then choose Hide When Inactive, Always Hide, or Always Show in the list box.

5. When you're finished changing the notification entries, click OK.

6. On the Taskbar tab, click OK (or Apply).

✔ Tips

- If Hide Inactive Icons is checked, you can customize notifications directly. Right-click blank space on the notification area; then choose Customize Notifications.

Figure 2.36 A tall or vertical taskbar displays the day, the date, and more icons.

Figure 2.37 A < button indicates that Windows has hidden some notification-area icons (refer to Figure 2.33). Click the button to expand the notification area and display all icons, as shown here. (Note that the button becomes a >.)

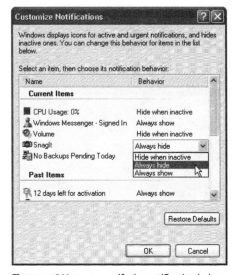

Figure 2.38 You can specify the notification behavior for items displayed currently as well as in the past.

- To restore the standard behavior of the notification-area icons, click Restore Defaults in the dialog box.

Adding Toolbars to the Taskbar

Specialized toolbars are available on the taskbar (**Figure 2.39**):

Address. A text box that accepts any address on the Web, on your network, or on your computer. Entering a Web address launches or activates Internet Explorer (or your default browser); a program name launches the program; a filename and path opens the file in its associated program (launching the program if necessary); and a folder name opens a Windows Explorer window.

Links. Links to Internet Explorer's Favorites folder. You can drag file or Web-page shortcuts onto this toolbar or right-click to delete links.

Desktop. Links to all desktop shortcuts, so that you don't have to minimize all windows to reach them.

Quick Launch. Provides one-click access—much quicker than the Start menu—to commonly used items. It also lets you minimize all windows to show the desktop.

✔ Tips

■ By default, only Quick Launch is displayed on the taskbar.

■ Address and Links also appear in Windows Explorer and Internet Explorer.

(continues on next page)

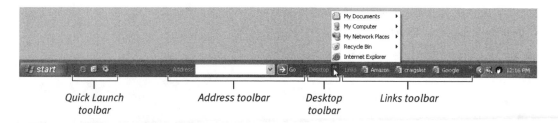

Quick Launch toolbar   *Address toolbar*   *Desktop toolbar*   *Links toolbar*

Figure 2.39 Toolbars occupy a lot of taskbar space. Click the >> button that appears at the toolbar's right end to display a menu of items or commands that won't fit on the taskbar.

- The Address toolbar auto-completes—that is, proposes matching entries that you've typed before. You can keep typing, or you can use the down-arrow key to select a match and then press Enter. If you type something that Windows doesn't understand, Windows searches and either finds what you want or displays an error message.

- If your desktop is crowded, it may be faster to click Show Desktop on the Quick Launch toolbar than to use the Desktop toolbar.

- Many tasks in this section require an unlocked taskbar. Right-click blank space on the taskbar. If Lock the Taskbar is checked, uncheck it.

Figure 2.40 You can hide or show each toolbar independently of the others.

To show or hide taskbar toolbars:

- Right-click blank space on the taskbar; point to Toolbars; then check or uncheck a name in the submenu to toggle that toolbar (**Figure 2.40**).

✔ Tips

- Drag the vertical rib at the toolbar's left end to resize or move the toolbar. A toolbar dragged onto the desktop can float freely or dock against any screen edge.

- To create a custom toolbar, right-click blank space on the taskbar; choose Toolbars > New Toolbar; specify a folder whose contents you want to make into a toolbar; then click OK. Sadly, this toolbar vanishes when you close it; you repeat the New Toolbar process to get it back.

- To create a toolbar quickly, drag a folder to the edge of the desktop and drop it.

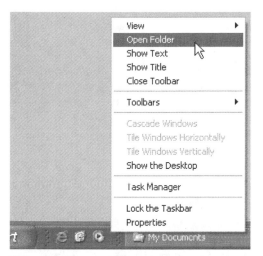

Figure 2.41 The Open Folder command works with only the Links and Quick Launch toolbars (and with custom toolbars created with New Toolbar).

Figure 2.42 The left button launches Internet Explorer (Chapter 13). The Show Desktop button (center) minimizes all windows to make the desktop visible. The right button launches Windows Media Player (Chapter 10).

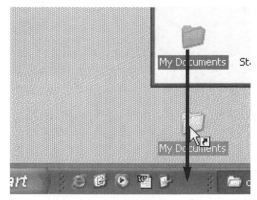

Figure 2.43 A vertical black line shows where the item will land when it's dropped.

To customize a taskbar toolbar:

◆ Right-click blank space on the toolbar; then choose one of these commands at the top of the shortcut menu (**Figure 2.41**):

View. Shows large (double-height) or small (default) toolbar icons.

Open Folder. Opens the folder that the toolbar represents. Adding, changing, and deleting shortcuts in the folder can be easier than manipulating the toolbar's small icons.

Show Text. Displays a text label next to each toolbar icon, which takes a *lot* of room. This feature is on by default for Links but not for Quick Launch.

Show Title. Shows the toolbar name—generally a waste, except as extra blank space for right-clicking or dragging.

Close Toolbar. Closes the toolbar.

✔ Tips

■ Quick Launch begins with three Microsoft-supplied buttons (**Figure 2.42**). You can add buttons for instant access to favorite programs and files, or delete buttons that you don't need.

■ Click Show Desktop a second time to restore all windows to their original positions.

■ You can press Windows logo key+D (if your keyboard supports it) once to show the desktop and twice to restore windows.

To add a button to Quick Launch:

1. Locate the item (icon) that you want to place on the toolbar, and drag it over.
   When the icon hovers over the toolbar, a black I-bar appears where it will land.

2. Drop the icon where you want it (**Figure 2.43**)

ADDING TOOLBARS TO THE TASKBAR

✔ Tips

- You can add almost any item to Quick Launch: a program, document, folder, disk, device, Control Panel, and so on.

- Drag buttons within the toolbar to shuffle their order.

To delete a button from Quick Launch:

1. Right-click the button; then choose Delete.

2. If a confirmation dialog box appears, click Yes.

✔ Tips

- Deleting a shortcut doesn't remove the file it represents.

- *Don't* delete the Show Desktop button; it's a command, not a shortcut.

- You can drag an unwanted button from the toolbar to the Recycle Bin.

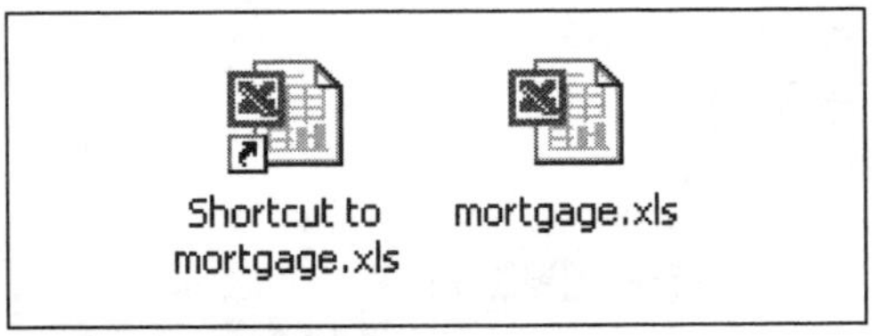

Shortcut to   mortgage.xls
mortgage.xls

Figure 2.44 You can distinguish a shortcut from the file to which it's linked by the small curved arrow.

Managing Shortcuts

I've covered creating, editing, and deleting shortcuts in the Start menu and Quick Launch toolbar. Shortcuts also can appear on the desktop and in folders. A shortcut can link to a program, document, folder, disk, printer or other device, Web address (URL), or system folder (such as My Computer). When you double-click a shortcut, its linked file opens. You can create and modify a short cut to any item, and store it anywhere; it's a tiny file.

Windows offers two types of shortcut files: *Windows* shortcuts (.lnk files) and *Internet* shortcuts (.url files). A shortcut shares the icon of the original but adds a small boxed arrow in one corner (**Figure 2.44**).

✔ Tips

■ You can make several shortcuts to an object and store them in different places.

■ You can make shortcuts to network-accessible items, not just local items.

■ Word to the wise: The Web Document tab of an Internet shortcut displays the number of times its site has been visited from your computer.

■ Don't confuse a shortcut *icon,* which is a placeholder for an object, with a shortcut (command) *menu* or *keyboard* shortcut, which is a command keystroke.

To create a shortcut:

1. Locate the item (icon) that you want to add as a shortcut.

2. Right-drag the icon to a destination (typically, the desktop or a folder); then choose Create Shortcut(s) Here from the shortcut menu.

   or

   Right-click the icon; then choose Send To > Desktop (Create Shortcut) (**Figure 2.45**).

   or

   Right-click the icon; then choose Create Shortcut.

   This method creates a shortcut in the same location as the original. You can move the shortcut anywhere.

   or

   Alt-drag the icon to a destination.

   or

   Ctrl-Shift-drag the icon to a destination.

✔ Tips

- If you want to create a shortcut to a program (.exe file), look for programs supplied with Windows—such as Notepad—in the \Windows or \Windows\System32 folder. For other programs, look in a folder nested in \Program Files.

- If you create a shortcut to a shortcut, the new shortcut points to the original target.

To display system-folder shortcuts on the desktop:

1. Right-click blank space on the desktop; then choose Properties.

2. Choose Desktop tab > Customize Desktop.

3. In the Desktop Icons section, check the boxes for the shortcuts that you want on the desktop (**Figure 2.46**); then click OK.

4. On the Desktop tab, click OK (or Apply).

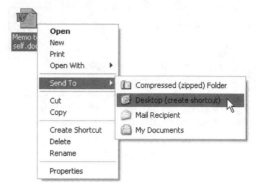

Figure 2.45 The shortcut menu provides a quick way to create a desktop shortcut.

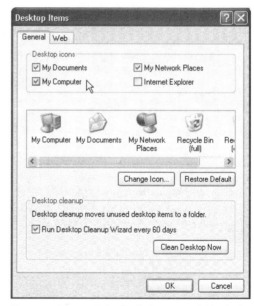

Figure 2.46 You can bring back the system-folder desktop shortcuts that Microsoft removed.

✔ Tip

- The Desktop Icons dialog box lets you change a system item's icon. Select the item; then click Change Icon to choose a new icon. (To restore the original icon, select the item; then click Restore Default.)

Figure 2.47 Getting rid of *Short-cut to* is often the objective in renaming.

Figure 2.48 The Properties dialog box of Windows shortcuts (to documents and programs) has a Shortcut tab, whereas...

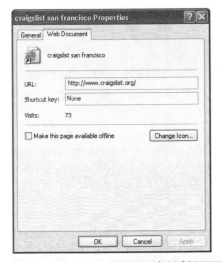

Figure 2.49 ...Internet shortcuts (URLs) have a Web Document tab. For details, see the sidebar.

To rename a shortcut:

1. Right-click the shortcut; then choose Rename.

   or

   Select (highlight) the shortcut; then press F2.

   or

   Click the shortcut's title (not its icon) twice slowly; don't double-click.

2. Retype or edit the name; then press Enter (**Figure 2.47**).

✔ Tips

■ Shortcut names can include letters, numbers, spaces, and some punctuation marks, but not these characters: \ : / * ? " > < |.

■ You can rename a shortcut in the General tab of the shortcut's Properties dialog box.

To delete a shortcut:

◆ Right-click the shortcut; then choose Delete.

   or

   Select (highlight) the shortcut; then press Delete.

✔ Tips

■ You can delete several shortcuts at a time by selecting the icons, right-clicking the selection, and choosing Delete.

■ To recover (undelete) a shortcut from the Recycle Bin, see "Deleting Files and Folders" in Chapter 5.

To view or change a shortcut's properties:

◆ Right-click the shortcut; then choose Properties.

   or

   Highlight the shortcut; then press Alt+Enter (**Figures 2.48** and **2.49**).

✔ Tips

- Some targets—printers and My Computer, for example—can't be modified.

- Shortcut keys work only for desktop and Start-menu shortcuts, and they won't work at all if they conflict with program-defined or other shortcut keys.

- Run Maximized is useful for programs that "forget" to run in full-screen mode when you start them from the shortcut.

- Run Minimized makes Startup folder less intrusive; programs start automatically as taskbar buttons, and your screen isn't cluttered with windows.

- You can rewrite the target (path) of the object that a shortcut points to, but it's usually easier to create a new shortcut.

Shortcut Properties

Information in a Properties dialog box depends on what the shortcut represents. Here are some common properties.

Target. The name of the item that the shortcut points to. A shortcut to a file needs the full path to its location (unless the file is in a Windows system folder).

Start In. The folder in which the program looks for files to open or save, by default.

Shortcut Key specifies the keyboard shortcut with which to open (or switch to) the program. Press any key to make Ctrl+Alt+key appear here. You can assign Ctrl+Alt+E to Windows Explorer, for example, to open it without hunting for its shortcut. A shortcut key requires at least two of Ctrl, Shift, and Alt but can't use Esc, Enter, Tab, spacebar, Print Screen, Delete, or Backspace.

Run tells the program to open in a normal (restored), minimized, or maximized window.

Comment provides the descriptive text (tool tip) that appears when your pointer hovers over the shortcut.

Find Target opens the folder containing the file that the shortcut points to. The file will be selected in the folder window.

Change Icon allows you to change the default icon of a shortcut, which is the same as that of the target. Changing this icon doesn't change the target's icon.

URL displays the address (URL) of a Web page in an Internet shortcut, as though it were the target of a Windows shortcut.

Make This Page Available Offline for Internet Shortcuts allows you to download the Web page for offline viewing. See "Browsing Tips" in Chapter 13.

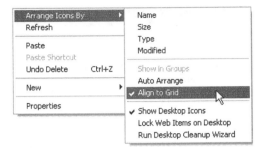

Figure 2.50 This submenu lets you sort your desktop shortcuts, align them, or hide them temporarily.

Tidying Your Desktop

Over time, shortcuts tend to accumulate on your desktop. Microsoft's productivity elves view a messy desk not as a sign of genius, but as a sign of a messy desk, so they've provided cleanup tools.

To arrange desktop shortcuts:

◆ Right-click blank space on the desktop; point to Arrange Icons By, then choose a command from the submenu (**Figure 2.50**):

Name. Sorts alphabetically by name.

Size. Sorts by file size, with the smallest first. If the shortcut points to a program, the size refers to the size of the shortcut file.

Type. Sorts by file type, which keeps files with the same file extension together (.doc for Word files or .exe for programs, for example).

Modified. Sorts by the date when the shortcut (not the original) was last modified, with the most recent first.

Auto Arrange. Places icons in neat columns, starting on the screen's left side. Uncheck this option to drag icons anywhere on your desktop. This option won't work if your desktop is full.

Align to Grid. Turns on an invisible grid that makes icons snap into equally spaced alignment when you move them. Uncheck this option to turn off the grid. (Useful only if Auto Arrange is turned off.)

Show Desktop Icons. Uncheck this option to hide all desktop icons; check it to show them.

✔ Tip

■ If your icons look grainy or badly drawn, right-click blank space on the desktop; then choose Refresh to redisplay icons.

To remove unused shortcuts:

1. Right-click blank space on the desktop; then choose Arrange Icons By > Run Desktop Cleanup Wizard.

or

Right-click blank space on the desktop; then choose Properties > Desktop tab > Customize Desktop > Clean Desktop Now (**Figure 2.51**).

2. Click Next to bypass the wizard's first screen.

3. Check the boxes of the shortcuts to remove from your desktop; then click Next (**Figure 2.52**).

4. Click Finish to confirm your choices.

The wizard doesn't actually delete the shortcuts but stores them in a folder named Unused Desktop Shortcuts on your desktop, where you can retrieve them if you need them.

✔ Tips

■ The Desktop Cleanup Wizard removes not only your personal shortcuts, but also shortcuts that appear on all users' desktops. To check whether a shortcut is shared, right-click the icon; choose Properties; then check the Location property in the General tab. If the path contains *All Users* (rather than your user name), it's a shared shortcut.

■ The Desktop Cleanup Wizard appears automatically every 60 days, with a list of shortcuts that you haven't used for the past two months. Uncheck Run Desktop Cleanup Wizard Every 60 Days if you don't want the wizard to run automatically.

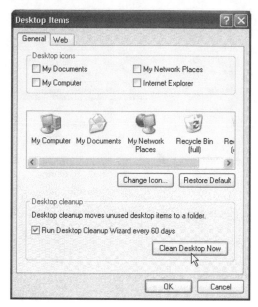

Figure 2.51 You can run the desktop cleanup program whenever you want or automatically, in two-month intervals.

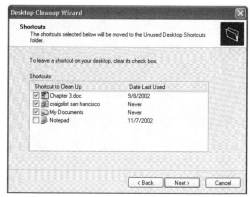

Figure 2.52 The wizard lists your desktop shortcuts, along with the last times you used them.

GETTING HELP

3

If you're already a Windows user, you may be tempted to skip this chapter because you've given up on Microsoft's anemic help system. Don't. A change of heart—closely related to what Microsoft spends on telephone support—has spawned XP's Help and Support Center, a cross between a Web portal and an on-disk help system. With it, you use Web-style links and searches to access:

◆ Standard documentation

◆ Animated tutorials

◆ Troubleshooting wizards

◆ Diagnostic and repair utilities

◆ Up-to-date configuration information about your system's hardware, software, and services

◆ Web pages at Microsoft's support site and Windows newsgroups (if you're connected to the Internet)

Also, XP's new Remote Assistance program lets a remote user view your screen—or even control your PC—to help you solve problems.

Starting Help and Support Center

The first stop in Help and Support Center is the home page (**Figure 3.1**), which includes links to basic information, external help resources, and common system tasks. Your home page may differ slightly from the one pictured because this help system isn't a static collection of pages; Microsoft and third parties, like PC manufacturers, are free to modify it. The "Did you know?" section in the bottom-right corner is the usual target for such changes.

To start Help Center:

◆ Choose Start > Help and Support.

or

Press Windows logo key+F1 (if your keyboard supports it).

✔ Tips

- If your desktop is active, press F1 to start Help Center.

- You can have multiple Help Center windows open.

- To get help for a specific Windows component, such as Internet Explorer or Solitaire, use that program's Help menu rather than Help Center.

- In Windows XP, the Help font size is independent of Internet Explorer's font size. To change font size in Help Center, choose Options (on the toolbar) > Change Help and Support Center Options (on the left panel) > Font Size Used for Help Content (see Figure 3.3 later in this chapter).

- The home page's left column replaces the Help Contents page of previous Windows Help systems.

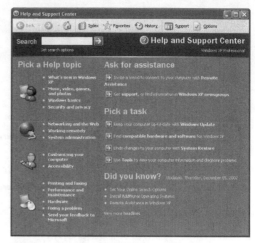

Figure 3.1 The left column lists common help topics. The green arrows in the right column mark links to support resources and system tools.

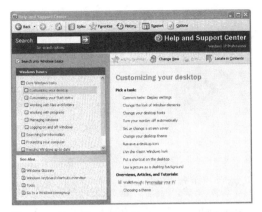

Figure 3.2 To get here from the home page, I clicked Windows Basics > Core Windows Tasks > Customizing Your Desktop. The right panel lists choices that let me drill down into the help system until I find the relevant help page.

Help and Support Center options

Select from the options below to customize your Help and Support Center experience.

- ☑ Show Favorites on the navigation bar
- ☑ Show History on the navigation bar

Font size used for Help content:

- ○ Small
- ◉ Medium
- ○ Large

Options for icons in the navigation bar:

- ○ Show all text labels
- ◉ Show only default text labels
- ○ Do not show text labels

Figure 3.3 You can change the appearance of the navigation bar.

Navigating in Help Center

Find your way around Help Center by using Web-like navigation. Help Center's toolbar, or *navigation bar*, looks and works like Internet Explorer's standard toolbar.

To navigate by clicking links:

1. On the home page, click a link below Pick a Help Topic.

   Help Center displays a subtopic list.

2. Keep clicking links to burrow to the topic you're looking for (**Figure 3.2**).

To navigate via the navigation bar:

◆ On the navigation bar, click one of the following buttons:

   Back (or press Alt+left arrow) or **Forward** (or press Alt+right arrow) to move through recently viewed topics.

   Home (Alt+H) to return to Help Center's home page.

   Index (Alt+N) to search by keyword.

   Favorites (Alt+A) to view Help pages that you've saved. To save a Help page, click Add to Favorites (just above the topic panel). These Favorites aren't the same ones in Internet Explorer.

   History (Alt+Y) to view pages that you've read during this Help session.

   Support (Alt+U) to launch Remote Assistance, contact a Microsoft support person, or visit the Windows newsgroups.

   Options (Alt+O) to set your own preferences for the Help system (**Figure 3.3**).

Searching for Help Topics

When you tire (quickly) of clicking and skimming among Help Center's 10,000 pages, you'll warm up to Help Center's search function. It's fast, easy, and usually finds a wide range of related topics, which can acquaint you with XP features that you were unaware of.

To search for help topics:

1. In Help Center, type or paste a search phrase in the Search text box; then press Enter or click the green arrow (**Figure 3.4**).

   Help Center conducts the search and divides the results into three categories.

2. Click one of the categories listed in the Search Results panel (**Figure 3.5**):

   Suggested Topics lists pages with *keyword* matches. Microsoft assigns invisible keyword tags to help topics.

   Full-Text Search Matches lists pages that contain the literal phrase you entered.

   Microsoft Knowledge Base (on the Internet) lists relevant articles that appear in Microsoft's massive support Web site.

✔ Tips

- If your search phrase contains multiple words, Help Center searches for pages that contain *all* the words. A search for *keyboard shortcuts,* for example, yields pages that contain *keyboard* and *shortcuts,* though not necessarily adjacent in the text. To find an exact phrase, enclose it in quotation marks (*"keyboard shortcuts"*).

- The toolbar just above the topic panel lets you add the page to your Help favorites; shrink the Help Center window; print the topic; or locate the topic in the Help table of contents.

- Search terms aren't case-sensitive.

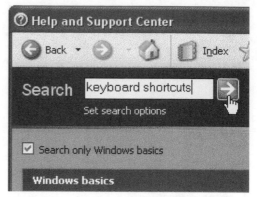

Figure 3.4 If you choose a category in Pick a Help Topic on the home page before starting your search, Help Center displays a Search Only check box below the Search text box. Check this box to narrow your search; uncheck it to search the entire Help system.

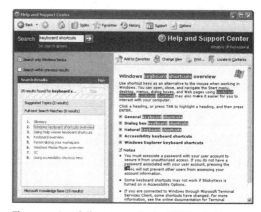

Figure 3.5 In a full-text search, the highlighted text shows matches for your search phrase.

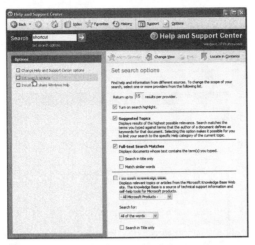

Figure 3.6 Help Center displays up to 15 results per category by default. Experienced users may want to increase this limit and accept longer Internet searches.

Customizing Help Center

Help Center's settings page lets you specify how to search and how to display results.

To set search options:

1. Click Options > Set Search Options (in the left panel) (**Figure 3.6**).

2. Set your choices in Set Search Options, working from **Table 3.1**.

Table 3.1

Help Center Search Options

SET SEARCH OPTIONS	SEARCH OPTION BEHAVIOR
Return up to *n* Results Per Provider	Type the number of results, per category, to display. Default is 15.
Turn on Search Highlight	Checked: Search phrases in result pages highlighted with dark rectangles (see Figure 3.5). Unchecked: Search results displayed without highlighting.
Suggested Topics	Checked: Search results sorted with the most relevant at the top, by comparing your query with a database of keywords. Unchecked: Search results sorted alphabetically.
Full-Text Search Matches	Checked: Displays any document containing your search terms. Unchecked: Lets searches be confined by other priorities (such as Suggested Topics).
Search in Title Only	Checked: Limits searches to topic titles and ignores body text. Unchecked: Allows search of entire documents.
Match Similar Words	Checked: Allows alternative and approximate forms of words (*network* and *networking*). Unchecked: Searches only on the exact terms entered (not case-sensitive).
Microsoft Knowledge Base	Checked: Include a search of Microsoft's vast, Web-compliant, keyword-oriented technical database. Unchecked: Omit this search. Uncheck if you're not connected to the Internet.
–All Microsoft Products–	Select a single Microsoft product to search on from a *giant* drop-down list, Search on all Microsoft products (default).
Search for:	*All of the Words:* Displays only documents that contain all your search terms. *Any of the Words:* Displays all documents that contain any of your search terms. *The Exact Phrase:* Displays all documents that contain your search terms in the order you give them (same as enclosing the phrase in quotes). *The Boolean Phrase:* Lets you use AND, OR, NOT, and NEAR operators to confine search phrases. (*Internet* NOT *Explorer* finds topics related to the Internet but not Microsoft's browser, for example.)
Search in Title Only	Checked: Ignores body text (within the Knowledge Base). Unchecked: Searches body text (within the Knowledge Base).

Using the Help Index

To search for help successfully, you must speak Microsoftese, not English. If you want to snuff a file on your hard drive, do you search for *erase? delete? remove?* The official term is *delete,* but any of these will work, thanks to Help Center's keyword searches, which include common synonyms. In other searches, you may not be so lucky. The best way to learn the Windows vocabulary is to browse the Help Center index.

To use the Help index:

1. On the navigation bar, click Index (or press Alt+N).

   Help Center displays a list of keywords, sorted alphabetically (**Figure 3.7**).

2. In the keyword text box, type a word.

   As you type, the highlighted selection jumps to the keyword that's the closest match.

3. Double-click a list entry to see its matching help page in the right panel.

   If an entry has subentries, double-click an indented subentry rather than the top-level entry.

✔ Tip

■ Type *troubleshooting* to see a list of XP's Troubleshooters. Use these wizardlike tools to identify and resolve hardware, software, and networking problems (**Figure 3.8**).

Figure 3.7 You can scroll through the massive index to see help topics.

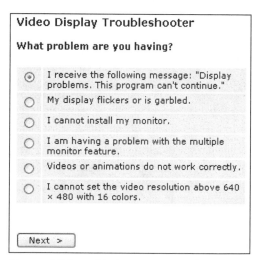

Figure 3.8 This troubleshooter steps you through help screens designed to help you fix display problems. Of course, if you're having *serious* display problems...

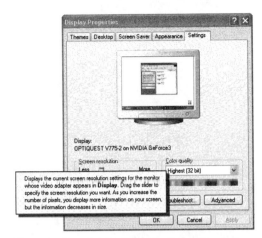

Figure 3.9 Here, I right-clicked the Screen Resolution slider for "What's This?" help. To dismiss the pop-up box, click it.

Getting Help in Dialog Boxes

XP's designers describe the function of check boxes, options buttons, lists, and other dialog-box elements in a few words. This concision yields obscurely worded labels, especially in crowded dialog boxes. Fortunately, there's "What's This?" help for pop-up tips on individual elements.

To get pop-up help for a dialog-box element:

◆ Right-click an element; then click "What's This?" (**Figure 3.9**).

or

Click the question mark in the top-right corner of the dialog box; then click an element.

✔ Tip

■ Right-click inside the pop-up box to print it or copy its contents to the clipboard.

Allowing Others to Connect to Your Computer Remotely

You'll appreciate XP's Remote Assistance function if you've ever endured the friendship-corroding stress of giving or receiving tech support over the phone. *Remote Assistance* lets you invite a friend or technical expert—anyone you trust who's running Windows XP—to help you by connecting to your PC over the Internet or a network. That person can swap messages with you, view your screen, or (with your permission) use his mouse and keyboard to control your computer.

Remote Assistance relieves novices of having to explain problems in jargon they haven't learned, and lets experts cut the chatter and work on the novice's machine directly. Experts can even install software, update hardware drivers, and edit the registry.

✔ Tip

■ **PRO** Remote Assistance isn't the same as XP Pro's Remote Desktop (see Chapter 18). Among other differences, in Remote Assistance, both parties must be present at their PCs and agree to the connection.

Before you start a Remote Assistance session, you should set invitation and time limits.

Security Concerns

Like all remote-control technologies, Remote Assistance has security implications beyond the ordinary issues of strong passwords and firewalls. When you invite someone to take control of your PC, you must balance your trust with others' inclinations toward malice. That person is free not only to fix your problem, but also to, say, erase your hard drive or steal your files. You can view everything he's doing onscreen and, if you don't like what you see, press Esc to break the connection immediately. Still, damage done in a moment may take ages to undo. Even if that person can't control your PC, you could follow his bad advice and delete critical files or disable security features yourself. Furthermore, you may not be able to confirm the identity of the other person.

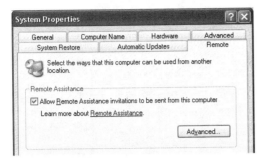

Figure 3.10 If you're paranoid, uncheck this box to disable Remote Assistance.

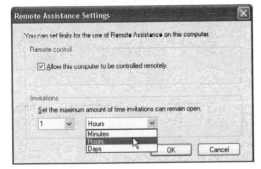

Figure 3.11 If you're concerned about security, you can shorten the maximum expiration period to a few minutes or hours. This setting affects the invitation-expiry choice in Figure 3.23.

To configure Remote Assistance:

1. Choose Start > Control Panel > Performance and Maintenance > System > Remote tab.

   or

   Press Windows logo key+Break (if your keyboard supports it); then click the Remote tab.

   Remote Assistance is enabled by default.

2. If it's clear, check Allow Remote Assistance Invitations to be Sent from This Computer (**Figure 3.10**).

3. Click Advanced to open Remote Assistance Settings (**Figure 3.11**).

4. If you're the novice, and you don't want the expert to control your computer, uncheck Allow This Computer to be Controlled Remotely.

   Even with this box checked, you must approve each request for control of your computer explicitly.

5. Use the two Invitations drop-down lists to specify the maximum duration of Remote Assistance invitations.

   The default setting is 30 days.

6. Click OK.

7. In the System Properties dialog box, click OK (or Apply).

In a Remote Assistance session, the two connected parties—the *novice* and the *expert*—must:

◆ Be using Windows XP (either Home or Pro edition)

◆ Be on the same local area network (LAN) or have active Internet connections

◆ Not be blocked by a firewall

(continues on next page)

ALLOWING OTHERS TO CONNECT REMOTELY

The order of events in a Remote Assistance session is:

1. The novice sends the expert an invitation via email or Windows Messenger.

2. The expert accepts the invitation.

3. Remote Assistance opens a window that shows the novice's desktop.

4. The expert views the novice's desktop and exchanges messages with the novice or, with permission, takes control of the novice's computer.

5. Either party disconnects to end the session.

It's faster and easier to send an invitation via Messenger, but you can use email if one of you prefers it. I'll describe both methods separately. Each step is marked by *Novice* or *Expert* to indicate who does what.

To get Remote Assistance by using Windows Messenger:

1. (**Novice**) Sign in to Messenger (choose Start > All Programs > Windows Messenger, or see Chapter 15).

2. (**Novice**) In Messenger, choose Actions > Ask for Remote Assistance (**Figure 3.12**).

3. (**Novice**) Specify the expert to invite; then click OK (**Figure 3.13**).

   Messenger invites the expert and opens a Conversation window (**Figure 3.14**).

4. (**Expert**) When an invitation pops up in your notification area (**Figure 3.15**), open Messenger and accept the invitation (**Figure 3.16**).

Figure 3.12 Windows Messenger makes it easy to extend a Remote Assistance invitation.

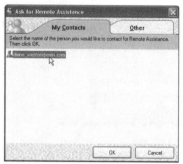

Figure 3.13 If the expert's email address isn't listed on the My Contacts tab, click the Other tab to enter it.

Figure 3.14 Wait for a response. If you change your mind or fix your problem while you're waiting, click Cancel (or press Alt+Q) to revoke the invitation.

Figure 3.15 When the expert receives an invitation, his Messenger taskbar button flashes, and this invitation pops up on his screen.

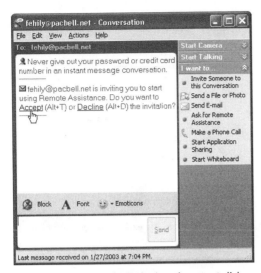

Figure 3.16 To accept the invitation, the expert clicks Accept (or presses Alt+T) in Messenger.

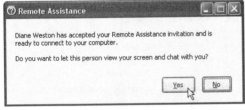

Figure 3.17 Just to be sure, Remote Assistance makes you confirm the connection one last time.

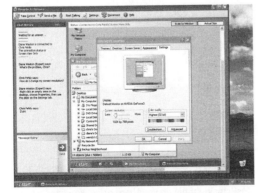

Figure 3.18 To compensate for screen-size and resolution differences, the expert can click Scale Actual or Scale to Window. Actual requires scrolling but usually presents a better image than Window, which distorts the novice's screen proportions to fit in the expert's Remote Assistance pane.

5. (**Novice**) Windows displays a message box when the expert accepts your invitation; click Yes (**Figure 3.17**).

6. (**Expert**) The novice's desktop appears in a Remote Assistance window (**Figure 3.18**).

7. (**Novice/Expert**) Both of you can communicate via Messenger (**Figure 3.19**).

8. (**Expert**) To ask permission to take control of the novice's computer (rather than just *view* the novice's desktop), click Take Control on the toolbar.

(continues on next page)

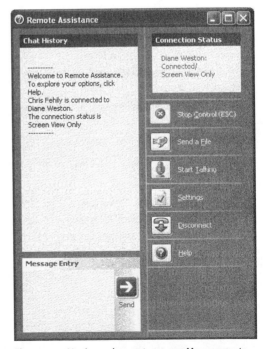

Figure 3.19 Novice and expert can use Messenger to communicate via instant messages, voice, files, or any of the methods described in Chapter 15. You also can bypass Messenger and just pick up the phone.

ALLOWING OTHERS TO CONNECT REMOTELY

9. (**Novice**) To relinquish control of your PC to the expert, click Yes in the message box that appears (**Figure 3.20**).

10. (**Novice/Expert**) To cancel control, either of you can press Esc or click Stop Control.

Canceling control still lets the expert view the novice's desktop. To sever the connection (so that the novice's desktop is no longer visible), click Disconnect.

✔ Tip

■ If you, the expert, want the Remote Assistance window out of your way briefly while you're helping the novice, don't *close* it, or you'll break the connection. *Minimize* it instead.

To get Remote Assistance by using email:

1. (**Novice**) Choose Start > Help and Support.

2. (**Novice**) Click Invite a Friend to Connect to Your Computer with Remote Assistance.

The Remote Assistance wizard steps you through the process of inviting an expert via email.

3. (**Novice**) Click Invite Someone to Help You.

4. (**Novice**) Type the expert's email address in the Type an E-mail Address box; then click Invite This Person (**Figure 3.21**).

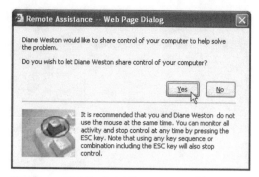

Figure 3.20 Click Yes to let the expert use *his* mouse and keyboard to fiddle with *your* computer. You'll see ghostly pointer movements, self-typing text, and self-opening windows as the expert fixes your problem.

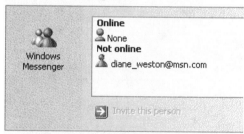

Figure 3.21 If you instead click Save Invitation As a File (Advanced), Windows saves the invitation as a .MsRcIncident file on your hard drive. You can transfer this invitation file over a network or via floppy instead of emailing it.

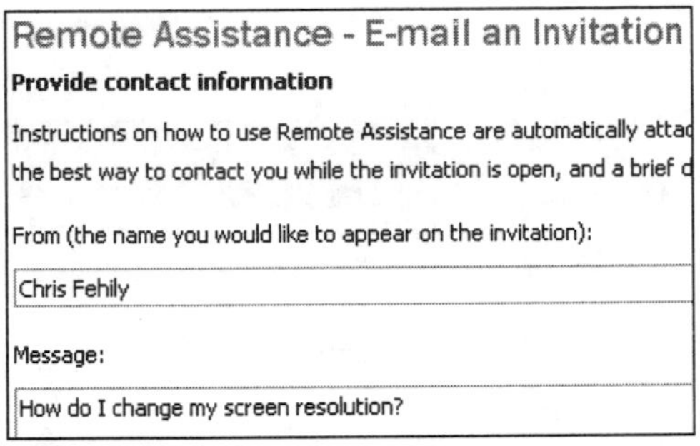

Figure 3.22 Remote Assistance adds your message to the boilerplate text that it generates in the email invitation to be sent to the expert. Your name appears in the Subject line.

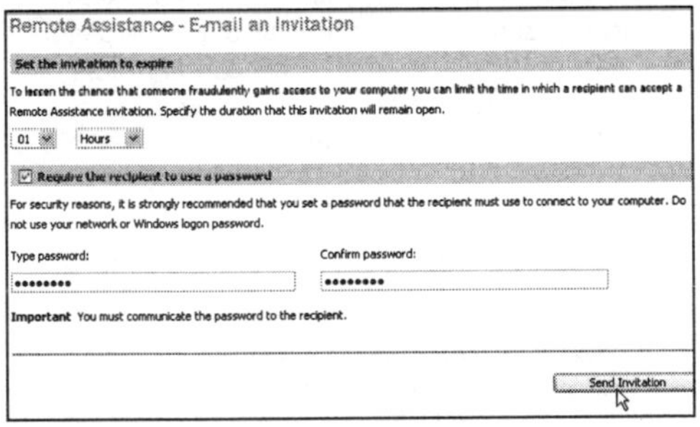

Figure 3.23 If the expert doesn't respond to your invitation within the specified time period, the invitation expires. If you're unconcerned about security, you can specify a longer time limit. To set the maximum expiration period, see Figure 3.11.

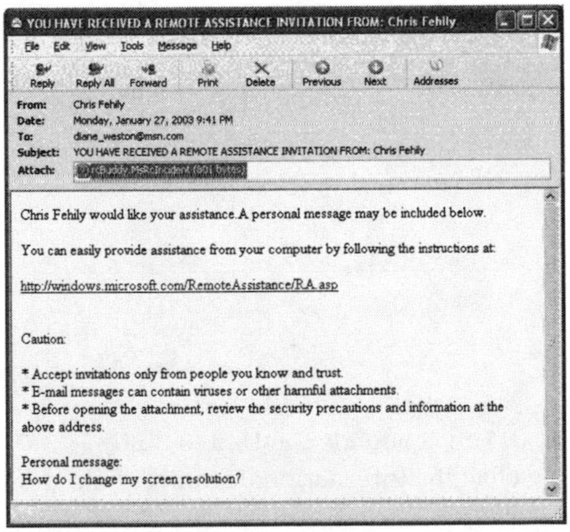

Figure 3.24 The file rcBuddy.MsRcIncident is attached to the emailed invitation. The expert opens (double-clicks) this file to accept the invitation, sending a message back to the novice.

5. (**Novice**) Type your name and a description of the problem; then click Continue (**Figure 3.22**).

6. (**Novice**) Set up your security options and make sure that you're online; then click Send Invitation (**Figure 3.23**).

7. (**Novice**) If a warning dialog box appears, click Send.

   Remote Assistance tells you if your invitation was sent successfully.

8. (**Expert**) When the invitation arrives from the novice, open the attachment to accept the invitation (**Figure 3.24**).

9. (**Novice**) When the expert accepts the invitation, a message box like Figure 3.17 appears; click Yes to start a Remote Assistance session.

✔ Tips

■ The expert can use (and re-use) an invitation until it expires (refer to Figure 3.23).

■ The dialog box in step 7 protects you from *worms*—nasty programs that transmit copies of themselves secretly via email.

■ When you invite an expert via email, you're actually transmitting your PC's IP address, which identifies your PC uniquely on the Internet. If you have a *dynamic* (rather than *static*) IP address, which changes every time you dial in to the Internet, the expert won't be able to connect to your PC if you've broken your Internet connection since sending the invitation, or if you share an Internet connection through a router (see Chapter 17). These issues don't arise for Messenger connections.

ALLOWING OTHERS TO CONNECT REMOTELY

Getting Help From Microsoft

When all else fails, you can get help—free or paid—from Microsoft directly:

Microsoft Support Web site. At Microsoft's online support pages at support.microsoft.com (**Figure 3.25**), you can:

◆ Get answers to frequently asked questions (FAQs)

◆ Download software updates, Service Packs, patches, and device drivers

◆ Ask non-technical questions about pricing, training, and other Microsoft products

◆ Search the Microsoft Knowledge Base of more than 250,000 support articles, if you don't want to reach it through Help Center

Free telephone support. If you purchased your copy of Windows XP separately—that is, it didn't come on your computer—you can call Microsoft for unlimited help *with installation*. After XP is up and running, you can call for free (but not toll-free) help with *two* more problems. In the United States, the number is 425-635-3311 (Redmond, Washington).

Paid telephone support. After you use up your "free" calls, the meter starts running. Microsoft charges you $35 (U.S.) per incident. (A single incident may span several phone calls.) The toll-free number is 800-936-5700 (**Figure 3.26**).

✔ Tips

■ When you call, Microsoft will want your 20-digit product ID number. To look it up, choose Start > Control Panel > Performance and Maintenance > System > General tab. The ID number is in the Registered To section.

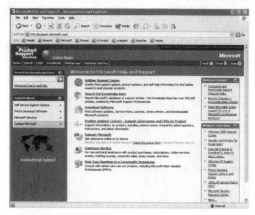

Figure 3.25 Click the Post Your Question to a Community Newsgroup link (at the bottom of the page) to post a technical question on a Microsoft Product Support Internet Newsgroup. You can check back later to see if anyone answered.

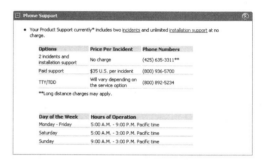

Figure 3.26 Here are the U.S. phone numbers and business hours for no-charge and paid Windows phone support.

■ If you're outside the United States, click the International Support link in Figure 3.25.

PERSONALIZING YOUR WORK ENVIRONMENT

With each new version of Windows, its designers make more assumptions about the preferences and abilities of the "average" user. Because this user doesn't exist, Microsoft lets you twiddle Windows XP's factory settings.

Hundreds of configuration options range from superficial to deep. Changes to graphics, colors, and fonts, for example, are cosmetic, whereas other settings—the language used or adaptations for disabled users—profoundly change the way you work with Windows.

Using Control Panel

Control Panel is a central container of customizing tools for changing preferences, configurations, and settings. These miniature programs are commonly called *applets* or *extensions*. Many experienced Windows users are familiar with the interface in **Figure 4.1**, now called *classic view*. Windows XP's Control Panel defaults to a novice-friendly interface called *category view* (**Figures 4.2** and **4.3**).

To open Control Panel:

◆ Choose Start > Control Panel.

✔ Tip

■ To start Control Panel from the Run command, type control; then press Enter.

■ To start Control Panel in the classic Start menu, choose Start > Settings > Control Panel.

■ To show Control Panel in the My Computer folder, choose Control Panel > Appearances and Themes > Folder Options > View tab > check Show Control Panel in My Computer check box (toward the bottom).

■ Control Panel can look quite different, depending on preferences set in a few scattered dialog boxes.

To open an item in category view:

◆ Click its icon or category name.

In some cases, such as Add or Remove Programs, the item opens in its own window. In others, such as Appearance and Themes, the category opens to a list of tasks and applets that you can click.

Figure 4.1 Classic view consolidates all Control Panel tools in one window.

Figure 4.2 Category view groups Control Panel tools into functional categories. Click a category to...

Figure 4.3 ...open an item or (as here) display a list of related tasks and Control Panel tools.

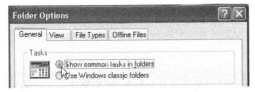

Figure 4.4 Select this option to make the task pane appear on the left side of the Control Panel window (as in Figures 4.1 and 4.2).

Figure 4.5 The Switch View option toggles according to the current view.

To open an item in classic view:

◆ Double-click the item.

or

Use the arrow keys to navigate to the desired item; then press Enter.

or

Press the key of the item's first letter; then press Enter.

To switch Control Panel views:

1. If the Control Panel task pane isn't displayed, choose Tools > Folder Options > General tab > Show Common Tasks in Folders (**Figure 4.4**).

2. In the task pane, click Switch to Category View or Switch to Classic View (**Figure 4.5**).

✔ Tips

■ If you can't find the item you want in category view, click Other Control Panel Options in the task pane (or switch to classic view).

■ In either view, hold your pointer over a category or item to view a pop-up description of it.

■ If multiple items share the same first letter, press that letter repeatedly until the desired item is highlighted; then press Enter.

■ Working from Control Panel, you can create desktop shortcuts to its applets, which are handy if (for example) you're setting up a network or a printer and need to launch one applet repeatedly. To create a shortcut, see "Managing Shortcuts" in Chapter 2.

Changing Your Desktop Background

You can change the image, or *wallpaper,* that appears under the icons on your desktop. If you don't like the desktop backgrounds that Windows provides in Control Panel > Appearance and Themes, you can use a file of your own.

To change the desktop background:

1. In Control Panel, choose Appearance and Themes > Display Properties > Desktop tab (**Figure 4.6**).

   or

   Right-click blank space on the desktop; then choose Properties > Desktop tab.

2. Select an image from the Background list or click Browse to hunt for an image file on your computer or the network.

   Windows looks for Background files in the My Pictures, \Windows, and \Windows\Web\Wallpaper folders.

3. Select the file's icon in Windows Explorer; then click Set As Desktop Background in the Picture Tasks section of the task pane (**Figure 4.7**).

4. From the Position drop-down list, choose one of these options:

   Center to center the image on the desktop background.

   Tile to repeat the image over the entire screen. This option works best with small images.

   Stretch to resize the image to fit your screen (with some distortion). This option works best with large images and photos.

Figure 4.6 Use the Desktop tab to select an image or browse for an HTML page as your desktop background.

Figure 4.7 A picture folder is one for which the Pictures or Photo Album folder-type template has been applied on the Customize tab of the folder's Properties dialog box.

5. Select a desktop color to fill the space unoccupied by a picture.

or

Select a predefined color or click Other to specify a custom color.

6. Click OK (or Apply).

✔ Tips

- To display a solid desktop color with no picture, select None in the Background list.

- To use an Internet Explorer image as wallpaper, right-click the image; then choose Set as Background. The downloaded image appears as Internet Explorer Background in the Background list. Each new Internet image you define as a background replaces the old one.

- To use an Internet Explorer image as your *permanent* background, right-click the image as it appears in your browser; choose Save Picture As; save the image in My Pictures or a folder of your own; then proceed as described.

- To place live Web content on your desktop, see the next section.

To Squish or Not to Squish?

The Stretch function of Display Properties can be handy, although the results are sometimes amusing. But a photo from a new digital camera can easily be larger than your computer's entire screen—demonstrating the lack of a matching Squish function. Here's how to detect and deal with the problem:

1. Right-click an empty area of your desktop; then choose Properties > Settings tab.

2. In the Screen Resolution box (bottom left), note the number of pixels (for example, 1024 x 768).

3. Find the icon or thumbnail of the image you want to use for wallpaper, and hover the pointer over it till its file information pops up.

   Dimensions will be its size in pixels (for example, 1600 × 1200)

If the image's dimensions are larger than your computer's screen resolution, Windows fills your screen with the center portion of the image, and the edges go wherever leftover pixels mysteriously go. This result may be fine with you; the edges of an image are often the least interesting part. But if you want the uncropped image to be your wallpaper, make a new copy, using the Resize function of your favorite graphics program to shrink it to the same size as your screen—or at least come closer.

Displaying Web Content on Your Desktop

The desktop background isn't limited to static images; you can embed a browser window in your desktop to display self-updating Web information such as weather reports, stock prices, and news (**Figure 4.8**). A fast, continuous Internet connection such as DSL or cable modem works best, but a regular dial-up modem works too, in a creaky sort of way.

You can work with desktop Web content (called Active Desktop in earlier Windows versions) just as if you were working in a browser window. When you click a link, Windows launches (or activates) a browser with the link's target displayed.

Web content is updated at intervals or when you request an update manually. You have several options that will keep Web content current.

To add a Web content item:

1. In Control Panel, choose Appearance and Themes > Display > Desktop tab > Customize Desktop > Web tab (**Figure 4.9**).

   or

   Right-click blank space on the desktop; then choose Properties > Desktop tab > Customize Desktop > Web tab.

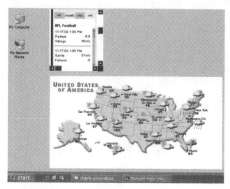

Figure 4.8 Some sports scores and a weather map on the desktop.

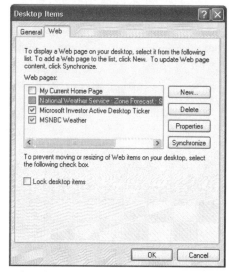

Figure 4.9 Use the Web tab to display Web pages on your desktop.

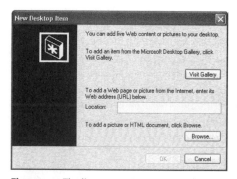

Figure 4.10 The live content's source can be a Web page, local file, or network file.

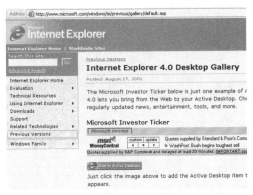

Figure 4.11 This Microsoft Web page contains live content designed especially for desktop display, including an investor ticker. Click Add to Active Desktop to add a particular item; then click Yes to confirm.

Figure 4.12 Click OK to accept the vendor's default update schedule. Click Customize to start the Offline Favorite Wizard and specify your own schedule for updating content.

2. Click New, and choose one of three options (**Figure 4.10**):

   Visit Gallery. Click Visit Gallery to visit Microsoft's Internet Explorer Desktop Gallery Web page (**Figure 4.11**); then choose items on the page.

   Location. If you know the item's Web address (URL), type it in the Location box.

   Browse. This option gives you access to several standard locations—including My Recent Documents, My Network, and your Internet Favorites folder—that contain potential items for your desktop.

3. Click OK to confirm your choices (**Figure 4.12**).

4. In the Desktop Items dialog box, click OK.

5. In the Display Properties dialog box, click OK (or Apply).

Wallpaper Image Formats

Any image to be used as wallpaper must be in one of these formats:

- ◆ .BMP or .DIB (Windows Bitmap)

- ◆ .JPEG or .JPG (Joint Photographic Experts Group)

- ◆ .GIF (Graphics Interchange Format, also called CompuServe graphics format)

- ◆ .PNG (Portable Network Graphics)

- ◆ .HTM or .HTML (Hypertext Markup Language)

HTML is the language used to code Web pages. Custom-design the .html file to fit your screen, as it won't have scroll bars, and its text and links will have to contend with desktop icons. Position options aren't offered for HTML backgrounds; an HTML file will always display as full-screen and centered.

A wallpaper graphic can be any size on disk; the file-size limit of earlier Windows versions doesn't seem to apply to XP.

DISPLAYING WEB CONTENT ON YOUR DESKTOP

To delete a Web content item:

1. Right-click blank space on the desktop;
then choose Properties > Desktop tab >
Customize Desktop > Web tab.

2. Select the item that you want to delete;
then click Delete.

✔ Tips

■ To display Web content on the desktop
quickly: Right-drag the link icon from
Internet Explorer's Address bar to the
desktop; then choose Create Active Desktop Items Here (**Figure 4.13**).

■ Windows stores Web content in the
\Windows\Offline Web Pages folder.

■ Some gallery items require you to download and install an ActiveX control, a
module available from Microsoft that
helps complex graphics display correctly.

To modify Web content:

1. Right-click blank space on the desktop;
then choose Arrange Icons By > Lock
Web Items on Desktop.

If this box is checked, uncheck it. Now
you can modify Web content.

2. Point to the item's top edge until a border
pops up from that edge (**Figure 4.14**).

3. To move the window, drag the top border.

or

To resize the window, drag the left, right,
or bottom border.

or

Click an icon on the top border
(**Figure 4.15**).

4. After you've set everything up, check
Lock Web Items on Desktop to prevent
accidental changes.

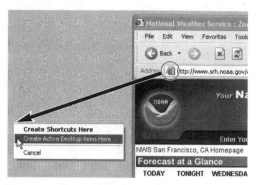

Figure 4.13 You can right-drag a Web page onto your
desktop directly from your browser.

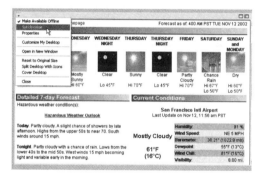

Figure 4.14 Web content items are displayed as
(slightly nonstandard) windows.

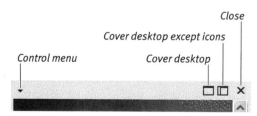

Figure 4.15 You can move, resize, close, or maximize
(but not minimize) Web content windows. The Full
Screen button becomes the Restore button when the
window is maximized.

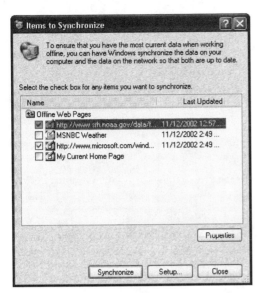

Figure 4.16 Check the items that you want to update (synchronize).

■ To redisplay a Web content window that you've closed, select its check box on the Web tab of the Desktop Items dialog box (refer to Figure 4.9).

To update Web content items:

◆ To update *all* items, right-click blank space on the desktop; then choose Properties > Desktop tab > Customize Desktop > Web tab > Synchronize (refer to Figure 4.9).

or

To update *some* items, choose Start > All Programs > Accessories > Synchronize; check one or more items; then click Synchronize (**Figure 4.16**).

or

To update *one* item, point to the item's top edge until a border pops up from that edge; click the down arrow in the top-left corner; then click Synchronize (refer to Figure 4.14).

To display a Web content item's properties:

◆ Point to the item's top edge until a border pops up from that edge; click the down arrow in the top-left corner; then click Properties.

or

Right-click blank space on the desktop, choose Properties > Desktop tab > Customize Desktop > Web tab; select an item; then click Properties.

or

Choose Start > All Programs > Accessories > Synchronize; select an item; then click Properties.

DISPLAYING WEB CONTENT ON YOUR DESKTOP

To change a Web content item's update schedule:

1. Display the item's properties.

2. On the Schedule tab, set the item's update schedule (**Figure 4.17**).

✔ Tips

■ To see when an item was last updated, choose Start > Accessories > Synchronize; then inspect the Last Updated column (refer to Figure 4.16).

■ You can disable updates of a Web content item, if you want to keep the contents you have. Display the item's properties; then, on the Web Document tab, clear the Make This Page Available Offline check box (**Figure 4.18**).

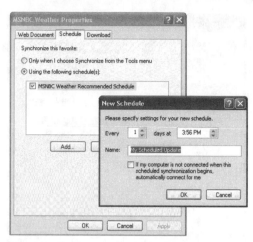

Figure 4.17 You can specify that updates occur manually or automatically and add, edit, or delete automatic schedules. Your computer can connect automatically at the times set for updating.

Figure 4.18 Clearing this check box hides the Web document's summary information and suppresses the Schedule and Download tabs.

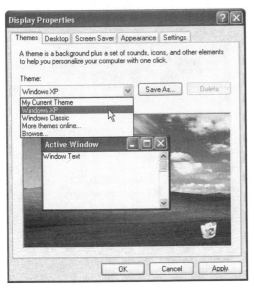

Figure 4.19 Each person with a user account can pick a distinct theme.

Themes and Control Panel

You can tailor individual theme elements by changing Control Panel settings directly. The elements that you can change, with the relevant Control Panel items, are:

◆ Background (Display > Desktop tab)

◆ Desktop icons (Display > Desktop tab > Customize Desktop)

◆ Windows and buttons (Display > Appearance tab)

◆ Colors and fonts (Display > Appearance tab and Display > Appearance tab > Advanced)

◆ Screen saver (Display > Screen Saver tab)

◆ Mouse pointers (Mouse > Pointers tab)

◆ Sounds (Sounds and Audio Devices > Sounds tab)

Choosing a Desktop Theme

Windows XP's default appearance and colors aren't to every taste, nor does Microsoft intend they should be. You can change them with a different desktop *theme*—a stored set of colors, icons, fonts, sounds, and other elements that help personalize your desktop and environment. Windows lets you pick a predefined theme or create your own.

To choose a theme:

1. In Control Panel, choose Appearance and Themes > Display > Themes tab.

   or

   Right-click blank space on the desktop; then choose Properties > Themes tab.

2. In the Theme list, select a new theme (**Figure 4.19**).

3. Click OK (or Apply).

✔ Tips

■ Microsoft includes only two themes on the Windows XP CD, but the popularity of XP means that gazillions of free themes are available on independent Web sites— some of which Microsoft promotes. Try www.themexp.org, for example.

■ Select the Windows Classic theme to restore the look of Windows 2000/98/Me.

■ The classic look of some windows (such as the command-prompt window) can't be changed with themes.

■ The Windows XP section of www.microsoft.com also offers Microsoft Plus! for Windows XP—a $30 (U.S.) enrichment pack that contains themes, screen savers, games, and add-ins for Media Player.

To create a custom theme:

1. In Control Panel, choose Appearance and Themes > Display > Themes tab.

   or

   Right-click blank space on the desktop; then choose Properties > Themes tab.

2. In the Theme list, select an existing theme as a starting point for creating a new one.

3. Set the relevant Control Panel options to change the theme (**Figures 4.20** and **4.21**).

4. When you're finished making changes, click Apply on the Themes tab (refer to Figure 4.19).

5. Click Save As; type a theme name; then click Save.

   Windows saves the theme in the My Documents folder.

6. In the Display Properties dialog box, click OK (or Apply).

✔ Tips

- If you modify a theme without saving it, Windows saves your changes with the name *Previous-theme-name* (Modified). Your modified theme is discarded if you select a different theme. If you modify a theme and save it, you must use a new theme name.

- To populate the Theme list, Windows looks in the My Documents and \Windows\Resources\Themes folders. Click Browse on the Themes tab to open a theme located elsewhere.

To delete a custom theme:

1. In Control Panel, choose Appearance and Themes > Display > Themes tab.

   or

   Right-click blank space on the desktop; then choose Properties > Themes tab.

2. In the Theme list, select the theme that you want to delete; then click Delete.

Figure 4.20 The Appearance tab lets you select the overall window and button style, color scheme, and font size.

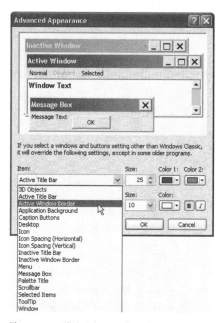

Figure 4.21 Click Advanced on the Appearance tab to fine-tune the font and color of individual interface elements.

✔ Tip

- You can delete only the themes that you created or installed, not the ones Windows provides.

Figure 4.22 Choose and set your screen saver carefully, so your boss won't realize how long it's been since you did any work.

Setting a Screen Saver

A *screen saver* is a utility that causes a monitor to blank out or display images after a specified time passes without keyboard or mouse activity. (Pressing a key or moving the mouse deactivates the screen saver.) Screen savers were originally developed to prevent hardware damage to your monitor, but today's monitors don't need that, so modern screen savers provide decoration or entertainment instead. A screen saver can also password-protect your computer and hide your screen when it takes effect.

To set a screen saver:

1. In Control Panel, choose Appearance and Themes > Display > Screen Saver tab (**Figure 4.22**).

   or

   Right-click blank space on the desktop; then choose Properties > Screen Saver tab.

2. Select a screen saver in the list.

   (To disable the screen saver, select None, click OK, and skip the remaining steps.)

3. Specify how long your computer must be idle before the screen saver activates.

   Try 10 to 15 minutes.

4. Click Settings to see any options for the selected screen saver—to change color or animation style, for example.

5. Check the On Resume, Password Protect (or On Resume, Display Welcome Screen) check box to display a logon window when you begin using your computer after screen-saver activation.

6. Click Preview to see a full-screen preview of the screen saver.

   Press a key or move your mouse to end the preview.

7. Click OK (or Apply).

SETTING A SCREEN SAVER

✔ Tips

- Your screen-saver password is the same as your logon password. If you have no logon password, you can't set a screen-saver password.

- Appearances aside, screen savers—particularly complex ones such as 3D Flying Objects and 3D Pipes—waste energy and processor time. To save resources, turn off your monitor manually or automatically after a certain period of inactivity. See "Conserving Power" later in this chapter.

To use personal pictures as a screen saver:

1. Make sure you have two or more pictures in a folder on your computer (usually, the My Pictures folder).

2. On the Screen Saver tab (refer to Figure 4.22), choose My Pictures Slideshow from the Screen Saver drop-down list.

3. Click Settings to specify the folder containing your pictures, define picture size, and set other options (**Figure 4.23**).

Figure 4.23 My Pictures Slideshow scrolls through all the pictures in the selected folder.

SETTING A SCREEN SAVER

Configuring the Monitor

Windows lets you get the most out of your display hardware with these settings:

Screen resolution is the amount (fineness) of detail in your screen's image, expressed in pixels wide by pixels high. (A *pixel* is the smallest building block of the display.) Conventional screens have resolutions of 640 × 480 (largely useless except in emergencies), 800 × 600, 1024 × 768, and 1152 × 864. High-end monitors support resolutions up to 2048 × 1536 and higher.

Color quality ranges from 16 ugly colors for archaic Standard VGA to 4 billion colors (32 bits per pixel) for the best monitors and video cards. The number of colors available correlates to your resolution setting—most video cards display fewer colors at higher resolutions—so you may have to reduce resolution to get higher color quality. The available resolution and color choices adjust automatically. If your digital photos look blotchy, increase color quality.

Refresh rate is the frequency at which the screen is redrawn to maintain a constant, steady image. Higher refresh rates yield less flicker. A refresh rate below 72 hertz, or 72 times per second, can tire your eyes if you look at the screen too long.

Color matching ensures that colors are represented accurately and consistently across color printers, scanners, cameras, monitors, and programs. Without color management, onscreen and printed colors can vary greatly: Orange can appear brown, green can appear blue, and so on. Graphic designers love color matching because it does away with trial and error in resolving color differences. Color matching requires a separate color profile (.icm file) for each device connected to your computer. This profile conveys the device's color characteristics to the color management system every time colors are scanned, displayed, or printed.

✔ Tips

- Changing these settings affects all users who log on to your computer.

- Don't always choose the maximum resolution available. If you spend most of your time typing Word documents or reading email, you may find that medium resolution reduces eyestrain. For general use, try 800 × 600 on a 15-inch monitor, 1024 × 768 on a 17-inch monitor, or 1152 × 864 on a 19-inch monitor.

- Flat-panel screen (laptop or desktop) images may look fuzzy at less-than-maximum resolutions.

- Video-card memory largely determines the maximum resolution and color quality that you can use. To see how much video memory you have, In Control Panel, choose Appearance and Themes > Display > Settings tab > Advanced > Adapter tab > Adapter Information section (**Figure 4.24**).

- To adjust the monitor for vision impairments, see "Accommodating Disabled Users" later in this chapter.

- For notes on installing and configuring peripherals, see Chapter 8.

To set screen resolution and color quality:

1. In Control Panel, choose Appearance and Themes > Display > Settings tab (**Figure 4.25**).

   or

   Right-click blank space on the desktop; then choose Properties > Settings tab.

2. Drag the Screen Resolution slider to set the display size.

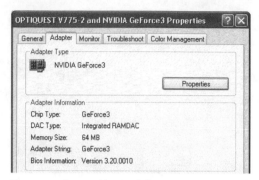

Figure 4.24 Better video cards have 32 MB or more of memory—overkill for word processing and email but barely enough for gaming.

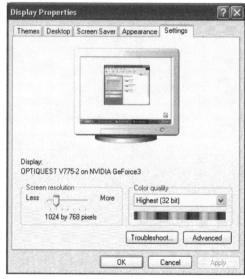

Figure 4.25 As you increase the number of pixels, you display more information on your screen, but the features—such as icon titles—get smaller.

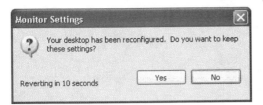

Figure 4.26 If your new screen settings look good, click Yes; otherwise, click No, or just wait, to revert to your previous settings.

3. From the Color Quality drop-down list, choose the number of colors.

Choose Medium (more than 65,000 colors), High (more than 16 million colors), or Highest (more than 4 billion colors).

4. Click Apply.

5. If Windows asks you to confirm settings, click OK.

Your screen briefly turns black and refreshes with the new settings.

6. After your settings change, you have 15 seconds to accept the changes (**Figure 4.26**).

✔ Tips

■ If you have more than one monitor (driven by multiple video cards or by a single card that supports multiple monitors), the Settings tab displays a monitor icon for each monitor. Click a monitor icon to activate it before choosing its resolution and color settings.

■ If you need a 256-color display to run an older game, don't set your entire system to 256 colors, even if it's available. Instead, use the Compatibility feature; see "Running Older Programs" in Chapter 6.

■ Click the Troubleshoot button to start the Display Troubleshooter, which helps you resolve flicker, installation, video, multiple-monitor, resolution, and other problems.

■ The Advanced button lets you view the hardware properties of your monitor and video card. You can adjust some settings usually don't need to unless you're installing a new driver, setting color matching, or changing the refresh rate.

CONFIGURING THE MONITOR

To set the refresh rate:

1. In Control Panel, choose Appearance and Themes > Display > Settings tab > Advanced > Monitor tab (**Figure 4.27**).

   or

   Right-click blank space on the desktop; then choose Properties > Monitor tab.

2. If you have multiple monitors, in the Monitor Type section, select the monitor that you're working with currently.

3. In the Monitor Settings section, choose a refresh rate from the drop-down list.

4. Click Apply.

5. If Windows asks you to confirm settings, click OK.

   Your screen briefly turns black.

6. After your refresh rate changes, you have 15 seconds to accept the change (refer to Figure 4.26).

✔ Tip

- Don't clear the Hide Modes That This Monitor Cannot Display check box to choose a higher refresh rate. A refresh rate that exceeds the capabilities of your monitor or video card can distort images and damage hardware.

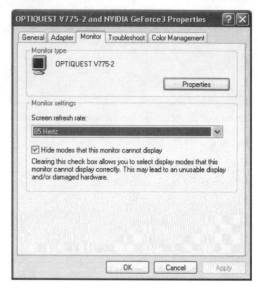

Figure 4.27 To reduce eyestrain, choose the highest refresh rate that your monitor and video card support, but check the documentation or the manufacturer's Web site to find out what the hardware will accept.

Figure 4.28 The Color Profiles list shows all color profiles associated with the current monitor and video card (none, in this case).

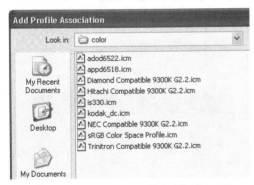

Figure 4.29 Color profiles installed with the monitor and video card are stored in the \Windows\System32\Spool\Drivers\Color folder.

To manage color profiles:

1. In Control Panel, choose Appearance and Themes > Display > Settings tab > Advanced > Color Management tab (**Figure 4.28**).

   or

   Right-click blank space on the desktop; then choose Properties > Color Management tab.

2. To add a color profile, click Add; then use the Add Profile Association dialog box to select a color profile to associate with the current monitor (**Figure 4.29**).

   or

   To remove a profile, select it; then click Remove.

   or

   To set a profile as the default for the current monitor, select it; then click Set As Default.

3. Click OK.

4. In the Display Properties dialog box, click OK (or Apply).

✔ Tips

- I've only touched on color management here. To learn more, search for *color management* in Windows Help and Support Center.

- Right-click a color profile (.icm file) in Windows Explorer to install it or associate it with a device.

CONFIGURING THE MONITOR

Configuring the Mouse

Use the Mouse utility in Control Panel to control settings such as button configuration, double-click speed, mouse pointers, responsiveness, and wheel behavior.

To configure the mouse:

1. In Control Panel, choose Printers and Other Hardware > Mouse (**Figure 4.30**).

2. To swap the left and right mouse-button functions, choose Buttons tab > check Switch Primary and Secondary Buttons.

3. If Windows often interprets your double-clicks as two single clicks, choose Buttons tab > push the Double-Click Speed slider toward Slow.

4. To make dragging easier, choose Buttons tab > check Turn on ClickLock; then you can select text or drag icons without holding down the mouse button continuously.

5. To customize mouse pointers, choose Pointers tab > Scheme to set or create a new pointer scheme (**Figure 4.31**). Use Customize to change individual elements.

   For information about the default pointer scheme, see "The Mouse" in Chapter 1.

6. On the Pointer Options tab, adjust how the pointer responds to the mouse's physical actions (**Figure 4.32**).

7. If your mouse or trackball has a wheel, on the Wheel tab, adjust its scroll behavior (**Figure 4.33**).

8. Click OK (or Apply).

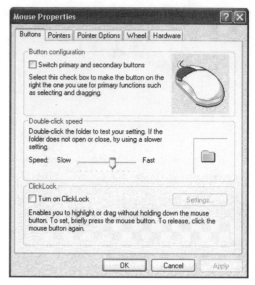

Figure 4.30 ClickLock is a mercy for touchpad users.

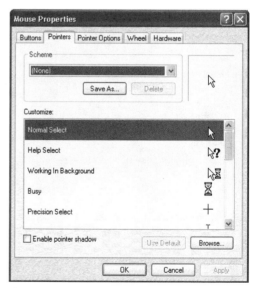

Figure 4.31 This tab lets you select predefined pointer schemes (which range from cute to practical), create your own pointer schemes, or browse to select an individual pointer (rather than an entire scheme).

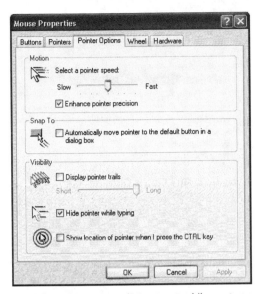

Figure 4.32 If the pointer distracts you while you type, check Hide Pointer While Typing. If you need to keep track of the pointer as it moves, check Display Pointer Trails (useful for laptop computers). Adjust the pointer's speed to have it respond more quickly or slowly to mouse movements.

Figure 4.33 A mouse wheel can stand in for scroll bars; roll the wheel to scroll up or down a list, document, or Web page. If your mouse has no wheel, these settings are ignored.

✔ Tips

- Some mice come with their own driver software. Installing these drivers adds new options and may change or replace some default mouse options. A cordless mouse may add a tab that indicates remaining battery life, for example.

- A computer with a special default pointing device—such as a touchpad on a laptop—replaces the Wheel tab with a tab of controls for that device.

- When you install an alternative pointing device such as a stylus or tablet, look for a Control Panel item devoted to that device.

- To adjust the mouse for mobility impairments, see "Accommodating Disabled Users" later in this chapter.

- To drag an icon with ClickLock turned on, point to the icon; press the left mouse button for the ClickLock interval; release the button; drag the icon to a destination; then press the button again for the ClickLock interval.

(continues on next page)

CONFIGURING THE MOUSE

- The Hardware tab (**Figure 4.34**) lists the pointing devices attached to your computer and provides access to the Properties dialog box, which is the same as the one in Device Manager.

- For general information about installing and configuring peripherals, see Chapter 8.

To access the mouse's device driver:

1. In Control Panel, choose Performance and Maintenance > System > Hardware tab > Device Manager (**Figure 4.35**).

2. Double-click Mice and Other Pointing Devices; then double-click the name of the mouse (**Figure 4.36**).

✔ Tip

- For information about Device Manager, see "Managing Device Drivers" in Chapter 8.

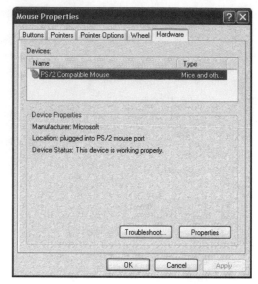

Figure 4.34 The Troubleshoot button connects you to Help and Support Center with step-by-step advice and tutorial.

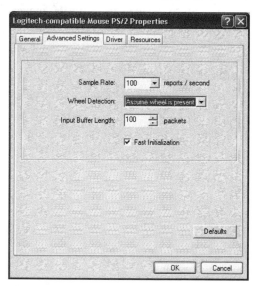

Figure 4.36 If you're having trouble activating your mouse wheel, the Wheel Detection setting on the Advanced Settings tab may help.

Figure 4.35 Like all peripherals, mice have device drivers that you may need to update or tweak from time to time.

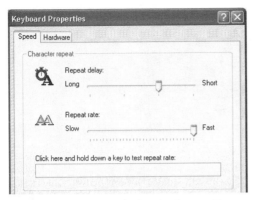

Figure 4.37 If you type rapidly, drag the Character Repeat sliders to the right to make your keyboard more responsive.

Figure 4.38 Keyboard malfunctions are rare, but the keyboard has its own Troubleshoot button to connect to Help and Support Center.

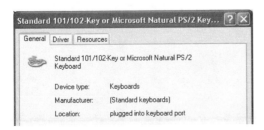

Figure 4.39 The keyboard installs a driver and claims system resources, like any other device.

Configuring the Keyboard

A keyboard should just work with no adjustments; but you can use Control Panel's Keyboard utility to change some settings.

To configure the keyboard:

1. In Control Panel, choose Printers and Other Hardware > Keyboard.

2. On the Speed tab (**Figure 4.37**), update the following settings:

   Repeat Delay controls the amount of time that elapses before a character begins to repeat when you hold down a key.

   Repeat Rate adjusts how quickly a character repeats when you hold down a key.

   Cursor Blink Rate controls the blink rate of the text cursor. To stop it from blinking, set this to None.

3. Click OK (or Apply).

✔ Tips

- Fancy keyboards with dedicated buttons and controls include their own driver software. Installing these drivers adds new options and may modify some keyboard defaults.

- The Hardware tab (**Figure 4.38**) provides access to the Properties dialog box, which is the same as the one in Device Manager.

- To adjust the keyboard for mobility impairments, see "Accommodating Disabled Users" later in this chapter.

- For an international keyboard layout, see "Localizing Your System" later in this chapter.

To access the keyboard's device driver:

1. In Control Panel, choose Performance and Maintenance > System > Hardware tab > Device Manager.

2. Double-click Keyboards; then double-click the name of the keyboard (**Figure 4.39**).

Configuring Sound and Audio Devices

Most computers have sound devices such as sound cards, microphones, and speakers, either built-in or external. Use Control Panel's Sounds and Audio Devices utility to configure the sounds and sound devices used in Windows.

✔ Tips

- For general information about installing and configuring peripherals, see Chapter 8.

- To adjust sounds for hearing impairments, see "Accommodating Disabled Users" later in this chapter.

To control sound volume:

1. In Control Panel, choose Sounds, Speech, and Audio Devices > Sounds and Audio Devices > Volume tab (**Figure 4.40**).

2. Move the slider left to lower the sound level or right to increase it.

   or

   Check the Mute box to turn off sound.

3. Check the Place Volume Icon in the Taskbar box to show a notification-area icon that you can click to change volume quickly.

4. Click OK (or Apply).

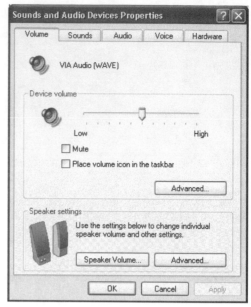

Figure 4.40 The slider in the Device Volume section is a master volume control for audio hardware.

Controlling Audio Hardware

When you choose Sounds and Audio Devices > Volume tab, the Device Volume Advanced controls are really a whole subordinate control panel for your audio hardware. In a typical installation, you may see these controls:

- **CD Player** controls the volume of audio CDs (if your CD drive is connected to the sound card directly with a three-conductor cable).

- **Line-In** controls the volume of the sound card's Line-in or Aux input (usually used to record from a stereo or other external playback device).

- **Mic** controls the sound card's microphone input volume (usually used with a microphone or dictation headset).

- **PC Speaker** controls the volume of your PC's built-in speaker, which is connected to the main board, not the sound card.

- **SW Synth** controls the volume of music produced by the sound card's MIDI synthesizer or wavetable.

- **Volume Control** is the master control—the same one shown in Figure 4.40.

- **Wave** sounds are generated by Windows, games, MP3s, Windows Media Player, and many other programs.

Depending on your computer's audio hardware, you may see all or some of these items, or some that aren't listed here. If you don't want to display all the available controls, turn them off or on individually (choose Options > Properties).

To control sound volume for individual devices:

1. In Control Panel, choose Sounds, Speech, and Audio Devices > Sounds and Audio Devices > Volume tab (refer to Figure 4.40).

2. In the Device Volume section, click Advanced to display the Volume Control dialog box (**Figure 4.41**).

3. Choose Options > Properties and check boxes to choose controls to show or hide audio devices; then click OK.

4. Drag the Balance and Volume sliders (or click Mute) to adjust each device individually.

5. Choose Options > Exit, or click the window's Close button.

6. In the Sounds and Audio Devices Properties dialog box, click OK (or Apply).

✔ Tips

- In the Volume Control dialog box, choose Options > Advanced Controls; then click one of the Advanced buttons to control bass, treble, and other settings.

- To adjust *recording* volume levels, choose Options > Properties; then select Recording in the Adjust Volume For section. The Volume Control dialog box changes to the Recording Control dialog box.

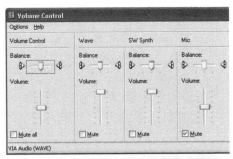

Figure 4.41 The Volume Control dialog box lets you adjust volume and balance for playback and recording devices individually.

CONFIGURING SOUND AND AUDIO DEVICES

Sound output

Your computer creates sound with several devices, including its own internal speaker, attached external speakers, headphones, and (less often) dedicated speech or synthesizer cards. These, too, are controlled by the Sounds and Audio Devices applet.

To configure speakers and headphones:

1. In Control Panel, choose Sounds, Speech, and Audio Devices > Sounds and Audio Devices > Volume tab (refer to Figure 4.40).

2. In the Speaker Settings section, click Speaker Volume to adjust the volume of each speaker separately; then click OK.

3. In the Speaker Settings section, click Advanced to select the speaker or headphone setup that you have on your computer (**Figure 4.42**); then click OK.

4. In the Sounds and Audio Devices Properties dialog box, click OK (or Apply).

Figure 4.42 The Advanced Audio Properties dialog box lets you tell Windows about your speaker setup and orientation, stereo separation, and much more.

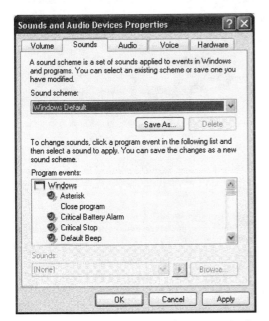

Figure 4.43 You can choose (or mute) each sound individually or use a sound scheme to apply a group of sounds.

The Sounds tab lets you customize system sound effects, which are audio clips (beeps, chords, or music snippets) associated with system events such as emptying the trash or error messages.

To configure system sound effects:

1. In Control Panel, choose Sounds, Speech, and Audio Devices > Sounds and Audio Devices > Sounds tab (**Figure 4.43**).

2. To choose a predefined group of sound effects, choose a scheme from the Sound Scheme drop-down list.

3. To change a sound for a particular event, select the event in the Program Events list; then select the sound in the Sounds list.

   or

   Select the event and click Browse to select another sound file (in .wav audio format) on your system.

   or

   Select (None) in the Sounds list to remove a sound.

4. To preview a sound for a particular event, select the event in the Program Events list; then click the Play button (the button with the right-pointing triangle).

5. To save a changed sound scheme, click Save As; type a name; then click OK.

6. To delete a custom sound scheme, select the scheme; then click Delete.

   You can delete only schemes that you created or installed, not the ones Windows provides.

7. Click OK (or Apply).

✔ Tip

■ Place .wav files in the \Windows\Media folder to have them appear in the Sounds list.

CONFIGURING SOUND AND AUDIO DEVICES

If your system has multiple input or output audio devices, the Audio and Voice tabs let you pick which device to use for sound playback, sound recording, MIDI or voice playback, and voice recording.

To configure audio and voice settings:

1. In Control Panel, choose Sounds, Speech, and Audio Devices > Sounds and Audio Devices.

2. On the Audio tab (**Figure 4.44**), select the default devices for audio playback and recording.

3. If your audio programs require the sound card selected in Default Device, check the Use Only Default Devices box; if your audio programs can use any sound card on your computer, clear the box.

4. On the Voice tab (**Figure 4.45**), select the default devices for voice playback and recording.

5. Click OK (or Apply).

✔ Tip

■ Some specialized multimedia devices, such as video capture cards, may appear in the Default Device lists on the Audio or Sounds tabs. If you have such a device and you're getting no sound, check these two tabs.

Figure 4.44 MIDI is the sound source normally used by games; it also plays music nicely without grabbing lots of disk space.

Figure 4.45 Click Test Hardware to start the Sound Hardware Test Wizard, which helps you make sure that your PC can play sounds and capture your voice.

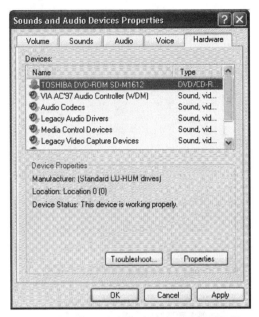

Figure 4.46 Audio and video devices are identified by make and model—crucial information when you're dealing with the manufacturer's Web support.

Figure 4.47 The Driver tab lets you inspect, update, roll back, or uninstall a device's driver.

To access an audio or video device's driver:

1. In Control Panel, choose Sounds, Speech, and Audio Devices > Sounds and Audio Devices > Hardware tab (**Figure 4.46**).

2. Choose an item from the Devices drop-down list; then click Properties > Driver tab (**Figure 4.47**).

✔ Tips

■ Each multimedia device on the Hardware tab has the same Properties dialog box that it does in Device Manager.

■ Unfortunately, getting audio output hardware to work in Windows—especially if you have a lot of it—can be complex and counterintuitive. Click the Troubleshoot button to open Help and Support Center's step-by-step trouble-shooting tutorial. If you know who made the sound component that's giving you trouble, try the manufacturer's Web site for tips, updated drivers, or patches.

Changing the Date and Time

Windows depends on accurate system time. Use Control Panel's Date and Time utility to adjust your system's clock, set its time zone, or turn on Internet-time synchronization.

To set the date and time:

1. In Control Panel, choose Date, Time, Language, and Regional Options > Date and Time.

2. On the Date & Time tab (**Figure 4.48**), adjust the date and time as needed.

3. On the Time Zone tab (**Figure 4.49**), select your time zone in the list.

    Windows assumes that you do want to Automatically Adjust Clock for Daylight Saving Changes. Uncheck this box if you don't want to use daylight saving time.

4. On the Internet Time tab (**Figure 4.50**), check the Automatically Synchronize With an Internet Time Server box to synchronize your computer clock with a highly accurate time server. Once a week is the only interval you get unless you click Update Now.

5. Click OK (or Apply).

✔ Tips

■ When your computer is shut down, its internal battery maintains the system clock.

■ Internet-time synchronization occurs regularly only if you have a full-time Internet connection, such as DSL or a cable modem. If you use dial-up, click Update Now while you're connected to the Internet to synchronize your clock immediately.

■ A time server won't adjust your computer's clock unless your PC's date is set correctly.

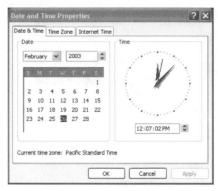

Figure 4.48 To set the time in the Time box, type new numbers; press the up- and down-arrow keys; or click the small up and down arrows.

Figure 4.49 The map is decorative; you can't click your location to specify your time zone.

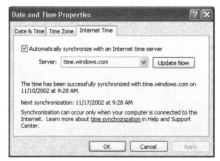

Figure 4.50 You can type the address of any time server in the Server box. Microsoft operates time.windows.com; the U.S. government operates time.nist.gov. Your network administrator or computer's manufacturer may have included other time servers in the list.

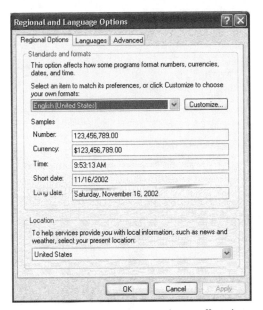

Figure 4.51 The language that you choose affects how programs format numbers, currencies, times, and dates.

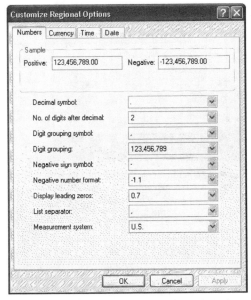

Figure 4.52 The Sample pane shows how selected settings affect the appearance of quantities.

Localizing Your System

Windows XP supports many international standards, formats, and languages. Use Control Panel's Regional and Language Options utility to adjust country-specific settings such as unit of measurement; currency, number, and date formats; and keyboard and display language.

To choose formats for numbers, currencies, times, and dates:

1. In Control Panel, choose Date, Time, Language, and Regional Options > Regional and Language Options > Regional Options tab (**Figure 4.51**).

2. In the Standards and Formats section, choose a language from the drop-down list.

3. To change individual settings, click Customize (**Figure 4.52**).

4. Click OK (or Apply).

✔ Tip

■ You can't save customized regional settings as though they were themes. If you customize and then choose another language in the list, you lose customized settings.

To choose a keyboard layout for a different language:

1. In Control Panel, choose Date, Time, Language, and Regional Options > Regional and Language Options > Languages tab > Details button > Settings tab (**Figure 4.53**).

2. Click Add; specify the language and keyboard layout to install; then click OK.

3. Repeat step 2 for each language that you want to add.

4. When you're done adding languages, click Apply.

5. In the Preferences section, click Language Bar; then check the Show the Languages Bar on the Desktop box.

6. Click OK.

7. In the Regional and Language Options dialog box, click OK (or Apply).

8. On the taskbar, click the Language bar to choose a keyboard layout (**Figure 4.54**).

✔ Tip

- Use Character Map to view the characters available on your keyboard; see "Using the Free Utility Programs" in Chapter 6.

Figure 4.53 Keyboard layouts rearrange the keys' character assignments. Pressing the [key on a U.S. keyboard with a German layout types the ü character, for example.

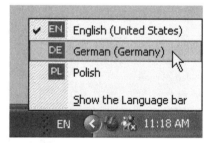

Figure 4.54 In the menu, choose the language or keyboard layout that you want to switch to, or switch by pressing the left Shift and left Alt keys at the same time.

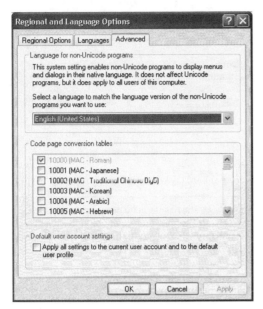

Figure 4.55 If an older program is unable to recognize your preferred language, Windows can swap the character set.

To specify the preferred language for older programs:

1. In Control Panel, choose Date, Time, Language, and Regional Options > Regional and Language Options > Advanced tab (**Figure 4.55**).

2. In the Language for Non-Unicode Programs section, choose your preferred language from the drop-down list.

3. If your word processor or Web browser isn't displaying foreign-language content correctly, in the Code Page Conversion Tables section, check the languages to install.

4. To apply your Regional and Language Options settings to your user account and to all new user accounts, check the box in the Default User Account Settings section.

5. Click OK (or Apply).

Accommodating Disabled Users

Windows XP can be set up to assist disabled users. *Accessibility* is Microsoft's umbrella term for tools that make a computer easier to use for people with poor eyesight, hearing, or mobility. Accessibility tools are:

◆ Accessibility Wizard

◆ Accessibility Options

◆ Magnifier

◆ Narrator

◆ On-Screen Keyboard

◆ Utility Manager

✔ Tip

■ Some accessibility tools are useful for everyone. Designers and developers can use Magnifier for pixel-level design work, for example.

Accessibility Wizard

Accessibility Wizard helps you choose accessibility options step by step. Use it to learn about Windows XP's accessibility functions without exploring each setting individually.

To run the Accessibility Wizard:

1. Choose Start > All Programs > Accessories > Accessibility > Accessibility Wizard.

2. Click Next.

   Accessibility Wizard guides you through the available accessibility options (**Figure 4.56**).

✔ Tip

■ Settings in the Accessibility Wizard also are available in Control Panel's Accessibility Options utility.

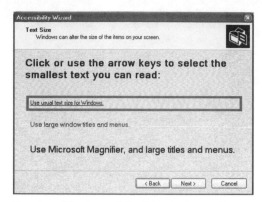

Figure 4.56 The Accessibility Wizard asks questions and sets accessibility options appropriately. In this introductory screen, you set the size of onscreen text.

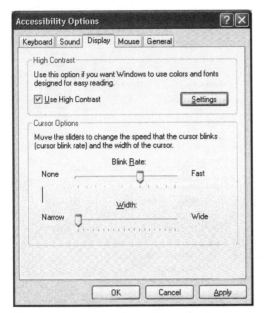

Figure 4.57 To toggle between high-contrast and standard colors, press Alt+Left Shift+Print Screen.

Figure 4.58 ShowSounds, which works a little like TV closed-captioning, substitutes text captions for speech and other sounds. Programs labeled "XP-Compatible" generally support this feature.

Accessibility Options

Control Panel's Accessibility Options utility lets you adjust accessibility settings for vision-, hearing-, or mobility-impaired users.

To set accessibility options for vision-impaired users:

1. In Control Panel, choose Accessibility Options > Accessibility Options > Display tab (**Figure 4.57**).

2. To make Windows and other programs use a color scheme that increases legibility, check the Use High Contrast box; then click Settings to pick the scheme.

3. To make the cursor (insertion point) blink faster or slower, drag the Blink Rate slider.

4. To make the cursor wider so that it's easier to see, drag the Width slider to the right.

5. Click OK (or Apply).

✔ Tips

■ Some high-contrast color schemes include large and extra-large fonts.

■ See also Magnifier and Narrator later in this section.

To set accessibility options for hearing-impaired users:

1. In Control Panel, choose Accessibility Options > Accessibility Options > Sound tab (**Figure 4.58**).

2. To display a signal onscreen when Windows plays a system sound (such as a warning beep or incoming-mail beep), check the Use SoundSentry box.

3. If SoundSentry is activated, select a visual signal, such as flashing the title bar or the entire screen.

4. To turn on captioning for programs that support it, check the Use ShowSounds box.

5. Click OK (or Apply).

To set accessibility options for mobility-impaired users:

1. In Control Panel, choose Accessibility Options > Accessibility Options > Keyboard tab (**Figure 4.59**).

2. To make the Shift, Ctrl, Alt, and Windows logo keys toggle on or off by pressing and releasing them (rather than holding them down), check the Use Sticky-Keys box.

3. To have Windows ignore brief or repeated keystrokes, check the Use Filter-Keys box.

4. To make the computer beep whenever you press Caps Lock, Num Lock, or Scroll Lock, check the Use ToggleKeys box.

5. To make programs display extra keyboard Help (if available), check the Show Extra Keyboard Help in Programs box.

6. Click the Mouse tab (**Figure 4.60**).

7. To use the numeric keypad to move the mouse pointer and to click, double-click, or drag, check the Use MouseKeys box.

8. Click OK (or Apply).

✔ Tips

- Click Settings to fine-tune the behavior of StickyKeys, FilterKeys, ToggleKeys or MouseKeys; each utility has several functions that you can choose individually.

- StickyKeys lets you use keyboard shortcuts such as Ctrl+Z or Ctrl+Alt+F1 without having to hold down multiple keys simultaneously.

- FilterKeys prevents rrrrrrrepeated keystrokes when you hold down a key. See also "Configuring the Mouse" earlier in this chapter.

Figure 4.59 StickyKeys is useful for people who have trouble pressing more than one key simultaneously. FilterKeys is for people who have trouble pressing keys quickly or lightly.

Figure 4.60 MouseKeys is designed for people who have trouble using the mouse, but it's handy for making precise moves in graphics programs, too.

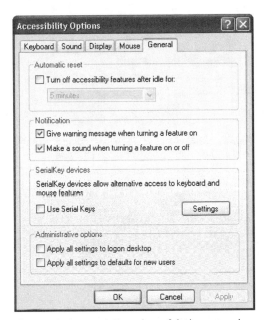

Figure 4.61 Automatic Reset is useful when several people use your computer but only some require accessibility options. Notification is useful to alert people who might turn on an accessibility feature accidentally. SerialKey is appropriate for people who can't use a standard keyboard or mouse.

■ If you watch the keyboard (rather than the screen) when typing, you may find ToggleKeys useful for warning you that you've TURNED ON CAPS LOCK ACCIDENTALLY.

■ In MouseKeys mode, press 2, 4, 6, or 8 on the numeric keypad to move the pointer. Press 5 to click, + to double-click, – to right-click, Insert to start dragging, or Delete to end dragging. Hold down Shift to move in small, precise increments or Ctrl to jump in large increments.

■ The keyboard shortcuts for toggling Accessibility options are:
StickyKeys. Press Shift five times in a row.
FilterKeys. Hold down the right Shift key for eight seconds.
ToggleKeys. Hold down the Num Lock key for five seconds.
MouseKeys. Press left Alt+left Shift+Num Lock.

■ See also "On-Screen Keyboard" later in this chapter.

To set general accessibility options:

1. In Control Panel, choose Accessibility Options > Accessibility Options > General tab (**Figure 4.61**).

2. To make Windows turn off all accessibility features after a period of inactivity, check the box in the Automatic Reset section, and select a length of time.

3. To display a confirmation message or beep every time you use a shortcut key to turn an accessibility feature on or off, check the boxes in the Notification section.

4. To turn on support for special input devices (keyboard and mouse replacements attached to a serial port), check the box in the SerialKey Devices section, and click Settings to define the device's chosen port name and data rate.

(continues on next page)

ACCOMMODATING DISABLED USERS

5. To apply these accessibility settings to all future logons or new user profiles, check the boxes in the Administrative Options section.

6. Click OK (or Apply).

Magnifier

Magnifier is a magnification program for visually impaired users; it displays a special panel at the top of the screen that shows an enlarged version of the area of the screen near the pointer or cursor (**Figure 4.62**). When you first open Magnifier, the Magnifier Settings dialog box appears (**Figure 4.63**).

To open and configure Magnifier:

1. Choose Start > All Programs > Accessories > Accessibility > Magnifier.

2. In the Magnifier Settings dialog box, select the magnification level; specify whether the magnified area tracks the mouse pointer, highlighted area, or text insertion point; or change the color scheme.

3. To hide the Magnifier Settings window, minimize it; to exit, click Close or Exit.

✔ Tips

■ The Magnifier window is docked to the top of the screen by default, but you can move it, resize it, or drag it to any screen edge to lock it in place.

■ Magnifier is a bare-bones utility, and even Microsoft suggests that you may need a more robust commercial program for full-time use. Even so, Magnifier is quite helpful if you can accept its limits.

Figure 4.62 Magnifier acts as a magnifying glass that follows the pointer or cursor around the screen.

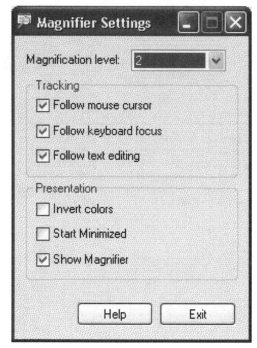

Figure 4.63 Select Invert Colors for a high-contrast color scheme that improves visibility in the magnification window.

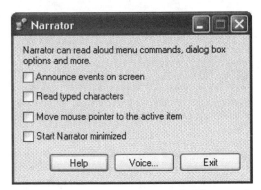

Figure 4.64 Narrator is designed to work with Notepad, WordPad, Control Panel programs, Internet Explorer, the Windows desktop, and Windows setup; it may not read words aloud correctly in other programs.

Narrator

Narrator is a text-to-speech program for visually impaired users; it uses a voice synthesizer and your system's audio hardware to read aloud the contents of the active window, menu options, text that you've typed, and text and captions of other screen elements. When you first open Narrator, the Narrator dialog box appears (**Figure 4.64**).

To open and configure Narrator:

1. Choose Start > All Programs > Accessories > Accessibility > Narrator.

2. In the Narrator dialog box, specify whether new windows, menus, or shortcut menus are read aloud when displayed; whether typed characters are read aloud; or whether the active item on your screen is read aloud.

3. Click Voice to adjust the synthesized voice's speed, volume, or pitch.

4. To hide the Narrator window, minimize it; to exit, click Close or Exit.

✔ Tips

■ Only the English version of Windows XP supports Narrator.

■ For fun, have Narrator read your email.

■ See also "Configuring Speech Recognition and Translation" later in this chapter.

■ Narrator, like Magnifier, is less capable than a full-featured commercial equivalent. If text-to-speech really boosts your ability to use a computer, consider investing in a third-party program.

ACCOMMODATING DISABLED USERS

On-Screen Keyboard

This virtual keyboard lets mobility-impaired users click the mouse (or other pointing device) to type. The program that's accepting your typed characters must be active while you're using On-Screen Keyboard.

To open and configure On-Screen Keyboard:

1. Choose Start > All Programs > Accessories > Accessibility > On-Screen Keyboard (**Figure 4.65**).

2. Use the Keyboard menu to choose the onscreen keyboard's layout.

3. Use the Settings menu to add a click when you select a key; choose a font; or set the typing mode.

4. To close On-Screen Keyboard, choose File > Exit (or click Close).

Utility Manager

Utility Manager manages Magnifier, Narrator, and On-Screen Keyboard from a central location.

To open and configure Utility Manager:

1. Choose Start > All Programs > Accessories > Accessibility > Utility Manager (**Figure 4.66**).

   or

   Press Windows logo key+U (if your keyboard supports it).

2. Select an accessibility tool; then click Start or Stop.

3. Use the check boxes to tell Windows to start any or all tools when you log on, lock your desktop, or start Utility Manager.

4. Click OK (or Apply).

Figure 4.65 On-Screen Keyboard displays a facsimile of a full keyboard that floats atop the active program.

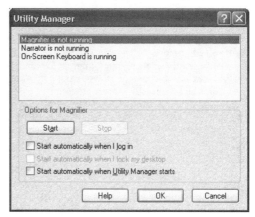

Figure 4.66 The first time that you open Utility Manager from the Start menu, a warning message tells you that some of Utility Manager's features are available only if you start it by pressing Windows logo key+U.

✔ Tip

- If your keyboard has no Windows logo key, use On-Screen Keyboard to open Utility Manager with the keyboard shortcut. This maneuver enables features that are otherwise unavailable.

Configuring Speech Recognition and Translation

Control Panel's Speech utility controls the speech-recognition and text-to-speech (speech synthesizer) features of Windows XP.

The Speech Recognition tab is visible only if you've installed a program that supports speech-recognition features such as voice dictation. Microsoft Word 2002 and later versions, for example, have this capability.

The Text-to-Speech tab controls the text-to-speech translation of the Windows speech synthesizer. The only built-in program that reads to you is Narrator, which has its own voice controls (see "Accommodating Disabled Users" earlier in this chapter).

✔ Tips

- Depending on the hardware installed on your computer, Speech may appear in Control Panel as its own applet or as part of the Sounds, Speech and Audio Devices applet.

- Windows XP's speech tools are immature. Try an established product such as Dragon Naturally Speaking (www.scansoft.com).

To configure speech recognition:

1. In Control Panel, choose Sounds, Speech, and Audio Devices > Speech > Speech Recognition tab (**Figure 4.67**).

2. Choose a speech-recognition engine from the Language drop-down list or click Settings (if available) to show additional engine properties.

3. Click New to create a new recognition profile for your voice.

   Several wizards run to help you set up the profile, calibrate your microphone and speakers, and train your profile.

4. In the Microphone section, set and configure your audio input device.

5. Click OK (or Apply).

To configure text-to-speech translation:

1. In Control Panel, choose Sounds, Speech, and Audio Devices > Speech > Text to Speech tab (**Figure 4.68**).

2. Choose one of the available Text-to-Speech voices or click Settings (if available) to display additional voice properties.

   The selected voice speaks the text in the Preview Voice section.

3. In the Voice Speed section, drag the slider to adjust the voice's rate of speech.

4. Click Audio Output to set the preferred device for voice playback.

5. Click OK (or Apply).

Figure 4.67 You must train a speech recognizer to adapt to the sound of your voice, word pronunciation, accent, and speaking manner.

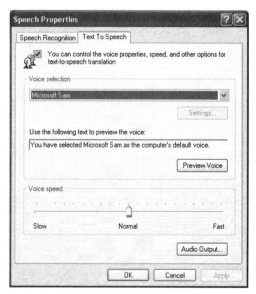

Figure 4.68 The robotic voice of Windows is named Microsoft Sam.

Figure 4.69 You can open items in folders and on the desktop by single-clicking them, just as you click a link on a Web page. To select an item without opening it, move the pointer over it.

Using Alternative Mouse Behavior

The mouse behavior described in "The Mouse" in Chapter 1 is the default. Windows' alternative setting is a Web-like interface, letting you open icons by single-clicking—instead of double-clicking, which can be awkward or confusing for beginners. (Right-clicking and dragging are unchanged.)

To open items with a single click:

1. In Control Panel, choose Appearance and Themes > Folder Options > General tab (**Figure 4.69**).

2. In the Click Items As Follows section, select Single-Click to Open an Item (Point to Select).

3. Choose icon title underlining: permanent, (like links on a Web page) or temporary (only when you point to icons).

4. Click OK (or Apply).

The instructions in this book assume that you use the default, but if you choose the alternative, be aware of the following differences:

◆ The entire concept of double-clicking is eradicated.

◆ To open an icon, click it.

◆ To select an icon, move the pointer over it—*don't* click.

◆ To select multiple icons, hold down the Ctrl or Shift key while moving the pointer over each desired icon—again, don't click. Ctrl selects individual icons; Shift selects a range of icons.

◆ To rename an icon, point over it; press F2; type the name; then press Enter.
or
Right-click it; choose Rename; type the name; then press Enter.

Conserving Power

Environmental and money concerns make power management an issue for desktop as well as laptop users. Control Panel's Power Options utility lets you configure hardware features that reduce power consumption, affect how the power switch works, and extend the life of computer parts by turning them off or switching them to a low-power state. The tabs and controls displayed in the Power Options Properties dialog box depend on the type of computer that you're using (**Figure 4.70**).

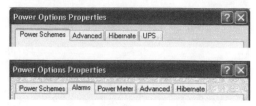

Figure 4.70 Power Options detects what's available on your PC and shows you only the options that you can control. A desktop computer has the top set of tabs; a laptop computer has the bottom set.

✔ Tips

■ To use your computer's power-management features, you may have to enable them in your system BIOS. When you boot your PC, you can configure the BIOS by pressing a key combination before Windows starts; consult the documentation that came with your computer or motherboard for details.

■ If your computer's components don't comply with the industrywide Advanced Configuration and Power Interface (ACPI) specification (also called OnNow), some power-management features may be unavailable or unpredictable. Older, non-ACPI-compliant computers have an APM tab (Advanced Power Management—an older standard) in the Power Options Properties dialog box.

Uninterruptible Power Supply

An Uninterruptible Power Supply (UPS) is a sealed backup battery—connected between the computer and the electrical outlet—that kicks in to keep your computer running if power fails. The UPS's *capacity* is expressed in minutes available to save your work and shut down normally during a power outage—about 5 minutes for a cheap UPS and up to about 30 minutes for a higher-priced one. UPSes usually protect against power surges, spikes, and brownouts (low voltage), too.

A UPS doesn't really *have* to interact with Windows, but Windows XP includes built-in support for monitoring that sounds power-failure alerts, displays remaining UPS-battery time, and—if power becomes dangerously low—shuts down the computer automatically. A UPS that plugs into a USB port will install its driver and make the Power Options UPS tab vanish, replacing it with Alarms and Power Meter tabs.

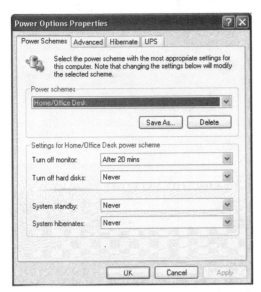

Figure 4.71 The timed power-savings settings depend on the power scheme you choose.

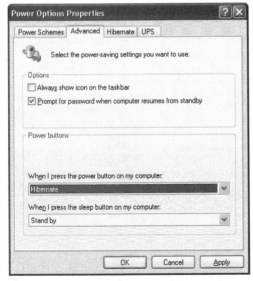

Figure 4.72 The Always Show Icon on the Taskbar option is useful if you're a laptop-computer user who changes between battery and electrical-outlet power occasionally.

To optimize your computer's power use, Windows uses a *power scheme*—a collection of settings that reduces the power consumption of certain system devices or of your entire system. You can use the power schemes provided with Windows or create your own, as you can a desktop theme.

To choose a power scheme:

1. In Control Panel, choose Performance and Maintenance > Power Options > Power Schemes tab (**Figure 4.71**).

2. In the Power Schemes section, choose a scheme from the drop-down list.

3. To customize a power scheme, in the Settings section, change the default time settings.

4. To create a new power scheme, select the time settings you want, click Save As; type a name; then click OK.

5. To delete a power scheme, select it in the Power Schemes list; then click Delete.

6. Click the Advanced tab (**Figure 4.72**).

7. To put a power-plug (or battery) icon in the notification area, check the Always Show Icon on the Taskbar box.

   Click this icon to choose a power scheme, or double-click it to open the Power Options utility.

8. To password-protect your computer during standby or hibernation, check the Prompt for Password box.

9. Click OK (or Apply).

✔ Tips

- On a laptop computer, the Power Schemes tab lets you choose independent settings for battery and plugged-in power.

(continues on next page)

CONSERVING POWER

127

- Move the mouse or press a key to bring your computer out of standby mode. Press the power button to bring it out of hibernation. Your disks may take a minute to awaken from standby.

- Turning off a monitor makes its screen go dark (and turns the green power light yellow). Turning off a hard disk makes it stop spinning.

- Windows puts a computer into System Standby more rapidly than it does into System Hibernate. This makes sense, because you'll want to put the system on standby if you're away briefly and have it hibernate automatically if you're away, say, overnight.

- The details of Stand By and Hibernate modes are listed in Table 1.1 in Chapter 1.

- Older systems may not support standby, hibernation, or software shutdown (powering off without the switch).

As described in "Logging on and Logging off Windows XP" in Chapter 1, you can choose Start > Turn Off Computer to stand by or hibernate manually, but it's faster to use the computer's power or sleep button.

To use the computer's power button to stand by or hibernate:

1. In Control Panel, choose Performance and Maintenance > Power Options > Hibernate tab (**Figure 4.73**)..

2. Check the Enable Hibernation box.

3. Click the Advanced tab (refer to Figure 4.72).

4. In the Power Buttons section, select the action your computer takes when you press the Power or Sleep button.

5. If you're using a laptop computer, choose Standby from the drop-down list below

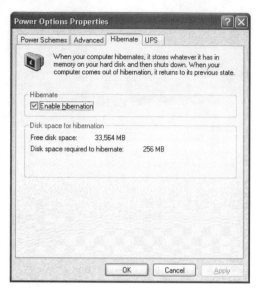

Figure 4.73 The Hibernate tab isn't available if your computer doesn't support this feature.

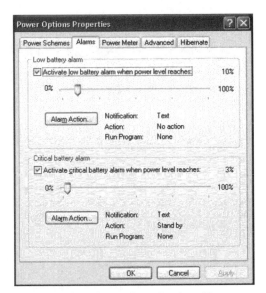

Figure 4.74 If your battery has a four-hour life, 3 percentage points is about seven minutes of use, but these settings are approximate.

Figure 4.75 At a critical power level, you put your computer in hibernation automatically (thus saving your work if you're away from your laptop when the battery dies).

When I Close the Lid of My Portable Computer.

6. Click OK (or Apply).

For laptop computers, you can set alarms that sound or appear when the battery is almost out of power. Windows gives two distinct warnings: a *low-battery alarm* and the more urgent *critical-battery alarm*. When you hear either, you should save your work immediately. The alarm options let you specify which alarms you want (low-battery, critical-battery, or both); how you want to be notified (text, sound, or both); and what the laptop should do in response to the alarm.

To set a warning alarm for a low- or critical-battery condition:

1. In Control Panel, choose Performance and Maintenance > Power Options > Alarms tab (**Figure 4.74**).

2. In the Low Battery Alarm and Critical Battery Alarm sections, check either or both boxes to set the alarms.

3. Drag the sliders to change the power-level thresholds.

   (Experience with the particular computer will help here.)

4. Click Alarm Action to specify what happens when an alarm goes off (**Figure 4.75**).

5. Click OK (or Apply).

✔ Tip

■ The Power Meter tab offers a graphical "fuel gauge" of remaining battery power, with a separate icon for each battery. Click an icon to get detailed information about that battery.

CONSERVING POWER

Managing Fonts

Windows XP includes dozens of fonts used to display text on the screen and in print. Most of these are *TrueType* or *OpenType* fonts that look smooth in all sizes and on all output devices. Windows also supports Adobe's Type 1 fonts for PostScript printers, with no need for Adobe Type Manager. You manage fonts in the Fonts folder.

✔ Tips

■ For more font information, visit www.microsoft.com/typography/.

■ Windows includes a few hideous bit-mapped fonts, called *raster* fonts, for compatibility with older programs.

■ OpenType fonts also are known as TrueType version 2 fonts.

■ To change the fonts used in icons, menus, and other screen elements, see "Choosing a Desktop Theme" earlier in this chapter.

To open the Fonts folder:

◆ In Control Panel, choose Appearance and Themes; below See Also in the task pane, click Fonts (**Figure 4.76**).

or

In Windows Explorer, open the \Windows\Fonts folder.

✔ Tips

■ To match the font names with their file-names, choose View > Details in the Fonts folder.

■ If you need more detail about the font than you can get by opening the icon, right-click it and choose Properties. (But be warned: Many Microsoft fonts have blank property sheets.)

Figure 4.76 The *O* icon indicates an OpenType font; *TT* indicates a TrueType font; and *A* indicates a raster or PostScript font.

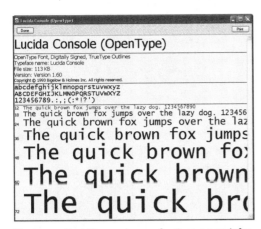

Figure 4.77 Font Viewer shows a font's summary information along with a preview.

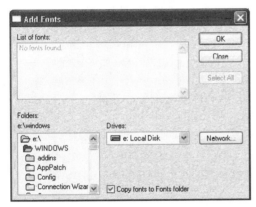

Figure 4.78 To install fonts from a network drive without using disk space on your computer, clear the Copy Fonts to Fonts Folder check box.

To view a font:

◆ In the Fonts folder, double-click the font's icon (**Figure 4.77**).

or

In the Fonts folder, select the font's icon; then press Enter (or choose File > Open).

Windows displays the font's statistics, the full alphabet, and a type sample at various sizes.

✔ Tips

■ To print a font sample, click Print in Font Viewer.

■ Font Viewer displays only a predefined set of characters. To display every character in a font, use Character Map. See "Using the Free Utility Programs" in Chapter 6.

■ Some fonts (Courier, Symbol, and Marlett, for example) are hidden because they're system fonts that Windows wants absolutely intact for use in program windows, dialog boxes, and menus. To view them, in the Fonts folder, choose Tools > Folder Options > View tab > Show Hidden Files and Folders.

■ To view fonts with a program other than Windows Font Viewer, right-click a font icon; choose Properties; then click Change.

To install a new font:

◆ In the Fonts folder, choose File > Install New Font; then navigate to and select the font files to install (**Figure 4.78**).

or

Drag a font file into the Fonts folder.

✔ Tips

■ After a font is installed, it appears in your programs' Font dialog boxes and lists.

■ Windows lets you install only these font types: TrueType (.ttf), OpenType (also .ttf), Adobe Type 1 (.pfm or .pfb), and raster (.fon).

■ If a new font appears unexpectedly in your Fonts folder, a recently installed program probably put it there.

To remove a font:

◆ In the Fonts folder, right-click the font's icon; then choose Delete.

   or

   In the Fonts folder, select the font's icon; then press Delete (or choose File > Delete).

   or

   Drag the font's icon out of the Fonts folder (to the Recycle Bin or another folder).

✔ Tip

■ If an icon in the Fonts folder has a shortcut arrow, the font is installed but located somewhere else.

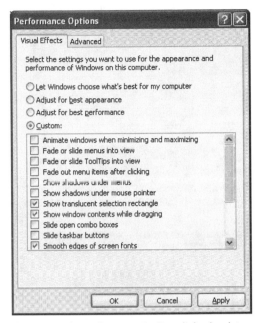

Figure 4.79 The Performance Options dialog box lets you turn off visual effects.

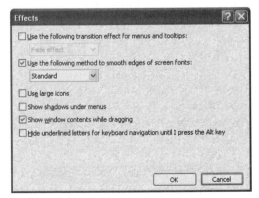

Figure 4.80 Show Window Contents While Dragging is the most useful effect here, but it can be a drag on responsiveness.

Managing Visual Effects and Performance

The Windows interface offers a lot of visual effects, such as animation, fading, and shadows. These effects are entertaining but chew up processor time and can degrade performance noticeably (particularly if you're short on RAM or video processor speed). Windows lets you disable individual visual effects; turning off some of them may make your system more responsive. It's worth experimenting.

To turn off visual effects:

1. In Control Panel, choose Performance and Maintenance > System > Advanced tab.

2. In the Performance section, click Settings > Visual Effects tab (**Figure 4.79**).

3. Select Custom; uncheck the boxes for the effects that you want to turn off; then click OK.

4. In the System Properties dialog box, click OK (or Apply).

5. In Control Panel, choose Appearance and Themes > Display > Appearance tab > Effects button.

6. Uncheck the boxes for the effects that you want to turn off; then click OK (**Figure 4.80**).

7. In the Display Properties dialog box, click OK (or Apply).

Restoring the Look of Previous Windows Versions

If you prefer the appearance of Windows 2000, 98, or Me to Windows XP's redesigned interface, you can revert to the classic look (**Figure 4.81**). I've collected the settings here for quick reference. They apply only to the logged-on user.

To switch to the classic Start menu:

◆ In Control Panel, choose Appearance and Themes > Taskbar and Start Menu > Start Menu tab > Classic Start menu option (**Figure 4.82**).

To switch to classic Control Panel view:

1. Choose Start > Control Panel.

2. In the task pane, click Switch to Classic View (**Figure 4.83**).

To hide the task pane in folder windows:

1. In Control Panel, choose Appearance and Themes > Folder Options > General tab.

2. In the Tasks section, select Use Windows Classic Folders (**Figure 4.84**).

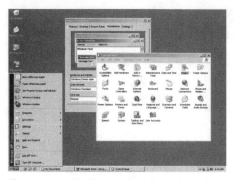

Figure 4.81 A Windows XP desktop with the classic Start menu, Control Panel, and visual style.

Figure 4.82 This setting activates the classic single-column Start menu.

Figure 4.83 Control Panel's task pane lets you remove the extra layer of fluff in category view.

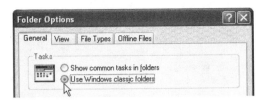

Figure 4.84 This option hides the space-consuming task pane in folder windows.

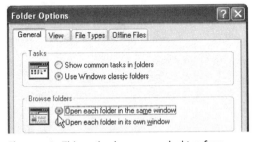

Figure 4.85 This option keeps your desktop from becoming cluttered with folder windows.

To browse folders by using a single window:

1. In Control Panel, choose Appearance and Themes > Folder Options > General tab.

2. In the Browse Folders section, select Open Each Folder in the Same Window (**Figure 4.85**).

To switch to the classic visual style for windows and buttons:

1. In Control Panel, choose Appearance and Themes > Display > Appearance tab.

2. From the Windows and Buttons drop-down list, choose Windows Classic Style (**Figure 4.86**).

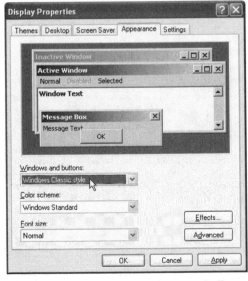

Figure 4.86 This setting restores the squared-off, muted look of windows and buttons.

To show My Computer, My Documents, and My Network Places on the desktop:

1. In Control Panel, choose Appearance and Themes > Display > Desktop tab > Customize Desktop button.

2. In the Desktop Icons section, select the icons to show (**Figure 4.87**).

To use earlier versions of desktop icons:

1. In Control Panel, choose Appearance and Themes > Display > Desktop tab > Customize Desktop button (refer to Figure 4.87).

2. Select an icon; click Change Icon; then browse to \Windows\system32\ shell32.dll, which contains most of the old icons (**Figure 4.88**).

✔ Tip

■ When you upgrade to Windows XP, the Windows Setup program hijacks your file-type associations—rudely and without telling you. Your default program for .html files, for example, is replaced with Internet Explorer. To change your settings back, In Control Panel, choose Appearance and Themes > Folder Options > File Types tab; select an extension; then click Change. For information about file types, see "Associating Documents with Programs" in Chapter 6.

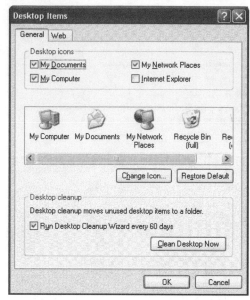

Figure 4.87 The Desktop Items dialog box lets you put system icons back on your desktop.

Figure 4.88 Windows XP still contains a treasure trove of classic-style icons, if you prefer them.

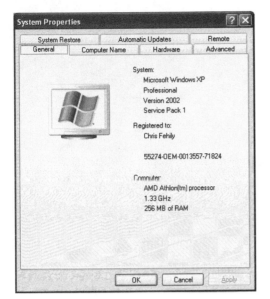

Figure 4.89 The General tab gives information about your Windows version, registration, processor, and RAM.

Getting General System Information

The General tab in Control Panel's System utility is a helpful, information-only window that displays:

◆ The version of Windows installed on your computer (including Service Packs)

◆ The Windows edition (Home, Professional, Server, and so on)

◆ Registration information that was entered during Windows Setup

◆ The type and speed of your computer's processor

◆ The total physical memory (RAM) installed on your computer

You'll need some or all of this information when you request tech support over the phone, particularly if you're talking to Microsoft.

To display general system information:

◆ In Control Panel, choose Performance and Maintenance > System > General tab (**Figure 4.89**).

✔ Tip

■ See also "Getting System Information" in Chapter 19.

ORGANIZING
FILES AND FOLDERS

Like all modern operating systems, Windows XP uses files and folders to organize your information, so that you aren't overwhelmed by long file lists and can distinguish one set of information from another. A *file* is the basic unit of computer storage; it can be a program, a program's configuration data, a log that the computer itself maintains, or a document that you create or receive. You organize files in containers called *folders* (or *directories*), which can hold additional folders (called *subfolders*) to form a treelike hierarchy. Folders in turn are stored on *disks*, or *volumes*—such as hard drives, floppy disks, CD/DVD drives, or Zip drives.

Windows creates a few system folders to store its own files and settings but otherwise doesn't care how you structure your tree of folders and files. In this chapter, I explain how to use Windows Explorer to navigate and manage your stored information.

Exploring Your Computer

My Computer (**Figure 5.1**), a top-level folder, is the window to your computer's data structure. From it, you can open all the files, folders, and disks on your computer (or network), which are categorized as follows:

Files Stored on This Computer lists folders for everyone with a user account on this computer. You see your personal files and folders here. All users can see the community folder named Shared Documents. If you double-click another user's folder, and you don't have permissions for it, you'll get an error message; see "Sharing Files" in Chapter 17.

Hard Disk Drives lists the hard drives installed on this computer.

Devices with Removable Storage lists floppy, CD-ROM, DVD, Zip, and other removable-disk drives.

Scanners and Cameras shows icons for installed digital cameras and scanners.

Depending on how your PC is configured, more categories (such as Other or Network Drives) may appear.

To see what's on your computer:

1. Choose Start > My Computer.

   or

   Press Windows logo key+E (if your keyboard supports it).

2. To see what's on a hard drive, in the Hard Disk Drives section, double-click the drive you want to see.

   or

   To find a file or folder on a floppy disk, CD-ROM, or other media, in the Devices with Removable Storage section, double-click the item you want to see. (You'll get an error message if there's no disk in the drive.)

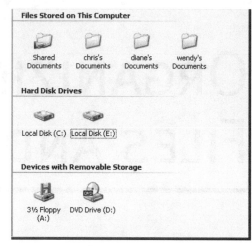

Figure 5.1 The My Computer window shows the top-level folders and disks on your PC, including network drives and other storage devices. Except on factory-fresh computers, no two My Computer folders are ever quite the same.

or

To find a file or folder, in the Files Stored on This Computer section, double-click a folder.

Keep double-clicking folders to burrow to the file or folder you want. (To return to the previous folder, press Backspace or click the Back arrow in the window's top-left corner.)

✔ Tips

- When you double-click a folder, Windows replaces the original window with a new one or opens a separate window atop the current one. Opening new windows makes it easy to move or copy files but clutters the screen quickly. To choose the behavior you prefer, in My Computer, choose Tools > Folder Options > General tab; then select an option in the Browse Folders section.

- Shift–double-click a My Computer disk or folder icon to jump to Windows Explorer view.

- To change how My Computer is displayed in the Start menu, see "Customizing the Start Menu" in Chapter 2.

- To show the My Computer icon on the desktop, see "Restoring the Look of Previous Windows Versions" in Chapter 4.

- To show Control Panel in My Computer, see "Using Control Panel" in Chapter 4.

- You can rename Hard Disk Drive icons.

- To see how much free space remains on a hard disk, right-click its icon; then choose Properties.

Drive Letters

Like all Windows versions, Windows XP inherits its drive-naming conventions from DOS. Drives are named by a letter followed by a colon:

A: is the first floppy-disk drive.

B: is the second floppy-disk drive (if present).

C: is the first hard-disk drive or the first partition of the first physical hard-disk drive. This drive usually contains Windows itself.

D: through Z: are assigned to other hard-disk drives, CD/DVD drives, mapped network drives, or removable storage devices such as Zip drives.

Windows assigns drive letters consecutively, but you can use Computer Management to change them; see "Managing Disks" in Chapter 19.

The My Computer folder is the master view of *Windows Explorer*, or simply *Explorer*, the key tool for working with files and folders on your local machine or network.

To open Windows Explorer:

◆ Choose Start > All Programs > Accessories > Windows Explorer (**Figure 5.2**).

or

Right-click the Start button; then choose Explore.

or

Choose Start > Run, type explorer; then press Enter.

✔ Tips

■ During installation, Windows XP creates three top-level system folders:

Documents and Settings contains a subfolder for each user account or for each user who has logged on to a network domain. These subfolders contain the users' personal settings and documents. If you're not an administrator, you can't open other users' subfolders (see Chapter 16).

Program Files contains all the programs—Word, Internet Explorer, or Photoshop, for example—that you or Windows Setup have installed, along with all the support files needed to run those programs. In general, you shouldn't need (or want) to touch files in this folder.

Windows (or **Winnt**, if you've upgraded from Windows 2000/NT) contains critical operating-system files. Look, but don't touch—with the exception of the Fonts subfolder, see "Managing Fonts" in Chapter 4.

■ If These Files Are Hidden appears when you click a system folder, click Show the Contents of This Folder to see the folder's contents.

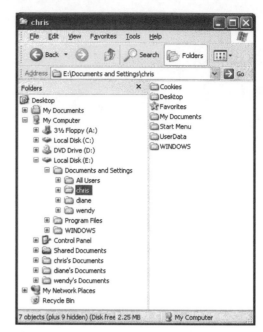

Figure 5.2 The right pane shows the selected folder's contents (or the results of a search). The left pane is the Explorer bar. The Folders bar (shown here) is displayed by default, but you can use the View menu to show Search, Favorites, and other bars.

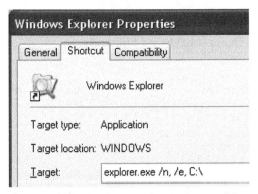

Figure 5.3 This setting opens Explorer at the root of the C: drive, but it's more common to specify a personal subfolder, such as `C:\Documents and Settings\<your name>\My Documents\My Novel`.

Pathnames

Windows locates and identifies each file or folder by its unique address, called its *pathname* or simply *path*. A pathname is a listing of the folders that lead from the top-level or *root* directory of a disk drive to a particular file or folder. `C:\` represents the C: drive's root directory, for example. A backslash (\) separates the pathname components. The pathname `C:\Documents and Settings\All Users\Documents\My Pictures\Sample Pictures\Water lilies.jpg` traces the route from the file `Water lilies.jpg` to the C: drive's root directory. For files on a network, the pathname may begin with a double-backslash and a computer name instead of a disk drive (`\\someserver` instead of `C:`, for example).

The Address toolbar in Windows Explorer displays the pathname of the selected folder. The Target box in document or program shortcut's Properties dialog box also displays a pathname. You can copy and paste these pathnames if you need them.

- If you choose Open (instead of Explore) from the Start button's shortcut menu, Explorer opens with the task pane (instead of the Folders bar) displayed.

- If you use Explorer's Favorites menu to view a Web page, the menus and toolbars change to those of Internet Explorer (see Chapter 13).

By default, Explorer opens with My Documents or Desktop highlighted, but you can modify Explorer's shortcut to highlight a folder of your choice initially.

To open Windows Explorer with a specific folder selected:

1. Right-click a Windows Explorer shortcut (in the Start menu or on the desktop); then choose Properties.

2. In the Target box, type:
   `explorer.exe /n, /e, C:\<folder>`
   `C:\<folder>` is the full pathname of the folder to select initially (**Figure 5.3**).

3. Click OK.
   When you double-click the shortcut, Explorer opens with the specified folder highlighted.

✔ Tip

- Another way to open Explorer in a specific folder: Choose Start > Run; type the folder's pathname; then press Enter.

Windows Explorer represents your files, folders, and disks as a hierarchical structure called a *tree* (shown in the Folders bar in the left pane in Figure 5.2). A fully expanded tree is unwieldy, so Explorer shows only the top few levels of the tree by default. Use the mouse or keyboard to collapse and expand individual branches selectively.

To navigate folders in Windows Explorer:

◆ To expand or collapse a branch, click the plus sign (+) or minus sign (-) next to a tree icon.

The selected folder's files and nested folders appear in the right pane.

✔ Tips

■ **Table 5.1** lists Explorer's keyboard shortcuts.

■ If no plus sign appears next to an icon, that branch can't be expanded further because it has no subfolders.

■ If the Folders bar isn't displayed, click Folders on the toolbar (or choose View > Explorer Bar > Folders).

■ If the Folders bar is too narrow to show its contents, drag its right edge to widen it, or use the horizontal scroll bar at bottom to shift its contents. If you point to a partially hidden folder, a pop-up tip displays its full name.

Table 5.1

Explorer Keyboard Shortcuts	
To	Press
Expand or collapse the selected branch	Right arrow or left arrow
Jump to parent branch *without* collapsing	Backspace
Jump from top to bottom of expanded branch	Alt+Right arrow
Jump from bottom to top of expanded branch	Alt+Left arrow
Move up visible branches	Up arrow
Move down visible branches	Down arrow
Expand all branches below selection	* (on numeric pad)
Go to a visible branch	The branch's initial letter
Cycle through visible branches with same initial letter	The initial letter repeatedly
Cycle between the icon pane, folder pane, and address bar	Tab or F6

- Explorer offers information beyond Folders via the View > Explorer Bar submenu. Search displays the XP search program; see "Searching for Files and Folders" later in this chapter. Favorites lists your Internet Explorer bookmarks; see "Bookmarking Pages" in Chapter 13. The Media bar, new in XP, contains controls for playing and managing music and video files; see "Browsing Tips" in Chapter 13. History lists recently visited Web pages and recently opened documents, sorted by date; see "Navigating the Web" in Chapter 13.

- If you notice that a folder is missing in Windows Explorer (or that a + appears next to a folder that has no subfolders), press F5 to refresh the display.

- To navigate by using the slightly different method of earlier Windows versions, turn off Simple Folder View. See "Setting Folder Options" later in this chapter.

EXPLORING YOUR COMPUTER

Displaying Links to Common Tasks

The *task pane*, new in XP, occupies the left side of an Explorer window and provides useful commands and links to related locations. Use it to move, copy, or email files; play music; jump to other folders quickly; or get file and folder details, for example (**Figure 5.4**). The task pane is displayed by default; if space is tight you may prefer to hide it.

To show or hide the task pane:

1. In Windows Explorer, choose Tools > Folder Options > General tab.

   or

   In Control Panel, choose Appearance and Themes > Folder Options > General tab.

2. Select one of the Tasks options (**Figure 5.5**).

3. Click OK (or Apply).

✔ Tips

- The task pane is on or off globally; you can't have it appear in some windows but not others.

- Any displayed Explorer bar replaces the task pane. You can't resize the task pane, as you can the Folders or Search bar.

- The task pane's Details section (at bottom) acts like a stripped-down Properties dialog box for the selected file or folder. If multiple files are selected, the number of selected files and their total size are displayed.

- At a low monitor resolution, you may have to scroll the task pane to see the lower sections.

- To expand or collapse a task-pane section, click the double arrow in the section's top-right corner.

Figure 5.4 The task pane changes dynamically, depending on the selected folder or file. Here, I've selected a music file.

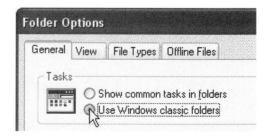

Figure 5.5 Choose Use Windows Classic Folders to hide the task pane in all windows.

Figure 5.6 The Windows Explorer status bar (along the bottom of the window) shows the number of objects selected, their combined size, and free disk space.

Displaying Summary Information

The *status bar* is the rectangular panel that runs along the bottom of an Explorer window and displays settings and statistics about the selected files, folders, or disks. The status bar is divided into sections, each of which shows different information. If you're used to an earlier Windows version, you'll notice that the status bar is *hidden* by default in XP.

To show or hide the status bar:

◆ In Windows Explorer, choose View > Status Bar to toggle the status bar on or off (**Figure 5.6**).

✔ Tips

■ The status bar displays a short explanation of any menu command that you point to.

■ Double-clicking the status bar's My Computer icon displays the Internet Security Properties dialog box...which makes little sense. Microsoft chose this behavior to make the Windows Explorer status bar act like the Internet Explorer status bar.

■ Status bars appear in many programs— all Microsoft Office applications, for example—but their layout and behavior depend on the program. Some sections respond to clicks, double-clicks, or right-clicks; no standard exists. Just try clicking.

Using Windows Explorer Toolbars

Windows Explorer has three toolbars that you can display in any combination (**Figure 5.7**):

Standard Buttons displays buttons for common Explorer tasks. You can customize these buttons.

Address Bar displays the name or pathname of the selected item. You can type a pathname in the Address text box and press Enter or click Go to go to that item.

Links displays links to Internet Explorer's Favorites folder. You can drag file or Web shortcuts onto this toolbar or right-click to delete links.

To show or hide a toolbar:

◆ In Windows Explorer, choose View > Toolbars; then, from the submenu, choose a toolbar to toggle.

  or

  Right-click any displayed toolbar; then choose a toolbar to toggle.

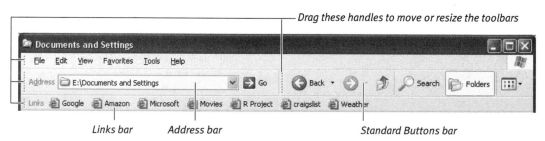

Drag these handles to move or resize the toolbars

Links bar   *Address bar*   *Standard Buttons bar*

Figure 5.7 The Windows Explorer toolbars.

✔ Tips

- To hide the menu bar and all toolbars (except Standard Buttons) and view Explorer full-screen, press F11. Press F11 again to restore toolbars.

- To remove the redundant Go button from the Address bar, right-click the Go button; then uncheck Go Button. (But don't hurry to do this; the Go button often works better than the Refresh icon, even though both items nominally do the same thing.)

- The Media bar replaces the earlier Radio toolbar. See "Browsing Tips" in Chapter 13.

- After you have the toolbars looking the way you want, you can lock them in place.

To move or resize a toolbar:

- ◆ Drag the vertical dimpled handle on the toolbar's left edge.

✔ Tips

- To put a toolbar on its own line, drag it up or down.

- To swap the positions of two toolbars on the same line, drag one of them down; then drag it up to the other side of the second toolbar.

- You can move the menu bar.

- If a toolbar is too long to fit in the window, a >> button appears on the toolbar's right edge. Click the button to display the buttons that don't fit.

- If you can't move or resize the toolbars, unlock them.

To lock or unlock the toolbars:

◆ Choose View > Toolbars > Lock the Toolbars.

or

Right-click any displayed toolbar; then choose Lock the Toolbars.

✔ Tip

■ The dimpled handle on a toolbar's left edge turns solid when the toolbar is locked.

To customize the Standard Buttons toolbar:

1. Choose View > Toolbars > Customize (**Figure 5.8**).

   or

   Right-click the Standard Buttons toolbar; then choose Customize.

2. To add a button, select it in the left list; then click Add (or drag it to the right list).

3. To change a button's position, select it in the right list; then click Move Up or Move Down (or drag it to the desired position).

4. To remove a button, select it in the right list; then click Remove (or drag it to the left list).

5. To reposition or hide the buttons' descriptive text, use the Text Options list.

6. To change the size of the toolbar icons, use the Icon Options list.

7. To restore the default set of buttons on the toolbar, click Reset.

8. Click Close.

Figure 5.8 If you change the appearance of folders a lot, add a Folder Options button to the Standard Buttons toolbar.

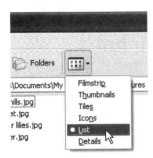

Figure 5.9 The View menu is available from the menu bar or the toolbar.

Viewing Files and Folders in Different Ways

Explorer lets you view the contents of a folder several ways. You can vary the size of icons, change the details displayed, or view miniature previews of graphics and files, for example. Each view has advantages.

To change the view of a folder's items:

◆ In Windows Explorer, select a folder; then choose a view from the View menu (**Figure 5.9**):

Filmstrip (new in XP) creates a slide show of image files, with the selected file shown as a larger image above the others (**Figure 5.10**).

Thumbnails displays large icons for easy identification (**Figure 5.11**).

Tiles (new in XP) displays large, colorful icons with three lines of text that describe each file (**Figure 5.12**).

Figure 5.10 In Filmstrip view, use the first pair of buttons below the larger image to run forward or backward through the other images. Use the second pair of buttons to rotate the current picture.

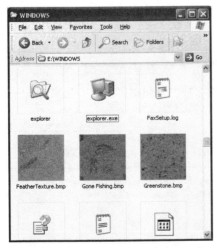

Figure 5.11 Thumbnails view is good for viewing photos, but it's also useful if you want a large icon to click.

Figure 5.12 In Tiles view, the information that appears depends on the file type.

Icons displays items the way icons are shown on the desktop (**Figure 5.13**).

List lists the names of files and folders, preceded by small icons (**Figure 5.14**).

Details displays a columnar list of files, folders, and their properties (**Figure 5.15**).

✔ Tips

■ You can right-click an empty area in Explorer's right pane to use the View submenu.

■ The Small Icons view of earlier Windows versions is gone.

■ Filmstrip view is unavailable in Windows Classic Folders. See "Restoring the Look of Previous Windows Versions" in Chapter 4.

■ In Filmstrip or Thumbnails view, right-click a picture to rotate it or set it as your desktop background via the shortcut menu. Double-click a picture to preview it in Windows Picture and Fax Viewer.

■ You can view pictures as a filmstrip in any My Pictures subfolder or any folder customized as a pictures folder. See "Customizing a Folder" later in this chapter.

■ To make all your folders use the same view, set up one folder the way you want it; then choose Tools > Folder Options > View tab > Apply to All Folders. You still can apply distinct views to individual folders afterward. (To return all folders to their default views, click Reset All Folders in the same dialog box.)

■ Windows remembers every folder's view each time you revisit the folder—although it tends to forget the view of seldom-visited folders. To make Windows always forget folder views between visits, choose Tools > Folder Options > View tab > Advanced Settings > uncheck Remember Each Folder's View Settings.

Figure 5.13 Icons view sorts items across rows.

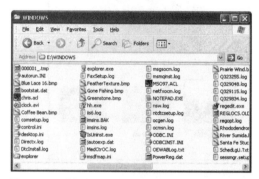

Figure 5.14 List view is the most compact display, showing the most files per window—but it's also the most difficult to select files from.

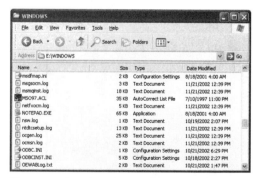

Figure 5.15 The column headings in Details view list the properties displayed for each file.

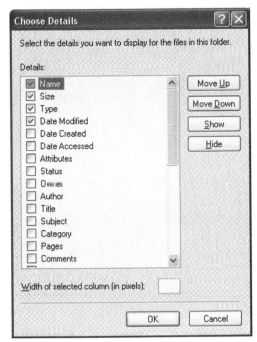

Figure 5.16 Explorer offers dozens of properties to display, but each file type will have only some of these properties.

Figure 5.17 This double-headed arrow appears as I'm resizing the Name column by dragging its vertical divider. To move a column, drag from the column heading's center, not its edge.

Changing the File Details Displayed

Details view contains the most information. By default, the columns displayed depend on the type of files in the folder—picture folders show date photographed and image dimensions, for example—but you can choose which columns appear.

To choose details to display:

1. In Windows Explorer, select a folder; then choose View > Details.

2. Choose View > Choose Details; then select the properties that you want to display (**Figure 5.16**).

3. Click OK.

✔ Tips

■ Right-click any column heading to choose which columns to display.

■ You can rearrange columns and set column widths through the Choose Details dialog box, but it's easier to make those changes in the Explorer window. To resize a column, drag the column heading's right edge left or right (**Figure 5.17**). To rearrange columns, drag the column headings horizontally.

■ Double-click a column's right edge to widen that column just enough to reveal that column's widest item.

Sorting Icons

By default, Windows Explorer sorts icons alphabetically by name (listing all folders first, followed by all files), but you can sort them in other ways.

To sort icons:

◆ In Windows Explorer, select a folder; choose View > Arrange Icons By; then choose a sorting priority from the submenu:

Name to sort alphabetically by name.

Size to sort by file size, with the smallest first. Folders aren't sorted by size.

Type to sort alphabetically by file type, which keeps files with the same file extension together (.doc for Word files or .exe for programs, for example).

Modified to sort by the date when the file or folder was last modified, with the most recent first.

✔ Tips

■ Right-click an empty area in Explorer's right pane to use the Arrange Icons By submenu.

■ In My Computer, you can sort by the disks' free space or total size.

■ The Auto Arrange and Align to Grid commands in the Arrange Icons By submenu arrange icons neatly, rather than sort them. See "Tidying Your Desktop" in Chapter 2.

Details view offers more sorting options than the other views. You can reverse-sort (from Z to A, for example), and you can sort by any visible column.

To sort icons in Details view:

◆ Click the heading of the column to sort by. To reverse the sort order, click the column heading again (**Figure 5.18**).

The sorted column's header shows a small arrowhead pointing up for ascending sort or down for descending sort.

Name	Size	Type	Date Modified
Blue hills.jpg	28 KB	JPEG Image	8/18/2001 4:00 AM
Sunset.jpg	70 KB	JPEG Image	8/18/2001 4:00 AM
Water lilies.jpg	82 KB	JPEG Image	8/18/2001 4:00 AM
Winter.jpg	104 KB	JPEG Image	8/18/2001 4:00 AM

Figure 5.18 Subtle shading indicates the sort column. A small arrow in the column heading points up or down to indicate the sort direction.

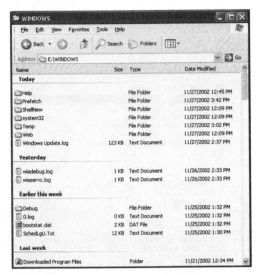

Figure 5.19 These icons are sorted by the dates they were changed. The Show in Groups feature categorizes them by Today, Yesterday, and so on.

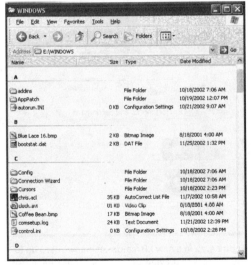

Figure 5.20 When the same icons are sorted by name, they're grouped like a book's index: A, B, C....

Grouping Icons

Windows XP's clever Show in Groups feature imposes grouping categories based on how icons are sorted. In a folder sorted by file type, for example, image files appear in one group, Microsoft Word files appear in another group, and Photoshop files in another. Sorting by size yields, say, Tiny, Small, Medium, and Large groups. Grouping is useful for scanning crowded folders.

To group icons:

◆ In Windows Explorer, select a folder; then choose View > Arrange Icons By > Show in Groups (**Figures 5.19** and **5.20**).

✔ Tips

■ You can right-click an empty area in Explorer's right pane to use the Arrange Icons By submenu.

■ Grouping isn't available in Filmstrip and List views.

■ Within each time period, the icons in Figure 5.19 are sorted alphabetically by name (listing all folders first, followed by all files).

Customizing a Folder

Windows XP drops the Customize This Folder Wizard of earlier versions in favor of the Customize This Folder command, with a dialog box that lets you apply folder templates or custom images. Most of the time, though, you'll be satisfied with the default folder settings.

To customize a folder:

1. In Windows Explorer, select a folder; then choose View > Customize This Folder (**Figure 5.21**).

   or

   Right-click a folder icon; then choose Properties > Customize tab.

2. Select a folder template from the list, and specify whether you want the template applied to all its subfolders as well.

   The Documents template is for generic folders. Other templates are designed for photo, music, or video folders.

3. To place a picture of your choice on a folder in Thumbnails view, click Choose Picture; then navigate to and select an image file.

   If you change your mind, click Restore Default to use default pictures.

4. To change the folder's icon in every view except Thumbnails, click Change Icon; then navigate to and select an icon.

   The icon replaces the standard folder icon.

5. Click OK (or Apply).

✔ Tips

- Right-click an empty area in Explorer's right pane to choose Customize This Folder.

- Customize This Folder isn't available for system folders such as Windows (or Winnt), Program Files, Shared Documents, My Documents, and other Shared and My folders.

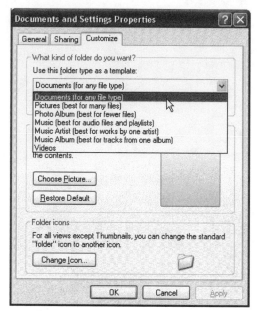

Figure 5.21 The template choice determines the view setting (Tiles, Thumbnails, and so on), task-pane commands, and background image for the folder.

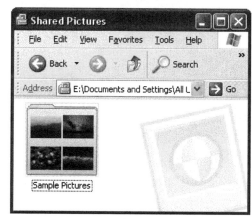

Figure 5.22 In a new XP feature, Windows uses up to four images to preview the contents of picture, music, and video folders. For videos, the first frame is displayed. For music downloaded from Windows Media Player, album art is displayed.

- In Thumbnails view, Windows uses the first four files in a picture, music, or video folder to identify it. The folder's sort order determines which files are displayed (**Figure 5.22**).

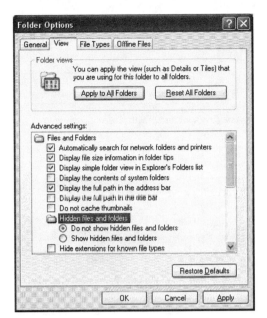

Figure 5.23 In Folder Options View Advanced, you may have to double-click the icons in the list to display subordinate options.

Setting Folder Options

Windows offers a trainload of options that control how folders appear and behave. Some options are trivial, but others are significant—and their default values can make Windows harder to use.

To set folder options:

1. In Windows Explorer, choose Tools > Folder Options > View tab (**Figure 5.23**).

   or

   In Control Panel, choose Appearance and Themes > Folder Options > View tab.

2. In the Advanced Settings list, select the desired options (**Table 5.2**, next page). Changes affect all Explorer windows.

3. To restore the settings to their factory values, click Restore Defaults.

4. Click OK (or Apply).

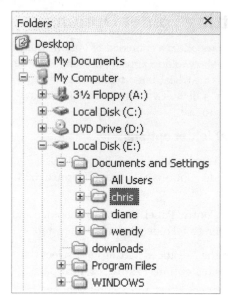

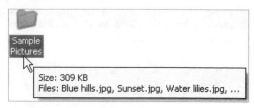

Figure 5.24 A folder tip with size and content information.

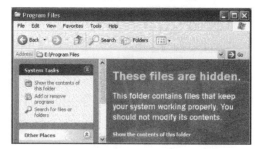

Figure 5.25 Turn off Simple Folder View to restore the vertical dotted lines that indicate how deeply a folder is nested.

Figure 5.26 If you click Show the Contents of This Folder in this screen, the warning never reappears, no matter how this option is set.

Table 5.2

Folder Options

Option	Description
Automatically Search for Network Folder and Printers	Turn this option off if you're rarely connected to a network and don't want Windows to scan for network printers, shared folders, and shared disks periodically.
Display File Size Information in Folder Tips	Shows size information in the folder tip that pops up when your pointer hovers over a folder icon (**Figure 5.24**). If you turn this off, you still get pop-up contents information; to disable folder tips, see Show Pop-Up Description for Folder and Desktop Items.
Display Simple Folder View in Explorer's Folders List	When turned on, Windows *expands* the folder you click and simultaneously *collapses* the folder you previously expanded. (To stop the previous folder from collapsing, click a plus-sign icon, not a name or folder icon.) Turning off this option restores the navigation method of earlier Windows versions, which never collapses folders automatically (**Figure 5.25**). Simple Folder View is helpful when you're working with many folders and subfolders.
Display the Contents of System Folders	By default, Windows displays a These Files Are Hidden screen when you try to open critical system folders such as Windows or Program Files (**Figure 5.26**). Microsoft installed this safety feature to prevent potentially disastrous changes. Turn off this option if you're an experienced user with legitimate business in system folders.
Display the Full Path in the Address Bar and Display the Full Path in the Title Bar	When these options are turned on, Explorer shows the selected folder's pathname in the Address bar (if it's showing) and title bar. As the path is quite informative, turn on at least one of these options. (For information about paths, see "Exploring Your Computer" earlier in this chapter.) If you display the full path on the title bar, Windows also displays the (usually truncated) full path on taskbar buttons too. Hover the pointer over the button to pop up the full path.
Do Not Cache Thumbnails	By default, Windows stores the images that appear in Thumbnails view in memory so that it can display them quickly when you revisit the folder. Check this box to free some memory, in exchange for a delay when opening folders in Thumbnails view.

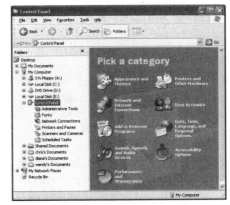

Figure 5.27 When I save Microsoft's complete home page in Internet Explorer (that is, visit www.microsoft.com, and choose File > Save As), IE creates an HTML file named `Microsoft Corporation.htm` and a folder named `Microsoft Corporation_files` that contains the accompanying image (GIF and JPEG) and script files.

Figure 5.28 You can open Control Panel in the Folders bar.

Table 5.2

Folder Options *(continued)*	
OPTION	**DESCRIPTION**
Hidden Files and Folders *and* Hide Protected Operating System Files	By default, Windows (wisely) hides critical files that it doesn't want you to move, delete, or rename. If you show these files, they appear as dimmed icons, so you remember to leave them alone. (Technically, a hidden file has its Hidden attribute set, and a system file has its System attribute set.)
Hide Extensions for Known File Types	By default, Windows hides the file extension on standard documents and files (.doc for Word files and .exe for programs, for example). Beginning users may want to leave this option on to make Windows appear less intimidating, but everyone else should turn it off for the reasons discussed in "Associating Documents with Programs" in Chapter 6.
Launch Folder Windows in a Separate Process	This option makes Windows run each folder window in segregated memory space (RAM). Turn this on only if Windows Explorer is crash-prone on your system; otherwise, leave it off to manage your RAM more efficiently.
Managing Pairs of Web Pages and Folders	When you save a complete Web page in Internet Explorer, the page's text is stored in one HTML file, and its images and scripts are stored in a folder named to match (**Figure 5.27**). To make Windows Explorer treat this file-and-folder pair as a single entity, select Show and Manage the Pair as a Single File or Show Both Parts but Manage as a Single File. If you move or delete one item, for example, Windows Explorer takes the same action on the other, maintaining the connection between them. To break the file-and-folder link, select Show Both Parts and Manage Them Individually.
Remember Each Folder's View Settings	Turn this on to make Explorer remember each folder's view settings independently. If you turn off this setting, each folder inherits the view setting from its parent folder.
Restore Previous Folder Windows at Logon	Turn on this option to make Windows Explorer reopen all your previously opened folder windows when you log on. This behavior was automatic in earlier Windows versions but is turned off by default in XP.
Show Control Panel in My Computer	Turn this on to make Control Panel appear in Windows Explorer, below My Computer (**Figure 5.28**).
Show Encrypted or Compressed NTFS Files in Color	Turn this on to show the names of NTFS-*encrypted* files and folders in green and the names of NTFS-*compressed* files and folders in blue. Turn this off to turn all names black. For information about compression, see "Compressing Files and Folders" later in this chapter.
Show Pop-Up Description for Folder and Desktop Items	Turn this option on to see pop-up information about almost any icon you point to. Turn this off if the little yellow pop-up boxes get in your way.
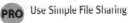 Use Simple File Sharing	See "Sharing Files" in Chapter 17.

Creating Folders

Here are a few ground rules for creating folder structure:

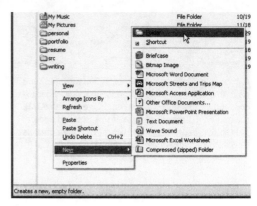

- ◆ You don't *have* to use My Documents as the root folder for your personal folders and documents, but it's the best choice because it's easy to open—via the Start menu, task pane, or Open and Save dialog boxes, for example. It's also easier to back up a centralized My Documents folder tree than folders scattered all over your drives. (By the way, you can rename My Documents as you would any folder.)

- ◆ Go ahead and nest folders deeply. If you create a shallow or "flat" folder structure, you're forced to use long, descriptive filenames rather than succinct ones. A flat structure also makes you fill folders with so many subfolders that it's hard to discern the structure quickly.

Figure 5.29 You can create a folder inside another folder, on the desktop, or at the root of a hard drive or floppy drive.

To create a folder:

1. In Windows Explorer, pick a location for a new folder.

2. Choose File > New > Folder.

   or

   Right-click blank space in the right pane; then choose New > Folder (**Figure 5.29**).

   or

   In the task pane, click Make a New Folder.

3. Type a name for the new folder; then press Enter.

✔ Tips

- ■ To create a new folder on the desktop, right-click an empty area; then choose New > Folder.

- ■ The File > New submenu lets you create some document files too, depending on which programs are installed.

Figure 5.30 To replace the current name, just start typing. To change a few characters in the existing name, use the arrow keys to move to a specific position and then insert, delete, cut, or paste characters.

Naming Files and Folders

You can rename a file or folder to make its name longer, shorter, or more explicit.

To rename a file or folder:

1. In Explorer or on the desktop, select the file or folder that you want to rename.

2. Choose File > Rename.

   or

   Right-click the file or folder; then choose Rename.

   or

   In the task pane, click Rename This File (or Rename This Folder).

   or

   Press F2.

   or

   Click the file or folder's title (not its icon) again.

3. Type a new name; then press Enter (or click outside the name area) (**Figure 5.30**).

✔ Tips

- You can rename a file or folder in the General tab of its Properties dialog box.

- Press Esc while editing to revert to the item's original name.

- If you select multiple items and rename one item, say, MyFile, Windows renames the others MyFile(1), MyFile(2), and so on.

- You can't rename certain system folders, such as Documents and Settings, Windows (or Winnt), and System32.

- If the Hide Extensions for Known File Types folder option is turned off, you must retype the file extension when renaming the file; otherwise, Windows tracks the file association automatically. See "Setting Folder Options" earlier in this chapter.

Legal File and Folder Names

A folder or filename can be up to 255 characters, including the extension (the part after the dot). Spaces and punctuation are allowed, but names can't contain the following characters, which are reserved for Windows' use:

`\ / : * ? " < > |`

A folder can't contain two items with the same name. Windows is case-insensitive (it considers `MyFile.txt` and `myfile.txt` to be identical), but it preserves the case of each letter you type.

Moving and Copying Files and Folders

You can move or copy files and folders to make backup copies in a safe location, or move files to Shared Documents to share them with other users. To copy or move items, you must select (highlight) them. For an icon-selection refresher, see "Icons" in Chapter 1.

To move or copy items by choosing a destination:

1. In Windows Explorer, select the item(s) that you want to move or copy.

2. To move the items, choose Edit > Move to Folder (or click Move This File or Move This Folder in the task pane).

   To copy the items, choose Edit > Copy to Folder (or click Copy This File or Copy This Folder in the task pane).

3. Navigate to the destination folder; then click Move (or Copy) (**Figure 5.31**).

To move or copy items by using cut, copy, and paste:

1. In Windows Explorer or on the desktop, select the item(s) that you want to move or copy.

2. To move the items, press Ctrl+X (or right-click a selected item and choose Cut).

   To copy the items, press Ctrl+C (or right-click a selected item and choose Copy).

3. Select the destination folder, disk, or window.

4. Press Ctrl+V (or right-click an empty area and choose Paste).

To move or copy items by dragging:

1. Make sure that the destination folder, disk, or window is visible.

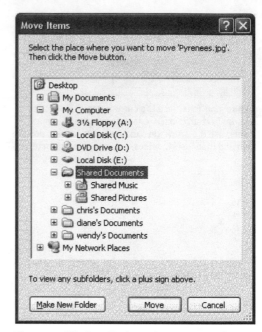

Figure 5.31 Windows Explorer gives you several ways to move and copy files, but using a highlighted target is the easiest and most consistent.

Figure 5.32 I'm dragging the file Pyrenees.jpg from Desktop to My Pictures. The destination folder in the left pane darkens automatically as the pointer moves over it. If you hover briefly over a folder that contains subfolders, it will expand.

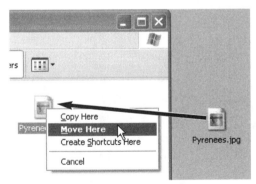

Figure 5.33 Right-dragging to copy or move items is safer than left-dragging.

2. In Windows Explorer or on the desktop, select the item(s) that you want to copy or move.

3. Right-drag the items to the destination; then release the right mouse button.

4. Choose Move Here or Copy Here from the shortcut menu (**Figures 5.32** and **5.33**).

You can use the *left* mouse button and drag normally to copy or move items (bypassing the shortcut menu), but the rules that determine whether an item is actually moved or copied are confusing:

◆ If you drag an item to another place on the same disk, it's moved.

◆ If you drag an item from one disk to another, it's copied, not moved.

◆ To copy an item instead of moving it, hold down Ctrl while dragging.

◆ To move the item instead of copying it, hold down Shift while dragging.

◆ If you drag a system icon such as My Computer or Control Panel, it's never moved or copied; instead, a shortcut is created.

Got all that? Me neither. That's why it's easier to *right*-drag to copy or move items.

✔ Tips

■ You can move or copy items anywhere on your computer or network, so long as you have permission to do so.

■ If you copy an item to the folder in which it already exists, Windows creates a duplicate named Copy of <*itemname*>.

■ You can drag items between Explorer windows, or cut or copy from one window and paste to another.

■ Items appear dimmed when they're cut, but they don't actually move until you paste them somewhere.

Sending Files and Folders

One of the handiest file-management tools is the Send To menu, which lets you send a copy of a file or folder quickly to:

◆ A floppy disk

◆ Your desktop (as a shortcut)

◆ Another person via email

◆ Your My Documents folder

◆ A compressed (zipped) folder (see "Compressing Files and Folders" later in this chapter)

◆ Other destinations, depending on the programs you have installed

To send an item:

1. In Windows Explorer or on the desktop, select the item(s) that you want to send.

2. Right-click one item; choose Send To; then choose a destination from the submenu (**Figure 5.34**).

✔ Tips

■ In Explorer, Send To is available in the File menu.

■ To move an item instead of copying it, hold down Shift when you right-click.

Figure 5.34 The Send To menu often is faster than dragging and dropping.

Figure 5.35 Here, I've added a few custom destinations to the standard ones. The Notepad shortcut opens any file in Notepad, regardless of the file's type. The Backups shortcut copies files to a safe place. The Printer shortcut prints documents with no need to open their associated applications.

If you perform the same file-management tasks regularly, you can add your own destinations to the Send To menu by adding new shortcuts to your Send To folder (which is hidden by default). Every user on your computer has a separate Send To folder. The destination determines what happens to the item being sent. If the destination is a program, for example, the program is launched with the selected file open. For folder and disk destinations, items are copied.

To add a destination to the Send To menu:

1. Choose Start > My Computer > Local Disk (C:) > Documents and Settings > *<your name>*.

   If Windows is installed on a drive other than C, choose that drive instead.

2. If the Send To folder is hidden, choose Tools > Folder Options > View tab > check Show Hidden Files and Folders > OK.

3. Add the desired shortcuts to the folder (or choose File > New > Shortcut) (**Figure 5.35**).

4. Close the window when you're done adding shortcuts.

✔ Tips

■ If you have a lot of destinations, you can nest folders to create Send To sub-submenus.

■ You can create Send To shortcuts to shared folders on other machines.

■ If you put a shortcut to the Send To folder in the Send To folder itself, you can create Send To destinations quickly by sending them to the Send To folder.

Deleting Files and Folders

When you delete a file or folder, it's not actually erased, but compressed and stored in the Recycle Bin on the desktop (**Figure 5.36**). The Recycle Bin is a safeguard from which you can restore (undelete) items if you change your mind or delete them permanently.

Figure 5.36 The Recycle Bin's icon tells you whether it contains deleted items.

To delete items:

1. In Windows Explorer or on the desktop, select the item(s) that you want to delete.

2. Press Delete.

or

Right-click one item; then choose Delete.

or

Choose File > Delete.

3. If an "Are you sure?" message appears, click Yes.

✔ Tips

■ You also can drag items to the Recycle Bin to delete them.

■ To suppress the "Are you sure?" message, right-click the Recycle Bin; choose Properties > Global tab; then uncheck Display Delete Confirmation Dialog.

■ To delete an item without sending it to the Recycle Bin, press Shift+Delete.

■ If you have perfect judgment, you can bypass the Recycle Bin so that all deleted files are erased immediately: Right-click the Recycle Bin icon; choose Properties > Global tab; then check Do Not Move Files to the Recycle Bin.

■ Some programs let you delete items within Open and Save As dialog boxes.

■ Items deleted from network drives, floppy disks, or removable disks (such as Zip disks) bypass the Recycle Bin, as do deletions via the command-line del and erase commands.

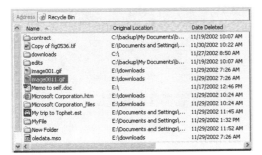

Figure 5.37 Details view tells you when items were deleted, and where from.

To empty the Recycle Bin:

1. Double-click the Recycle Bin icon (**Figure 5.37**).

2. To remove all items, choose File > Empty Recycle Bin (or click Empty the Recycle Bin in the task pane).

   or

   To remove only some items, Ctrl+click each item that you want to remove; then press Delete (or choose File > Delete).

3. Click Yes in the "Are you sure?" message.

✔ Tips

■ The Delete command also is available in a Recycle Bin item's shortcut menu.

■ To empty the Recycle Bin quickly without inspecting its contents, right-click its icon on the desktop; then choose Empty Recycle Bin. You can't suppress this "Are you sure?" message.

To restore items from the Recycle Bin:

1. Double-click the Recycle Bin icon (refer to Figure 5.37).

2. Ctrl+click the items that you want to restore (or click only one item).

3. To restore items to their original locations, choose File > Restore (or click Restore the Selected Items or Restore This Item in the task pane).

   or

   To restore items to a specific location, drag them out of the Recycle Bin to the desired folder (in an Explorer window or on the desktop).

✔ Tip

■ The Restore command also is available in a Recycle Bin item's shortcut menu.

The Recycle Bin stores deleted items until it runs out of space, at which point the items are removed automatically and forever, oldest first, to accommodate new items. By default, the size of the Recycle Bin folder is 10 percent of the hard drive, but you can change that percentage.

To change the Recycle Bin's capacity:

1. Right-click the Recycle Bin icon; then choose Properties (**Figure 5.38**).

2. On the Global tab, drag the slider to specify how much of each drive can be allocated to the Recycle Bin.

✔ Tips

- On high-capacity drives, 10 percent is a lot of space. On a 50 GB disk, for example, 10 percent is 5 GB of junk. Certainly, unless you manipulate incredible numbers of music or video files, 1 or 2 GB should be plenty.

- The Recycle Bin's status bar (choose View > Status Bar) shows how much space the deleted items occupy.

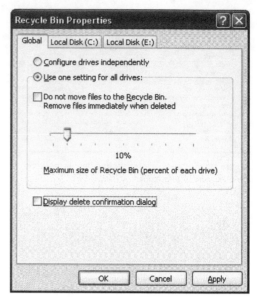

Figure 5.38 Every disk has its own Recycle Bin. If you have more than one drive, or have a partitioned drive, you can select Configure Drives Independently and click the separate tabs to set each disk's junk limit.

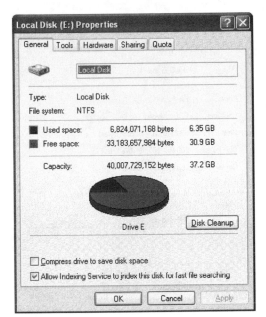

Figure 5.39 To determine whether a drive is formatted with NTFS, choose Start > My Computer; right-click a drive; then choose Properties. The file system appears on the General tab.

Compressing Files and Folders

Compressing files and folders reduces the space they occupy on your drives, or on removable storage. Windows XP offers two compression schemes: Microsoft's proprietary NTFS compression (the same as in Windows 2000) and industry-standard zipped folders (new in XP). You can use either scheme or both; each has its relative advantages. NTFS compression is simple, transparent, and suitable for everyday use, whereas zipped folders are best for:

◆ Emailing large attachments

◆ Archiving files that you no longer need regularly

◆ Transferring files over the Internet or via FTP

NTFS compression

Some important points about NTFS compression are:

◆ It's available only on NTFS-formatted drives, not FAT32 drives (**Figure 5.39**). See "Getting Ready to Install Windows XP" in Appendix A.

◆ You can compress individual files and folders or an entire NTFS drive.

◆ It's easy to use but doesn't save much disk space compared with Zip compression.

◆ NTFS-compressed files and folders act normally in Explorer, applications, and dialog boxes. XP decompresses and compresses files invisibly and on the fly when you open and close them, at the cost of a small (probably not noticeable) performance hit.

◆ Don't compress system files in the Windows (or Winnt) folder, as XP uses them frequently.

◆ If you send an NTFS-compressed file to a non-NTFS disk (via email or dragging, for example), XP expands it to its normal size automatically and invisibly. A file sent to a compressed folder or disk is compressed automatically.

◆ Windows XP disposes of the awful DriveSpace compression scheme from Windows 9*x*.

◆ **PRO** NTFS-compressed files can't be NTFS-encrypted.

To NTFS-compress a file, folder, or drive:

1. Close all files to be compressed.

2. To compress individual files or folders, select their icons in Windows Explorer; right-click one of the selected items; then choose Properties > General tab > Advanced > Compress Contents to Save Disk Space (**Figure 5.40**).

   or

   To compress a drive, right-click its icon in My Computer; then choose Properties > General tab > Compress Drive to Save Disk Space (refer to Figure 5.39).

3. In the Confirm Attribute Changes dialog box, indicate whether you want to compress subfolders too (**Figure 5.41**).

4. Click OK in each open dialog box.

✔ Tips

■ Compressing an entire hard disk may take hours. Close all programs before you start; otherwise, Windows halts mid-process to ask you to quit a program.

■ To display compressed file and folder names in a different color in Windows Explorer, choose Tools > Folder Options > View tab > check Show Encrypted or Compressed NTFS Files in Color.

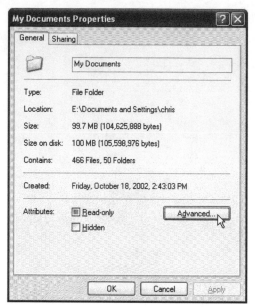

Figure 5.40 If the Advanced button is missing, the selected file or folder isn't on an NTFS drive.

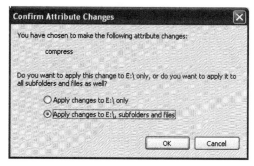

Figure 5.41 Usually, you'll want to compress all sub-folders too.

COMPRESSING FILES AND FOLDERS

Figure 5.42 An archive looks like a folder, except with a zipper. An archive has a .zip file extension.

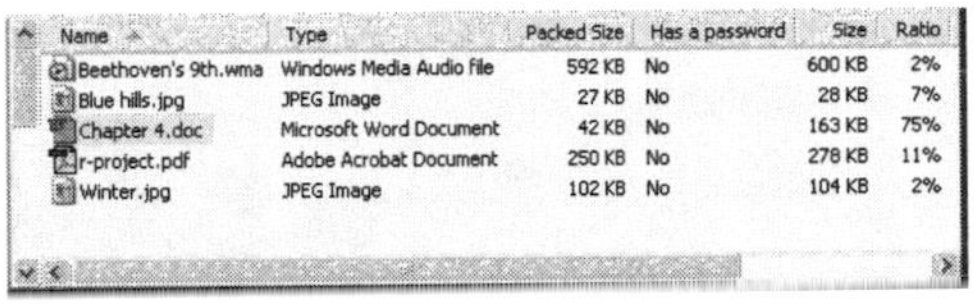

Name	Type	Packed Size	Has a password	Size	Ratio
Beethoven's 9th.wma	Windows Media Audio file	592 KB	No	600 KB	2%
Blue hills.jpg	JPEG Image	27 KB	No	28 KB	7%
Chapter 4.doc	Microsoft Word Document	42 KB	No	163 KB	75%
r-project.pdf	Adobe Acrobat Document	250 KB	No	278 KB	11%
Winter.jpg	JPEG Image	102 KB	No	104 KB	2%

Figure 5.43 Details view provides compression information about each file. The Ratio column tells you how much smaller a zipped file is relative to its uncompressed size.

Zipped folders

If you've used the popular WinZip program, you're familiar with the concept of compressing files and folders in Zip format. Some important points about Zip files are:

◆ A zipped folder, called an *archive,* is a collection of files compressed and combined into a single file (**Figure 5.42**).

◆ You can create archives on any drive, not just NTFS drives. Archives stay compressed when you send them elsewhere. Mac and Unix users can work with them, too (if they have a decompression utility).

◆ Zipping squashes files much smaller than NTFS compression does. Zipping most image and music files won't save much space, because they're already compressed, but word processing, spreadsheet, database, BMP image, and WAV audio files shrink a lot.

◆ Though they're actually files, zipped folders still behave like folders in several ways. Double-click an archive to see what's in it (**Figure 5.43**). Double-clicking a document in the archive opens a read-only copy of it; choose File > Save As to save a copy elsewhere. (Or extract it from the archive to work with the original.)

◆ You can password-protect archives to prevent others from extracting files.

To create a new zipped folder:

1. In Explorer, select where you want to create the new archive.

2. Choose File > New > Compressed (Zipped) Folder.

   or

   Right-click blank space in the right pane; then choose New > Compressed (Zipped) Folder.

3. Type a name for the new archive (keep the .zip extension, if it appears); then press Enter.

✔ Tip

■ To create a zipped folder on the desktop, right-click an empty area; then choose New > Compressed (Zipped) Folder.

To create a new zipped folder from existing files or folders:

1. In Explorer, select the file(s) or folder(s) that you want to archive.

2. Right-click one of the selected items; then choose Send To > Compressed (Zipped) Folder.

To add files or folders to a zipped folder:

1. In Explorer, select the zipped folder that you want to add files or folders to.

2. Right-drag the file(s) into the zipped folder; then choose Copy Here or Move Here.

To password-protect a zipped folder:

1. Select any item in a zipped folder (not the folder itself).

2. Choose File > Add a Password; then complete the Add Password dialog box.

   The password applies to every file in the archive.

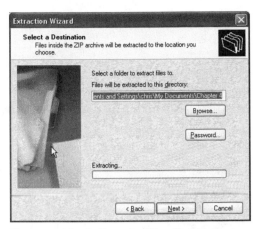

Figure 5.44 Use the Extraction Wizard to specify a destination folder.

✔ Tips

■ New files added to the zipped folder *aren't* password-protected. To protect them, choose File > Remove Password before adding new files; then reinstate the password. The Has a Password column (refer to Figure 5.43) indicates a file's password status.

■ Password-protection prevents only file *extraction*. Other people can still view a protected archive's filenames and even delete the files, bypassing the Recycle Bin.

To extract files and folders from a zipped folder:

◆ To extract only some files or folders, double-click the zipped folder to open it; then drag the files or folders to a new location, where they return to their original sizes.

   or

   To extract all files and folders, right-click the zipped folder in Explorer; then choose Extract All (**Figure 5.44**).

✔ Tip

■ If a zipped folder window is already open, click Extract All Files in the task pane.

Searching for Files and Folders

Even if you organize your files and folders logically, sooner or later, you'll need to find something—newly installed software, a download, or a file whose location you forgot, for example. Often, you'll also want to find all files that meet certain criteria—all or part of a filename, approximate size, modification date, type, and so on. Welcome to the expanded search function—called Search Companion—in Windows XP.

✔ Tip

- Search Companion can find printers, people, and other computers on your network. In this section, I describe how to find files and folders.

To open Search Companion:

- On the desktop, choose Start > Search, press F3, or press Windows logo key+F (if your keyboard supports it) (**Figure 5.45**).

  or

  In Explorer, press Ctrl+E, press F3, click the Search toolbar button, or choose View > Explorer Bar > Search.

✔ Tips

- To widen or narrow the search pane, drag its right edge.

- To get rid of the animated dog, click the dog itself; then click Turn Off the Animated Character in the menu that appears.

- I describe Search Companion's standard interface here. Windows veterans may prefer the more advanced Windows 2000-like interface, which offers the same search options without the handholding screens. To invoke it, in Search Companion, choose Change Preferences > Change Files and Folders Search Behavior > Advanced.

Figure 5.45 The Search Companion occupies the left pane of Windows Explorer, where it replaces the task bar or Folders bar when visible.

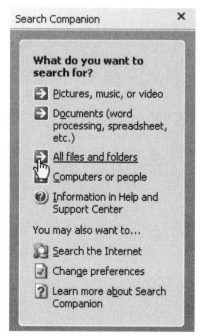

Figure 5.46 The initial Search Companion screen offers specialized searches for digital media (MP3s, JPEGs, WMAs, and so on) or documents (no folders and no program, hidden, help, or system files). Each search entails its own default settings and screens. All Files and Folders is the broadest, most versatile search.

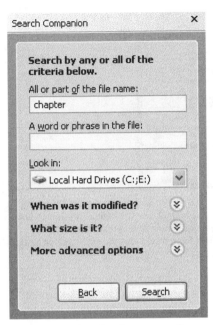

Figure 5.47 Each option that you specify narrows the search.

Figure 5.48 You can specify a range of dates when the file was modified, search for files of a specified size, or choose among advanced options. Subfolders and system folders are searched by default.

To search for a file or folder:

1. In Search Companion, click All Files and Folders (**Figure 5.46**).

2. Enter basic search criteria (**Figure 5.47**):

   To search by filename, type the filename or a distinctive part of it in the All or Part of the File Name text box.

   To search by text *inside* files (which is very slow without indexing), type a distinctive word or phrase in the A Word or Phrase in the File text box.

   From the Look In list, choose the drive, folder, or network to search.

3. To narrow this search, click the double down arrows to specify more criteria (**Figure 5.48**).

   (continues on next page)

4. Click the Search button.

Search Companion performs the search and returns a list of matches (**Figure 5.49**).

5. To open the selected item's parent folder, choose File > Open Containing Folder

Otherwise, you can sort the entries in the results list as you would in an ordinary Explorer window. Point to an item for pop-up information, double-click it to open it, drag an item to move or copy it, right-click it for its shortcut menu, and so on.

6. To save the current criteria for repeated searches, choose File > Save Search.

Search Companion creates a .fnd file (by default in My Documents). To search again, double-click a .fnd file; then click Search.

✔ Tips

■ Search Companion searches the Recycle Bin too.

■ The results list sometimes contains duplicate entries for files in My Documents.

■ You can use *wildcard characters* to represent one or more filename characters when you don't know what the real character is or don't want to type the entire name. ? substitutes for any single character, and * substitutes for zero or more characters. Type *.do?, for example, to find all files that end in .doc (Word documents) or .dot (Word templates). chapter*.doc finds all Word documents that begin with the word *chapter,* followed by any characters (or no characters).

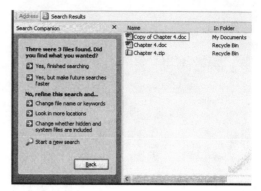

Figure 5.49 If Search Companion returns the wrong match (or no match), use the Refine This Search links to try again with more or less restrictive criteria. (Refine This Search performs the *entire* search again; it doesn't look in only the current results.)

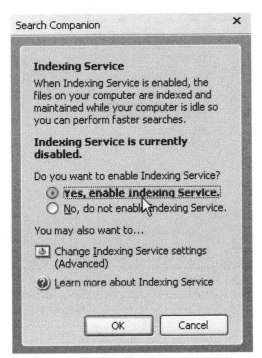

Figure 5.50 Indexing Service updates and maintains its indexes automatically, without your intervention. If the service is busy updating itself, Search Companion performs an ordinary, unindexed search. Updates take lots of time and power but occur only when your PC has been idle for a while.

As described in step 2 of "To search for a file or folder," Search Companion lets you search for text *inside* files whose contents you remember but whose names you forget. Fortunately, Windows XP's indexing service accelerates the glacial pace of exhaustive string searches (typically, by a factor of 10 or more). Indexing Service, which is turned off by default, collects information from the documents on your hard drive and compiles a database, or *catalog*, of contents in HTML files (their text only), text files, Microsoft Office documents (Office 95 and later), email, and Internet news. Third-party software firms may provide snap-in filters for indexing their documents, too. The tradeoff for slashing search time is a catalog file that's about 25 percent of the size of the indexed files.

To enable Indexing Service:

◆ Open Search Companion; then choose Change Preferences > With Indexing Service (for Faster Local Searches) > Yes, Enable Indexing Service (**Figure 5.50**).

✔ Tips

■ Indexing Service indexes only *your* documents and shared documents. It ignores other users' documents.

■ Indexing Service ignores case. Search Companion can't perform case-sensitive searches with the service running.

■ Indexing Service ignores "noise" words, such as *a, the, to, be* and common pronouns, prepositions, conjunctions, and articles. You can include these words in the search text, but Search Companion treats them as placeholders rather than literal words.

■ Administrators and power users can control Indexing Service in the Computer Management window. In Control Panel, choose Performance and Maintenance > Administrative Tools > Computer Management > Services and Applications > Indexing Service.

Copying Files and Folders to CDs

If your PC has a recordable (CD-R) or rewritable (CD-RW) CD drive, Windows XP lets you copy—or *burn*—files or folders to a recordable CD without the need for third-party software. CDs are excellent for backing up files (they're durable, capacious, and inexpensive) or for exchanging files with Unix and Mac users (CDs are cross-platform).

This section talks about copying *data* files to CDs. To burn *music* CDs, use Windows Media Player. See "Burning Music CDs" in Chapter 10.

To copy files and folders to a CD:

1. Insert a blank CD into the recordable CD drive (**Figure 5.51**).

2. In Windows Explorer, right-click a file or folder (or selection of files and folders) that you want to copy to the CD; then choose Send To > CD Drive.

3. Repeat step 2 for all the items that you want to copy.

4. Activate the CD Drive window or, if it has disappeared, choose Start > My Computer; then double-click the CD icon (**Figure 5.52**).

5. In the task pane, click Write These Files to CD to start the CD Writing Wizard (**Figure 5.53**).

6. Name the CD, and click Next to start writing files to the CD.

   A progress screen appears.

7. When the wizard finishes writing the CD, click Finish (**Figure 5.54**).

Figure 5.51 When you insert a blank CD, Windows displays this dialog box. Click OK to open a temporary folder that acts as an intermediate staging area for the items to be copied to the CD.

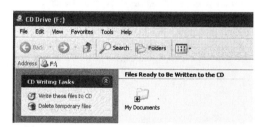

Figure 5.52 The CD Drive window contains the queue of files ready to be copied to the CD. A small down-arrow marks items that are ready to be burned.

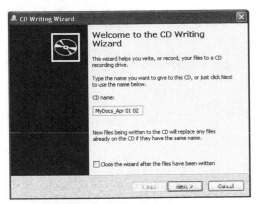

Figure 5.53 This screen allows you to give the CD a name (up to 16 characters) more meaningful than the current date. You can't change even the name of a CD-RW disc after it has been recorded the first time.

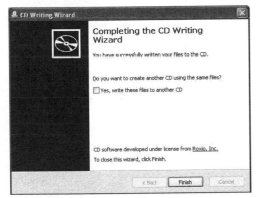

Figure 5.54 In the final screen, you can make another copy of the same CD. Click Finish to close the wizard, or start copying again, as appropriate.

✔ Tips

■ As an alternative to the Send To command in step 2, you can drag items into the CD Drive folder or use the Copy and Paste commands.

■ To burn a CD, you need *temporary* free disk space at least twice the size of the items to be copied; otherwise, you'll get a "Cannot complete writing" error from the wizard.

■ The items in the Files Ready to Be Written to the CD list (refer to Figure 5.52) are stored in the hidden folder Local Disk (C:)\ Documents and Settings\<*your name*>\ Local Settings\Application Data\ Microsoft\CD Burning.

■ Calculate the total size of the items before you start copying: In the CD Drive window, press Ctrl+A, then inspect Total File Size in the task pane's Details box. Standard CDs hold around 650 MB. A high-capacity CD holds 800 to 850 MB.

■ After you create a CD, test it immediately to see whether the disc can be used. CD-writing drives are distressingly unreliable.

■ If you decide not to create the CD, in the CD Drive window, click Delete Temporary Files to clear the storage area.

■ Some files contain extra information called *metadata*—the bit rate of an audio track or the dimensions of an image, for example—that can't be copied to a CD. If you get a stream-loss error from the wizard, you may want to copy the file without the metadata rather than skip it entirely.

■ For more recording features, buy a commercial CD-burning program such as Roxio Easy CD & DVD Creator (www.roxio.com).

Making Network Files and Folders Available Offline

The Offline Files feature isn't available in Windows XP Home edition.

Offline Files is designed for travelers who work with a laptop computer that's often disconnected from the network. When you make a file or folder available offline, Windows makes a temporary copy of it on your laptop; you can work with this copy as you would the original. When you reconnect to the network, Windows *synchronizes* your laptop documents with the network originals, so you have up-to-date versions in both places.

✔ Tips

- If you upgraded from Windows 98/Me, you'll find Offline Files easier to use than the Briefcase of those OSes.

- To use Offline Files, you must disable Fast User Switching. In Control Panel, choose User Accounts > Change the Way Users Log On or Off > uncheck Use Fast User Switching.

- Fast User Switching and Offline Files can't be used at the same time, as Windows warns you with a dialog box.

To enable offline files:

1. In Windows Explorer, choose Tools > Folder Options > Offline Files tab (**Figure 5.55**).

2. Check Enable Offline Files.

3. Check Synchronize All Offline Files Before Logging Off to be sure that you have the latest versions of offline files on your laptop when you log off.

4. Click OK (or Apply).

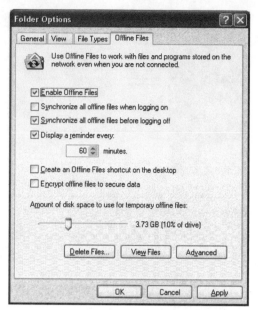

Figure 5.55 Set up your computer to use offline files with this dialog box.

To make a file or folder available offline:

1. In My Network Places (on your laptop), right-click the files or folders that you want to be available offline; then choose Make Available Offline.

   The first time you do this, the Offline Files Wizard helps you configure your settings.

2. If you select a folder that contains subfolders, specify whether to include the subfolders.

✔ Tips

- Instead of using My Network Places, you can double-click a shared network drive icon in My Computer.

- If My Network Places or My Computer contains no network drive icons, choose Tools > Map Network Drive to assign a local drive letter.

- You *must* log off, or shut down, to effect synchronization. If you simply disconnect from the network, Windows won't have time to synchronize files.

- You open offline files as though you were working with them online, but Windows displays a special icon to remind you that you're working offline.

- Synchronization is at Windows' discretion by default. If you've disabled that feature, you can synchronize manually when you're connected to the network: Choose Start > All Programs > Accessories > Synchronize.

- To view a list of available offline files, choose Tools > Folder Options > Offline Files tab > View Files.

- To make an item *un*available offline, right-click it; then choose Make Available Offline again to clear the check mark.

- I've covered only the basics here. For a complete description of offline files, search for *offline files* in Help and Support Center.

FILES AND FOLDERS: WORKING OFFLINE

INSTALLING AND RUNNING PROGRAMS

Windows, like all operating systems, is a launching pad for programs, or *applications*. More programs from more software firms are available for Windows than for any other OS. Fortunately, Microsoft and sound design enforce substantial consistency, so you can apply knowledge of a few common operations to many programs. Most programs share user-interface elements—scroll bars, copy-and-paste functions, and so on—as well as setup and management options.

In this chapter, you'll learn how to install, remove, launch, and manage Windows programs. You'll also learn about *documents,* which are self-contained pieces of work (files) that you create with programs.

Installing Programs

If you've upgraded to XP, you'll find some improvements in the installation process. Windows 9x users will find that Microsoft has improved the Add or Remove Programs dialog box. More important, XP won't let poorly designed programs harm your system by installing outdated drivers and system files. Windows 2000 users will find improved compatibility; many programs (especially games) that acted cranky or refused to run under Windows 2000 will run under XP properly. Most installations go smoothly, but be aware of a few things:

Be an Administrator. XP is a multiuser OS that supports Administrator, Limited, and Guest user accounts (see "Setting up User Accounts" in Chapter 16). Only Administrators can install programs without restriction (**Figure 6.1**).

Set a restore point first. Create a System Restore point before you install new software. If the new program causes problems, you can undo the installation and return your system to its previous working condition. See "Restoring Your System" in Chapter 19.

Make sure the program is XP-compatible. XP is compatible with fewer programs than Windows 9x but more programs than Windows 2000. Look for an XP compatibility statement or the Designed for Windows XP logo on the software's package or Web site (and look for patches or updates while you're there). You also can check Microsoft's Web site for XP-compatible programs: Choose Start > Help and Support > Find Compatible Hardware and Software for Windows XP; then search for your program.

Figure 6.1 To install software, you need certain permissions. XP-certified programs give these clear instructions, but older Windows 9x-aware programs may display a vague or puzzling message when you try to install them. XP allows a Limited user or Guest to log on as an Administrator to install a program.

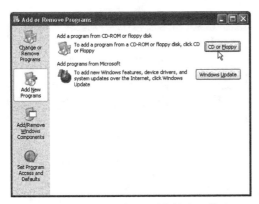

Figure 6.2 Experienced users avoid this installation method; it's quicker to double-click the disk's Setup program (typically, setup.exe) in Windows Explorer.

Close open programs first. Exit all open programs before you install so that support files won't be open—and, therefore, locked—when Setup tries to replace them. If you have a virus scanner, turn it off; otherwise, it may interpret your new program as being harmful.

✔ Tips

- Your PC's manufacturer may have added software—Microsoft Office or Works, for example—at the factory. Check the Start > All Programs menu before you install new stuff.

- If you upgraded an earlier Windows version to XP, Windows Setup configured your existing programs to run; you don't have to reinstall them. If an older program doesn't run in XP, see "Running Older Programs" later in this chapter.

- If you upgraded from Windows 2000, you can install programs if you're a Power Users group member, rather than an Administrator.

These days, you install most commercial software from a CD. XP's *AutoPlay* feature runs the CD's Setup program automatically when you insert the CD into its drive. But you can use Control Panel to add programs if AutoPlay is disabled, you're installing from a floppy, or AutoPlay can't find the Setup program.

To install a program from CD or floppy disk:

1. Choose Start > Control Panel > Add or Remove Programs.

2. Click Add New Programs (**Figure 6.2**).

3. Insert the program's setup disk into the CD or floppy drive.

(continues on next page)

4. Click CD or Floppy; then follow the prompts that appear.

Windows usually can find the Setup program, even if it's not in the top-level folder or named `setup.exe`; it may be an .ini or .inf file instead.

✔ Tips

- Setup programs usually require you to specify a destination folder, accept a license agreement, choose which components to install, and type a serial number or product key from the CD's envelope or registration card.

- Software publishers create Setup programs with third-party programs such as InstallShield, Wise Installer, or Microsoft's Windows Installer, so you'll see those program names in title bars.

- After installation, the program's shortcuts are highlighted in orange in the Start > All Programs menu.

- If you're on an office network, the Add New Programs tab may contain a list of administrator-approved programs available for installation.

- Some programs include a Click Here for Support Information link in the Add or Remove Programs dialog box. Click this link to display technical support information (**Figure 6.3**).

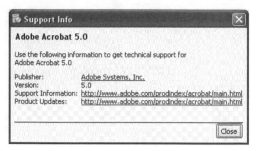

Figure 6.3 Support information usually includes the software company's name, the program's version number, and links to relevant Web pages.

Who Can Use the Program?

A program installed by you—or any Administrator—is available to *all* users by default; its shortcuts appear in everybody's All Programs menu. The shortcuts may end up in your *personal* All Programs menu because you (inadvertently) told Setup to do so or because Setup gave you no choice. Recall from "Using the Start Menu" in Chapter 2 that XP inspects two folders to build the All Programs menu: one for All Users and another for the logged-on user. To make a program available to everyone (instead of only you), do the following:

1. Choose Start > All Programs.

2. Right-click the item that you want everyone to be able to access; then choose Copy.

3. Right-click Start; then choose Open All Users.

4. Right-click the Programs folder; then choose Paste.

Now the program appears in everyone's All Programs menu. If this method doesn't work, or if a program requires per-user settings, log on to each user account and rerun Setup.

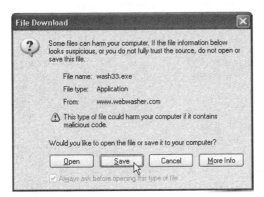

Figure 6.4 This dialog box appears when you click a link to download a file. Blame virus writers worldwide for the paranoid tone of the message.

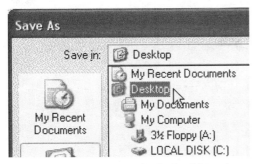

Figure 6.5 Choose or create a destination folder where you won't lose the downloaded file. Desktop is a good choice.

The Internet is the preferred (sometimes only) distribution method for many software vendors. You can use Internet Explorer (Chapter 13) to download any of the thousands of commercial, shareware, demo, and free programs (and updates) available at vendors' Web sites and sites such as www.download.com.

To download and install software:

1. In Internet Explorer, click a link that initiates a download.

2. In the File Download dialog box, click Save (**Figure 6.4**).

3. In the Save As dialog box, select a destination folder for the download (**Figure 6.5**).

   The download almost always will be an executable (.exe) file or a compressed (.zip) file.

4. After the download completes, double-click the file in Windows Explorer.

   If the download is an executable file, Setup starts automatically. If it's a Zip archive, extract its files (see "Compressing Files and Folders" in Chapter 5); then double-click the installer program (usually named setup.exe) among the extracted pieces.

✔ Tips

- You can delete the download file after installation.

- Some software download sites offer the choice of installing the program directly online, rather than locally from the archive. Generally, this option isn't the best idea. Installing from the downloaded file gives you more control of the installation and leaves you a copy of the archive if you ever have to reinstall.

Removing Programs

When you install a program, it scatters its components all over your folder structure, not just in the Program Files subfolder it creates. Only the uninstall utility of an unwanted program has the ability to remove it completely. Don't just delete the program's folder; if you do, you'll leave behind short-cuts, support files, hidden folders, registry entries, and other litter on your hard drive.

✔ Tip

■ Always exit the program that you're going to remove. If you're using Fast User Switching (see "Logging on and Logging off Windows XP" in Chapter 1), make sure that no other logged-on users are using the program.

To remove a program:

1. Choose Start > Control Panel > Add or Remove Programs > Change or Remove Programs.

2. In the Currently Installed Programs list, click the program that you want to remove (**Figure 6.6**).

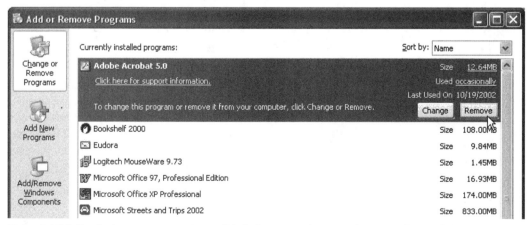

Figure 6.6 This list displays a program's size on disk, its frequency of use over the past 30 days, and the date you last used it. If you have a lot of programs, use the Sort By list (top-right corner) to select a sorting option.

REMOVING PROGRAMS

3. Click the Change/Remove button (or Remove button), and confirm the removal if a message box appears.

Windows runs the program's uninstall utility (which varies by program). Follow any directions onscreen.

✔ Tips

■ Some uninstallers let you remove program components selectively; others eradicate the entire program.

■ The folder that contained the program may persist after uninstallation, usually because it contains documents created with the program. If you don't need those documents, you can delete the folder and its files safely.

■ Most uninstallers display a progress bar, explain what they're removing or not removing, and tell you whether you must restart your computer to complete the removal.

■ You may get a midprocess message asking whether Windows should remove a shared file that other programs may need. Beginners should keep such files; power users may delete them unless they know a specific reason not to.

■ If your program doesn't appear in the Currently Installed Programs list, try contacting the vendor or reading the program's readme.txt file (if any) for removal instructions. As a last resort, drag the program's folder into the Recycle Bin.

REMOVING PROGRAMS

Adding and Removing Windows Components

The default XP installation omits some accessory programs that Microsoft deemed inessential—mostly, network and administration tools. If you feel otherwise, you can install them from the Windows CD. You also can remove optional Windows components if disk space is tight or you don't want them cluttering your All Programs menu.

To add or remove Windows components:

1. Choose Start > Control Panel > Add or Remove Programs > Add/Remove Windows Components.

2. In the Components list, check a box to install its item; clear a box to remove it (**Figure 6.7**).

3. Click Next.

4. If you're prompted for the Windows CD, insert it and continue.

✔ Tips

■ To learn about a component, click its name (not its check box). A description appears below the list.

■ To the right of each component name is the space it occupies on your hard disk.

■ For some installations, Windows might ask you to restart your PC.

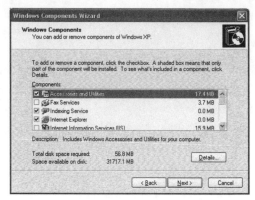

Figure 6.7 Some list items, such as Internet Explorer, are single features; others, such as Accessories and Utilities, are entire categories. If you choose a category, click the Details button to install or remove that category's programs individually.

Figure 6.8 Here, I've highlighted the program listings for Microsoft Office applications. Finding programs by name takes a little hunting, because the names of many executable (.exe) files are cryptic holdovers from DOS days, when all names were no more than eight characters long.

Launching Programs

XP gives you more ways to launch (open) a program than any other operating system. If you're familiar with Windows, you may know most of them.

To start a program:

◆ Choose Start > All Programs; then click the program's icon.

or

On the left side of the Start menu, click the program's icon (if it appears).

or

On the Quick Launch bar, click the program's icon (if it appears).

or

Choose Start > My Computer > Local Disk (C:) > Program Files. In the program's subfolder, double-click the program's icon (or select the icon and press Enter) (**Figure 6.8**).

or

Right-click the program's icon; then choose Open.

or

Press the keyboard shortcut that you assigned to the program's icon.

(continues on next page)

or

Choose Start > Run (or press Windows logo key+R); type the program's name; then press Enter (**Figure 6.9**).

You may have to include the path. See "Exploring Your Computer" in Chapter 5.

or

Type the program's name in the Address toolbar (in Windows Explorer, Internet Explorer, or on the taskbar); then press Enter.

Again, you may have to include the path.

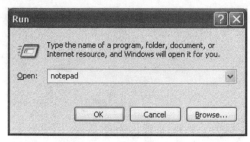

Figure 6.9 The Run dialog box (or the Address toolbar) may seem old-fashioned, but for many experienced users (and rapid typists), it's the fastest way to open a program or document.

✔ Tips

- You can use any of these methods to open a document with its associated program. If you created the document stuff.doc in Microsoft Word, for example, double-click the document's icon to start Word and open that file automatically.

- Most Setup programs put an icon in the All Programs menu or on the desktop. To customize these locations, see "Using the Start Menu" in Chapter 2.

- To customize the Quick Launch bar, see "Adding Toolbars to the Taskbar" in Chapter 2.

- To assign a keyboard shortcut to a shortcut icon, see "Managing Shortcuts" in Chapter 2.

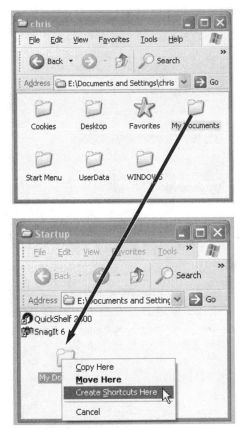

Figure 6.10 Items in the Startup folder open automatically when Windows starts. It's a common practice to put a My Documents shortcut in Startup.

Unwelcome Startup Programs

Too many programs add their own shortcuts silently to the All Users Startup folder. Many of these programs are unnecessary, slow the boot process, and run invisibly in the background, chewing up processor time. If you know that you can delete a Startup shortcut without affecting your system or a program adversely, do so. (You'll want to keep some programs, such as virus scanners.) If you have trouble identifying a Startup item, visit www.pacs-portal.co.uk/startup_index for help.

Launching Programs Automatically

The Start > All Programs > Startup folder contains programs that open automatically every time you start Windows. To save yourself a few clicks or keystrokes every time you log on, you can place your own shortcuts to programs or documents in this folder.

To open an item each time you start Windows:

1. Choose Start > All Programs, right-click Startup, and choose Open.

   Choose Open All Users (instead of Open) to change the Startup folder that applies to *all* users, not only yourself.

2. In Windows Explorer or My Computer, navigate to the item that you want to open automatically.

   You can select a disk, folder, program, or document.

3. Right-drag the item to the Startup window; then choose Create Shortcuts Here (**Figure 6.10**).

4. Close the windows you've opened.

   From now on, the item opens each time you (re)start your PC or log on.

✔ Tip

- For an uncluttered desktop when you boot up, open Startup programs as taskbar buttons (minimized), rather than standard or full-screen (maximized) windows. Right-click a Startup shortcut; choose Properties > Shortcut tab; then choose Minimized in the Run list.

Running Older Programs

If you upgraded from XP's forebear, Windows 2000, you know that its designers sacrificed some compatibility for stability; many Windows 9x programs (games in particular) just won't run on 2000. With XP, Microsoft made a heroic effort—largely successful—to run older programs written for Windows 9x and even Windows 3.1/DOS. But if XP has trouble running a program that ran fine in Windows 9x, NT, or 2000, you can try tricking the program into thinking that it's running on the older OS.

To run a troublesome older program:

1. Right-click a program's shortcut icon; then choose Properties > Compatibility tab (**Figure 6.11**).

2. Change the compatibility settings for the program; then click OK.

   The next time you open the program, XP tries to fool it into running.

✔ Tips

■ Never try to coerce obsolete hardware-level system utilities to run on XP. Upgrade to the latest version of your virus scanner, backup program, hard-disk partitioning tool, CD burner, or whatever.

■ The Compatibility tab is available only for programs installed on your hard drive. If the program is on a CD, floppy, or network drive, use Program Compatibility Wizard instead: Choose Start > All Programs > Accessories > Program Compatibility Wizard.

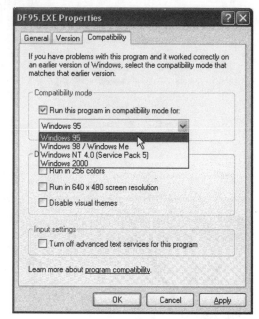

Figure 6.11 Choose the previous version of Windows that the old program was made for.

Running 16-Bit Programs

Windows 3.1 and DOS programs are called *16-bit programs*. Programs written for Windows 95, NT, and later are called *32-bit programs*. 16-bit programs run slowly because XP confines them in a leakproof, emulated space called a *virtual machine* which is a common memory pool. If one 16-bit program crashes, they all crash. To run DOS programs, choose Start > All Programs > Accessories > Command Prompt. See "Killing Unresponsive Programs" and "Using the Free Utility Programs" later in this chapter.

If XP displays an incompatibility message when you try to install or run a 16-bit program, don't ignore it. Either find a patch (update) or scrap the program.

Google - Microsoft Internet Explorer

Figure 6.12 Alt+Tab pops up a small array of icons representing running programs. Hold down Alt and press Tab repeatedly to highlight a program. If you press and release Alt+Tab quickly, you swap between only two programs instead of cycling through all of them.

Switching Programs

Working in Windows, you'll probably have multiple programs running simultaneously so that you can juggle, say, a word processor, email program, and Web browser. You have several techniques for switching programs.

To switch between running programs:

◆ If the program's window is visible in the background, click it. (But click blank space, not a button or menu, lest you activate it accidentally.)

or

Click the program's taskbar button. (The darkest button indicates the active program.)

or

Hold down Alt; press Tab repeatedly until the desired program is highlighted in the pop-up window; then release both keys (**Figure 6.12**).

or

Hold down Alt; press Esc repeatedly until the desired program appears; then release both keys.

✔ Tips

■ Alt+Esc, unlike Alt+Tab, has no pop-up window; doesn't cycle through *minimized* programs; and doesn't swap between two programs. (It simply sends the active program to the bottom of the pile.)

■ Windows logo key+Tab is equivalent to Alt+Tab.

■ Shift+Alt+Tab or Shift+Alt+Esc cycles *backward* through running programs.

■ If a program's taskbar button shows a small arrow and a number, button grouping is active. Clicking the button doesn't activate the program but displays a menu of documents.

Exiting Programs

When you finish using a program, you should exit (or quit or close) it, to get it out of your way and to let Windows reclaim its memory for other use.

To exit a program:

◆ Choose File > Exit (**Figure 6.13**).

or

Click the program's Close button (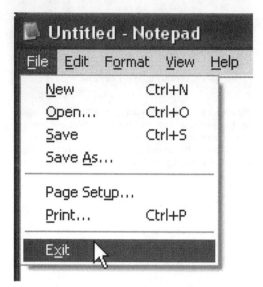).

or

Double-click its control-menu icon (at the left end of the title bar).

or

Right-click its taskbar button; then click Close.

or

Press Alt+F4.

or

Press Alt+spacebar; then press C.

✔ Tip

■ Before exiting, the program prompts you to save any unsaved work.

Figure 6.13 File > Exit is the usual way to quit a program. To choose it with the keyboard, press Alt+F to drop the menu; then press X.

Killing Unresponsive Programs

Even in Windows XP, the most stable version to date, programs occasionally crash or lock up. Such errant programs are said to be "not responding," in Microsoft vernacular; you can move the pointer within the program's window, but the program itself won't respond to clicks or keystrokes. If you're coming from Windows 9x, you'll be glad to hear that an unresponsive program rarely forces you to restart your computer. Instead, use Task Manager (inherited from Windows 2000) to send the frozen program to its grave.

✔ Tip

- Before you kill a program, make sure that it's really not responding. Wait a minute or two; Windows may be struggling to allocate extra memory. If you're running a Visual Basic macro in, say, Word or Excel, the program may appear frozen while VB has control. Global reformatting or find-and-replace can keep a word processor hypnotized for minutes. An open dialog box may prevent you from doing anything else in the program; look for one hiding behind another window.

Desperate Measures

If killing an unresponsive program as described doesn't work, you still have these options, in order of preference:

- Click the Processes tab in Task Manager; click the program's image name; then click End Process.

- Exit all other programs, and log off.

- If you can't log off but other users are logged on, right-click another user in Task Manager's Users tab; choose Connect to switch to that user; then use Task Manager to log off (Disconnect) *yourself.*

- If none of these measures works, press your PC's Reset button.

To kill an unresponsive program:

1. Press Ctrl+Alt+Del or Ctrl+Shift+Esc to open Task Manager.

   or

   Right-click an empty area of the taskbar; then choose Task Manager.

2. On the Applications tab, select the name of the unresponsive task (**Figure 6.14**).

3. Click End Task.

4. In the End Program dialog box, click End Now (**Figure 6.15**).

Figure 6.14 After Windows terminates the program, you can usually launch it again immediately without repercussions.

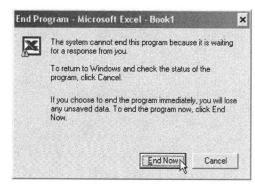

Figure 6.15 If you're lucky, Windows will ask whether you want to save your unsaved work before it kills the program. Sometimes, alas, even if Windows gives you the chance, the program itself won't.

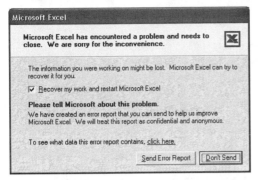

Figure 6.16 A "Please tell Microsoft" dialog box appears after a program crashes or after you reboot following a Windows "blue screen" system error. Click Send Error Report to transmit the error details to Microsoft; otherwise, click Don't Send. Sometimes, as shown here, you can have Windows try to recover your unsaved work.

Figure 6.17 You can choose to report only Windows system errors, or only program errors, or both. Click Choose Programs if you want to report errors for some programs but not others.

Reporting Errors to Microsoft

When a program or Windows itself terminates abnormally, a new XP feature lets you report the error to Microsoft over the Internet (**Figure 6.16**). If enough people report the same error, in theory, Microsoft will fix the bug—or at least post a Knowledge Base article. Microsoft swears that only technical information is sent, for purely technical purposes—not for, say, marketing or license compliance. You can fine-tune error reporting or turn it off.

To configure error reporting:

1. Choose Start > Control Panel > Performance and Maintenance > System > Advanced tab > Error Reporting (**Figure 6.17**).

   or

   Press Windows logo key+Break; then choose Advanced tab > Error Reporting.

2. To turn off error reporting, select the Disable Error Reporting option.

   or

   To report errors, select the Enable Error Reporting option; then select the types of errors that you want to report.

3. Click OK.

4. In the System Properties dialog box, click OK (or Apply).

Using the Free Utility Programs

The All Programs menu teems with free programs that are part of the standard XP installation. Some of these programs (such as Internet Explorer and Outlook Express) are heavy hitters that rate their own chapters. But Microsoft also includes some useful utility programs, described here.

✔ Tips

- These programs are available in the Start > All Programs > Accessories menu (**Figure 6.18**) or Start > All Programs > Games, if appropriate.

- To get program-specific help for a utility program, use its Help menu (or press F1).

Address Book

Address Book offers a centralized directory where you can store names, mailing and email addresses, phone numbers, and other contact information (**Figure 6.19**). You can retrieve this information from programs such as Outlook Express, Outlook, Fax, and Start > Search > Computers or People.

Calculator

In Standard mode, Calculator offers add, subtract, square root, invert, and other basic functions. In Scientific mode (**Figure 6.20**), it boasts trigonometric, statistical, logarithmic, and base functions. To operate Calculator, click its buttons with your mouse or press the corresponding keyboard keys. Help > Help Topics gives keyboard shortcuts for Scientific mode.

Figure 6.18 Launch utility programs from the Start > All Programs > Accessories menu or one of its submenus.

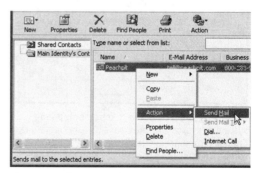

Figure 6.19 Choose File > Import > Other Address Book to import names from other popular address-book programs and formats.

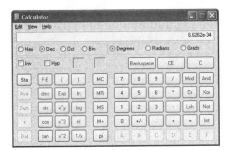

Figure 6.20 Choose View > Scientific to reveal Calculator's geeky secret identity.

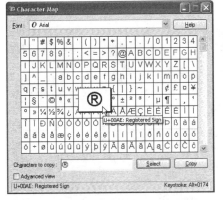

Figure 6.21 Here are the characters for the Arial font. Double-click characters to put them in the Characters to Copy text box; then click Copy. Now you can Edit > Paste them into any document. The pop-up tip is for typography experts and programmers: it shows the character's hexadecimal code.

```
E:\Documents and Settings\chris>dir
 Volume in drive E is Local Disk
 Volume Serial Number is 80EB-78C0

 Directory of E:\Documents and Settings\chris

11/07/2002  09:00 AM    <DIR>          .
11/07/2002  09:00 AM    <DIR>          ..
12/11/2002  02:01 PM    <DIR>          Desktop
12/10/2002  07:24 PM    <DIR>          Favorites
12/05/2002  07:26 PM    <DIR>          My Documents
11/04/2002  01:44 PM    <DIR>          Start Menu
10/19/2002  11:25 AM    <DIR>          WINDOWS
               0 File(s)              0 bytes
               7 Dir(s)  33,173,069,824 bytes free

E:\Documents and Settings\chris>
```

Figure 6.22 Hundreds of commands are available; search for *command-line reference* in Help Center. To quit Command Prompt, type exit; then press Enter.

Character Map

Character Map (**Figure 6.21**) displays all characters and symbols for a particular font. Use it to copy and paste diacritical marks, currency symbols, copyright signs, and all the other characters that don't appear on your keyboard.

Command Prompt

Command Prompt, formerly called DOS Prompt, lets you type commands rather than point and click (**Figure 6.22**). New users usually find this feature cryptic and intimidating, but experience teaches them to appreciate its efficiency. Command Prompt is handy for many routine tasks, but it really shines when it's impractical to use a graphical interface. (Network administrators don't add 1,000 user accounts by pointing and clicking, for example.) You also can use Command Prompt to (try to) run your old 16-bit DOS programs and games.

Games

The Games menu offers several games, including world-class productivity killers Solitaire, FreeCell, and Minesweeper. You also can play a few games with strangers over the Internet; the games match you with other players on www.zone.com.

HyperTerminal

HyperTerminal (in the Communications submenu) lets you connect to remote computers via modem. In days of yore, people used HyperTerminal to dial into bulletin-board services; now they use it to access remote systems that offer text-only Telnet service. Two nearby computers with identical HyperTerminal settings can swap files over an Ethernet connection or null-modem cable. Unfortunately, while HyperTerminal is robust, it's *not* intuitive to use.

Notepad

Notepad, a bare-bones text editor, is one of the most useful tools in Windows (**Figure 6.23**). Use it to open, create, or edit *text files,* which contain only printable characters—no fonts, formatting, "invisible" characters, colors, graphics, or any of the clutter usually associated with a word processor. Notepad is the default program for .txt and .log files, but you can use it to edit .html files (saved Web pages), .ini files (program initialization settings), or any other text-based file types.

✔ Tips

■ Notepad *does* offer a choice of fonts, but this formatting is stored elsewhere on your computer and won't appear when you open the file in other text editors.

■ Notepad is quite limited. You may want to explore the many excellent shareware and commercial editors (search for *text editors* at www.download.com).

Paint

Paint is a no-frills image editor with a few drawing, color, and manipulation tools (**Figure 6.24**). Use it to create your own works of art or to view or touch up graphic files that were created in other programs (such as Photoshop) or that you scanned or downloaded. Paint supports bitmap (.bmp), JPEG, GIF, TIFF, and PNG file formats.

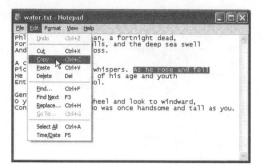

Figure 6.23 If you find Notepad too limiting, you can find many excellent shareware and commercial editors; search for *text editors* at www.download.com.

Figure 6.24 The Image menu lets you flip, rotate, and stretch images.

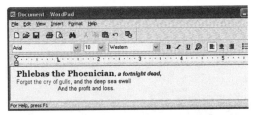

Figure 6.25 Like any word processor, WordPad lets you apply formatting (italics, justification, colors, fonts, and so on) to text. The Insert > Object command lets you embed images, sounds, movies, charts, spreadsheets, and other objects in your document.

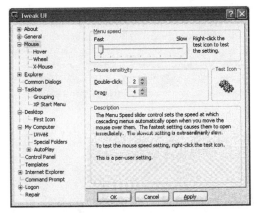

Figure 6.26 The most useful PowerToy is TweakUI, which lets you change many aspects of the standard user interface without the risk of messing with the Windows registry directly.

WordPad

WordPad (**Figure 6.25**) is a simple, stripped-down word processor associated with .doc files (unless Microsoft Word is installed on your PC), .rtf files (Rich Text Format), and .wri files (Microsoft Write). You also can use it to edit plain-text files, but Notepad is more appropriate for that task.

✔ Tip

■ WordPad's native file format is an obsolete Microsoft Word version called 6.0/95. Most versions of MS-Word will handle files made with WordPad, but the converse is not true.

PowerToys

PowerToys is a suite of utility programs, *not* on the Windows XP CD, that Microsoft felt experienced users would appreciate. They're free and available for download at www.microsoft.com/windowsxp/pro/downloads/powertoys.asp. PowerToys includes tools for changing the user interface, supercharging existing features, viewing images, and more (**Figure 6.26**). Some of them alter Windows on very deep levels and should be used carefully.

Saving Documents

Most programs let you save your work as documents, which you can return to later, print, send to other people, back up, and so on. Documents generally are thought of as being word-processed materials, but they can be graphics, spreadsheets, presentations, databases, email, or any other user-created work. Nearly all programs use Windows' standard Save dialog box. The first time you save a document, Windows asks you to name it and pick a folder to store it in. (Two files in the same folder can't have the same name.)

Figure 6.27 The Save dialog box appears the first time you save a file, or when you choose File > Save As.

To save a document:

1. Choose File > Save (**Figure 6.27**).

    or

    To save a copy of a file under a different name or in a different folder, choose File > Save As.

Save Your Work in My Documents

When Microsoft introduced the My Documents folder in Windows 98, many Windows veterans seethed at being told where to store their files and sniffed at its silly name (which, by the way, you can change; just right-click the folder and choose Rename). If you're one of these stalwarts, you might reconsider and use My Documents to store your folders and files because it:

◆ Is easy to access from the Start menu or Explorer task pane.

◆ Is where most programs expect you to save and open files.

◆ Segregates documents and programs (which are stored in Program Files), obviating accidental document deletion when programs are removed or upgraded.

◆ Makes it easier to back up your work by archiving only My Documents (and its subfolders) rather than folders scattered about your hard disk.

◆ Keeps your personal files private. To share files, move them to the Shared Documents folder. (Shared Documents isn't available on a network domain.)

◆ Has two specialized personal subfolders (My Pictures and My Music).

If your user name is, say, John, your My Documents folder appears as John's Documents to other logged-on users (who can't access it without permission).

Figure 6.28 From left to right, these buttons go to the last folder visited, go up one level in the folder hierarchy, create a new folder, and change the view of the listed files and folders in the dialog box. Extra buttons in Microsoft Office programs let you search the Web, delete files, map network drives, and more.

- The Save dialog box must be closed before you can use another part of the program.

- Some older programs use the old-style Save dialog box, which lacks some of the navigation features of the new dialog box.

- You can't save your work in some utility and game programs, such as Calculator and Solitaire.

2. Navigate to the folder where you want to store the document.

You have several ways to navigate. Double-click folder icons in the folder box to drill down the folder hierarchy. Use the left-side buttons to go to a common destination quickly. Use the top-side Save In list to pick a different drive. The toolbar also helps you navigate (**Figure 6.28**).

3. In the File Name box, type the name of the file.

For file-naming rules, see "Naming Files and Folders" in Chapter 5.

4. To save a file in a format other than the program's default format, choose a format from the Save As Type list.

This feature lets you, say, save a Microsoft Word document as Text (.txt), Rich Text Format (.rtf), or HTML (.html) so that users without Word can open it in Notepad, WordPad, or Internet Explorer.

5. Click Save.

✔ Tips

- To bypass step 2, type the filename's full path in step 3. See "Exploring Your Computer" in Chapter 5.

- The folder box lists documents as well as folders. Click a document to make its name appear in the File Name box; then click Save to overwrite the existing document or edit the name to save a new document. The latter technique saves typing when you're saving similarly-named documents.

- The folder box acts like an Explorer window. You can right-click any item to, say, rename or delete it. You can even drag items into and out of this box or use the standard navigation keys.

SAVING DOCUMENTS

Opening Documents

You have several ways to reopen a document that you've already named and saved.

To open a document:

◆ In the program that created the document, choose File > Open; navigate to the document; then click Open (**Figure 6.29**).

   or

   In Windows Explorer, double-click the document's icon (or select it and then press Enter).

   or

   If the document was opened recently, choose it from the Start > My Recent Documents menu.

   My Recent Documents is turned off by default. To enable it, see Table 2.1 in "Customizing the Start Menu" in Chapter 2.

   or

   Choose Start > Run (or press Windows logo key+R); type the document's name and full path; then press Enter.

✔ Tips

■ Like the Save dialog box, the Open dialog box must be closed before you can use another part of the program.

■ To open a file that's not associated with a particular program, right-click the file; choose Open With; then select the name of a program. See "Associating Documents with Programs" later in this chapter.

■ If you open a document that somebody else already has open, the program usually will warn you or open a *read-only* copy of the document, unless it's a multiuser document, such as a database.

■ Explorer's Favorites menu lets you add documents—not only Web pages—to your Favorites list, which you can access quickly in the Open and Save dialog boxes.

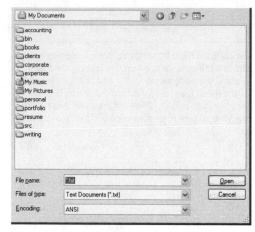

Figure 6.29 The Open dialog box works like the Save dialog box described in the preceding section. Upgraders note that the old Save In and Save As Type lists are now called Look In and Files of Type.

Table 6.1

Common File Extensions

EXTENSION	DESCRIPTION OR PROGRAM
.avi	Windows Media Player
.bmp	Bitmap image
.dll	System file (not a document)
.doc	Microsoft Word (or WordPad)
.exe	Program (not a document)
.gif	GIF image
.htm/.html	Web page (Internet Explorer)
.jpg/.jpeg	JPEG image (for photos)
.mdb	Microsoft Access
.pdf	Adobe Portable Document Format
.ppt	Microsoft PowerPoint
.qxd	QuarkXPress
.tmp	Temporary file
.txt	Text file (Notepad)
.wpd	WordPerfect
.xls	Microsoft Excel
.zip	Compressed Zip file

Associating Documents with Programs

When you double-click a Microsoft Word document, Windows launches Word with that document open. Windows knows to launch Word—rather than, say, Paint or Outlook Express—because a document's file type is embedded in its filename, as the (usually three, except for *.html* and *.jpeg*) characters appearing after the name's last dot. These characters—called a *file extension*—associate a document with a particular program. **Table 6.1** gives a short list of common file extensions; visit **www.filext.com** for a comprehensive list.

Microsoft hides file extensions by default to make Windows appear friendlier. But even beginners appreciate visible extensions for a few reasons:

◆ An icon alone can be insufficient to specify a file's type (particularly the tiny icons in Details view).

◆ Extensions supply the types of like-named files quickly (`resume.doc` vs. `resume.txt` vs. `resume.html`, for example).

◆ You may, for example, want to choose among Photoshop, Paint, Internet Explorer, and Windows Picture and Fax Viewer to open JPEG files.

◆ If a newly installed program hijacks a file extension's association without asking your permission (which is both rude and quite common), you can reassociate the extension with your preferred program.

◆ If you don't learn about file extensions, you'll remain mired in beginner status, forever pestering your friends and colleagues with trivial problems.

To show file extensions:

◆ In Windows Explorer, choose Tools > Folder Options > View tab > Advanced Settings list > uncheck Hide Extensions for Known File Types (**Figures 6.30** and **6.31**).

Figure 6.30 Clear this check box to show file extensions in Explorer, on the desktop, and in dialog boxes.

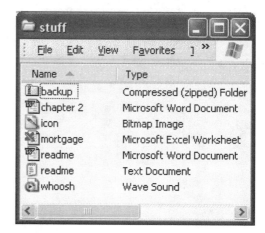

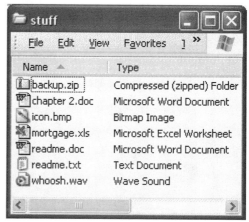

Figure 6.31 An Explorer window with (top) and without (bottom) file extensions hidden.

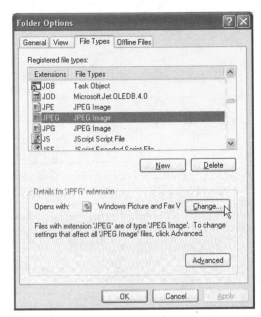

Figure 6.32 Each program must register its file type(s) with Windows to appear in this list.

Figure 6.33 At the top of the list are programs that Windows thinks appropriate for the selected file type, but you can choose or browse for a different program.

To change the program associated with a file extension:

1. In Windows Explorer, choose Tools > Folder Options > File Types tab (**Figure 6.32**).

2. In the Registered File Types list, select the extension that you want to change.

3. Click Change.

4. In the Open With dialog box, select another program to associate the extension with; then click OK (**Figure 6.33**).

5. In the Folder Options dialog box, click Close.

✔ Tips

■ The Details section in Explorer's task pane contains file-type information for the selected file.

■ Some file types have multiple extensions (.htm/.html and .jpg/.jpeg, for example). Repeat the association for each form of the extension.

(continues on next page)

- If you double-click a file with an unknown extension, Windows lets you select the name of the program you want or try to look up the extension on Microsoft's Web site (**Figure 6.34**).

- If you want to open a file with a program other than the associated one (without actually reassigning the file type), right-click the file's icon; then choose a program from the Open With submenu (**Figure 6.35**).

- To change the icon for a file type, follow steps 1 and 2; then click Advanced > Change Icon (**Figure 6.36**). You can also find individual icons by using Search to look for *.ico files. Unfortunately, almost all icon collections in XP are hidden in .dll files whose names—other than shell32.dll—aren't exactly public knowledge.

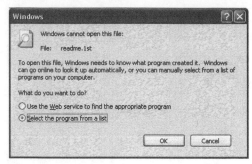

Figure 6.34 This dialog box appears when you double-click a file with an extension that Windows doesn't recognize. A file with an unknown extension (or no extension) often is a text file; try opening it in Notepad before asking Windows to hunt for a program.

Figure 6.36 You can't change the icon for an individual file, but you can change it for a file *type* (JPEG files, here). If you don't like any of the replacement icons Windows offers, you can browse.

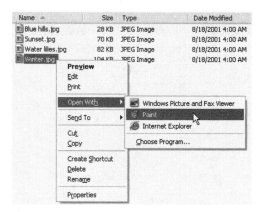

Figure 6.35 The Open With menu lists programs capable of opening the selected file. Click Choose Program to pick a program that's not in the menu.

Printing and Faxing

Paperless office? Hardly. Computer users have felled entire forests to feed inexpensive, quality printers and preserve a paper trail "just in case". Under Windows XP, the operating system, rather than individual programs, handles printing. When you print something in any application, you activate XP's intermediary printing system, which accepts print jobs from programs and feeds them to the printer. This process, called *background printing*, lets you keep working in your program during printing.

Printer installation and configuration is easy. After hardware connection and setup, you can print individual documents with the default settings or override them for special purposes. In this chapter, I'll discuss basic printer properties, printing tasks, and a few topics beyond the usual routine. I'll also describe how to *save* paper by using XP to send and receive faxes without a fax machine.

Installing a Printer

A *local printer* connects directly to your computer through a USB, parallel, serial, or infrared port. Your printer's manual describes how to attach it to the back of your computer —it's quite simple. Newer printers attach through a USB (Universal Serial Bus) port; older ones attach through a parallel or (rarely) serial port. You can use a cableless infrared connection if both your printer and computer (typically, a laptop) have infrared lenses. For information about ports, see "Connecting Devices to Your Computer" in Chapter 8.

When you connect a printer to your computer, XP often recognizes the device and searches its extensive collection of built-in drivers to run printers. A *printer driver* is software that enables programs to give commands to a particular printer. If your printer doesn't appear on XP's built-in list, you can use the driver on the CD or floppy that came with the printer. If you upgraded from an earlier Windows version, XP inherited the existing printer driver and settings, and your printer *may* work fine. In any case, check the printer manufacturer's Web site for a more recent driver.

✔ Tips

- You must be an Administrator to install a printer. See "Setting Up User Accounts" in Chapter 16.

- Turn off your PC before connecting or disconnecting a parallel or serial cable. (Your PC can remain on for USB and infrared connections.)

- Skim the manual before installation. Some manufacturers supply software to be used instead of XP's Add Printer Wizard.

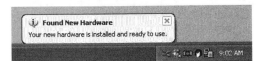

Figure 7.1 You'll see this notification-area message for Plug and Play printers. It means that Windows completed the installation automatically. Go ahead and start printing.

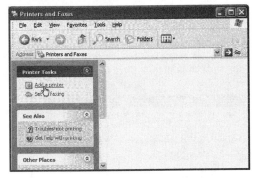

Figure 7.2 When Windows says *printer*, it means *printer driver*.

Figure 7.3 The Add Printer Wizard tells you not to use it if your printer connects to a USB or IEEE 1394 (FireWire) port.

■ Installation is trivial for printers that support Plug and Play, which lets Windows detect and configure a connected device automatically. Printers that use USB or infrared connections always support Plug and Play. Parallel connections *might* support it; serial connections *never* do. For more information about Plug and Play, see "Installing Plug and Play Devices" in Chapter 8.

To install a local printer:

1. Connect your printer to the appropriate port, and turn on the printer.

   On the Windows desktop, one of three things happens:

   ▲ A Found New Hardware alert appears (**Figure 7.1**), meaning that Windows knows about your printer and has installed the appropriate driver. You're ready to print; skip the rest of these steps.

   ▲ The Add Printer Wizard appears, meaning that Windows detected the printer but lacks a driver for this model. Skip to step 7.

   ▲ Windows didn't detect the printer and does nothing. Continue to step 2.

2. Choose Start > Control Panel > Printers and Other Hardware > Printers and Faxes.

3. In the task pane, click Add a Printer (**Figure 7.2**).

   The Add Printer Wizard opens.

4. On the Welcome page, click Next (**Figure 7.3**).

(continues on next page)

5. On the Local or Network Printer page, select Local Printer Attached to This Computer; uncheck Automatically Detect and Install My Plug and Play Printer; then click Next (**Figure 7.4**).

6. On the Select a Printer Port page, select a port from the list (**Figure 7.5**); then click Next.

In almost all cases, LPT1: (the default) is the correct port.

7. On the Install Printer software page, select the manufacturer and model of your printer; then click Next (**Figure 7.6**).

or

If your printer model isn't listed, insert the printer's installation CD or floppy; click Have Disk; then follow the onscreen instructions to install your printer.

(If Windows disdains your installation disk, download the current printer driver from the printer manufacturer's Web site.)

8. On the Name Your Printer page, type a name for your printer or accept the default name; then click Next (**Figure 7.7**).

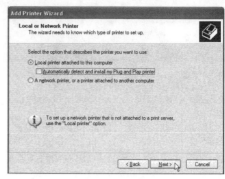

Figure 7.4 Uncheck the Automatically Detect box to spare Windows a fruitless search for your non-Plug and Play printer.

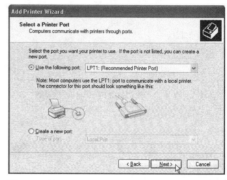

Figure 7.5 For most printer setups, you can accept the default settings. Windows refers to a parallel port as an *LPT port* and a serial port as a *COM port*.

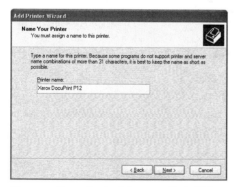

Figure 7.7 Use a short printer name that will fit easily in messages and dialog boxes. If you're going to print from an old DOS-based program, use a name with eight or fewer letters (no spaces or punctuation).

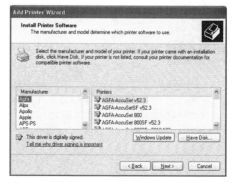

Figure 7.6 Clicking an entry in the Manufacturer list (left) displays XP's standard drivers for that manufacturer in the Printers list (right). The Windows Update button connects you to Microsoft's Web site for drivers that were updated since XP came out.

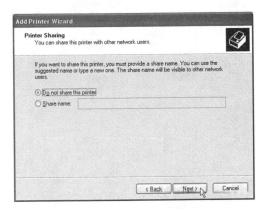

Figure 7.8 To share a printer on a network, see the next section in this chapter.

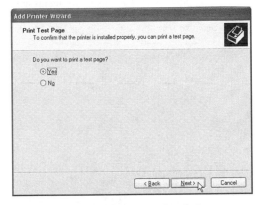

Figure 7.9 Print a test page to confirm that your printer is working properly.

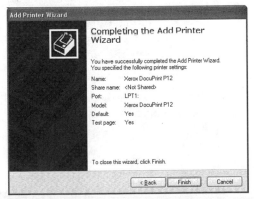

Figure 7.10 This page echoes the settings you've chosen in the Add Printer Wizard.

9. On the Printer Sharing page, select Do Not Share This Printer; then click Next (**Figure 7.8**).

10. On the Print Test Page page, choose Yes to print a test page; then click Next (**Figure 7.9**).

11. On the completion page, click Finish (**Figure 7.10**).

12. In the pop-up confirmation dialog box, click OK if the test page printed or Troubleshoot if it didn't (**Figure 7.11**).

(continues on next page)

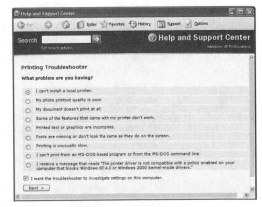

Figure 7.11 If the test page looks garbled (or doesn't print at all), click Troubleshoot to have Windows help you try to solve the problem.

After successful installation, the printer's icon appears in the Printers and Faxes window (**Figure 7.12**).

✔ Tips

- If the manufacturer provides no XP driver for your printer, try the Windows 2000 driver. If no 2000 driver exists, try the Windows NT driver. No luck? Try a NT/ 2000/XP driver for a different printer from the same manufacturer—but keep it in the family; inkjet printers can't use laser-printer drivers, for example. *Still* no luck? Try *printer emulation:* Check the manual to see whether your printer can mimic a different printer, and use *that* printer's driver. Many non-Hewlett Packard laser printers can work with HP LaserJet drivers, for example.

- To remove a printer that you no longer use, right-click its icon in the Printers and Faxes window; then choose Delete.

- For information about installing fonts, see "Managing Fonts" in Chapter 4.

- To put a Printers and Faxes shortcut in the Start menu, see "Making Programs Appear in the Start Menu" in Chapter 2.

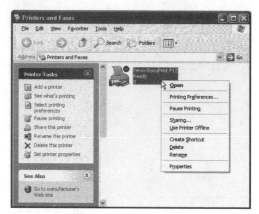

Figure 7.12 Right-click a printer icon to show common printer tasks (many of which are duplicated in the task pane at left). Tiles view (shown here) and Details view display printer status information. Note the link to the printer manufacturer's Web site in the task pane's See Also section.

Same Printer. Different Purposes.

You can install multiple drivers with different settings for the same physical printer, then switch between "virtual" printers to suit what you're printing. If your printer has two paper trays, create "Letterhead" and "Plain" printers; to switch between printing high-resolution graphics and low-resolution text documents, create "1200 dpi" and "300 dpi" printers. Separate "Landscape" and "Portrait" printers are popular too. To create another printer:

1. Install the printer again, but under a different name that indicates its purpose (see step 8).

2. After installation, right-click the printer's icon in the Printers and Faxes dialog box (refer to Figure 7.12), choose Printing Preferences; then select settings appropriate to its role.

3. In the Printers and Faxes dialog box, right-click the icon for the printer that you use most of the time; then choose Set As Default Printer.

    A check mark appears on the default printer's icon.

From now on, you can choose the appropriate printer in any program's Print dialog box. See "Printing Documents" later in this chapter.

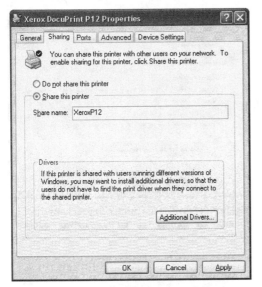

Figure 7.13 Type a short name without spaces or punctuation.

Figure 7.14 You can install additional printer drivers on your system so that users running other Windows versions can connect to your printer without being prompted to install missing drivers.

Sharing a Network Printer

If you have several computers connected over a network (see Chapter 17), they can share the same printer. Step 9 of the preceding section showed you how to use the Add Printer Wizard to set up a shared network printer, but that option isn't available if you let Windows detect your Plug and Play printer automatically. Here's how to set up a network printer manually.

To share a printer:

1. At the computer attached to the printer to be shared, choose Start > Control Panel > Printers and Other Hardware > Printers and Faxes.

2. Right-click a printer; choose Sharing.

3. Select Share This Printer; then type a share name for the printer (**Figure 7.13**). You can make up this name, but it has to be unique on the network.

4. To share the printer with users using different Windows versions or computer hardware, click Additional Drivers; choose the environment and operating system for the other computers; then click OK (**Figure 7.14**).

5. Click OK (or Apply).

After you've set up a shared printer, other users on the network can add it to their own Printers and Faxes window and print with it.

To use a shared printer:

1. Choose Start > Control Panel > Printers and Other Hardware > Printers and Faxes.

2. In the task pane, click Add a Printer (refer to Figure 7.2); then click Next.

3. On the Local or Network Printer page (refer to Figure 7.4), select A Network Printer, or a Printer Attached to Another Computer; then click Next.

4. If you don't know the printer's address, select Browse for a Printer (**Figure 7.15**); then click Next.

    or

    Select the second option to type a network path (such as \\server_name\printer_name); then click Next.

    or

    Select the third option to type an Internet address (URL); then click Next.

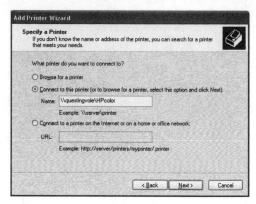

Figure 7.15 Browse for a printer on your network or, for extra geek points, select it by its network address or URL.

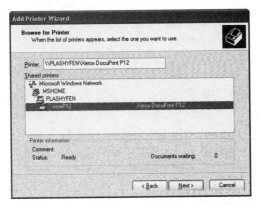

Figure 7.16 When you browse for a printer, the Shared Printers list appears, empty. Wait a few seconds for Windows to populate it with the names of available network printers.

5. If you selected Browse for a Printer in the preceding screen, select the printer to use (**Figure 7.16**); then click Next.

6. Enter your user account name and password if you're asked.

7. If you have more than one printer installed, specify the one to be your default (primary) printer.

8. Click Finish.

   The shared printer appears in the Printers and Faxes dialog box.

✔ Tips

- **Table 7.1** shows how a printer's icon reflects its status.

- If you share a printer with DOS or Windows 3.x computers, use eight or fewer letters for the printer's share name (no spaces or punctuation); a network share is named with the same rules as a file.

- The terms *shared printer* and *network printer* are synonymous.

- When you share a printer connected to your PC, everybody's print jobs go through *your* copy of Windows, draining your system resources. Busy networks use a computer dedicated to printing *(print server)* to arbitrate complex print requests.

Table 7.1

Printer Icons	
ICON	**DESCRIPTION**
🖨	A local printer has a normal printer icon.
🖨	A shared local printer has a hand below it.
🖨	A remote printer on the network has a cable below it.
🖨	The default printer has a check mark on it.

Setting Printer Properties

You can change a printer's default settings through its Properties dialog box. This dialog box varies by printer model because the manufacturer supplies the drivers whose features appear there. Options common to all printers include those in the General and Advanced tabs.

To change a printer's default settings:

1. Choose Start > Control Panel > Printers and Other Hardware > Printers and Faxes.

2. Right-click a printer icon; then choose Properties.

3. On the following tabs, set the printer's default properties:

   General. Change the printer's name, location, or comments. To test the printer, click Print Test Page (**Figure 7.17**).

   Sharing. See "Sharing a Network Printer" earlier in this chapter.

   Ports. Review the printer's port assignment and configuration. You'll rarely want to change these settings.

   Advanced. Change settings such as printer access hours and spooling (queuing) behavior. (*Don't* select Print Directly to the Printer; it disables background printing.) Click Printing Defaults to view or change the default document properties for all users. Click Separator Page to add or change a separator page that prints between documents (**Figure 7.18**).

   Device Settings. These options differ by printer model depending on its features (**Figure 7.19**).

4. Click OK (or Apply).

✔ Tip

- To set print server properties that affect *all* networked printers, right-click an empty area of the Printers and Faxes dialog box; then choose Server Properties.

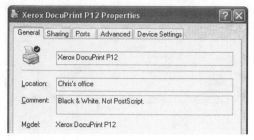

Figure 7.17 If you're sharing a printer, add its location and a few helpful comments for other network users to see.

Figure 7.18 With shared printers, separator pages make it easy to find your documents among others at the printer. You can create custom separator pages.

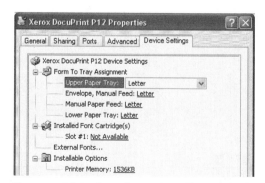

Figure 7.19 Printer-dependent settings affect such things as color, tray selection, fonts, printer memory, and duplex printing.

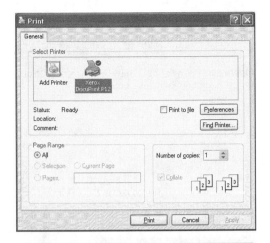

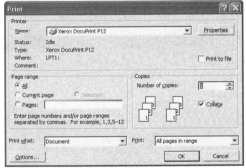

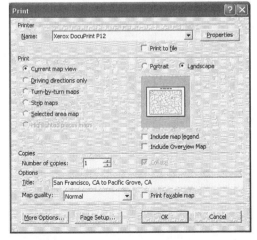

Figure 7.20 Print dialog boxes vary by program and printer model, but you'll find some common settings. Here are Print dialog boxes for Notepad (top), Microsoft Word (middle), and Microsoft Streets & Trips (bottom).

Printing Documents

After your printer is up and running, printing a document is a simple operation.

To print a document:

1. Open the document that you want to print.

2. Choose File > Print (or press Ctrl+P).

3. In the Print dialog box (**Figure 7.20**), select the printer and print options.

   This dialog box varies by printer model and program, but the basic settings are:

   Select Printer. Choose a local or network printer from the list or scrolling panel. If you've created several icons for different modes of the same printer, choose among them here.

   Preferences/Properties. Click this to open the Preferences or Properties dialog box (**Figure 7.21**).

   (continues on next page)

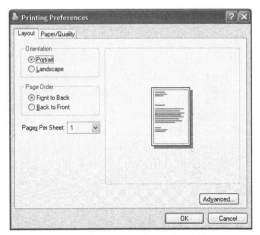

Figure 7.21 This dialog box lets you specify paper size (for multiple trays), orientation (landscape or portrait), print quality (dots per inch), and so on. These settings apply to the current printout, not to the printer in general.

Page Range. Specify which pages of the document to print. The Selection option is dimmed if you didn't highlight any text before you opened the Print dialog box.

Copies. Specify the number of copies to print. You'll usually want to turn on collation for multiple copies.

Program-specific settings. Any program can add extra features to the Print dialog box. Right-click an option; then click What's This? for pop-up help.

4. Click Print or OK (or press Enter).

✔ Tips

■ During printing, a status icon appears in the notification area (**Figure 7.22**).

■ To bypass the Print dialog box and use the default printer and settings to print, click the Print button on a toolbar (**Figure 7.23**).

■ Internet Explorer's Print dialog box lets you print a Web page's frames and links (**Figure 7.24**).

■ You can print a document right from Windows Explorer or the desktop without opening it; right-click the document's icon and choose Print. Or drag a document's icon to a printer icon in the Printers and Faxes dialog box, to a print spooler window, or to a desktop printer shortcut.

■ Most programs have additional print commands in the File menu or a toolbar. Page Setup sets margins, orientation, and other layout options. Print Preview shows how a document will look when you print it.

■ If you have a color printer, see the discussion of color management in "Configuring the Monitor" in Chapter 4.

■ **PRO** If you're a domain member, the Print dialog box has a Find Printer button that you can click to search the network for a particular printer.

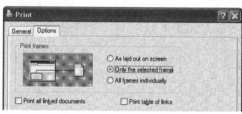

Figure 7.22 Point to this icon (without clicking) to pop up the number of print jobs pending.

Figure 7.23 The standard Print toolbar button (shown here in Microsoft Office) looks like this. The pop-up tip displays the destination printer.

Figure 7.24 Click the Options tab in IE's Print dialog box. If a Web page is divided into independent rectangular sections (frames), you can print them selectively. You also can print all the linked pages and a table at the end of the printout that lists all the page's links.

Printer Troubleshooting

When you're having trouble printing, you want to determine whether the problem lies with the printer, Windows XP, or a particular program. Here are some things to check:

◆ Make sure that the printer is plugged in and turned on. Check for snug cable connections on the printer and computer ports. (Most printer hardware problems involve the cable.)

◆ Remove the paper tray, pop the printer's lid, and check for a jammed paper path.

◆ Streaks of white space in printouts mean you're low on toner (ink).

◆ Turn the printer off and on to clear its memory.

◆ Create a file in Notepad, and print it from the command prompt. Choose Start > All Programs > Accessories > Command Prompt; type print *filename.txt*; then press Enter. (Replace *filename.txt* with the name of your homemade text file.) If it prints, you have a software problem; otherwise, you have a hardware problem.

◆ Consult the printer's manual and print a test page. (If it prints, delete and reinstall the printer driver.)

◆ Use XP's built-in troubleshooter: Choose Start > Help and Support > Printing and Faxing topic > Fixing a Printing Problem (in the left pane) > Printing Troubleshooter (in the right pane). (Refer to Figure 7.11.)

If you still can't determine the problem's source, you may have a malfunctioning port (somewhat complex) or motherboard (get out your wallet).

Controlling Printouts

When you print a document, it's intercepted by an intermediary program, called the *print spooler,* on its way to the printer. The print spooler holds your documents (on disk or in memory) until your printer can accept them. The delay is short for text files but may be substantial for large graphics files. The spooler puts each document in a *print queue* (or just *queue*), where it waits its turn to be printed. You can change the order of queued documents, pause or resume printing, or cancel specific print jobs. Spooling occurs in the background, so you can keep working in your program—or even quit the program—and documents still print.

To manage the print queue:

1. Choose Start > Control Panel > Printers and Other Hardware > Printers and Faxes; then double-click a printer icon.

   or

   Double-click the notification-area printer icon (refer to Figure 7.22).

2. In the print spooler window, do any of the following (**Figure 7.25**):

   To cancel printing a document, right-click that document; then choose Cancel.

   To cancel printing all documents, choose Printer > Cancel All Documents.

   To pause (or resume) printing a document, right-click that document; then choose Pause (or Resume).

   To pause (or resume) printing all documents, choose Printer > Pause Printing. (Choose it again to resume printing.)

   To add another document to the queue, drag the document's icon from Explorer or the desktop into the printer-spooler window.

   To rearrange the printing order, right-click a document; choose Properties; then drag the Priority slider. Higher-priority documents print before lower-priority documents.

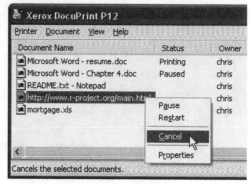

Figure 7.25 The print-spooler window lists the documents waiting to print. The first document is printing, the second one is paused, and I'm about to cancel the fourth one. By default, you can pause, resume, restart, or cancel your own documents but not those of other users.

Faxing

XP's nifty Fax program lets you send and receive faxes through your PC, without an actual fax machine. You'll need a phone line and almost any modem. Even an oldish 33.6 Kbps modem can send a multipage fax in a minute or two.

✔ Tips

- Install the modem *before* you start the Fax setup process. Make sure that the modem is connected to a phone line and the phone line is connected to a working jack.

- You *can't* use your DSL or cable connection for faxing...yet...but a new technology called *VoIP* (Voice Over Internet Protocol) may change this.

- To fax documents that aren't computer files, you'll need a scanner (see Chapter 9). Faxes are sent in black and white at a default resolution of 150 x 150 dpi, which any scanner can manage.

- If you don't want buy a modem or tie up your phone line, consider one of the Internet-based fax services listed at http://directory.google.com/Top/Computers/Internet/Internet_Fax/.

PC-Based Faxing Advantages

Faxing through Windows offers these advantages over a traditional fax machine:

- Conserves paper.

- Saves money on paper and fax-machine cartridges.

- Faxes documents without printing them.

- Faxes from your computer via the File > Print command.

- Lets you read incoming faxes onscreen or print them automatically.

- Lets you manage incoming faxes as you would any documents; read, save, or delete them, or attach them to email.

- Generates cleaner, more legible faxes than ones sent via fax machine.

FAXING

Fax is ignored by default during Windows Setup; you have to install it manually. Exception: If you upgraded to XP from a Windows version that had a Fax component, the XP Fax component was installed automatically during the upgrade. You can import your existing faxes into Fax. Choose Start > All Programs > Accessories > Communications > Fax > Fax Console. In Fax Console, choose Help > Help Topics; then read the topic Fax After Upgrading to Windows XP.

To install Fax:

1. Choose Start > Control Panel > Printers and Other Hardware > Printers and Faxes > Set Up Faxing (in the task pane) (**Figure 7.26**).

2. Insert your Windows XP CD when prompted, close the blue Welcome to Windows screen when it appears, and continue.

3. When the installation is complete, a Fax icon appears in the Printers and Faxes dialog box (**Figure 7.27**), and new fax programs appear in Start > All Programs > Accessories > Communications > Fax.

Before you can send or receive faxes, you must use the Fax Configuration Wizard to configure Fax.

To configure Fax:

1. Choose Start > All Programs > Accessories > Communications > Fax > Fax Console.

2. On the Fax Configuration Wizard's Welcome page, click Next.

3. On the Sender Information page, type your name or business name and your fax number (**Figure 7.28**); then click Next.

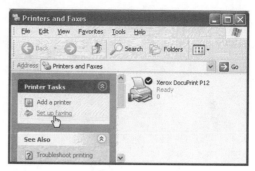

Figure 7.26 Use Control Panel's Add or Remove Programs extension to install Fax. See "Adding and Removing Windows Components" in Chapter 6.

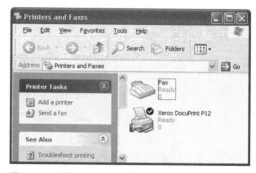

Figure 7.27 When you install XP's Fax Services component, a fax icon appears in your Printers and Faxes dialog box.

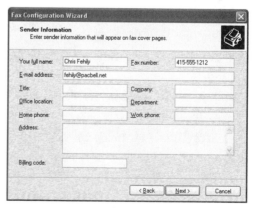

Figure 7.28 *All* these fields are optional, but information from here appears on the fax cover sheet, so include enough for the recipient to contact you if a fax doesn't go through.

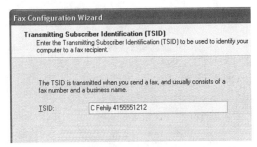

Figure 7.29 The TSID is mandatory in some areas. This identification information usually appears in the header area of a received fax and serves to identify the sending fax machine. Some fax-routing software depends on TSIDs to determine where to direct incoming faxes.

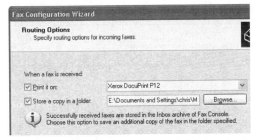

Figure 7.30 Check Print It On if you want each received fax to be printed automatically (on the selected printer). Check Store a Copy in a Folder to create a backup copy of each fax (in addition to the copies saved by Fax Console).

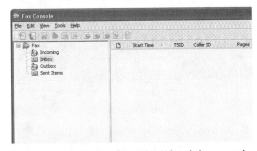

Figure 7.31 The Fax Configuration Wizard closes, and the Fax Console window opens. Now the computer is configured to send or receive faxes.

4. On the Select Device for Sending or Receiving Faxes page, make sure that your modem is selected; set send and receive options; specify whether you'll answer incoming faxes manually or automatically; then click Next.

5. On the Transmitting Subscriber Identification (TSID) page, enter your business name and fax number (**Figure 7.29**); then click Next.

6. On the Called Subscriber Identification (CSID) page, enter your business name and fax number again; then click Next.

   The CSID is displayed on the sending fax machine. This helps to confirm that the fax is being sent to the correct recipient.

7. On the Routing Options page, specify how incoming faxes will be handled; then click Next.

   All faxes are stored in Fax Console automatically, but you can print a copy or store it in a local or shared folder (**Figure 7.30**).

8. Confirm the settings; then click Finish (**Figure 7.31**).

FAXING

227

To send a fax:

1. Open the document that you want to print.

2. Choose File > Print (or press Ctrl+P).

3. In the Print dialog box, click the Fax icon or choose Fax from the list; then click Print or OK, or press Enter (**Figure 7.32**).

4. On the Send Fax Wizard's Welcome page, click Next.

5. Type the recipient's name and fax number (**Figure 7.33**); click Add to send a fax to multiple recipients; then click Next.

   or

   Click Address Book; select one or more recipients; then click Next.

6. Select a cover page, if you want one; add a subject line and a note to appear on the cover page; then click Next.

7. Specify when you want to send the fax and its priority; then click Next.

   Priority determines the sending order if you're stacking a bunch of faxes to send at a particular time.

8. Confirm the settings; then click Finish.

   Click Preview Fax if you want to inspect the fax. For multipage faxes, you can preview only the first page.

   If you're sending the fax now, the Fax Monitor window appears after a few seconds (**Figure 7.34**).

✔ Tips

- To fax from a Microsoft Office program (such as Word or Outlook), choose File > Send To > Fax Recipient. The Office Fax Wizard asks for information and then hands off to the Send Fax Wizard.

- To fax someone a one-page note, choose Start > All Programs > Accessories > Communications > Fax > Send a Fax.

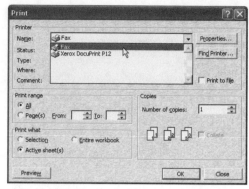

Figure 7.32 After configuration, a Fax icon appears in the Printer list of each program's Print dialog box.

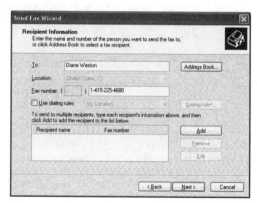

Figure 7.33 If Use Dialing Rules is turned off, type the recipient's fax number as it should be dialed. (Parentheses, commas, and hyphens are ignored.) If Use Dialing Rules is turned on, click Dialing Rules, and choose one of the dialing setups, or click Add to create one.

- Cover pages help when you send to big institutions where the fax might be misrouted. You can make an impressive cover page by designing your own: In Fax Console, choose Tools > Personal Cover Pages > New.

FAXING

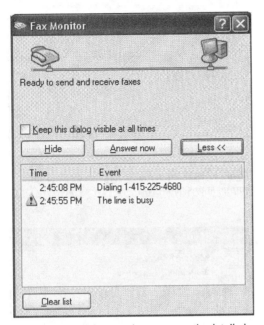

Figure 7.34 Click the More button to see the detailed status of each outgoing fax. Click Hide if you prefer Windows to do its faxing invisibly. A pop-up message appears when a fax is sent successfully (or fails).

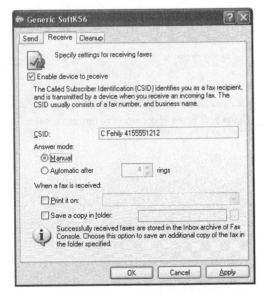

Figure 7.35 Select Manual answer mode if you receive a fax occasionally on a telephone line that you use mostly for talking.

To receive a fax, you must have checked Enable Receive in the Fax Configuration Wizard in step 4 of "To configure Fax." To change that setting (and others) without walking through the wizard again, in the Printers and Faxes dialog box (refer to Figure 7.27), right-click the Fax icon; then choose Properties > Devices tab > Properties button > Receive tab (**Figure 7.35**).

Faxes received in Automatic answer mode (best for dedicated fax lines) appear in the Fax Console's Inbox, discussed next. You'll prefer Manual answer mode if your computer and telephone share a line.

To receive a fax manually:

1. When the phone rings, click the message that appears in the notification area (**Figure 7.36**).

2. To see the received fax, look in the Fax Console's Inbox, discussed next.

Figure 7.36 If you're expecting a fax, click this message; Fax Monitor (refer to Figure 7.34) appears and downloads the fax. If you're expecting a person to call, just pick up the phone, and this message disappears.

To manage and view faxes:

1. Choose Start > All Programs > Accessories > Communications > Fax > Fax Console (**Figure 7.37**).

2. In the left pane, expand the Fax folder, if it's not already expanded.

   Fax contains the following subfolders:

   Incoming contains faxes that are being received now.

   Inbox contains faxes that have been received.

   Outbox contains faxes that are scheduled to be sent.

   Sent Items contains faxes that have been sent successfully.

3. In the left pane, click the folder that you want.

4. In the right pane, right-click the fax that you want; then choose a command.

To control fax-transmission behavior:

1. In the Printers and Faxes dialog box (refer to Figure 7.27), right-click the Fax icon; then choose Properties.

2. On the Tracking tab, set options for notifications and when the Fax Monitor should open.

3. On the Archives tab, specify whether incoming and outgoing faxes should be saved and, if so, where.

4. On the Devices tab, click the Properties button.

5. On the Send tab, specify the number of times to retry sending a fax and how long the program should wait between tries (**Figure 7.38**).

6. Click OK (or Apply).

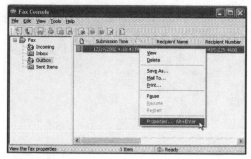

Figure 7.37 The Properties dialog box displays the current status of the fax.

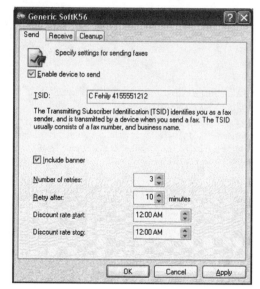

Figure 7.38 When a fax doesn't go through the first time, Fax tries again later.

SETTING UP HARDWARE

In the broadest sense, *hardware* is your computer and whatever connects to it; everything else is software. Windows generally uses the term to refer to a *peripheral*—nowadays usually called a *device*—which is any part of a computer other than the processor (CPU), motherboard, and memory (RAM and ROM). Your monitor, mouse, keyboard, hard disks, and printer, for example, are devices, as are *external devices* such as digital cameras, backup drives, video recorders, speakers, and PDA synchronization cradles.

Windows treats *any* gadget connected to your PC as a device, and requires you to install the software that controls it, called its *device driver* or simply *driver.* A driver acts like a translator between specialized commands for the device and the requests from the Windows programs that use it. Fortunately, XP makes installation a snap for modern Plug and Play devices, and offers wizards to help you install older non-Plug and Play devices.

Installing Plug and Play Devices

When you buy any hardware made since 1995, chances are that it's a *Plug and Play* (or *PnP*) device, which means that you can install it (plug it in) and use it (play with it) immediately—no configuration needed. To work properly, Plug and Play requires a few things:

◆ A Plug and Play-compliant operating system, which XP is.

◆ A device that identifies itself to Windows and lets Windows configure it and install its drivers. Look for the "Designed for Windows" logo when you buy.

◆ The PC's system startup software (called the *BIOS*) must be Plug and Play-compatible. Almost any computer with enough horsepower to run XP has a PnP BIOS.

The port or slot (discussed next) that a device plugs into may indicate its compatibility:

◆ *All* USB, IEEE 1394 (FireWire), Bluetooth, and PCMCIA (PC Card) devices support Plug and Play fully.

◆ *Most* PCI and parallel devices are Plug and Play-compliant.

◆ *No* ISA or serial devices are Plug and Play-compliant. Most such devices are quite old, and if their manufacturers still exist, you might check their Web sites for a Windows XP/2000/NT4.0 driver. If there's no such driver, resign yourself to buying a new gizmo.

✔ Tip

■ Remember that the *serial* in *serial port* and the *serial* in *Universal Serial Bus* (USB) are *not* the same thing. A serial port has a D connector with one row of five pins and one row of four. A USB port is a small rectangular hole that accepts a shiny metal plug with no pins.

Hardware Compatibility List

Windows XP's hardware compatibility is better than that of its parent, Windows 2000, but worse than that of its cousins, Windows 9x. If you've upgraded from 98 or Me, you may find that hardware that worked fine before abruptly ceases to.

First, check the manufacturer's Web site for updated drivers. Then browse `www.microsoft.com/hcl/` to inspect Microsoft's Hardware Compatibility List (HCL), a huge list of equipment that's certified to work with XP by Microsoft's Windows Hardware Quality Labs (WHQL). Also look for the "Designed for Windows XP" logo on the product's package or Web site.

If your errant device isn't on this HCL, however, it might still work with XP. The manufacturer may have declined to pay WHQL the (hefty) fee for XP-specific certification. Many devices that were WHQL-certified for Windows 2000 or Me work just fine with XP and an XP driver.

Connecting Devices to Your Computer

When you install a new device for your computer, you'll either connect it to a port on the back of the computer, or insert it into a slot inside the computer case. The port or slot provides the channel that the computer and device use to exchange data.

Ordinarily, there's more to installing a device than just connecting it, but I'll cover *connecting* here and the larger process of *installing* in the next section.

External devices

External devices—ones that you can connect without opening your PC's case—plug into *ports* on (generally) the back panel or (possibly) the front panel of your computer. **Table 8.1** lists the commonest ports on a PC, but yours may have others, depending on its age and its peripherals.

If you set up your own computer, you're familiar with ports, because the monitor, keyboard, mouse, and printer all have cables that connect to ports. Different shapes for different port types make it hard to plug a cable into the wrong port; but *always examine the plug and port* and *never force a connection.* Forcing might bend the pins in the port or connector.

Table 8.1

PC External Port Types	
PORT	**DESCRIPTION**
Parallel (DB-25)	A long narrow port with 25 holes along 2 rows. If your printer doesn't plug into a USB port, it plugs into this port (usually called a *printer port*). Older Zip, tape, CD, and other external drives use this port too. Windows calls it an *LPT port*. USB connections are supplanting parallel connections (slowly).
Serial	A short, slightly D-shaped port with 9 pins along 2 rows, used for any type of *serial device*—say, an older mouse, external modem, or serial printer. Windows calls it a *COM port*. USB connections, much faster than serial connections, have replaced them on new hardware.
PS/2	A small, round, female port with six holes. If your mouse and keyboard don't plug into USB ports, they plug into two PS/2 ports. Look for small pictures of a mouse and a keyboard, each next to its proper port. USB connections gradually are replacing PS/2 ports.
USB (Universal Serial Bus)	A small, thin, rectangular port that accepts almost all Plug and Play devices: mice, Zip drives, scanners, digital cameras, keyboards, printers, and so on. Almost every PC made since 1998 has two USB ports, but you can buy a USB *hub* with extra ports if you need them. USB ports are *hot-pluggable,* allowing you to connect and disconnect devices without shutting down your PC; Windows automatically loads or unloads the drivers as needed. USB ports provide power as well as data to the devices they connect.
IEEE 1394	A small, rectangular, very fast port with a tapered (>-shaped) plug, also called *FireWire, i.Link,* and *Lynx.* Few PCs have these ports, which are ideal for video, external disk, multiplayer gaming, and network devices. Like USB, FireWire supports Plug and Play and hot plugging, and provides power to peripherals.
Wireless (infrared or IrDA)	A small, usually red lens on laptops that uses infrared light to transfer data from the computer to a similarly equipped device (such as an infrared PDA or printer) without cables.
Video (VGA)	A rectangular, female port with 15 tiny holes along 3 rows. Your monitor plugs in here.

To connect an external device:

◆ If the device is hot-pluggable (USB or IEEE 1394), simply plug the device's cable into the appropriate port.

or

If the device isn't hot-pluggable (parallel, serial, or PS/2), turn off the computer and the device; plug the device's cable into appropriate port; then turn on the computer and device.

✔ Tips

■ Table 8.1 lists only the built-in ports. You get even more ports when you install expansion cards. Installing a network interface card (NIC) adds an Ethernet port (see Chapter 17). An internal modem lets you run a telephone line from the wall to your computer for faxing or dial-up connections. A sound card lets you connect external speakers, headphones, microphones, audio sources, and gaming devices (such as joysticks) to your PC.

■ XP supports the newer USB 2.0 specification only if you've installed Windows XP Service Pack 1 (SP1) or later (see "Updating Windows XP" in Chapter 19). To learn more about XP's USB support, see www.microsoft.com/hwdev/bus/usb/.

PS/2 Connectors x2

Unfortunately, it *is* possible to confuse two port types because they have the same—or nearly the same—connector. The keyboard and mouse, as noted, may both have PS/2 connectors. If you get them swapped by mistake, your computer may halt on the first screen with the message Attach Keyboard and Press F1 to Continue, or it may not boot at all.

A VGA monitor cable and an old-style serial cable both have a small D connector, but the VGA cable has 15 pins, and the serial cable has 9. *If you try to insert a VGA cable into a serial port, you will mangle the pins hopelessly.* Actually, the pins of a VGA cable are so thin that even putting them in the *right* port can be tricky.

A parallel (printer) cable and a *very* old serial cable both have a DB-25 or "big D" connector, with a row of 13 pins and a row of 12. If you plug a serial device's cable into a parallel port, it won't work. If your serial device is old enough to need a 25-pin cable, it probably will never work under XP anyway.

Internal devices

Internal devices are connected inside your PC's case. Storage devices such as CD, floppy, tape, Zip, and hard drives are mounted on stacked shelves in the case's front, called *bays*. Printed circuit boards with edge connectors—such as sound cards, video adapters, graphics accelerators, internal modems, and Ethernet (network) adapters—are called *expansion boards* or *cards*. These cards plug into *expansion slots* (or simply *slots*) on the main circuit board (*motherboard*). **Table 8.2** lists the common PC slots. You must open your computer's case to see which slots are empty.

Each type of slot has a different shape—and, usually, color—so you're unlikely to insert a card into the wrong slot. (But remember: Never force an insertion.)

Table 8.2

Slots	
SLOT	DESCRIPTION
PCI	A white-cased socket about 3.25 inches (8.25 cm) long, with a white crossbar about three-quarters of the way down the slot. PCI (Peripheral Component Interconnect) slots, developed by Intel but supported by almost all manufacturers, are the most common type.
ISA	A black-cased socket about 5.25 inches (13.3 cm) long, with a black crossbar about two-thirds of the way down the slot. Many computers include both ISA (Industry Standard Architecture) slots for slower devices and PCI slots for faster ones.
AGP	A brown-cased slot about 3 inches (7.6 cm) long, with a brown crossbar about one-third of the way down the slot. AGP (Accelerated Graphics Port) is based on PCI but gives 3D graphics cards faster access to main memory than PCI. A PC has only one AGP port, occupied by a video card or accelerated graphics card.
PCMCIA (PC Card)	A slot on the side or back of a laptop computer that accepts a metal *PC Card* about the size of a credit card. A PC Card adds a particular feature to a laptop: a modem, Ethernet port, wireless antenna, or extra memory, for example. PCMCIA supports Plug and Play and hot plugging, and provides power to peripheral devices.

Bluetooth

Bluetooth is a new wireless technology that provides short-range (about 30 feet) radio links among desktops, laptops, PDAs, mobile phones, printers, digital cameras, and all other Bluetooth-equipped devices. It aims to eliminate cable clutter while simplifying communications and data synchronization between computers and devices. Bluetooth doesn't need a line-of-sight connection (as infrared does), so you can, say, listen to MP3 music from the laptop in your briefcase on a hands-free headset.

To enable Bluetooth, you plug a Bluetooth adapter into any available USB port on your computer. XP supports Bluetooth only if you've installed Windows XP Service Pack 1 (SP1) or later (see "Updating Windows XP" in Chapter 19). To learn more about XP's Bluetooth support, browse to www.microsoft.com/hwdev/tech/network/ bluetooth/. Bluetooth is an open standard (that is, it's not owned by Microsoft or anyone else); see also www.bluetooth.com.

✔ Tips

■ Before touching the motherboard or handling a card outside its protective packaging, touch a grounded metal surface (such as the computer case or a pipe) to discharge static electricity.

■ Plugging a card into an expansion slot connects it to the *bus*—the shared collection of hardware conductors that allows computer components to exchange data.

■ Because PC Cards are hot-pluggable, you don't have to power down your laptop to connect them.

To connect an expansion card:

1. Shut down Windows, turn off the computer, and unplug the power cord.

2. Remove the computer's cover.

3. Remove the cover plate of an empty slot (to let the card's ports protrude from the computer case).

4. Seat the card in the slot firmly, according to the manufacturer's instructions.

5. Replace the screw that held on the cover plate, tightening it through the hole in the bracket on the back of the card.

6. Replace the cover, reconnect the power cord, and turn on the computer.

CONNECTING DEVICES TO YOUR COMPUTER

Installing a New Device

Installing a new device requires both new hardware and new software. The steps you take depend on the device's Plug and Play status and whether Windows has an appropriate driver on hand.

✔ Tips

- Windows stores thousands of drivers on your hard drive (in the file `\Windows\Driver Cache\i386\driver.cab`) and many more on the Windows CD. Running Windows Update adds new drivers as Microsoft certifies them. See "Updating Windows XP" in Chapter 19.

- After hardware installation, Windows— or the device manufacturer's instructions —may ask you to restart your computer.

- You must be an Administrator to install hardware. See "Setting up User Accounts" in Chapter 16.

To install a new device:

1. Run the device's setup program (if any). Many new devices come with a Setup CD or floppy that includes driver files. Run this program *before* you connect the device so that Windows can copy the drivers to your hard drive, and have them handy for the next steps.

2. Connect the device to your PC, as described in the preceding section. On the Windows desktop, one of the following three things will happen:

    - ▲ A Found New Hardware pop-up message appears (**Figure 8.1**), meaning that Windows has installed the appropriate driver for your Plug and Play hardware. You're done.

Figure 8.1 When you install a Plug and Play device, Windows pops up messages in the notification area. You might see several such messages, ending with the one shown here. If you do, you're in luck—the new hardware is ready to use.

Driver Information (.inf) Files

When Windows searches for a driver, it's actually looking for an information (.inf) file, which lists the driver files to use and Registry entries to make. Windows veterans may recognize that .inf files and Windows 9*x* initialization (.ini) files are quite similar. But .inf settings are subtler than .ini settings. Never edit an .inf file to try to solve your driver problems.

Hardware setup software may include an .inf file; a .sys file (the actual driver); and subordinate library (.dll), Help (.hlp), Control Panel (.cpl), and Web page (.htm) files. Some device drivers are *only* .inf files. A monitor, for example, may be set up by a single .inf file comprising the legal resolution, color quality, refresh rate, and other display settings.

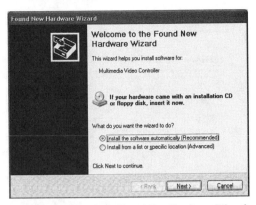

Figure 8.2 You'll see the Found New Hardware Wizard if your device isn't Plug and Play—or if it is, but Windows can't find an appropriate driver. This wizard helps you install the driver manually.

Figure 8.3 You have two choices here; click Finish to give up the installation (at least for now), or click Back to enter the driver's specific location. Check Don't Prompt Me if you don't want to be nagged to install this particular piece of hardware each time you restart Windows.

▲ The Found New Hardware Wizard appears (**Figure 8.2**), meaning that Windows detected the device but can't find an appropriate driver. Follow one of the procedures in the "To install a device driver" sections later in this chapter.

▲ Windows does nothing, meaning that it didn't detect the device. See the next section, "Installing Non-Plug and Play Hardware."

✔ Tip

■ The driver packed with the hardware may enable specific features that the Windows driver doesn't. If you want to use the manufacturer's unsigned driver instead of a signed driver included with Windows, follow "To install a device driver from a specific location" later in this chapter. (See the later tip about unsigned drivers.)

To install a device driver from an installation CD or floppy:

1. Insert the device's setup disk into a drive.

2. On the Welcome page (refer to Figure 8.2), select the first option, Install the Software Automatically (Recommended); then click Next.

   The wizard searches the CD, floppy, and all removable drives.

   If the wizard finds one compatible driver, it installs the driver automatically. If it finds several compatible drivers, it lets you choose one from a list. If it can't find any compatible drivers, the wizard displays **Figure 8.3**.

To install a device driver downloaded from the Internet:

1. On the Welcome page (refer to Figure 8.2), choose Install from a List or Specific Location (Advanced); then click Next.

2. On the Search page (**Figure 8.4**), choose Search for the Best Drivers in These Locations.

3. Check Include This Location in the Search.

4. Type or browse to the location (full pathname) of the folder that contains the downloaded driver and information (.inf) files.

5. Click Next.

   The wizard searches the specified location for the driver.

6. Follow the instructions on your screen.

✔ Tip

■ A downloaded driver usually comes as a self-extracting executable (.exe) file or a compressed (.zip) file that you must decompress before installation. Look for setup instructions on the Web page or, after unzipping, in a `readme.txt` file.

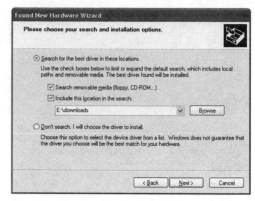

Figure 8.4 If you've downloaded a driver to a local or network drive, use this dialog box to specify its location.

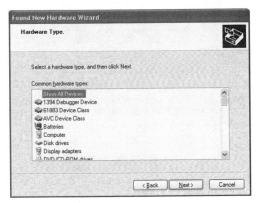

Figure 8.5 If you're installing drivers from a CD or floppy, it's not important to pick the correct hardware type; the .inf file will specify that.

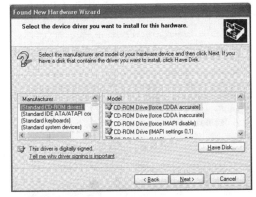

Figure 8.6 Clicking an entry in the Manufacturer list makes the Model list display the drivers that XP has on tap for that manufacturer. Click Have Disk to install a driver from a CD or floppy.

To install a device driver from a specific location:

1. On the Welcome page (refer to Figure 8.2), select Install from a List or Specific Location (Advanced); then click Next.

2. On the Search page (refer to Figure 8.4), select Don't Search, I Will Choose the Driver to Install; then click Next.

3. On the Hardware Type page, select the type of hardware that you're installing (**Figure 8.5**); then click Next.

   If the device doesn't fit any entry in the list, select Show All Devices.

4. On the Select Device Driver page, choose a manufacturer and model (**Figure 8.6**); then click Next.

   You're probably in this screen, however, to install a driver that Windows *doesn't* have. In that case, click Have Disk; type or browse to the location (full pathname) of the manufacturer's installation disk; then click Next.

5. Follow the instructions on your screen. You may be asked to choose among several drivers, select settings or a port, or insert the Windows CD. When you click Finish, you may be prompted to restart your PC.

INSTALLING A NEW DEVICE

✔ Tips

■ If Windows doesn't think you've picked the correct driver, it displays an Update Driver Warning nag screen (**Figure 8.7**).

■ When you try to install an *unsigned driver,* Windows displays **Figure 8.8**. A *signed driver* is one that Microsoft has digitally stamped to certify that it works properly with Windows XP and that it hasn't been tampered with since its creation. Microsoft's driver-signing program attempts to combat the sloppily written, system-destabilizing, third-party drivers that plagued earlier Windows versions.

■ Windows uses the icon 🖥 to identify a signed driver.

■ Unsigned drivers are adventures. They may work perfectly (particularly those that worked fine in Windows 2000), or they may cause system lockups and blue screens. To synchronize your driver security policy with your own degree of paranoia, choose Start > Control Panel > Performance and Maintenance > System > Hardware tab > Driver Signing (**Figure 8.9**).

■ Windows maintains its own list of drivers known to cause serious stability problems. XP's driver-protection feature refuses to install these drivers, regardless of your security policy. Windows warns you when such a driver is blocked (**Figure 8.10**).

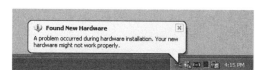

Figure 8.10 Windows displays several warnings when it blocks a driver, culminating with this one. You also may see an Incompatible Hardware or Software message box that provides details about the bad driver.

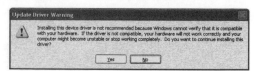

Figure 8.7 This nag appears if Windows thinks you've chosen a driver that won't work with your new device. Click Yes if you're sure that you want to install the driver; click No otherwise.

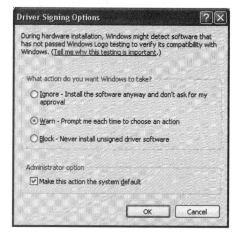

Figure 8.8 The most stable systems run only signed drivers; installing an unsigned driver is a gamble. If you see this message, check the device manufacturer's Web site for an updated driver. If you decide to click Continue Anyway, create a System Restore checkpoint first (see "Restoring Your System" in Chapter 19).

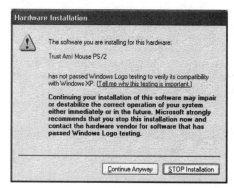

Figure 8.9 Ignore lets you install an unsigned driver without having to click through a warning message. Warn (the default) lets you install after you override the warning message. Block prohibits installation of any unsigned driver.

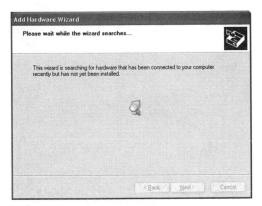

Figure 8.11 You can't skip this search for non-Plug and Play hardware, even though it's unsuccessful in most cases.

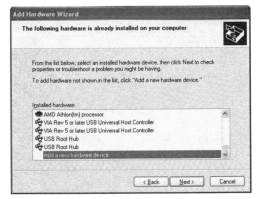

Figure 8.12 If your device doesn't appear in the list of installed devices, scroll to the bottom of the list and choose Add a New Hardware Device.

Installing Non-Plug and Play Hardware

You'll need to use the Add Hardware Wizard to set up older, non-Plug and Play devices. This wizard is a lot like the Found New Hardware Wizard, described in the preceding section, but it's not automatic.

✔ Tip

■ You must be an Administrator to install hardware. See "Setting up User Accounts" in Chapter 16.

To install a non-Plug and Play device:

1. If the device includes a setup program on CD or floppy, or if you've downloaded one from the manufacturer's Web site, run it now.

2. Connect the device to your PC, as described in "Connecting Devices to Your Computer" earlier in this chapter.

3. Choose Start > Control Panel > Performance and Maintenance > System > Hardware tab > Add Hardware Wizard.

4. Click Next to skip the Welcome page. The wizard searches for the new device (**Figure 8.11**).
   If the wizard finds it, you can install the correct driver, follow the onscreen instructions to finish the wizard, and skip the rest of these steps. Most of the time, the wizard won't find the device and instead prompts *you* to find it; continue to the next step.

5. On the Is the Hardware Connected page, select Yes, I Have Already Connected the Hardware; then click Next.

6. On the next page, select the device that you're trying to install (**Figure 8.12**).

(continues on next page)

7. On the next page, specify how you want to install the device:

   ▲ To search your computer's ports and slots for non-Plug and Play devices, select Search for and Install the Hardware Automatically (Recommended) (**Figure 8.13**).

   ▲ To skip the automated detection process, select Install the Hardware That I Manually Select from a List (Advanced).

8. On the next page, select a hardware type in the list, or select Show All Devices (refer to Figure 8.5); then click Next.

9. On the next page, select the device manufacturer and correct model (**Figure 8.14**); then click Next.

10. Follow the instructions on your screen.

    You may be asked to choose among several drivers, select settings or a port, or insert the Windows CD. When you click Finish, you may be prompted to restart your PC.

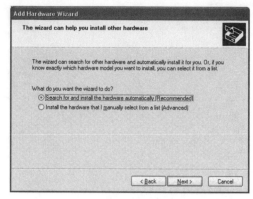

Figure 8.13 If you select this option and Windows finds the new device, it installs the driver automatically, and you're done. If Windows doesn't find the device, proceed to the next step.

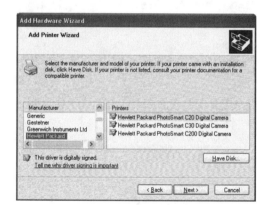

Figure 8.14 Click Have Disk if the driver resides on a local or network drive, a CD, or a floppy.

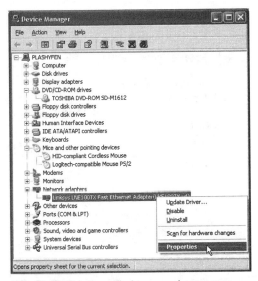

Figure 8.15 Click a + symbol to expand a category branch and list all installed devices that fit into that category. Right-click a particular device for a shortcut menu.

Managing Device Drivers

Device Manager is a powerful tool that lets you inspect, manage, and troubleshoot drivers for the hardware already installed on your computer. It lists every device in, or attached to, your system in an Explorer-like tree (**Figure 8.15**).

✔ Tip

■ You must be an Administrator to perform many Device Manager tasks. See "Setting up User Accounts" in Chapter 16.

To open Device Manager:

◆ Choose Start > Control Panel > Performance and Maintenance > System > Hardware tab > Device Manager.

or

Right-click My Computer (in the Start menu); then choose Properties > Hardware tab > Device Manager.

or

Choose Start > Run; type devmgmt.msc; then press Enter.

✔ Tips

■ Choose View > Show Hidden Devices to display *legacy* (non-Plug and Play) devices.

■ To expand all branches of the Device Manager tree, select the top-level (root) entry; then press *.

MANAGING DEVICE DRIVERS

Like any file, a device driver has properties that determine its behavior.

To show a device's properties:

◆ In Device Manager, right-click the device; then choose Properties (refer to Figure 8.15)

or

Double-click the device's name.

The tabs of the Properties dialog box vary by device. The standard ones are:

General shows the name, type, physical location, and status of the device (**Figure 8.16**).

Advanced (if it appears) contains device-specific properties. A network adapter, for example, may have a connection-type property.

Driver shows information about the currently installed driver and has buttons that let you manage it (**Figure 8.17**).

Resources lists the system hardware resources (such as interrupts and memory range) that the device uses.

✔ Tip

■ Some devices have their own extension installed in Control Panel by Setup, which lets you see additional properties.

Figure 8.16 The General tab tells you whether a device is working properly. If you're having problems, click Troubleshoot to display Help Center's troubleshooting wizard.

Figure 8.17 The Driver tab tells you the driver's provider (which, unhelpfully, is its distributor, not its manufacturer), its date and version, and whether it has a signature.

MANAGING DEVICE DRIVERS

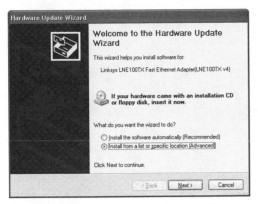

Figure 8.18 Choose the second option on the Welcome page to point the wizard to the new driver's location.

You can use Device Manager to install a driver that's newer than the current one. But newer doesn't always mean better—or more stable. If a driver isn't broken, don't bother to update unless the improvement will be significant.

To update a device driver:

1. In Device Manager, right-click the device whose driver you want to update; then choose Update Driver (refer to Figure 8.15).

2. Use the Hardware Update Wizard to install the new driver (**Figure 8.18**).

This wizard uses the same screens as the Found New Hardware and Add New Hardware wizards.

✔ Tip

■ Some devices have proprietary update programs that don't support the Hardware Update Wizard.

If a fresh driver causes more problems than it solves—common for unsigned drivers and prerelease beta drivers—XP's driver rollback feature lets you uninstall the current driver and replace it with the previous one.

To roll back a device driver:

◆ In Device Manager, right-click the device whose driver you want to roll back; then choose Properties > Driver tab > Roll Back Driver (refer to Figure 8.17).

✔ Tips

■ The rollback feature is available only if the driver has been updated since Windows was installed.

■ Remember that when you install a prerelease driver, you're really helping the software developer—which is noble but risky. Unless a beta driver claims to fix a flaw that's bugging you, don't bother with it.

MANAGING DEVICE DRIVERS

You can remove a driver permanently and erase all the configuration settings for its device. Generally, you uninstall a driver if you've removed the hardware from your PC to conserve system resources. But you can remove a troublesome driver completely, to scrap it or to reinstall it from scratch.

To uninstall a device:

◆ In Device Manager, right-click the device whose driver you want to uninstall; then choose Uninstall (refer to Figure 8.15).

✔ Tips

■ You can uninstall a Plug and Play device's driver only if the device is plugged in, because otherwise, the driver isn't in memory. To reinstall the driver without unplugging, in Device Manager, choose Action > Scan for Hardware Changes.

■ If Device Manager displays icons for duplicate devices (such as two mice), uninstall *both* of them; then restart your PC. If you uninstall only one, Windows detects it again when you restart. Click No if Windows asks you to restart after you uninstall the first duplicate; restart manually after removing the second.

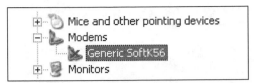

Figure 8.19 A red X means that a device isn't working, either because you've disabled it or because it's incompatible with Windows or your PC. Check the Resources and General tabs of the Properties dialog box for an explanation of the problem.

Figure 8.20 A yellow ! means that you (or Windows) installed the wrong driver; that the device is trying to use the same resources as another device; or that the driver can't find its device, perhaps because it's been removed or disconnected.

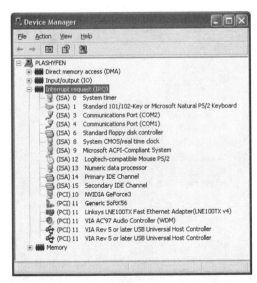

Figure 8.21 Choose View > Resources by Connection to see different devices sharing the same IRQ—11 in this case.

If you want to turn off a device without the hassle of removing it, you can disable it. Windows ignores a disabled device's existence and releases the system resources that it uses.

Generally, you disable and enable devices to create hardware profiles (see the next section), but you also can use this technique to resolve device conflicts. If two devices are competing for the same resource, disable one of them; restart; and then see whether the other one starts working.

To disable a device:

◆ In Device Manager, right-click the device that you want to disable; then choose Disable (refer to Figure 8.15).

A red X appears on the disabled device's icon (**Figure 8.19**).

✔ Tips

■ To enable a disabled device, repeat the procedure. (The Disable command becomes the Enable command.)

■ A black-on-yellow ! on the icon of a malfunctioning device (**Figure 8.20**) indicates a driver problem.

■ In Windows 9*x*, annoying conflicts were frequent because too many devices fought over scarce IRQs. An *IRQ,* or *interrupt request,* is a hardware line that a device uses to communicate with the CPU. XP Plug and Play copes with this headache by letting devices share IRQs when possible (**Figure 8.21**).

MANAGING DEVICE DRIVERS

Using Hardware Profiles

A *hardware profile* tells Windows which devices to start when you boot your computer. Profiles are especially useful if you're a traveling laptop user. When you're in the office, you want your laptop to recognize your network card, external mouse, keyboard, and monitor. When you're in transit, you don't want your laptop to waste time and battery power by looking for these devices. You can create a profile for each situation.

To create a hardware profile:

1. Choose Start > Control Panel > Performance and Maintenance > System > Hardware tab > Hardware Profiles (**Figure 8.22**).

2. Select an existing profile in the list; then click Copy.

    The copied profile serves as a starting point for the new one.

3. Type a name for the new profile; then click OK.

4. In the Hardware Profiles Selection section, specify how Windows should load a profile during startup; then click OK.

5. Restart your computer.

6. On the startup screen (a black, DOS-like text screen), choose the profile that you want to modify.

7. Open Device Manager (see the preceding section), and adjust the settings for each device that you want to enable or disable (**Figure 8.23**).

8. Close Device Manager.

9. To modify other profiles, repeat steps 6–8 for each profile.

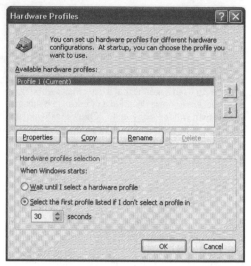

Figure 8.22 Windows names the default hardware profile Profile 1. If you have a laptop with a Plug and Play docking station, you'll see Docked and Undocked profiles too. Give new profiles meaningful names, such as In the Office or On the Road.

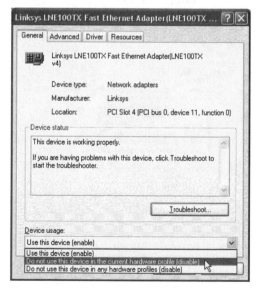

Figure 8.23 The General tab of a device's Properties dialog box lets you enable or disable that device in the prevailing hardware profile.

CAMERAS AND SCANNERS

Windows XP offers a slew of programs and features that make it easy—well, easier, at least—to download, view, and manage digital images on your computer.

The **Scanner and Camera Wizard** transfers digital photos from your camera to your computer. Other wizards help you print pictures or publish them on the Web.

Windows Explorer enhancements help you organize image files. Filmstrip view, for example, lets you browse miniature versions of your photos.

Windows Picture and Fax Viewer lets you view, rotate, magnify, and annotate images—and put up a slide show—without opening an image-editing program.

XP can also make your scanner behave (somewhat) like a digital camera and manipulate scanned documents and images just like digital photos.

Transferring Photos to Your Computer

After connecting your camera to your PC, you can use the Scanner and Camera Wizard to download and save pictures in your My Pictures folder or any folder you choose.

Most modern cameras come with a cable that plugs into your PC's USB port. XP includes and installs drivers for many camera models, sparing you the chore of manual setup. If your camera is too old to understand XP's automated download features, your best bet is to buy an inexpensive external *card reader* that plugs into a USB port. Insert a memory card into the reader, and Windows treats it like a floppy disk (**Figure 9.1**).

✔ Tips

- For information about USB and connecting hardware to your computer, see Chapter 8.

- Installed cameras also are accessible in Control Panel's Scanners and Cameras extension. Choose Start > Control Panel > Printers and Other Hardware > Scanners and Cameras.

To transfer photos to your computer:

1. Connect your digital camera to your computer with the USB cable, or connect your card reader to your computer and insert a memory card.

   If the Scanner and Camera Wizard doesn't appear, see the sidebar in this section.

2. If the wizard asks you which action you'd like to perform, choose Copy Pictures to a Folder; then click OK (**Figure 9.2**).

Figure 9.1 If you connect a digital camera to your PC, the top icon appears in the My Computer window. If you connect a card reader (SmartMedia or Compact-Flash), the bottom icon appears.

Figure 9.2 Check Always Do the Selected Action if you don't want to be nagged by this dialog box every time you download photos. If you've installed photo-management software—which probably came with your camera—you may see a similar dialog box for launching it.

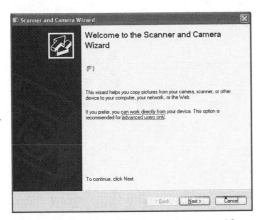

Figure 9.3 Instead of walking through the wizard (by clicking Next), you can click the Advanced Users Only link to work with individual photo files in Windows Explorer.

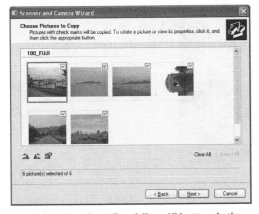

Figure 9.4 The Select All and Clear All buttons in the bottom-right corner are handy if you want to include or exclude only a few pictures. The bottom-left buttons let you rotate pictures and see their properties.

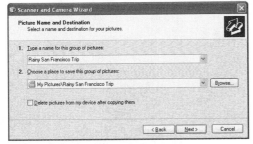

Figure 9.5 Check Delete Pictures from My Device After Copying Them if you want to erase your camera or memory card after the transfer.

3. On the Welcome page, click Next (**Figure 9.3**).

4. On the Choose Pictures to Copy page, choose the photos you want to work with on your computer (**Figure 9.4**); then click Next.

5. On the Picture Name and Destination page, name the group of pictures and specify a folder to copy them to (**Figure 9.5**); then click Next.

   If you name the group, say, My Bar Mitzvah, Windows creates the folder My Pictures\My Bar Mitzvah and puts the photos in it unless you click Browse or type a different pathname.

   The wizard displays a progress page (**Figure 9.6**).

(continues on next page)

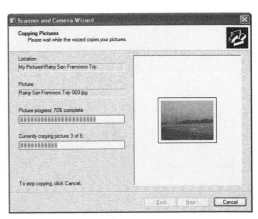

Figure 9.6 Twiddle your thumbs while Windows copies the photos to your hard drive. You can click Cancel to stop copying.

6. On the Other Options page, select the third option, Nothing, I'm Finished Working with These Pictures (**Figure 9.7**); then click Next.

7. You're done; click Finish (**Figure 9.8**).

The wizard tacks serial numbers onto the group name to create each photo's file name (Picture 001.jpg, Picture 002.jpg, and so on). You can rename the photos as you would any files.

✔ Tip

■ It's usually easier to copy *all* the photos from your camera to your hard disk (in step 4) and then delete the ones you don't want in Windows Explorer, which displays larger preview images.

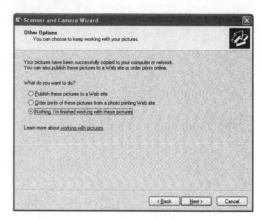

Figure 9.7 The first two options cost money.

Figure 9.8 Before clicking Finish, you can click the link to open the folder that contains your downloaded photos.

Figure 9.9 With these options selected, Windows automatically creates a subfolder in the specified folder (by using the current date), copies all the photos from the camera to that folder, and erases the pictures from the camera's memory.

If you find the Scanner and Camera Wizard cumbersome, you may prefer an option that downloads your pictures automatically to a specified folder whenever you plug in your digital camera.

To transfer photos to your computer automatically:

1. With the camera connected and powered on, choose Start > My Computer.

2. Right-click the camera icon; then choose Properties > Events tab.

3. Adjust the settings as shown in **Figure 9.9**.

4. Click OK (or Apply).

✔ Tip

■ This option doesn't apply to memory cards (removable disks).

Installing a Camera Driver Manually

The Scanner and Camera Wizard won't appear when you connect your camera to your PC if:

◆ It's an older (pre-2000) camera that doesn't comply with the WIA (Windows Image Acquisition) standard.

◆ The camera's driver didn't come preinstalled in XP.

In either case, you can install the necessary software manually by using the CD that came with the camera:

1. Choose Start > Control Panel > Printers and Other Hardware > Scanners and Cameras.

2. Below Imaging Tasks (in the task pane), click Add an Imaging Device.

3. In the Scanner and Camera Installation Wizard, click Next.

4. Click Have Disk.

5. Insert the disk containing the camera software; then follow the onscreen instructions.

You can also install a camera driver through the Add Hardware Wizard in Control Panel. See Chapter 8.

Viewing and Managing Photos

Windows XP's official storage locations for photos are the My Pictures folder and any subfolders that you create for it. You can store your pictures elsewhere, but My Pictures is easy to open from the Start menu and Explorer's task pane. It's also where most programs and wizards assume that you'll save and open image files.

My Pictures offers many options for viewing and managing digital pictures. From within this folder, you can view photos at different sizes, view a slide show, rotate photos, print them, email them, or publish them. Don't miss the special list of tasks in the task pane on the left side of the window (**Figure 9.10**).

To view photos as a filmstrip:

1. Choose Start > My Pictures.

2. Double-click the subfolder containing your photos, if you made one.

3. Choose View > Filmstrip (**Figure 9.11**).

✔ Tips

- If My Pictures doesn't appear in your Start menu, right-click the Start button; choose Properties > Customize > Advanced tab; then choose Display As Link (below My Pictures) in the Start Menu Items list.

- In step 3, choose View > Thumbnails to see the images presented as miniatures arranged in rows and columns (**Figure 9.12**).

- To free screen space for displaying photos, press F11. Press F11 again to return to normal screen layout.

Figure 9.10 The Picture Tasks links give you quick access to common image tasks. The Get Pictures link relaunches the Scanner and Camera Wizard, for example. You also can right-click an image to see specialized photo tasks, as well as the usual file tasks (Copy, Rename, Properties, Delete, and so on).

Figure 9.11 The enlarged image shows the selected photo. To select another one, click the left or right arrows below the large image, click one of the smaller images in the bottom row, or press the left- or right-arrow keys.

Figure 9.12 You can drag and drop photos to rearrange their order in Thumbnails view. If you're viewing 50 photos, for example, you can drag your favorites— one by one or in groups—to the top of the folder. When you reopen that folder, you still see all 50 photos, but the first few are your favorites.

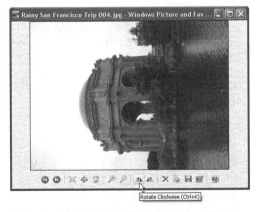

Figure 9.13 If your photo is flopped sideways (because you held the camera sideways when you took it), you can rotate it in 90-degree increments.

- To use a photo as your desktop background, select a photo; then click Set As Desktop Background in the task pane (refer to Figure 9.10).

- To use your photos as a screen saver, see "Setting a Screen Saver" in Chapter 4.

- You can edit images in Paint; choose Start > All Programs > Accessories > Paint.

- For more information about viewing Images in Explorer, see "Viewing Files and Folders in Different Ways" and "Customizing a Folder" in Chapter 5.

To start a slide show:

1. In the task pane on the left, in the Picture Tasks section, click View As a Slide Show (refer to Figure 9.10).

   Your screen fills with a self-advancing slide show of every picture in the folder.

2. View the slide show, using appropriate controls.

   As the slide show begins, an onscreen toolbar offers controls to start, pause, advance, reverse, or stop the show. You can also use the left- and right-arrow keys to move backward and forward, or click the photo itself to advance. To stop the show, click Exit on the toolbar or press the Esc key.

To rotate a photo:

◆ In Filmstrip or Thumbnails view, right-click the photo that you want to rotate; then choose Rotate Clockwise or Rotate Counterclockwise.

   or

   Double-click the photo to open it in Windows Picture and Fax Viewer; then click the Rotate Clockwise or Rotate Counterclockwise button at the bottom of the window (**Figure 9.13**).

VIEWING AND MANAGING PHOTOS

✔ **Tip**

■ Sometimes, Windows warns you that you may reduce image quality if you rotate a photo. This roughening usually is imperceptible, but if you're worried, make a copy of the image before rotation.

To zoom in or zoom out on a photo:

◆ In My Pictures, double-click the photo to open it in Windows Picture and Fax Viewer; then click the Zoom In or Zoom Out buttons at the bottom of the window as many times as you need to scale it properly.

✔ **Tip**

■ When you click Zoom In, the pointer turns into a magnifying glass. Wherever you place the pointer before you click becomes the new center of the displayed image when you click. This method is very handy when you're examining details before editing the image.

Windows Picture and Fax Viewer

Windows Picture and Fax Viewer (refer to Figure 9.13) isn't a freestanding program—you won't find it in the Start menu—but a window applet that appears only when you double-click an image file. The Viewer is associated by default with .emf, .gif, .jpg, .bmp, .png, .tif, and .wmf files unless you've assigned them otherwise (see "Associating Documents with Programs" in Chapter 6).

At the bottom of the Viewer window are buttons for advancing, reversing, rotating, zooming, printing, and deleting images, among other things. To learn what a button does, hover the pointer over it for a pop-up tip. When you view a TIFF file, the toolbar sprouts extra buttons for navigation, drawing, and annotation.

Windows Picture and Fax Viewer is quick and convenient but too lightweight for serious use. Without leaving Windows, you can view images in Paint and Internet Explorer; if you manage a *lot* of photos, consider a commercial alternative such as ACDSee (www.acdsee.com) or ThumbsPlus (www.cerious.com).

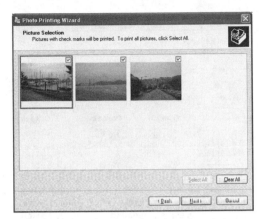

Figure 9.14 This page shows you the selected photos or, if you made no selection, all the current folder's photos.

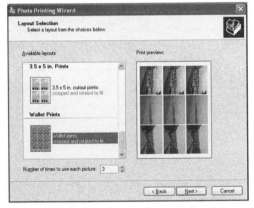

Figure 9.15 The wizard rotates, sizes, and crops images to fit. To prevent unpleasant surprises, the layout preview shows you which parts of the images you'll lose on paper.

Printing Photos

XP's Photo Printing Wizard walks you through the printing process and lets you print multiple photos per page, saving you money on expensive photo-quality paper.

To print photos:

1. Choose Start > My Pictures; then choose the subfolder (if any) containing your photos.

2. Select one or more photos that you want to print.

3. In the task pane on the left, click Print This Picture or Print the Selected Pictures, if you selected more than one (refer to Figure 9.10).

4. On the Welcome page of the Photo Printing Wizard, click Next.

5. On the Picture Selection page, check the box above each thumbnail you want to print; clear the others (**Figure 9.14**); then click Next.

6. On the Printing Options page, choose a printer; then click Next.

   If you're using photo-quality paper, also click Printing Preferences to set paper tray, color, and resolution options.

7. On the Layout Selection page, specify how you want the photos arranged on the page (**Figure 9.15**); then click Next.

8. Click Finish.

   The wizard sends your photos to the printer.

Ordering Prints Online

The Online Print Ordering Wizard walks you through getting digital photos printed via the Internet. You select the photos to be uploaded to an online photo processor (such as Fujifilm or Kodak) and enter credit-card and shipping information. Your prints arrive by mail in about a week.

To order prints via the Internet:

1. Choose Start > My Pictures and then the subfolder (if any) containing your photos.

2. Select the photos that you want to order.

3. In the task pane at the left, click Order Prints Online (refer to Figure 9.10).

4. On the Welcome page of the Online Print Ordering Wizard, click Next.

5. On the Change Your Picture Selection page, check or clear the box above the thumbnails to choose the prints to order; then click Next.

6. On the Select a Printing Company page, select a company to print your photos; then click Next.

7. Select the pictures, print sizes, and quantities that you want (**Figure 9.16**); then click Next.

8. Follow the onscreen instructions to complete the wizard.

   You'll be prompted for shipping and payment information.

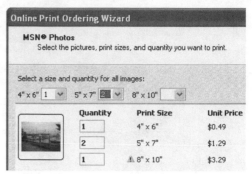

Figure 9.16 This screen varies by print processor. Heed the warning icons (such as the yellow ! shown here) next to print sizes; they mean that the image's resolution is too low to produce good print quality at that size. The same file may make a good 4" x 6" print but a grainy 5" x 7" print, for example.

ORDERING PRINTS ONLINE

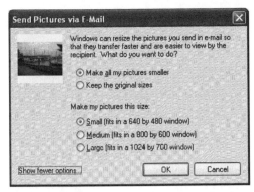

Figure 9.17 The default settings compress and resize images to 640 x 480 pixels, which is fine for onscreen viewing. A larger size shows more detail, at the cost of bigger files and slower emailing.

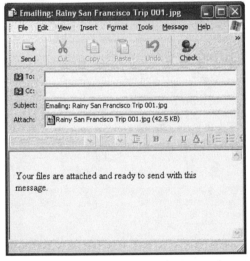

Figure 9.18 Windows opens your email program, creates a new message, and attaches the compressed files. You type the recipient's address, add your own text, and send the message.

Emailing Photos

A group of photos to be printed can be too large for emailing. You may have trouble sending photos if your (or your recipient's) ISP or mail service bounces attachments larger than 1 MB or 2 MB. Even if the transfer is successful, you may overload your recipients' inboxes and annoy them. Windows copes with this problem by offering image-shrinking tools.

To email photos:

1. Choose Start > My Pictures and then the subfolder (if any) containing your photos.

2. Select the photos to send.

3. In the task pane at the left, in the File and Folder Tasks section, click E-Mail This File or E-Mail the Selected Items, if you selected more than one.

4. In the Send Pictures via E-Mail dialog box, click Show More Options to expand the dialog box (**Figure 9.17**).

5. Make a selection, and click OK (**Figure 9.18**).

✔ Tips

- Windows compresses bitmap (.bmp) and TIFF (.tif) files before resizing them. GIF (.gif) and JPEG (.jpg) files already are compressed, so Windows resizes them without more compression.

- If you want to compress photos *without* emailing them, select the icons in the Attach header of the email message (refer to Figure 9.18) and drag them to the desktop or to any folder other than My Pictures.

Publishing Photos on the Web

The Web Publishing Wizard lets you compress photos and post them on selected Web sites for the world to see. MSN and some of the other sites are free.

To post photos on the Web:

1. Choose Start > My Pictures and then the subfolder (if any) containing your photos.

2. Select one or more photos, or a whole folder, to post.

3. In the task pane at the left, in the File and Folder Tasks section, click the Publish to the Web link.

4. On the Welcome page of the Web Publishing Wizard, click Next.

5. Check or clear the boxes above the thumbnails to choose the photos to post; then click Next.

6. Select an Internet service provider to host your Web site (**Figure 9.19**); then click Next.

7. Follow the onscreen instructions for your chosen service provider.

   When you arrive at **Figure 9.20**, you'll generally want to choose Small image sizes.

   After Windows uploads your photos to the Web site, the wizard's final screen opens your browser to the new Web page.

✔ Tips

- After you publish a file or folder to the Web, Windows creates a shortcut to that site in Internet Explorer's Favorites menu.

- You can use the Web Publishing Wizard to post other types of files, such as Word documents.

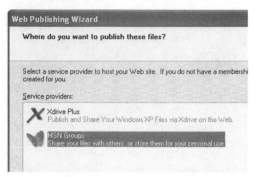

Figure 9.19 Suggested sites are configured specifically to hook into the Web Publishing Wizard. MSN is free, but its storage limit is 3 MB (about a dozen photos), and it requires a .NET Passport (see "Getting a .NET Passport" in Chapter 15). You can't use the wizard to publish to sites hosted by other ISPs.

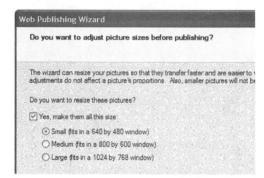

Figure 9.20 Large images on the Web increase page-loading times and waste server space. Choose Small to reduce your photos to Web-friendly sizes.

Table 9.1

Image-File Formats

FORMAT	DESCRIPTION
Bitmap	Windows bitmap (.bmp) images tend to be large, because this format can't be compressed. BMP is almost always the *wrong* choice for scanned documents and photos.
JPEG	Joint Photographic Experts Group (.jpg/.jpeg) files are highly compressed and an excellent choice for scanning photos, particularly if you're going to post them on the Web. But the JPEG process sacrifices image detail permanently during compression. In most cases, the loss is invisible for onscreen viewing.
PNG	Portable Network Graphics (.png) files, which all modern browsers support, is patent- and license-free and retains all detail during compression.
TIFF	Tagged Image File Format (.tif) files are compatible with most image-editing programs, even ancient ones. TIFF is a good choice for scanning text documents and grayscale images. TIFF's compression, like PNG's, preserves detail but results in larger files than JPEG or GIF. You can scan multiple pages into a single TIFF file; the XP Fax program does this to store faxes.

Using Scanners

When you connect a Plug and Play scanner to your PC, the Scanner and Camera Wizard appears, just as it does for a camera. The wizard's screens are similar to those described in "Transferring Photos to Your Computer" earlier in this chapter, with these differences:

◆ On the Choose Scanning Preferences page, specify black-and-white, color, or grayscale scanning and the part of the page you want scanned.

◆ On the Picture Name and Destination page, select an image format listed in **Table 9.1**.

✔ Tip

■ If you save an image in the wrong format, you can open it in Paint and save it in another format by choosing File > Save As. To open Paint, choose Start > All Programs > Accessories > Paint.

WINDOWS MEDIA PLAYER

Windows Media Player is Microsoft's free program that plays most of your digital media, including music, videos, CDs, and DVDs. It also acts like a digital jukebox that helps you find and organize digital media files. XP's Media Player is more versatile than the anemic attempts in previous Windows versions; it lets you listen to Internet radio stations, rip tracks from audio CDs to your hard drive, create custom CDs, download songs to your portable music player, and more.

✔ Tip

■ Most Windows XP installations include Media Player 8. This chapter covers Media Player 9, which Microsoft released in January 2003. You can download the latest version free via Windows Update or at www.microsoft.com/windowsmedia.

Getting Started with Media Player

The density of gee-whizzery in Media Player makes the interface and controls rather cluttered, as you see in **Figure 10.1**. Fortunately, you can let your mouse pointer hover over any control for a pop-up tip. The interior section changes depending on the Media Player feature that you're using; Figure 10.1 shows Media Guide.

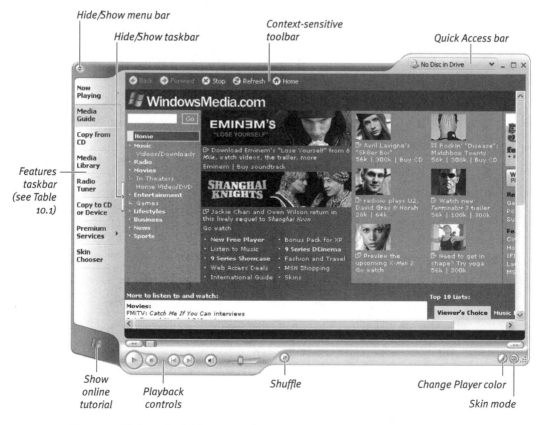

Figure 10.1 Windows Media Player controls.

Table 10.1

Features Taskbar Buttons	
CLICK	TO
Now Playing	View a video, visualization, or information about the item that's playing
Media Guide	Go online to WindowsMedia.com, which is updated daily with links to the latest movies, music, and video
Copy from CD	Copy tracks from a music CD to your hard drive
Media Library	Organize digital music and video files by using a Windows Explorer-like interface or compile your media files into sets of favorite songs and videos (playlists)
Radio Tuner	Find and listen to radio stations around the world by using your Internet connection
Copy to CD or Device	Create (burn) your own music CDs from the tracks stored on your hard drive or copy tracks to a portable music player
Premium Services	Get digital music and movies by subscribing to online, third-party subscription services
Skin Chooser	Change Media Player's appearance by using skins

To start Media Player:

◆ Choose Start > All Programs > Windows Media Player.

or

Click the Media Player icon on the Quick Launch toolbar, located on the taskbar.

or

Double-click any associated media file.

✔ Tips

■ Naturally, you need speakers (or headphones) and a sound card to *hear* anything. Most new computers come with preinstalled sound cards. If you have no sound card, they're cheap and easy to install.

■ The Features taskbar on the left edge has buttons for quick access to Media Player's main features. See **Table 10.1** for a summary, and later sections for details.

■ When you start Media Player, it goes online—by default, to the WindowsMedia. com Web site. If you're not online or have a slow connection, you can tell it not to: Choose Tools > Options > Player tab; then uncheck Start Player in Media Guide.

(continues on next page)

GETTING STARTED WITH MEDIA PLAYER

- To see the file types that Media Player will open by default, choose Tools > Options > File Types tab (**Figure 10.2**). For information about file-type associations, see "Associating Documents with Programs" in Chapter 6.

- Media Player doesn't play QuickTime, RealAudio, or RealVideo files. Free players for those formats are available at www.apple.com/quicktime/ and www.real.com.

You may notice that Media Player's odd-shaped window seems to have no menu bar. It's there, though, waiting to appear.

To summon the Media Player menu bar:

◆ Move the mouse pointer to where the menu bar *should* be (**Figure 10.3**).

or

Press and release the Alt key.

or

Click the double-headed arrow button in the top-left corner.

✔ Tips

- Use the View > Full Mode Options submenu to set menu-bar preferences.

- The controls shown in Figure 10.1 also are available in the View and Play menus.

Figure 10.2 Double-clicking any of these file types opens Media Player. Click a file-type name (not its check box) to make a description appear below the list. A dimmed check box means that a file type was configured to launch a different player.

Figure 10.3 The menu bar springs into existence when you move your pointer above the window's top edge. To toggle the menu bar on permanently, click the double-headed arrow button (shown here below the pointer).

Figure 10.4 Normally, you'll want to play the CD. You also can copy tracks to your hard drive (covered later), open a standard folder window with an icon for each song, or have the CD sit in the drive silently.

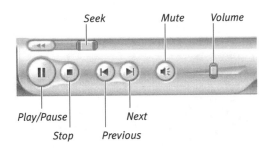

Figure 10.5 Media Player features the standard playback controls used on VCRs and other consumer toys. You can drag the Seek slider to move to a different place within the item that's playing.

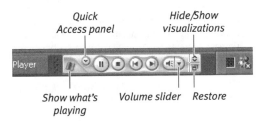

Figure 10.6 When you've enabled mini-Player mode and minimized Media Player, the playback controls appear in the Windows taskbar.

Playing Music CDs

Playing a music CD on your PC isn't too different from playing it on a conventional CD player. You can play music while you're working with other programs.

You can set your CD/DVD drive's *AutoPlay* options to make Windows detect various disks when you insert them.

To play a music CD:

1. Insert a music CD into your computer's CD or DVD drive.

2. If Media Player is open already, the CD starts playing automatically.

   or

   If **Figure 10.4** appears, select Play Audio CD; then click OK.

3. Click the Now Playing button on the Features taskbar to show artist, title, and track information, if you like (see the next section).

✔ Tips

- The buttons and slider in **Figure 10.5** control playback.

- If Media Player is minimized, you can use the mini-Player toolbar to perform basic playback functions. To enable mini-mode, right-click an empty area on the Windows taskbar; then choose Toolbars > Windows Media Player (**Figure 10.6**).

(continues on next page)

- Media Player plays through the playlist (**Figure 10.7**) in order, once, unless you turn on Shuffle (Play > Shuffle or Ctrl+H) to randomize the tracks or Repeat (Play > Repeat or Ctrl+T) to play them forever. If the playlist is hidden, choose View > Now Playing Options > Show Playlist.

- If Media Player doesn't play your CD automatically—or if it plays something else—choose your CD from the Quick Access drop-down list (refer to Figure 10.7); then click Play or press Ctrl+P.

- To eject a CD, choose Play > Eject or press Ctrl+E. You also can use this command to open and close the CD tray.

- If the music skips too much (assuming that your CD is clean and unscratched), try switching to analog playback: Choose Tools > Options > Devices tab; select your CD drive; click Properties; then choose Analog (below Playback). If that doesn't work, choose Digital again; then check Use Error Correction.

To change the AutoPlay behavior of a CD or DVD drive:

1. Choose Start > My Computer.

2. Right-click the icon for the CD or DVD drive; then choose Properties > AutoPlay tab.

3. From the drop-down list, choose a disk type (**Figure 10.8**).

4. In the Actions section, choose the action that you want Windows to take every time you insert that disk type.

5. Click OK.

Figure 10.7 The playlist lists the CD's track names and durations. Point to a track for pop-up information, or right-click a track for properties and related commands (such as skipping tracks). The first item in the Quick Access box (the drop-down list at top) is the CD in the drive. Click the album art for detailed album information.

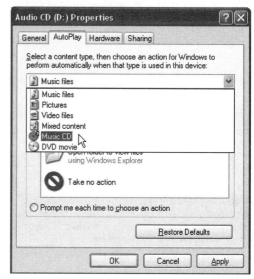

Figure 10.8 You can specify the action that Windows takes when you insert a specific type of disk, thus suppressing dialog boxes like Figure 10.4. Choose the Prompt Me Each Time option if you don't want Windows to do the same thing each time.

Customizing the Now Playing Area

The Now Playing area has several panes that you can use to view videos, visualizations, media information, audio and video controls, and the current playlist. **Figure 10.9** shows these panes, which you can show or hide to suit your needs. **Table 10.2** describes each pane.

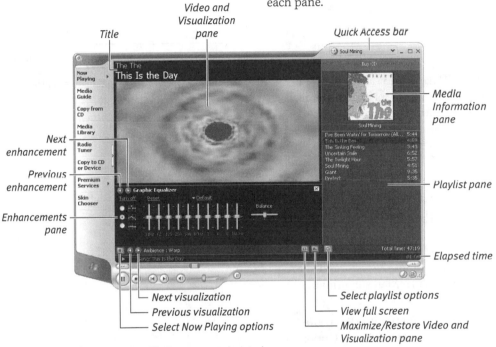

Title

Video and Visualization pane

Quick Access bar

Next enhancement

Previous enhancement

Enhancements pane

Media Information pane

Playlist pane

Elapsed time

Next visualization

Previous visualization

Select Now Playing options

Select playlist options

View full screen

Maximize/Restore Video and Visualization pane

Figure 10.9 Now Playing panes and controls.

Table 10.2

Now Playing Panes

Pane	Description
Video and Visualization	Displays the current video or visualization that you're playing. If you're playing a video or DVD, rather than music, this pane appears automatically.
Info Center View	Displays detailed information—if available—about the item that you're playing (**Figure 10.10**, next page).
Enhancements	Contains several controls that you can use to adjust graphic-equalizer levels, video settings, audio effects, play speed, and the color of Media Player. You also can use this pane to share a streaming media clip with a friend. Figure 10.9 shows the graphic equalizer.
Media Information	Displays summary information—if available—about the item that you're playing. For music copied from a CD, for example, this pane displays the album art and album title.
Playlist	Displays the current playlist. For a CD, this pane displays the track names and durations. For a DVD, it displays the title and chapter names.

To show the Now Playing area:

◆ Click Now Playing, at the top of the Features taskbar.

or

Choose View > Go To > Now Playing.

To show or hide Now Playing panes:

◆ To show the **Video and Visualization pane**, choose View > Visualizations; then choose a visualization from the submenu (see the next section).

or

To show the **Info Center View pane**, choose View > Info Center View > Show Always (or Show Only When Detailed Media Information Is Available to show a visualization when no information about the current item is available).

or

To show or hide the **Enhancements pane**, choose View > Enhancements > Show Enhancements.

or

To show or hide the **Media Information pane**, choose View > Now Playing Options > Show Media Information.

or

To show or hide the **Playlist pane**, choose View > Now Playing Options > Show Playlist.

✔ Tips

■ You can't display the Video and Visualization pane and the Info Center View pane at the same time.

■ Right-click any pane to show its shortcut menu. In the Playlist pane, right-click a specific item in the playlist.

■ To resize panes, drag the gray lines that separate them. If the lines are hidden, choose View > Now Playing Options > Show Resize Bars.

Figure 10.10 Click the links at the top of the Info Center View pane to display specific information, such as artist information, album information, and lyrics.

■ If you're connected to the Internet, Media Player retrieves CD information and album art from the All Music Group Web site (www.allmusic.com) and displays it in the Info Center View and Media Information panes. (If AMG's information is inadequate, try www.gracenote.com.)

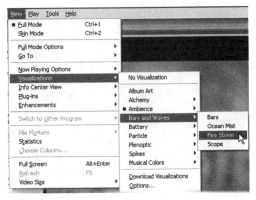

Figure 10.11 To play Media Player's scores of prein- stalled visualizations: Choose Tools > Visualizations and follow the submenus down. If you want more from the Internet, choose Tools > Visualizations > Down- load Visualizations.

Viewing Visualizations

Media Player lets you not only hear music but also see it with *visualizations*—splashes of color and shape that follow the music's beat. The Video and Visualization pane dis- plays the current visualization.

To view a visualization:

1. Play an item.

2. Click Now Playing on the Features task- bar (at the left).

3. Choose View > Visualizations; then choose a visualization from the submenu (**Figure 10.11**).

   or

   If you're already viewing one, click the Previous/Next Visualization buttons (refer to Figure 10.9) to cycle through available visualizations.

✔ Tips

- You can click the Select Now Playing Options button (refer to Figure 10.9) to choose a visualization.

- To fill your screen with a visualization, choose View > Full Screen (or Alt+Enter). To return to normal, click the mouse or press Esc (or Alt+Enter again).

- To show or hide the CD's title in the Video and Visualization pane, choose View > Now Playing Options > Show Title.

- Choose Album Art from the Visualiza- tions submenu to show the CD's album cover instead of an abstract visualization.

Changing Player Appearance with Skins

You can change Media Player's appearance by applying design schemes called *skins*. Each skin offers the essential controls—Play/Pause, Stop, Previous Track, Next Track, and Volume, along with the usual Minimize, Maximize, and Close buttons—but skin appearance and features vary. Some skins link to visualizations or include playlists and audio controls; play around to see which skin has what.

To apply a skin:

1. Click Skin Chooser on the Features taskbar.

2. Select a skin from the list (**Figure 10.12**).

3. Click Apply Skin on the toolbar.

When you apply a skin, the player's user interface is in *skin mode* (**Figure 10.13**, for example). You can return easily to *full mode*—the default state in which all features are displayed.

To switch modes:

◆ To switch to full mode: Press Ctrl+1 or click the Full Mode button ().

or

To switch to skin mode: Press Ctrl+2 or click the Skin Mode button (in the bottom-right corner of the Media Player window; refer to Figure 10.1).

✔ Tips

■ In Skin Chooser, click More Skins on the toolbar to download skins from Microsoft's Web site.

■ To delete a skin from the skins list, select it; then press Delete or click the red *X* in the toolbar.

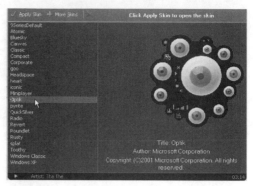

Figure 10.12 A preview of the skin appears in the right pane. Some skins are a triumph of form over function; it may take some hunting to find the Play button and other controls.

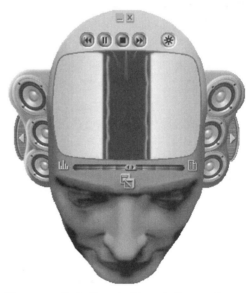

Figure 10.13 Media Player in skin mode. You can change skins as often as you like, but you must be in full mode to do so.

■ To make a player in skin mode float over all other windows, choose Tools > Options > Player tab; then check Display on Top When in Skin Mode.

■ Right-click a skin to display its shortcut menu.

Figure 10.14 Media Guide is more than just pandering, celebrity-driven gossip. Click a link along the page's left edge for news, business, sports, and other subjects. The search box (top-left corner) searches only the WindowsMedia.com site, not the entire Web.

Finding Digital Media on the Internet

If you're connected to the Internet, you can use Media Player's Media Guide and Premium Services to find digital media on the Web.

Media Guide is a live, frequently updated Internet "magazine" hosted by Windows-Media.com, containing links to the latest movie trailers, music, and video, all of which can play on Media Player.

To find digital media on the Internet:

1. Click Media Guide on the Features taskbar.

2. To view or listen to an item, click a link (**Figure 10.14**).

   or

   To find an item, use the search feature on the Web page.

✔ Tips

- If the player displays a Getting Started page instead of WindowsMedia.com, click the Go to Media Guide link on that page.

- If moving around Media Guide in Media Player feels cramped, visit www.windows media.com in Internet Explorer instead.

- Small icons below the pictures indicate the media format. A filmstrip icon means a video, a speaker icon means an audio clip, and two overlapping rectangles means that clicking the link launches a new Web page in Internet Explorer.

- Many videos let you choose your modem speed with the links 56k | 100k | 300k. Click 100k or 300k if you have a DSL, cable, or T1 connection; click 56k if you have a dial-up modem. 56K videos play haltingly but usually sound fine. You can right-click a video to change its size, which may improve playback.

Premium Services integrates subscription services such as PressPlay (music), FullAudio (music), and CinemaNow (movies) into Media Player (**Figure 10.15**).

To find digital media by using a subscription service:

1. Click Premium Services on the Features taskbar.

2. Follow the onscreen instructions.

To remove a subscription service:

1. Click Premium Services.

2. Click the subscription service that you want to remove.

3. Click Remove Service on the toolbar.

4. Follow the onscreen instructions.

✔ Tips

■ Digital media files from a subscription service may be available only as long as you're a subscriber to that service.

■ You may not be able to copy downloaded media files to non-DMAT-compliant portable music players. (DMAT, or Digital Music Access Technology, is a trademark for hardware that includes certain antipiracy features.)

■ If you subscribe to multiple services, access them by clicking the right arrow next to the Premium Services button.

■ Downloaded media files are listed in Media Library in the Premium Services category, as well as in the All Music and All Video categories. See "Organizing Your Media Library" later in this chapter.

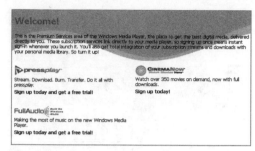

Figure 10.15 After you register or subscribe to a subscription service, you can stream, download, manage, play, and (in some cases) copy digital media files. Check back periodically for new services.

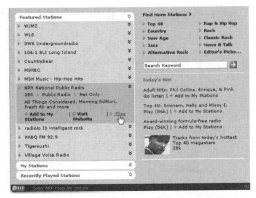

Figure 10.16 Radio Tuner's left side is divided into three expandable sections: Featured Stations (starter stations chosen by Microsoft), My Stations, and Recently Played Stations. The right side contains genre links and a search feature.

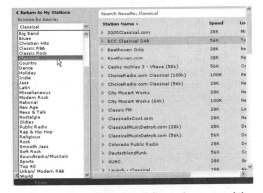

Figure 10.17 You can browse radio stations around the world by genre. Hidden by the expanded drop-down list are two search boxes that let you find stations by keyword (enter a talk-show host's name, for example) or zip code (U.S. only). Advanced search criteria such as country, language, and call sign also are available.

Listening to Radio Stations

Media Player, an Internet connection, and speakers will bring in stations from around the world without a radio or extra software or hardware. Add favorite stations to a preset list to access them quickly.

To listen to an Internet radio station:

1. Click Radio Tuner on the Features taskbar.

2. To listen to a featured, preset, or recently played station, click the arrow to the left of the station's name (**Figure 10.16**).

   or

   To find a radio station, click Find More Stations on the right side (**Figure 10.17**).

To add a radio station to a preset list:

1. Click the station's name or the down chevron to the right of the name.

   The station name expands to show details and links (refer to Figure 10.16).

2. Click Add to My Stations.

   The station is added to the My Stations section of the Radio Tuner home page.

✔ Tips

- You may have to wait up to 30 seconds for a station to tune in.

- The Speed column lists the stations' streaming speeds. Faster means better sound. Don't listen to a 56K station with a 28K modem.

- Presets also are added to Media Library in the My Favorites section of the Radio category. See "Organizing Your Media Library" later in this chapter.

- Playing a station may also open that station's Web site in Internet Explorer.

Copying CDs to Your Hard Drive

Media Player lets you copy (*rip*) an entire album or selected tracks from a music CD to your hard drive. Each track winds up as a double-clickable file in your My Music folder. Disk-based music means no more CD hunts; you can use your CD drive for other things while you play music files. You can organize your tracks into custom playlists, burn them on custom music CDs, or copy them to your portable music player.

Before you copy your first CD, you'll want to set a few default options.

To adjust the default quality settings for copying CDs:

1. Choose Tools > Options > Copy Music tab.

2. Select the music location and copy settings (**Figure 10.18**).

3. Uncheck Copy Protect Music.

4. Click OK.

✔ Tip

- By default, Media Player creates audio files only in Microsoft's proprietary Windows Media Audio (WMA) format (.wma). To create files in the vastly more popular MP3 (.mp3) format, click the Learn More About MP3 Formats link (refer to Figure 10.18) to launch a Web page that lists MP3 utilities (**Figure 10.19**).

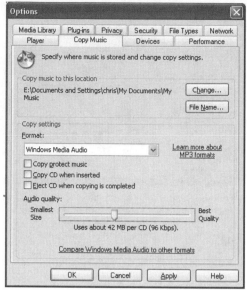

Figure 10.18 Click Change if you want to store the tracks somewhere other than your My Music folder. To save disk space, Media Player compresses music files automatically, at the cost of reduced sound quality. Drag the slider to the middle of the range (96 Kbps or 128 Kbps) for a good sound-quality/file-size trade-off or experiment with different settings to see what suits your ears.

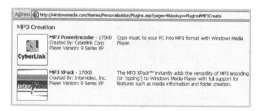

Figure 10.19 This Web page lets you buy, for about $10 (U.S.), a plug-in software module that adds MP3-creating capabilities to Media Player. If you'd rather use a stand-alone program, you can find WMA-to-MP3 converters (free or otherwise) on the Web.

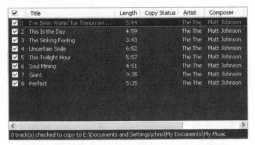

Figure 10.20 To rename a song title, right-click it; then choose Edit. (You also can change the artist, composer, and genre this way.) To rearrange the tracks, drag the titles up or down the list.

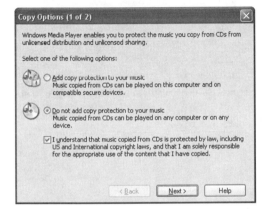

Figure 10.21 Copy protection? Feh! If you copy-protect your music, you won't be able to transfer it to other computers or your portable music player.

To copy tracks from a music CD:

1. Insert a music CD into your computer's CD or DVD drive.

 Media Player probably starts playing the CD on insertion. The player can play and copy tracks at the same time, but click Stop if you prefer silence while you copy tracks.

2. Click Copy from CD on the Features taskbar.

 If you're connected to the Internet, the player gleans the album's title and track names from AMG (www.allmusic.com) and lists them in the window (**Figure 10.20**). If AMG doesn't recognize your CD, see the sidebar in this section.

3. Clear the check boxes for the tracks that you *don't* want to copy.

 The topmost check box selects or clears all the tracks.

4. Click Copy Music on the toolbar.

 The first time that you click Copy Music, **Figure 10.21** appears.

5. Specify whether you want to add copy protection to your music (typically, you don't).

6. Click Next.

7. In the second dialog box, select the Change My Current Format Settings option only if your want to change the default settings (refer to Figure 10.18).

8. Click Finish.

 Media Player begins copying tracks to your hard drive. The Copy Status column shows its progress.

 The Copy Music button changes to Stop Copy, which you can click to stop the current copy operation.

✔ Tips

- The selected tracks are copied by default to a My Music subfolder. The subfolder is labeled with the artist's name or labeled Various Artists, if more than one artist is on the album.

- The copied tracks are listed in Media Library. See "Organizing Your Media Library" later in this chapter.

- If you have more than one CD drive, choose File > Copy > Copy from Audio CD; then choose the desired drive.

If AMG Doesn't Recognize Your CD

If you lack an Internet connection or if AMG doesn't recognize your CD, the album title *Unknown Album* appears in Figure 10.18, along with the tracks Track 1, Track 2, and so on, all by Unknown Artist. At this point, you can accept the default names and copy the tracks anyway; they'll sound fine, but you'll have a hard time finding them in Windows Explorer or Media Library. Instead, take the time to type the names yourself before you copy the tracks.

To do so, click Find Album Info on the toolbar. A wizard appears to help you search for the CD in AMG's online database. If you still can't find it, click the wizard's Edit button; enter the album and track information in the text boxes; then click Next to accept the names.

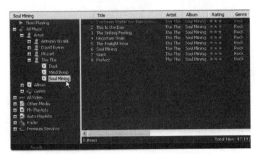

Figure 10.22 Media Library uses a Windows Explorer-like display of categories and subcategories. The left pane lets you access your music by artist, album, or genre, for example. The right pane displays details about the current selection.

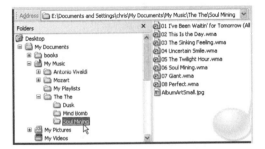

Figure 10.23 Note that the folder structure of My Music matches the Media Library list in Figure 10.22.

Figure 10.24 Media Player can populate the Media Library list by searching your drives for media files.

Organizing Your Media Library

Over time, your hard drive will become crowded with music and video files that you've copied or downloaded. Media Player's Media Library is a master list that helps you play and keep track of all your media files.

To show Media Library:

◆ Click Media Library on the Features taskbar (**Figure 10.22**)

✔ Tips

■ Behind the scenes, Media Player populates Media Library by inspecting your My Music folder (among other locations). Choose Start > My Music to see the folder (**Figure 10.23**).

■ Media Library also lists your Radio Tuner presets and Premium Services subscriptions.

Before you can create playlists, burn CDs, or copy files to portable music players, you must add (to Media Library) links to digital media files. CDs copied to your hard drive become part of the library automatically. You can add links to other media files in several ways.

To add media files to Media Library:

◆ Choose Tools > Search for Media Files (or press F3) (**Figure 10.24**).

or

Click Add on the toolbar; then choose an item to add.

or

Drag items from the desktop or an Explorer window to the right pane of Media Library.

✔ Tips

- By default, the Search function ignores small audio and video files to filter system files used by XP (such as the logon melody). To change the search settings, choose Tools > Options > Media Library tab.

- To add files to Media Library automatically when played (either on your computer or from the Internet), choose Tools > Options > Player tab; then check Add Music Files to Media Library When Played.

- You can't add other users' media files to your Media Library if you lack permission to read the folders containing those files. See "Sharing Files" in Chapter 17.

- To delete an item, right-click it; then choose Delete. You can choose whether to delete the item from only the Media Library list or from your hard drive as well (to land in the Recycle Bin).

- Now Playing lists the item that's playing currently even if that item hasn't been added to Media Library.

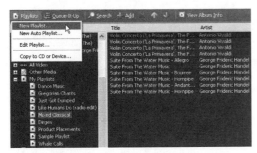

Figure 10.25 Playlists let you mix and match songs from different albums for different purposes. The My Playlists category in the left pane shows your existing playlists; the right pane shows the items in the selected playlist.

Figure 10.26 You can use the *X* and arrow buttons below the right list to delete and rearrange playlist items.

Working with Playlists

A *playlist* is a list of media files that you want to watch or listen to. Media Player generates a temporary playlist automatically when you play a CD (refer to Figure 10.7), but you also can create your own playlists that group any mix of songs and videos in the order in which you want them to be played. You can create a playlist that includes several tracks from various CDs, a radio-station link, and a video clip, for example. Classical-music fans use playlists to compare the same piece performed by different artists. You also can use playlists to burn your own CDs or copy files to portable music players.

An *auto playlist* is a playlist that Media Player compiles automatically, based on criteria that you specify. Auto playlists are updated each time you open them.

To create a playlist:

1. In Media Library, choose Playlists > New Playlist (**Figure 10.25**).

2. In the View Media Library By list, click the category that you want to use to sort the contents of Media Library.

3. Click an item in the Media Library list to expand it and to locate the individual file that you want to add.

4. Click the individual file to add it to the playlist (**Figure 10.26**).

5. Repeat steps 3 and 4 until you're done adding items.

6. In the Playlist Name box, type the name of the new playlist.

7. Click OK.

   The new playlist appears in the My Playlists category.

To create an auto playlist:

1. In Media Library, click Playlists > New Auto Playlist (refer to Figure 10.25).

2. In the Auto Playlist Name box, type the name of the new auto playlist.

3. Specify criteria for the items in the auto playlist (**Figure 10.27**).

4. Click OK.

   The new auto playlist appears in the Auto Playlists category (**Figure 10.28**).

To add an item to an existing playlist:

♦ In Media Library's right pane, right-click an item; choose Add to Playlist; then select the desired playlist.

   (Before right-clicking, you can Ctrl+click to select multiple items.)

   or

   Drag the item from Media Library's left or right pane to the playlist.

   or

   Drag the item from Windows Explorer or the desktop to a playlist.

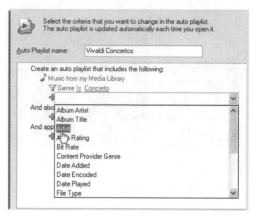

Figure 10.27 You can specify multiple filters for items to be included in (or excluded from) an auto playlist. Media Player updates the list automatically each time you open it.

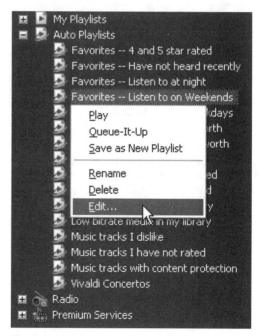

Figure 10.28 You can explore the auto playlists that come with Media Library to get ideas for your own auto playlists.

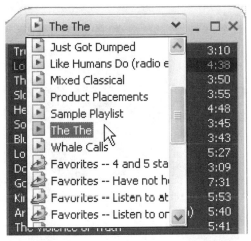

Figure 10.29 Your playlists and auto playlists are available to play even if you're not in Media Library.

To play a playlist:

◆· Choose a playlist or auto playlist from the Quick Access drop-down list (**Figure 10.29**).

  or

  In Media Library, expand My Playlists or Auto Playlists; then double-click a playlist (or select a playlist and click the Play button).

✔ Tips

■ With a playlist or playlist item selected, click the red *X* button on the toolbar to delete the playlist, the playlist item, or the media file from your hard drive.

■ With a media item selected, click Queue-It-Up on the toolbar to add it to the current playlist.

■ Use the up-arrow and down-arrow buttons on the toolbar rearrange playlist items.

■ Right-click a playlist or auto playlist to rename, delete, or edit it (refer to Figure 10.28).

■ Media Player plays through the playlist in order, once, unless you turn on Shuffle (Play > Shuffle or Ctrl+H) to randomize the tracks or Repeat (Play > Repeat or Ctrl+T) to play them forever.

■ To save an auto playlist as a regular playlist, right-click the auto playlist; then choose Save as New Playlist (refer to Figure 10.28). The playlist no longer auto-updates after conversion.

■ By default, playlists are stored in the My Playlists folder inside your My Music folder.

Burning Music CDs

If you're a fan of heavy-metal bands, you're aware that they insist on putting at least one cringe-inducing ballad on every album. If you have a CD burner, you can take your revenge by creating personal CDs of music that *you* like, without appalling filler tunes.

To burn a music CD:

1. As described in the preceding section, create a playlist of tracks to be burned, in the desired playback order.

2. Click Copy to CD or Device on the Features taskbar.

3. In the Items to Copy pane on the left, select the playlist or category of tracks that you want to copy.

4. Clear the check boxes for tracks you *don't* want to copy.

5. Insert a blank CD-R or CD-RW into your CD drive.

6. In the Items on Device pane on the right, select the type of CD you want to create (**Figure 10.30**).

7. Click Copy.

   The process takes a bit of time and disk space. You should leave Media Player alone until it ejects the completed CD.

✔ Tips

- Burning an *audio* CD with Media Player differs from burning a *data* CD with Windows Explorer (see "Copying Files and Folders to CDs" in Chapter 5). For details, choose Help > Help Topics > Index tab; type the keyword *burning*; then double-click the Audio vs. Data CDs subtopic.

- To burn a CD without first creating a playlist, browse Media Library; right-click each desired song; then choose Copy to CD or Device.

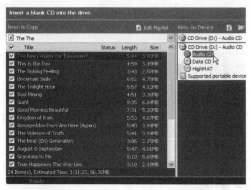

Figure 10.30 If "Will not fit" appears in the Status column (left pane) for some tracks, you must clear some check boxes until all the selected tracks fit. "Will not fit" appears even if the length of the selected tracks exactly matches the CD length, because Media Player inserts seconds (spaces) between tracks.

- Unless your CD-burner drive and software are very reliable (unlikely), you might want to *disconnect* from the Internet *while* the drive burns the CD, so that your computer doesn't have to manage two fat data streams at the same time.

- You can't copy additional tracks to the CD after copying is completed.

DVD Decoders

DVD playback requires a software *decoder.* If you bought your system with XP and a DVD drive preinstalled, you probably can play any DVD on your PC as is. If you have an older system, you may have to download and install a decoder from the Internet. If Media Player is unable to play a DVD, it displays an error message that links you to Microsoft's Web site, where you can purchase (for about $15 U.S.) and download a DVD Decoder Pack. But first check your computer or DVD-drive manufacturer's Web site for free, updated XP DVD decoders.

Playing DVDs

If you have a DVD drive, you can use Media Player to watch DVD movies. The Play menu lets you display closed captions and subtitles, choose a language track, and use other movie-specific features.

To play a DVD:

1. Insert a DVD into your computer's DVD drive.

2. Depending on the AutoPlay settings that you made (refer to Figure 10.8), Media Player opens automatically or offers to do so.

   If not, open Media Player; then choose Play > DVD, VCD or CD Audio > *[your DVD drive]*.

3. In the Playlist pane on the right, click a DVD title or chapter name, if appropriate.

   If the playlist is hidden, choose View > Now Playing Options > Show Playlist.

4. To enlarge the picture to fill the screen, press Alt+Enter (or choose View > Full Screen).

   To return to normal, press Esc or Alt+Enter again (**Figure 10.31**, next page).

Copying Music to a Portable Player

The process for copying music to a portable player, such as a Rio or Nomad, is the same as the process for burning a music CD. Just connect the player to your PC and choose its name from the drop-down list at the top of the right pane (in step 6). If your player requires MP3 files and can't play WMA files, see "Copying CDs to Your Hard Drive" earlier in this chapter.

PLAYING DVDS

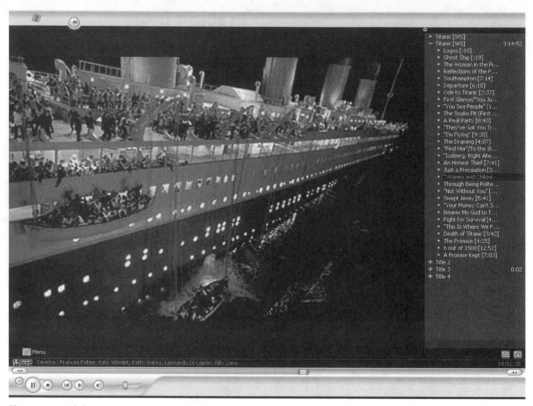

Figure 10.31 In full-screen mode, the playback controls appear automatically when you move the mouse and disappear after the mouse is idle for a few seconds. You can pin the controls onscreen by clicking the button in the top-left corner. Alternatively, you can right-click the movie or use the keyboard shortcuts listed in **Table 10.3**. The playlist (on the right) divides the movie into discrete chapters; double-click a chapter to jump to a particular scene.

Table 10.3

DVD Keyboard Shortcuts	
TO	PRESS
Play/pause	Ctrl+P
Stop	Ctrl+S
Rewind	Ctrl+Shift+B
Fast-forward	Ctrl+Shift+F
Previous/next chapter	Ctrl+B/Ctrl+F
Louder/quieter	F9/F10
Mute	F8
Eject	Ctrl+E

WINDOWS MOVIE MAKER

XP's Windows Movie Maker lets you transfer audio and video to your computer from a video camera, VCR, Web camera, or other video source and use that as raw material for your own movies. You can combine footage, still photos, music tracks, videos, voice-over narratives, and other media files. Then you can edit; add titles, video transitions, and special effects; and save the result as a stand-alone file in Windows Media Audio/Video (.wmv) format. Your movie is ready to play or to share with friends and enemies via email, Web, or disk.

✔ Tips

■ Movie Maker is a bare-bones video editor; it's no substitute for professional editors from, say, Adobe, Avid, or Pinnacle.

■ Video editing is a compute-intensive activity that requires at least a 1.5 GHz processor and 256 MB of RAM. You'll need a lot of free disk space, too; video consumes about 250 MB per *minute*.

■ Most copies or installations of Windows XP include Movie Maker 1. In January 2003, Microsoft released Movie Maker 2, which is covered in this chapter. You can download the latest version free via Windows Update or at **www.microsoft.com/windowsxp/moviemaker/**.

Getting Started with Movie Maker

Like all video-editing software, Movie Maker is a complex program; using it effectively isn't a simple matter of opening, editing, saving, and closing a document. Before you work with Movie Maker, you'll need to explore the interface and grasp a few concepts. **Figure 11.1** shows Movie Maker's main sections, which are described in **Table 11.1**. You can point (without clicking) to any Movie Maker control for a pop-up tip.

Figure 11.1 Movie Maker is divided into three main sections: the menu bar and toolbar, the panes, and the storyboard/timeline.

To start Movie Maker:

◆ Choose Start > All Programs > Windows Movie Maker.

or

Choose Start > All Programs > Accessories > Windows Movie Maker.

✔ Tips

■ You can't display the Movie Tasks pane and the Collections pane, or Storyboard view and Timeline view, at the same time. Use the View menu or toolbar buttons to show, hide, or toggle panes and views.

■ Right-click any section (or specific item in a section) to show its shortcut menu.

■ To resize the sections, drag the blue horizontal or vertical lines that separate them.

■ Choose Tools > Options to change Movie Maker's default settings.

Table 11.1

Movie Maker Sections	
FEATURE	**DESCRIPTION**
Movie Tasks pane	Lists common moviemaking tasks, such as capturing or importing video, editing a movie, adding effects, and saving or sending a movie.
Collections pane	Displays your collections in an Explorer-like tree. A *collection* is a container of video clips, audio clips, and pictures that you've captured or imported. Each *clip* is a smaller continuous segment of audio and video. (Not everything in a collection must appear in a final movie.) See "Organizing Your Clips" later in this chapter.
Contents pane	Displays the clips that are contained in the selected collection, including all the video, audio, pictures, video transitions, and video effects that you can add to the storyboard/timeline to include in your movie.
Storyboard view	Displays the sequence of the clips in your project and lets you rearrange them easily. This view also lets you see any video transitions or video effects that you've added.
Timeline view	Lets you review or modify the timing of clips in your project. You can zoom in or out on project details, record narration, add background music, adjust audio levels, and trim unwanted portions of a clip, among other things. See "Editing a Project" later in this chapter.
Monitor	Plays individual clips or an entire project. Use this to preview your project before saving it as a movie.

Capturing and Importing Content

You edit and create movies with Movie Maker by using footage transferred from camera to computer. *Capturing* is the process of recording audio and video as digital data in a file.

✔ Tip

- Captured and imported content appears in the My Videos folder inside your My Documents folder. My Videos also contains sample video files that you can practice on. To view My Videos, choose View > My Videos Folder.

To capture video:

1. Connect your camera to your computer (see the sidebar in this section).

2. Choose File > Capture Video (or press Ctrl+R).

   or

   In the Movie Tasks pane, below Capture Video, click Capture from Video Device.

3. Follow the onscreen directions in the Video Capture Wizard.

   The wizard lets you choose a capture device, specify video settings, and select a capture method (**Figures 11.2** and **11.3**). You can capture:

   - ▲ The entire video from a tape in a DV camera

   - ▲ Parts of video from a tape in a DV camera

   - ▲ Video from tape in an analog camera or VCR

   - ▲ Live video

   The captured content is imported into a new collection with the same name as the specified video file.

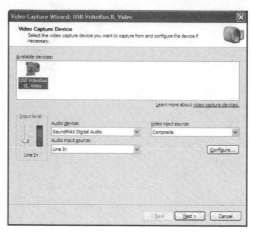

Figure 11.2 The Video Capture Wizard helps you download audio and video from your analog or digital camera to your computer.

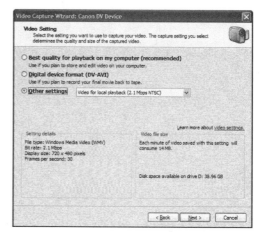

Figure 11.3 The quality level that you choose determines how big the video file will be.

✔ Tips

- For help choosing video settings, choose Help > Help Topics > Index tab; type the keyword *video;* then double-click the *capturing* subtopic.

- Copy-protected tapes may show up as onscreen garbage.

Your movie can combine footage that you've captured from your video camera with audio clips, still photos, and other video files that you've downloaded from the Internet, copied from CDs, transferred from a digital camera, or scanned into your computer.

To import existing pictures, sounds, and video:

1. Choose File > Import into Collections (or press Ctrl+I).

   or

   In the Movie Tasks pane, below Capture Video, click one of the Import links.

2. Locate the file that you want to import. You can import these types of files:

   Audio and music files: .aif, .aifc, .aiff .asf, .au, .mp2, .mp3, .mpa, .snd, .wav, .wma.

   Picture files: .bmp, .dib, .emf, .gif, .jfif, .jpc, .jpcg, .jpg, .png, .tif, .tiff, .wmf

   Video files: .asf, .avi, .m1v, .mp2, .mp2v, .mpe, .mpeg, .mpg, .mpv2, .wm, .wmv.

   For a description of each file type, visit http://support.microsoft.com and search for Knowledge Base article 316992, "Windows Media Player Multimedia File Formats".

3. If you're importing a video file, check Create Clips for Video Files to have Movie Maker separate the video automatically into smaller, more manageable clips.

   Clear the box to import the video as one whole clip.

4. Click Import.

✔ Tips

- When you capture or import a file, a new clip appears in the Contents pane (**Figure 11.4**).

- If you create clips in step 3, Movie Maker uses *clip detection* to begin a new clip each time it encounters a substantial change from one frame of the video to the next. (The minimum duration of a clip is 1 second.) To create clips *after* you've imported or captured a video, select the clip in the Contents pane; then choose Tools > Create Clips.

- Imported files actually remain in their original locations. Movie Maker doesn't create copies; instead, a clip in the Contents pane is a shortcut that points to the source file. If you move, rename, or delete a source file after you import it, you'll break the link. Movie Maker tries to find moved or renamed files automatically, but sometimes, you'll have to import them again.

- Movie Maker 2 imports and upgrades your Movie Maker 1 clip collections automatically, so you don't have to reimport files. To import a Movie Maker 1 collection manually, choose Windows Movie Maker 1.x Collection Files from the Files of Type list in the Import File dialog box (step 2).

Figure 11.4 Imported and captured clips appear as thumbnails in the Contents pane. Icons indicate the clip type: The top-left clip is an audio file, the top-right clip is a still photo, and the bottom five clips are videos. The five video clips actually come from a single file; I let Movie Maker divide the video into smaller segments during import, so they're ready to edit.

Connecting a Video Camera to Your Computer

A variety of hardware *capture devices* can transfer content to your computer from your analog video camera, VCR, digital video (DV) camera, or webcam. These are only guidelines about connecting; specific configuration will depend on your hardware. See Chapter 8 for tips on installing hardware.

Analog cameras and VCRs. Connect a VCR or analog camcorder (which uses VHS, 8mm, or Hi-8 tapes) to a *video capture card* installed in your PC, which provides extra video and probably audio ports. For video capture, you can connect your camera's video line-out to the card's video line-in. For audio capture, you could then connect the left and right audio lines (usually, through RCA-style single-channel connectors to a 3.5mm stereo plug Y-adapter) to the line-in on a sound card or a video capture card with audio ports. If both your camera and video capture card have *S-video* connectors, you can attach those connectors to record video while the attached audio connectors capture sound.

Digital cameras. Connect a digital camera (which uses miniDV, microMV, or Digital8 tapes) to an *IEEE 1394* or *FireWire* card in your PC, which provides one or more ports. (Newer PCs may already have built-in IEEE 1394 ports.) FireWire ports provide high-quality content very quickly because they're designed to transmit digital data like your camera's audio and video information. Use a special IEEE 1394 cable to connect the camera's DV-out port to the card's FireWire port. The cable transfers both audio and video. Many digital cameras also have analog outputs, which you can connect to a video capture card to transfer video and audio to your computer; but converting the signal from digital to analog and back again will degrade picture and sound quality.

Web cameras. A webcam connects to a USB port, to an IEEE 1394 port, or (if it's a video composite camera) to a video capture card. Some webcams have a built-in microphone for capturing audio too.

To capture audio only, you can use a stand-alone microphone connected to a sound card's line-in port or to a USB port. You can capture video from TV if you have a TV tuner card installed in your computer.

CAPTURING AND IMPORTING CONTENT

Organizing Your Clips

After capturing or importing clips, you can organize them in *collections*—Explorer-like folder hierarchies (**Figure 11.5**). A collection doesn't apply to any specific movie project; you can use it many times over in different movies.

To create a collection:

1. If the Collections pane is hidden, choose View > Collections.

2. In the Collections pane, right-click the collection folder where you want to add your new collection; then choose New Collection (refer to Figure 11.5).

3. Type a name for the collection; then press Enter.

✔ Tips

■ Right-click a collection to rename or delete it. Deleting a collection or clip deletes only pointers; source files remain in their original locations on your hard drive.

■ Collections are stored as .dat files in the hidden folder \Documents and Settings\ *<user_name>*\Local Settings\Application Data\Microsoft\Movie Maker. Again, backing up a collection file doesn't back up the source files.

To store a clip in a particular collection folder, just drag the clip's icon from the Contents pane to the folder. You can sort the clips in the Contents pane.

To arrange clips:

1. In the Collections pane, click the collection folder that contains the clips that you want to arrange.

   The clips appear in the Contents pane.

2. To change how much detail is displayed, choose View > Details or View > Thumbnails.

3. Choose View > Arrange Icons By; then choose a property to display (**Figure 11.6**).

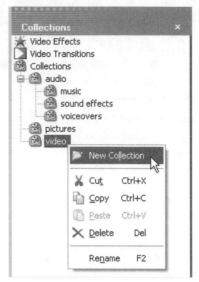

Figure 11.5 Here's a reasonable way to organize clips in a collection hierarchy. Alternatively, you can organize your clips by event, rather than by clip type. If you have only a few clips, you can stick them all in one collection folder.

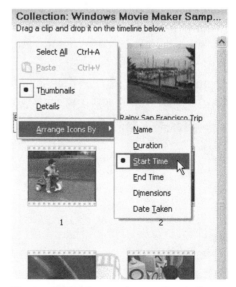

Figure 11.6 You also can arrange clips via the shortcut menu; just right-click an empty area of the Contents pane.

Figure 11.7 You can specify values for different properties (except Duration, which is preset) and use Windows Explorer to search for specific projects or organize them according to title, author, and so on.

Creating a Project

Your works in progress in Movie Maker are stored in *projects*. A project (.mswmm) file is *not* an end-result movie but a framework containing the arrangement and timing information of audio and video clips, video transitions, video effects, and titles that you've added to the storyboard/timeline. Project files also have properties that you can define and use to organize your projects.

You open and save existing projects with the usual Open, Save, and Save As commands in the toolbar or File menu.

To create a new project:

◆ Choose File > New Project.

✔ Tips

■ You can have only one project open at a time.

■ Project files are saved by default in the My Videos folder inside your My Documents folder (choose View > My Videos Folder).

■ Like most Microsoft applications, Movie Maker opens by default with a blank, untitled project. If you'd rather start editing where you left off, choose Tools > Options > General tab; then check Open Last Project on Startup.

To view a project's properties:

◆ Choose File > Properties (**Figure 11.7**).

✔ Tips

■ The properties that you enter become part of the project file *and* of your final, saved movie. Don't enter any information in the Project Properties dialog box that you don't want others to see.

■ To view an individual clip's properties (such as duration and source file), right-click the clip; then choose Properties.

Editing a Project

Now comes the fun. To begin editing your project, you add captured or imported video, audio, or pictures to the storyboard/timeline. The storyboard/timeline clips become the contents of your project and future movie.

The storyboard and timeline both display your work in progress, but each provides a different perspective. The storyboard displays the *sequence* of clips (**Figure 11.8**); the timeline displays the *timing* of clips (**Figure 11.9**).

You can preview your entire project or a particular clip in the Monitor.

To switch between storyboard and timeline view:

◆ Press Ctrl+T (or choose View > Storyboard or View > Timeline).

 or

 Click the Show Storyboard/Timeline button.

✔ Tips

■ Timeline time is displayed as hours: minutes:seconds.hundredths of a second (h:mm:ss.hs).

■ Some editing tasks can be performed in both storyboard and timeline views; others, in only one view.

To add a clip to a project:

1. In the Collections pane, click the collection that contains the clip you want to add to your project.

2. In the Contents pane, click the clip you want to add (or Ctrl+click to select multiple clips).

3. Drag the clip (or multiple clips) onto the storyboard/timeline in whatever order you like (or choose Clip > Add to Storyboard/Timeline).

Figure 11.8 Use the storyboard to look at the sequence of clips in your project and rearrange them, if necessary. You can preview all the clips and see any video effects or video transitions that you've added. Audio clips aren't displayed on the storyboard, but they are in the timeline.

Figure 11.9 Use the timeline to review or modify the timing of clips; use its buttons to change the view, zoom in or out, record narration, or adjust audio levels. Click the small + icon next to the Video track to expand it and display Transition and Audio tracks.

✔ Tips

- To rearrange your clips, just drag them to a different location on the storyboard/timeline. You also can move or duplicate clips with the usual Cut, Copy, and Paste commands in the Edit menu.

- To move a clip only slightly, select it; then choose Clip > Nudge Left/Right.

- To remove a clip from the storyboard/timeline, right-click it; then choose Delete (or select it and press Delete). To remove *all* clips, press Ctrl+Delete or choose Edit > Clear Storyboard/Timeline.

- If the timeline's clips become too cramped or too spread out, you can zoom to change the level of detail displayed. From the View menu, choose Zoom In, Zoom Out, or Zoom to Fit (or press Page Down, Page Up, or F9, respectively).

To preview a project or clip:

- To preview a project, choose Play > Play Storyboard/Timeline.

  or

  To preview a clip, select the clip; then choose Play > Play Clip.

✔ Tips

- The Play menu and the Monitor's playback controls let you play the current selection continuously or frame by frame.

- Press Alt+Enter to preview in full-screen mode. Press Esc (or Alt+Enter again) to go back to normal.

Timeline Tracks

Each timeline track (refer to Figure 11.9) shows specific items that you've added to a project:

Video. Shows video clips, pictures, and titles. If you add video effects to a clip, a small star icon appears on that clip.

Transition. Shows video transitions between clips.

Audio. Shows the audio that's included in any video clips.

Audio/Music. Shows audio clips that aren't part of the video track, such as narration and background music.

Title Overlay. Shows any titles or credits.

EDITING A PROJECT

Movie Maker's AutoMovie feature creates a movie quickly and automatically based on the selected clips or collection.

To create a movie automatically:

1. Select a collection in the Collections pane, or select multiple clips in the Contents pane.

   The selected clips must contain video and/or pictures that have a combined duration of at least 30 seconds. (An audio clip must be at least 30 seconds long.)

2. Choose Tools > AutoMovie.

3. Select an AutoMovie editing style.

4. If desired, click the More Options links to enter a movie title and select audio or background music (**Figure 11.10**).

5. Click Done, Edit Movie.

✔ Tip

■ After you create an AutoMovie, you can save it with the Save Movie Wizard or make further edits, just as you would when creating a project and movie manually.

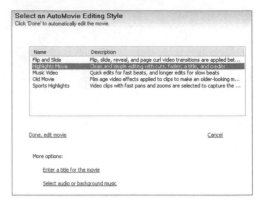

Figure 11.10 AutoMovie analyzes the selected video, audio, and picture clips, and combines them to make one movie based on the automatic editing style that you choose.

Editing Clips

You have several ways to edit the clips that you've arranged on the storyboard/timeline.

You can *split* an audio or video clip into smaller, more manageable clips. By splitting a clip, you can, say, insert a video transition or title into the middle.

To split a clip:

1. In the Contents pane or on the storyboard/timeline, select the clip that you want to split.

2. Press spacebar to play the clip; then press spacebar again to pause at the point at which you want to split the clip.

    or

    On the Monitor, move the seek bar to the point at which you want to split the clip.

3. Choose Clip > Split (or press Ctrl+L).

Conversely, you *combine* an audio or video clip that's divided into small clips. You can combine only contiguous clips. (The second clip's start time immediately follows the first clip's end time.)

To combine a split clip:

1. In the Contents pane or on the storyboard/timeline, hold down the Ctrl key; then select two or more contiguous clips that you want to combine.

2. Choose Clip > Combine (or press Ctrl+M).

You can *trim* a clip to hide its unwanted parts. By trimming an audio or video clip, you edit its starting and ending points, and therefore its length. Trimmed content isn't removed but merely hidden from the movie's audience.

To trim a clip:

1. Choose View > Timeline.

2. Select the clip that you want to trim.

3. Drag the trim handles to set the start and end trim points (**Figures 11.11**).

✔ Tips

- For precise trimming, use the Monitor's playback controls to pause at a trim point; then use the Clip menu's Set Trim Point commands.

- To clear trim points, select the trimmed clip on the timeline; then choose Clip > Clear Trim Points.

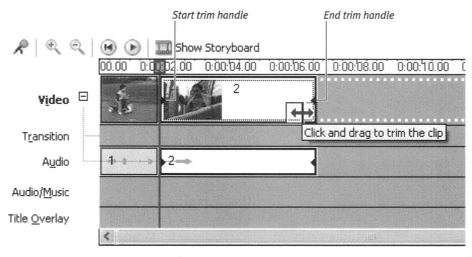

Figure 11.11 Drag the trim handles to set start and end trim points. The start trim point determines when the clip will begin to play; the end trim point determines when the clip will stop playing.

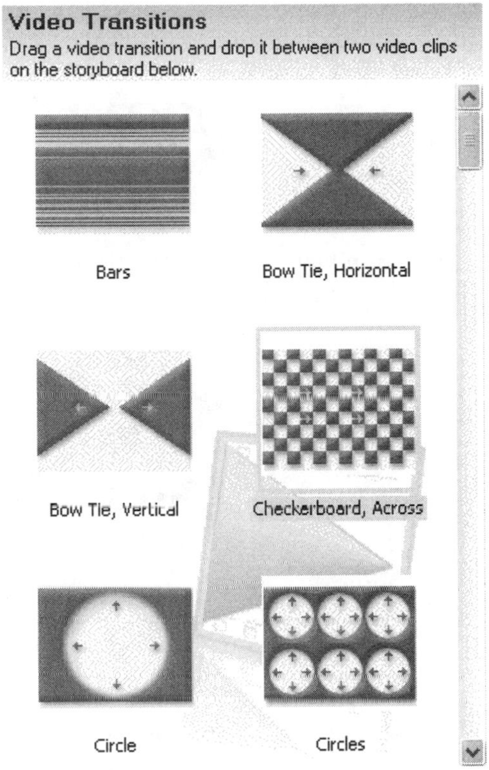

Video Transitions

Drag a video transition and drop it between two video clips on the storyboard below.

Bars

Bow Tie, Horizontal

Bow Tie, Vertical

Checkerboard, Across

Circle

Circles

Figure 11.12 Several video transitions appear in the Contents pane. Double-click a transition to test it in the Monitor.

Figure 11.13 The box between these clips shows a checkerboard transition, which plays before the first clip ends and while the other clip starts to play. In Timeline view, you can drag the transition's left edge to change its duration. The starred boxes in each clip's bottom-left corner indicate video effects. You can right-click a transition or effect to delete it.

Adding Visual Content

You can embroider your movies with video transitions, video effects, and titles and credits.

A *video transition* controls how your movie plays from one video clip or picture to the next.

A *video effect* is a special effect that determines how a video clip, picture, or title appears in a movie. The effect lasts for the clip's entire duration.

Titles and credits add text-based information, such as a movie title or your name, to a movie. You can add multiple titles to a track at different points in a movie. The titles overlay the video.

To add a video transition:

1. Choose Tools > Video Transitions (**Figure 11.12**).

2. In storyboard view, drag a video transition to the video-transition marker between two video clips or pictures (**Figure 11.13**).

   or

   In Timeline view, drag a video transition between two clips on the Video track.

To add a video effect:

1. Choose Tools > Video Effects (**Figure 11.14**).

2. In storyboard view, drag a video effect to a clip's video-effects cell (refer to Figure 11.13).

   or

   In Timeline view, drag a video effect to the Video track.

To add a title or credit:

1. Choose Tools > Title and Credits.

2. Select where you want to add text.

3. Type the text.

   The More Options links can tailor the text's appearance.

4. Click Done, Add Title to Movie.

Video Effects

Drag a video effect and drop it on a video clip on the storyboard below.

Fade In, From White   Fade Out, To Black

Fade Out, To White   Film Age, Old

Film Age, Older   Film Age, Oldest

Figure 11.14 These effects are maintained when you split, cut, copy, or move a video clip or picture. You can add multiple video effects to each clip.

Figure 11.15 You can drag an audio clip left or right to adjust its position in the movie or drag the clip's left or right edge to trim its length. (The Audio track—above the Audio/Music track—holds the *video's* audio track.) You can add video clips to the Audio/Music track if you want the audio, but not the video, to play in your movie.

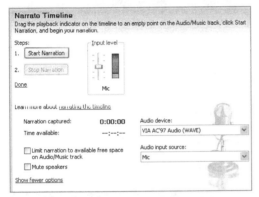

Figure 11.16 Click Show More Options to set additional recording options. If the Limit Narration to Available Free Space on Audio/Music Track check box is cleared, you can keep talking past the end of the movie.

Figure 11.17 Sound Recorder is a free—and under-rated—Windows program. You can record, mix, play, and edit sounds with it; choose Help Topics from its Help menu for instructions.

Adding Audio Tracks

If you've imported music or audio files, you can add them to your movie as background music or sounds.

If you have a microphone connected to your PC, you can add an audio narration to video clips. Your narration is synchronized with the video automatically, so the narration describes the action in your movie as it plays.

To add audio:

1. Choose View > Timeline.

2. In the Collections pane, click the collection that contains the audio clip that you want to add to your project.

3. Drag the clip from the Contents pane to the timeline's Audio/Music track (**Figure 11.15**).

To narrate the timeline:

1. Choose View > Timeline.

2. Move the timeline's playback indicator (the square with a vertical line; refer to Figure 11.15) to an empty point on the Audio/Music track where you want to begin your audio narration.

3. Choose Tools > Narrate Timeline (**Figure 11.16**).

4. Click Start Narration; then speak into the microphone to narrate the movie as it progresses.

5. Click Stop Narration.

6. Save the file.

✔ Tips

- You can record audio clips in Sound Recorder and import them into your project. To start Sound Recorder, choose Start > All Programs > Accessories > Entertainment > Sound Recorder (**Figure 11.17**).

- Right-click an audio clip to adjust its volume levels or to delete it.

Saving a Movie

Now you're ready to use the Save Movie Wizard to save your final project as an actual movie. The wizard lets you choose among several destinations: You can store the movie on your computer, burn it on a CD-R or CD-RW, send it as an email attachment, post it on the Web with a video hosting provider, or record it to a tape in your DV camera. The wizard's screens vary by the destination. In this section, I'll describe how to save a movie on your hard drive.

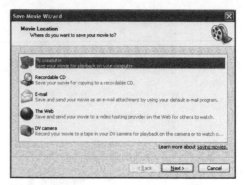

Figure 11.18 The Save Movie Wizard simplifies and automates the process of assembling your clips and compressing digital video to create movies.

To save a movie to your computer:

1. Choose File > Save Movie File (or press Ctrl+P).

2. Select My Computer (**Figure 11.18**); then click Next.

3. Type a file name and choose a location for the saved movie (**Figure 11.19**); then click Next.

4. Select the settings for your new movie (**Figure 11.20**); then click Next.

5. After your movie is saved, click Finish.

   By default, your movie plays in Windows Media Player.

Figure 11.19 Your My Videos folder is the movie's default location, but you can store it anywhere on your hard drive.

✔ Tips

- Movies are saved in Windows Media Audio/Video (.wmv) format. You can watch them in Windows Media Player version 7 or later, Internet Explorer, or any media player that can play .wmv files.

- You also can start the Save Movie Wizard from the Finish Movie section of the Movie Tasks pane.

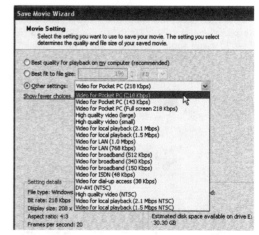

Figure 11.20 Movie Maker suggests a setting for intended use, bit rate and display size, but you can choose any setting you like. The setting details and the estimated movie-file size appear in the bottom half of this screen.

SAVING A MOVIE

CONNECTING TO THE INTERNET

People using a computer may *have* to write memos, create spreadsheets, and cook their books, but they *want* to browse the Web, pirate music, send email, and chat online. To do the fun stuff, you have to have your computer connected to the Internet. The New Connection Wizard simplifies this task, but honestly, hooking up to the Internet induces stress even in hardened network administrators.

As an individual, you can't leave your self-contained PC world and connect to the Internet directly. You must pay a go-between *Internet service provider* (*ISP*) and rely on it to provide setup information, turn on your service, equip and maintain dependable connections, and help you when things go wrong.

In this chapter, I'll describe the options for connecting to the Internet and show you how to set up a connection automatically or manually. Subsequent chapters show you how to browse, send email, and chat after you're hooked up.

Understanding Connection Types

First, you can skip this chapter if:

- **You upgraded from a previous Windows version that had Internet access.** Windows Setup preserved the configuration; your XP connection should work fine.

- **You want to transfer Internet connection settings from another PC.** Use the Files and Settings Transfer Wizard; see "Transferring Existing Files and Settings" in Appendix A.

- **Your PC is on a local area network (LAN) at work or school.** You have Internet access through the network. Ask your network administrator about connection details.

- **You want to share an Internet connection provided by another computer.** Use Internet Connection Sharing (or a router), see "Sharing an Internet Connection" in Chapter 17.

If you're not in any of these situations, you can set up your own Internet connection by using:

- A *dial-up connection* through an analog modem over ordinary phone lines, or

- A high-speed *broadband connection* such as DSL or cable.

Picking a Connection Type

If you want to get online but don't know the best way to do it, here's some help.

Dial-up connections are the most popular type. Each time you connect to the Internet, your analog modem dials your ISP over a standard phone line. (If you have only one line, callers can't reach you while you're online.) Compared with broadband, dial-up connections are tedious to set up and slow, but they're a good choice for frequent travelers, because big ISPs provide local access numbers over large geographic areas. In some areas, dial-up is your *only* choice. Dial-up service costs about $20 (U.S.) a month for unlimited access (plus your cost for the calls).

DSL and cable (broadband) connections are growing in popularity because they're:

- *Fast.* Broadband modems are 10 to 50 times faster than dial-up modems.

- *Persistent.* Broadband connections are *always* on. No dialing is involved.

- *Easy to set up.* In many cases, a technician comes to your home to install and configure everything. Otherwise, the ISP will mail you a kit with equipment and setup instructions.

continues on next page

For either connection type, you'll need an account with an ISP. If you have one already, see "Setting up an Existing Internet Account" later in this chapter. If not, ask a friend or colleague to recommend one; find a Web-enabled PC and visit www.dslreports.com or www.boardwatch.com; or look in your local Yellow Pages under, say, *Computers—Online Services*. After you've signed up, see "Setting up an Existing Internet Account" later in this chapter.

If you'd rather skip the ISP hunt and sign up online with a Microsoft-recommended ISP, see "Creating a New Internet Account" later in this chapter.

✔ **Tip**

■ Internet junkies like *traditional ISPs*, which provide direct, unsanitized Internet access. Beginners like *online services*, such as America Online (AOL) and Microsoft's MSN, because they're easier to use and set up, and they have their own little nonhostile online communities. Online services give you an all-in-one application to browse, email, create Web sites, and so on. With traditional ISPs, you choose your programs: Internet Explorer for browsing, Outlook Express for email, and so on. XP includes a fairly complete suite of Internet software.

Picking a Connection Type
(continued)

◆ *Cheaper (maybe)*. Broadband service costs about $30 to $50 a month for unlimited access (plus one-time setup and equipment costs, ranging from zero to a few hundred dollars). Dial-up's $20 monthly fee is cheaper, but with broadband, you don't need to pay for a second phone line for Internet access.

DSL (Digital Subscriber Line) uses a DSL modem to operate over a standard phone line without interfering with normal voice calls. DSL is available if you're no more than 3 miles from a phone-company central office. (The closer you are, the faster the connection speed.)

Cable uses a cable modem to operate over a cable TV line (coaxial cable). If you're wired for cable TV, you can get a connection through your cable company. Cable speed can drop precipitously when too many people in your area use the system.

Other connection types include satellite or ISDN (an older, slower sort-of-DSL). If your connection doesn't fit neatly into a particular category, your setup still may be similar to those described in the following sections. In any case, your ISP will provide equipment and instructions.

UNDERSTANDING CONNECTION TYPES

Creating a New Internet Account

Read this section if you don't have an Internet account and want to use Microsoft's referral service to sign up with an ISP online. This service lists only ISPs that cut a special deal with Microsoft; with a little legwork, you probably can find a better deal with a local ISP (in which case, skip to the next section).

✔ Tip

- You need a modem for this procedure. See "Dial-up connections" later in this chapter.

To create a new Internet account:

1. Choose Start > All Programs > Accessories > Communications > New Connection Wizard.

2. Click Next to skip the first screen.

3. Select Connect to the Internet; then click Next.

4. Select Choose from a List of Internet Service Providers (ISPs); then click Next.

5. To use Microsoft as your ISP, select Get Online with MSN; then click Finish.

   or

   To choose a different ISP, choose Select from a List of Other ISPs (**Figure 12.1**); then click Finish.

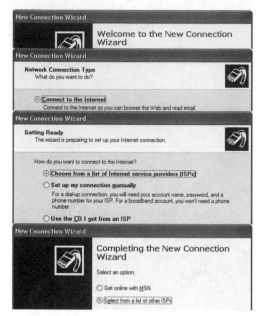

Figure 12.1 This wizard also lets you set up a network or connect to a small network. Here, you'll use it to establish an Internet account.

6. If you choose MSN, the MSN wizard starts.

or

Double-click Refer Me to More Internet Service Providers in the Online Services folder window that appears. The Internet Connection Wizard starts (**Figure 12.2**).

7. Follow the onscreen instructions.

When you're done, a new connection icon appears in the Network Connections window. Choose Start > All Programs > Accessories > Communications > Network Connections. Double-click the icon to go online, or right-click it to see its properties.

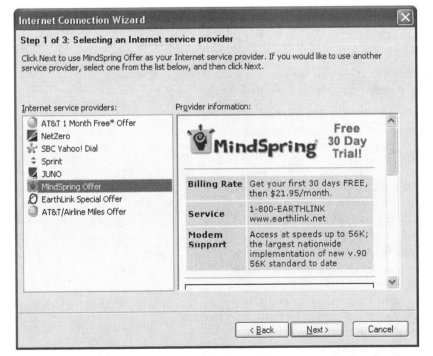

Internet Connection Wizard

Step 1 of 3: Selecting an Internet service provider

Click Next to use MindSpring Offer as your Internet service provider. If you would like to use another service provider, select one from the list below, and then click Next.

Internet service providers:

- AT&T 1 Month Free* Offer
- NetZero
- SBC Yahoo! Dial
- Sprint
- JUNO
- MindSpring Offer
- EarthLink Special Offer
- AT&T/Airline Miles Offer

Provider information:

MindSpring Free 30 Day Trial!

Billing Rate	Get your first 30 days FREE, then $21.95/month.
Service	1-800-EARTHLINK www.earthlink.net
Modem Support	Access at speeds up to 56K; the largest nationwide implementation of new v.90 56K standard to date

< Back   Next >   Cancel

Figure 12.2 The listed ISPs basically are identical; use price and the availability of local dial-up numbers as your selection criteria. During the sign-up process, Windows dials a toll-free number to send your name, address, credit-card number, chosen email address, and other information to your new ISP. If Windows can't find an ISP in your area, you'll have to find one yourself and set it up manually (see the next section).

Setting up an Existing Internet Account

Read this section if you have an existing dial-up or broadband Internet account that you want to set up manually or if your PC connects to the Internet through your company's network. The setup procedure depends on whether you have a dial-up connection or a DSL, cable, network, or other high-speed connection.

✔ Tips

- Look in the Network Connections window for existing connections; choose Start > Control Panel > Network and Internet Connections > Network Connections (refer to Figure 12.7).

- Type descriptive connection names when you're prompted. The names appear as icon labels in the Network Connections window.

- Always favor your ISP's own instructions over the generic instructions given here.

- To add a connections submenu to the Start menu, see "Customizing the Start Menu" in Chapter 2.

- A *firewall* is a secure boundary between your computer (or network) and the Internet, protecting you against external threats such as hackers, viruses, and malicious programs. Firewalls vary in their capability to resist attack, but generally, the more robust a firewall is, the more intrusive it can be to use. Windows has built-in firewall software (**Figure 12.3**), but consider a third-party firewall such as ZoneAlarm for added security; it's free at www.zonealarm.com.

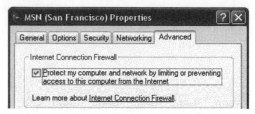

Figure 12.3 As you'll see, you can turn on the Internet Connection Firewall (ICF) in the New Connection Wizard. Alternatively, you can right-click a connection icon in the Network Connections window; choose Properties > Advanced tab; then check the ICF box.

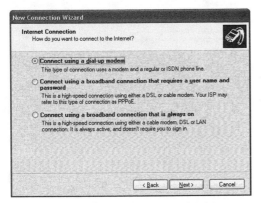

Figure 12.4 The different types of connections are described in the sidebar in "Understanding Types of Connections" earlier in this chapter.

Dial-up connections

You need an analog modem for a dial-up connection. Plug the telephone cable from your wall jack into the modem's *Line* (not *Phone*) jack. If you have to run your modem and a phone off the same line at the same jack, run a second piece of cable from the modem's *Phone* jack to the telephone's *Line* jack. If your PC didn't come with a built-in modem, buy a 56 Kbps model and install it (see Chapter 8).

To set up a dial-up connection:

1. Choose Start > All Programs > Accessories > Communications > New Connection Wizard.

2. Click Next to skip the first screen.

3. Select Connect to the Internet; then click Next.

4. Select Set up My Connection Manually (refer to the first three screens of Figure 12.1); then click Next.

   Detour: If you have an AOL or other installation CD, select Use the CD I Got from an ISP; click Next; click Finish; insert the CD; then follow the onscreen instructions and skip the rest of these steps.

5. Select Connect Using a Dial-Up Modem (**Figure 12.4**); then click Next.

6. Type a connection name; then click Next. If you're a traveler with multiple dial-up connections on your laptop, use names like *MSN (New York)* or *MSN (San Francisco)*.

7. Type the phone number that connects your PC to your ISP (including a prefix and area code, if necessary); then click Next.

(continues on next page)

SETTING UP AN EXISTING INTERNET ACCOUNT

8. Type your user name and password; check or uncheck the connection options; then click Next (**Figure 12.5**).

Check Use This Account Name and Password When Anyone Connects to the Internet from This Computer to let *all* logged-on users use this connection; uncheck it if you don't want to share the connection.

Check Make This the Default Internet Connection if this connection is the one that you use most often to dial up the Internet.

Check Turn on Internet Connection Firewall for This Connection to protect your PC from incoming attacks; uncheck it if you use other firewall software or have a router.

9. Review your settings; then click Finish.

A new connection icon appears in the Network Connections window (refer to Figure 12.7). Double-click the icon to go online, or right-click it to see its properties.

✔ Tips

■ The Connect dialog box is shown in **Figure 12.6**; to suppress it, right-click the connection icon, choose Properties > Options tab, then uncheck Prompt for Name and Password, Certificate, Etc.

■ To have Windows connect automatically when needed, right-click the connection icon and choose Set as Default Connection. Next, choose Start > Control Panel > Network and Internet Connections > Internet Options > Connections tab; Then select Always Dial My Default Connection.

■ To add alternative dial-up numbers to a connection, right-click its icon; then choose Properties > General tab > Alternates.

Figure 12.5 Contact your ISP if you don't know your user name and password.

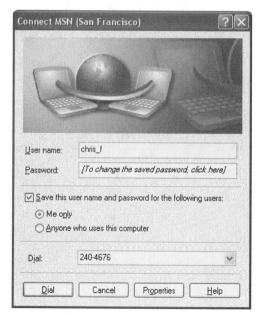

Figure 12.6 This dialog box appears when you start a connection.

■ To create another connection quickly, right-click an existing connection icon; choose Create Copy; then right-click the new icon and edit its properties.

High-speed connections

As noted earlier, normally someone sets up a broadband or network connection for you, but you may have to set up or repair one yourself some day. Before setup, make sure that your PC's Ethernet (network) adapter card is connected to a DSL modem, a cable modem, or a network jack. The correct lights on the modem should be lit (refer to your documentation).

Next, ask your ISP or network administrator if you have a static or dynamic IP address. An *IP address* identifies your computer uniquely on the Internet. A *static* (or *fixed*) IP address stays the same every time you connect; a *dynamic* IP address changes each time. Unlike a static IP connection, a dynamic IP connection (also called a *PPPoE, DHCP,* or—rarely—*DDNS* connection) requires a user name and password, and must be initiated (*leased*) each time you reconnect to the Internet. For some providers, your connection hardware can handle reconnection; for others, you have to initiate it yourself, like a dial-up connection.

Windows often refers to *connection* as *enabling* and to *disconnection* as *disabling.*

Hanging Up

A notification-area icon ( ) reminds you that you're online; if you don't see it, check the Show Icon box in the connection's Properties dialog box (refer to Figure 12.8). You can point to or click the icon for connection status.

When you close your browser or other Internet program, your dial-up connection doesn't hang up automatically; it ties up your phone line until you disconnect it manually. To hang up, right-click the notification-area icon; then choose Disconnect.

To make a connection hang up automatically after an inactivity period, right-click the connection icon in the Network Connections window; choose Properties > Options tab; then select a time limit from the Idle Time Before Hanging Up list.

SETTING UP AN EXISTING INTERNET ACCOUNT

To set up a dynamic IP connection:

1. Choose Start > All Programs > Accessories > Communications > New Connection Wizard.

2. Click Next to skip the first screen.

3. Select Connect to the Internet; then click Next.

4. Select Set up My Connection Manually (refer to the first three screens of Figure 12.1); then click Next.

5. Select Connect Using a Broadband Connection That Requires a User Name and Password (refer to Figure 12.4); then click Next.

6. Type your ISP's name; then click Next.

7. Type your user name and password; check or uncheck the connection options; then click Next (refer to Figure 12.5).

8. Review your settings; then click Finish.

   A new connection icon appears in the Network Connections window (refer to Figure 12.7). Double-click the icon to go online, or right-click it to see its properties.

✔ Tip

■ To suppress the Connect dialog box (refer to Figure 12.6) or to have Windows connect automatically when needed, see the Tips in "To set up a dial-up connection" earlier in this chapter.

To set up a static IP connection:

1. Choose Start > Control Panel > Network and Internet Connections > Network Connections.

2. Right-click the Local Area Connection icon; then choose Properties (**Figure 12.7**).

Figure 12.7 Your Ethernet (network) adapter card appears in the LAN or High-Speed Internet section of the Network Connections window.

Why Dynamic IP Addresses?

Dynamic IP addresses are more complicated than static ones but they're needed because of the IP-address shortage. About 4.3 billion addresses exist (ranging from 0.0.0.0 to 255.255.255.255), but the growing number of networked computers, "IP-aware" cell phones, car navigation systems, shipping containers, and other devices are swallowing them up.

The problem with static addresses is that once an IP address is allocated to a particular computer or device, it's off the market—even when that machine is offline. With dynamic addressing, an online machine asks the server "Got an IP address I can use temporarily?", and the server replies, "Take this one while you're here." It's a technically more difficult but more efficient use of a scarce resource.

Figure 12.8 TCP/IP is the standard protocol for computer communications over the Internet.

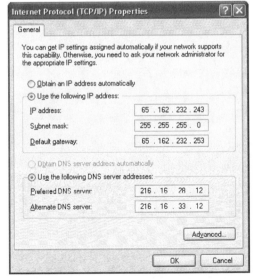

Figure 12.9 Most people type these settings while they've got their DSL provider, cable company, or network administrator on the phone.

3. Double-click Internet Protocol (TCP/IP) in the connections list (**Figure 12.8**).

4. Select Use the Following IP Address; select Use the Following DNS Server Addresses; then type your IP addresses (**Figure 12.9**).

5. Click OK.

✔ Tip

■ If Windows ever prompts you to connect to the Internet, choose Start > Control Panel > Network and Internet Connections > Internet Options > Connections tab; then select Never Dial a Connection.

BROWSING THE WEB WITH INTERNET EXPLORER

After your Internet connection is working (see Chapter 12), use Internet Explorer (IE) to browse the Web. If you've used IE before, turn the page; otherwise, you need to improve your vocabulary:

◆ The *Internet* is a global network that connects millions of computers. Unlike online services like AOL, the Internet is decentralized—by design. You can use to it exchange data, news, opinions, ideas, and things (you can buy or sell almost anything on it).

◆ The *World Wide Web*, or simply *Web*, is a way of viewing and sharing information over the Internet via specially formatted documents—*Web pages*—that support text, graphics, sounds, video, and links to other Web pages. A *Web site* is a group of related Web pages.

◆ A *Web browser* is an application that locates and displays Web pages, and downloads files to your hard drive.

■ IE is the most popular browser because it's included with Windows. Free alternatives include Mozilla (www.mozilla.org) and Opera (www.opera.com).

■ The Web isn't sacrosanct; most of what's written online is at a dreadfully low intellectual level.

✔ Tips

■ The Web is a *portion* of the Internet. (They're not synonyms.) The Internet contains not only the Web, but also channels for email and newsgroups (Chapter 14), as well as instant messages (Chapter 15).

Getting Started with Internet Explorer

Figure 13.1 shows Internet Explorer's main controls. You can point (without clicking) to any control for a pop-up tip. The important part of IE is not the program itself but the Web pages and resources that it gives you access to. You'll spend most of your browsing time working within the Web itself—reading, scrolling, clicking links, filling out forms, downloading files—rather than twiddling IE's controls and menus.

To start Internet Explorer:

◆ Choose Start > Internet Explorer (or Start > All Programs > Internet Explorer).
or
Click the Internet Explorer icon on the Quick Launch toolbar (on the taskbar).
or
Double-click an Internet shortcut.

IE vs. Windows Explorer

Web pages are .html files that sit on a dedicated computer called a *Web server.* Requesting a page makes the server upload it to IE for display. When you're on a planetwide network, it's silly to treat files differently depending on where they're located. Why use IE to access files on a Web server's hard drive and Windows Explorer (Chapter 5) to access files on a local drive or network drive? In fact, the two are two "faces" of the same program, and Windows blurs the distinction between local and remote files by letting you access *any* file from IE *or* Windows Explorer. Choosing a Web site in Windows Explorer's Favorites menu, for example, makes Windows Explorer transform into IE and display the site. Similarly, using IE's Search or Favorites bar to locate or manage files on your PC's hard drive makes IE morph into Windows Explorer.

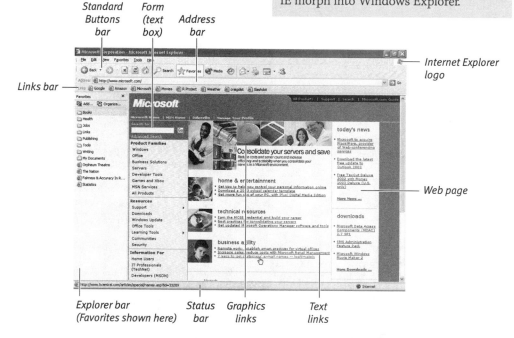

Standard Buttons bar / Form (text box) / Address bar / Internet Explorer logo

Links bar

Explorer bar (Favorites shown here) / Status bar / Graphics links / Text links / Web page

Figure 13.1 Internet Explorer's main panel shows a Web page (Microsoft's home page, in this case).

Figure 13.2 The Address bar displays the address (URL) of the current Web page. Type a new address to go to a different page.

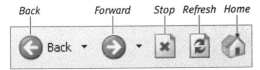

Figure 13.3 The Standard Buttons toolbar's navigation buttons.

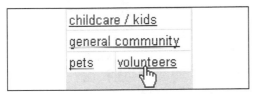

Figure 13.4 Links take you to a new Web page (or another place on the same page). Text links are typically underlined blue phrases. Pictures and buttons also can be links. Some links sprout a menu when you point to them. If links are hard to spot at first, watch your pointer; wherever it turns from an arrow into a finger-pointing hand, you've discovered a link.

Table 13.1

Web-Site Sampler	
TOPIC	SITE
Auctions	www.ebay.com
Classifieds	www.craigslist.org
Dating	www.match.com
Encyclopedia	www.wikipedia.org
Geek talk	www.slashdot.org
Great books	www.bartleby.com
Jobs	www.monster.com
Music (MP3s)	www.kazaa.com
Reference	www.refdesk.com
Searching	www.google.com
Shopping	www.amazon.com
Software	www.download.com
Weather	www.srh.noaa.gov
Web design	www.useit.com
Web terms	www.webopedia.com

Navigating the Web

You have three ways to move among Web pages:

◆ Type a Web address (URL) (**Figure 13.2**)

◆ Click a navigation button (**Figure 13.3**)

◆ Click a *link*, or *hyperlink* (**Figure 13.4**)

✔ Tips

■ To show or hide toolbars, use the View > Toolbars submenu. To move, resize, lock, or customize toolbars, see "Using Windows Explorer Toolbars" in Chapter 5.

■ To visit a page on a particular site, go to the site's home page; then use *the site's* search and navigation tools to find your target. **Table 13.1** lists a few sites to get you started.

■ If an error message ("Cannot find server" or "The page cannot be displayed") appears instead of a Web page, you may have mistyped the URL; the Web page may have been moved or removed; or the server may be down.

■ The status bar shows IE's progress ("Opening page..." or "Done") and displays the target URL of any link that you point to. If the status bar is hidden, choose View > Status Bar.

■ While the XP flag (top right) is waving, your PC is downloading a Web page. (Your ISP may replace the Windows flag with a spinning globe or blinking logo.)

To visit a Web page by typing a URL:

1. Click the Address bar (or press Alt+D).

2. Type the URL; then press Enter (or click Go).

✔ Tips

■ The Address bar auto-completes—that is, proposes a list of matching sites that you've visited recently. Keep typing, or use the down-arrow key to select a match; then press Enter. To show or hide the Address list manually, press F4.

■ Typing shortcut: To visit a commercial site, type only the business name; then press Ctrl+Enter. IE adds the `http://www.` and `.com` bits automatically. (Even without this shortcut, IE adds `http://` if you don't.)

■ When you're editing a URL, Ctrl+left arrow or Ctrl+right arrow will jump back or forward to the URL's next logical break (dot or slash).

To visit a Web page via navigation buttons or links:

◆ Click a link on a Web page.

or

Click a link in an email message or document.

or

To revisit the page that you were just on, click Back on the toolbar (or Backspace or Alt+left arrow) (**Figure 13.5**).

or

To return to a page you've visited in the past few weeks, click History on the toolbar (or Ctrl+H); then click a link on the History bar (**Figure 13.6**).

or

After you've clicked Back, click Forward on the toolbar (or Alt+right arrow) to return to the page you were on when you clicked Back.

URLs

A *URL* (Uniform Resource Locator) is an address that identifies a Web page uniquely. The URL for Microsoft's home page, for example, is `http://www.microsoft.com`. The transmission standard for all Web pages is `http://`, so you don't type it (IE fills it in for you). The rest of the address specifies the Web page's location. Some URLs don't need the `www.`, and others require additional dot-separated elements.

The suffix tells you about the Web site's owner or country. `.com` is a commercial business, `.gov` is a government, `.edu` is an educational institution, and `.org` is an nonprofit organization, for example. `.uk` is a United Kingdom site; `.ca` is a Canadian site, and so on. Like your own documents, Web-page files are organized in folder trees, so a long URL (`www.microsoft.com/windowsxp/support`, for example) works like a pathname. Note that URLs use forward slashes, not backslashes as in Windows pathnames.

By the way, articulate each letter: *U–R–L*; don't say *earl*.

Figure 13.5 Click the Back button's small triangle to reveal a menu that lets you jump back several pages. The Forward button has a similar menu.

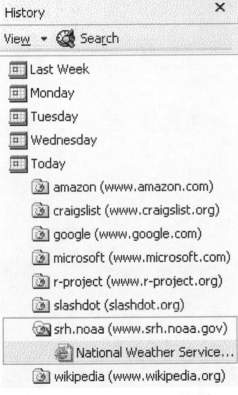

Figure 13.6 The History bar is an organized list of pages that you've visited recently. Click a time-period icon to list the Web sites visited during that period; then click a Web-site icon to view each page visited within that site. To sort the sites, click the View button (at top) and choose By Date, By Site, By Most Visited, or By Order Visited Today.

or

To go to a bookmarked page, choose it from the Favorites menu (see "Bookmarking Pages" later in this chapter).

✔ Tips

■ To stop downloading a page, click Stop on the toolbar (or press Esc).

■ To reload a stale or incomplete page, click Refresh on the toolbar (or press F5). But Refresh decides for itself what and what not to fetch from the Web server; Ctrl+Refresh forces a reload of everything and may bring you newer content.

■ To change the number of days that pages are saved in the History list, choose Tools > Internet Options > General tab > History section (**Figure 13.7**).

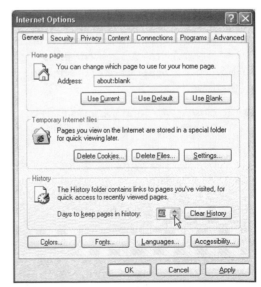

Figure 13.7 If you don't want people peeking at the sites you've visited, click Clear History; then set Days to Keep Pages in History to 0, thus covering your tracks and disabling the History feature.

You can move around a Web page by using scroll bars, but it's faster to use keyboard shortcuts or the mouse wheel. Almost all Web scrolling is up/down; some poorly designed pages or large images will make you scroll left/right.

To move around a Web page:

◆ To scroll up or down incrementally (or line by line), press the up- or down-arrow key.

or

To scroll up or down by a windowful, press Page Up or Page Down.

or

To scroll to the beginning or end, press Home or End.

or

To move the cursor forward or back through Web-page items, the Address bar, and the Explorer bar, press Tab or Shift+Tab.

If a link is highlighted, press Enter to activate it.

✔ Tips

■ If the insertion point isn't blinking in a text box or the Address bar, press spacebar or Shift+spacebar to scroll up or down.

■ To close a page (and IE), press Ctrl+W. To launch a new IE session, press Ctrl+N.

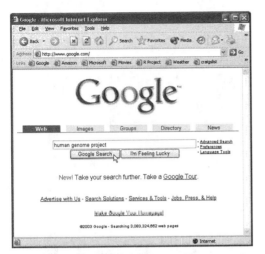

Figure 13.8 At www.google.com, type a search phrase in the text; then click Google Search (or press Enter) for a list of relevant Web pages (see Figure 13.9). Click the Advanced Search link to narrow your searches. The Google Tour link offers a tutorial.

Searching the Web

Billions of Web pages are indexed by *search engines*, the most popular being Google (**Figures 13.8** and **13.9**). The Web grows so fast that no search engine can keep up, and no one engine knows about every page. Alternatives include www.alltheweb.com, www.teoma.com, and search.msn.com Find search-engine recommendations, news, and tips at www.searchenginewatch.com. You also can use IE's Search Companion to search the Web.

Figure 13.9 Search engines are quite fast. Here, the Google results bar proclaims almost half a million matches for *human genome project* in about a tenth of a second. Search engines rank pages by using proprietary (and competing) "relevance" formulas.

To search the Web:

1. 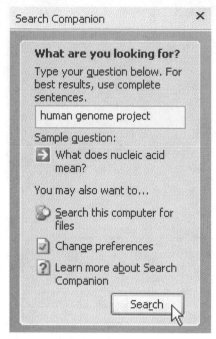 Click Search on the toolbar (or press Ctrl+E).

2. Type a search phrase in the text box; then click Search (**Figure 13.10**).

✔ Tips

■ Search Companion uses MSN Search by default. To use a different search engine, click Change Preferences (in Figure 13.10); click Change Internet Search Behavior; select With Classic Internet Search; then select an engine.

■ To search directly from the Address bar, press Alt+D; type go, find, or ?, followed by a search phrase; then press Enter.

■ After you go to a Web page, choose Edit > Find (on This Page) or Ctrl+F to search for specific text on that page.

■ Beware of advertisements posing as "sponsored links" interlaced in results. Reputable search engines like Google color-code paid links and set them apart from legitimate results.

■ A *metasearch engine* or *metaengine* queries other search engines and compiles the results that it receives. Try www.surfwax.com or www.vivisimo.com.

Figure 13.10 The search results appear in the pane to the right of the Search Companion.

Figure 13.11 Press Ctrl+D to make the current page appear instantly at the bottom of your Favorites list (bypassing the dialog box in step 3).

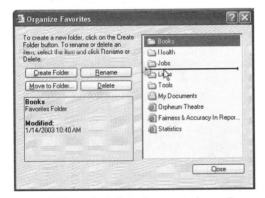

Figure 13.12 To edit the Favorites menu, choose Favorites > Organize Favorites. Drag shortcuts up or down to organize the list. Click a list item and use the buttons at left to rename it, delete it, or stick it in a folder.

Figure 13.13 You can drag a link to the Links folder in your Favorites list. If the Links bar is hidden, choose View > Toolbars > Links. Right-click a link to rename it, delete it, or see its properties. Drag links around the Links bar to rearrange them.

Bookmarking Pages

You can keep track of Web pages that you like and open them quickly in the future.

You can add a page to your Favorites list. Any time that you want to open that page, click Favorites on the toolbar (or Ctrl+I); then click the shortcut in the Favorites list. (Or use the Favorites menu.)

To add a page to your Favorites list:

1. Go to the page that you want to add.

2. Choose Favorites > Add to Favorites (**Figure 13.11**).

3. Type a new name for the page, if you like.

✔ Tip

■ As your Favorites list grows, you can organize it into folders (**Figure 13.12**).

You can add a few pages that you visit often to the Links bar for one-click access.

To add a page to your Links bar:

1. Go to the page that you want to add.

2. Drag the page icon from the Address bar to the Links bar (**Figure 13.13**).

Your *home page* (not the same as a Web site's home page, and sometimes called your *start page* to prevent confusion) appears every time you open IE. When you first open IE, you may see msn.com or your PC manufacturer's page, but you can change that.

To change your home page:

1. Go to your desired home page.

2. Choose Tools > Internet Options > General tab > Home Page section; then click Use Current (refer to Figure 13.7).

✔ Tip

■ To go to your home page, click Home on the toolbar (or Alt+Home).

Browsing Tips

This section contains tips for browsing the Web and using Internet Explorer's features.

Shortcut menus. Right-click toolbars, Explorer bars, shortcuts, or links to select commands quickly (**Figure 13.14**).

Keyboard shortcuts. For a complete list of IE's keyboard shortcuts, choose Help > Contents and Index > Index tab; type the keyword *keyboard;* then double-click the subtopic *shortcuts.*

Frames. Some Web pages are divided into rectangular sections called *frames* (**Figure 13.15**). To move forward between frames, press Ctrl+Tab or F6; to move backward, press Shift+Ctrl+Tab.

Text size, font, and color. To change the size of text displayed in Web pages, choose a relative size from the View > Text Size submenu. Press F5 to refresh the page, if necessary. If you have a mouse wheel, hold down Ctrl and spin the wheel to resize text.

To change the text's typeface or hyperlink colors, click the Fonts or Colors button (refer to Figure 13.7). Some rude Web pages won't let you change text properties. To override this restriction, click Accessibility (refer to Figure 13.7).

Full-screen browsing. Press F11 to toggle between full-screen and normal view. In full-screen view, you can right-click the Standard Buttons toolbar at the screen's top edge and choose Auto-Hide. The toolbar will vanish, and you'll have *real* full-screen browsing; when you bring the pointer close to the screen's top edge, the toolbar reappears.

Figure 13.14 This shortcut menu appears when you right-click an image link. Note that you can save a copy of a Web image on your own disk.

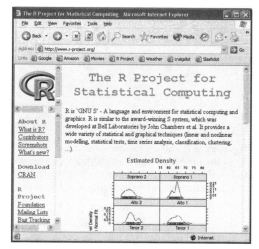

Figure 13.15 Each frame here is really a separate Web page. The sets of scroll bars show that this page has three frames. On some pages, frame boundaries are invisible.

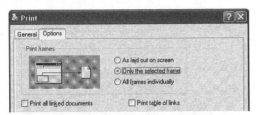

Figure 13.16 The Print dialog box's Options tab lets you print a Web page's frames and links.

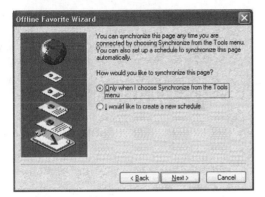

Figure 13.17 If you make, say, weather and news pages available offline, you can update them periodically to get the latest forecasts and headlines. (Web pages saved with File > Save As, by comparison, are static.)

Printing Web pages. To preview a Web page before printing, choose File > Print Preview; then use the toolbar to view each page to be printed. To set margins, headers, footers, and other printing options, choose File > Page Setup. To print a Web page, choose File > Print (or press Ctrl+P) (**Figure 13.16**); or click Print on the toolbar to bypass the Print dialog box.

Saving pages. To save a Web page on your hard drive, choose File > Save As. From the Save As Type drop-down list, choose Web Archive, Single File (*.mht) to save the page as a single file. If you want to edit the page, rather than simply view it, use one of the other options to save the page as a group of files or save only parts of the page. To open the saved Web page, double-click it or choose File > Open in IE. To specify how Windows treats saved Web pages, see "Setting Folder Options" in Chapter 5.

Viewing pages offline. IE takes saved Web pages one step further with *offline viewing,* which lets you *update* saved pages automatically to synchronize their contents with what's on the Web site. To make a page available offline, right-click it in the Favorites menu or Links bar (see "Bookmarking Pages" earlier in this chapter); choose Make Available Offline; then use the Offline Favorite Wizard to set up a synchronization schedule (**Figure 13.17**). To get the latest version of your pages before you go offline, choose Tools > Synchronize. When you're ready to work offline, choose File > Work Offline.

Graphics features. Right-click a picture to save it, email it, print it, or use it as a static or updating desktop image (refer to Figure 13.14). Or use the pop-up toolbar that appears when you point to an image (**Figure 13.18**). IE resizes large images automatically to fit in your browser window; click the pop-up Resize button to restore the image to its original size. To turn off the image toolbar and image resizing, choose Tools > Internet Options > Advanced tab; then uncheck the Enable Image Toolbar (Requires Restart) and Enable Automatic Image Resizing boxes. For faster browsing with *no* graphics, uncheck Show Pictures. (To see a particular picture, right-click it; then choose Show Picture.)

Suppressing advertisements. Advertising infests the Web. *Banner ads* are rectangular "billboards" at the edges of a page. *Pop-up* and *pop-under ads* are separate windows that appear uninvited above or beneath the browser window. When you visit a new Web page and the taskbar starts sprouting new buttons, you have pop-unders. Kill this pestilence with third-party programs (**Figure 13.19**).

Figure 13.18 The Image toolbar appears when you point to a picture. Click the Resize button (bottom-right corner) to toggle a picture between its normal and shrink-to-fit sizes.

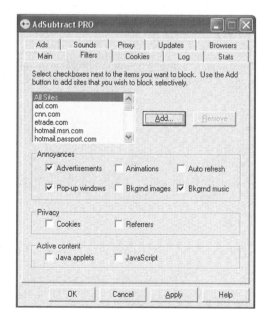

Figure 13.19 AdSubtract (www.adsubtract.com) is an ad-blocking program that suppresses pop-up windows, hides banner ads, and protects privacy. WebWasher (www.webwasher.com) is a similar program. Also try Ad-Aware (www.lavasoftusa.com) to find "spyware" placed on your PC surreptitiously by Web-savvy advertisers.

BROWSING TIPS

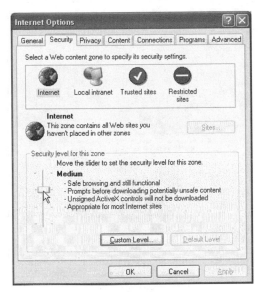

Figure 13.20 Moving this slider to the top provides the safest way to browse but may inactivate some Web sites. Click the Custom Level button to specify custom security settings for plug-ins, downloads, scripting, and more.

Figure 13.21 Drag the slider to the right to increase the size of the cache folder, so that revisited pages load faster. If IE displays stale pages from the cache instead of fresh ones from the Web, select an option that makes IE check for newer versions more frequently than "Automatically"

In a new low, advertisers abuse Windows' Messenger service (different from Windows Messenger; see Chapter 15) to put text ads in pop-up alert boxes on PCs with broadband connections. To stop them, Microsoft recommends that you install or turn on a firewall; see "Setting up an Existing Internet Account" in Chapter 12. For more information, visit http://support.microsoft.com and search for Knowledge Base article 330904, "Messenger Service Window That Contains an Internet Advertisement Appears".

Security settings. IE's security features help to prevent intruders from seeing your personal information, such as credit-card numbers that you enter when shopping online. Security features also can protect your PC from unsafe software (**Figure 13.20**).

Temporary files. When you visit a page, IE stores, or *caches* (say "cashes"), temporary Internet files on your hard disk. These files speed the display of pages you visit frequently or have already seen, because IE can open them from your hard disk instead of from the Web. To view or manage these files, choose Tools > Internet Options > Settings (**Figure 13.21**). To delete existing files, click Delete Files (refer to Figure 13.7).

Cookies and privacy. *Cookies* are messages given to IE by Web sites and stored in text files on your hard disk. A cookie's main purpose is to identify you and possibly prepare customized Web pages for you. When you enter shopping preferences and personal information at, say, Amazon.com, they're stored in a cookie, which Amazon can read when you return. (*Other* sites can't read the Amazon cookie.) Most cookies are innocuous and spare you from having to fill out forms repeatedly, but some unethical sites and advertisers use cookies to track the pages you've visited and violate your privacy. To control how IE handles cookies, choose Tools > Internet Options > Privacy tab (**Figure 13.22**). To delete existing cookies, click Delete Cookies (refer to Figure 13.7).

Content Advisor. IE's Content Advisor (Tools > Internet Options > Content tab > Content Advisor section > Enable) purportedly filters material (sex, violence, nudity, language) that you may find offensive or not want your kids to see. Don't bother—Content Advisor and all programs that make similar claims are 21st-century snake oil. They invariably filter legitimate topics (such as breast cancer) and let offensive stuff through.

AutoComplete. You met AutoComplete earlier in this chapter when you typed an address in the Address bar (refer to Figure 13.2). IE also can auto-complete forms (text boxes), user names, and passwords. To turn AutoComplete on or off, choose Tools > Internet Options > Content tab > AutoComplete (**Figure 13.23**).

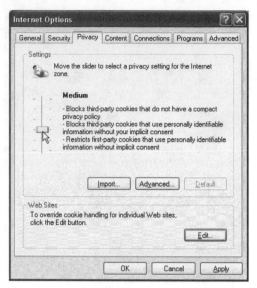

Figure 13.22 The more paranoid you are, the higher you should move this slider. Tip: Always block third-party cookies, which come from spying advertisers. Click the Edit button to specify Web sites that are always or never allowed to use cookies, regardless of your privacy-policy setting.

Figure 13.23 AutoComplete shows a list of suggested matches based on the previous entries you've typed. For security, uncheck the User Names and Passwords on Forms box.

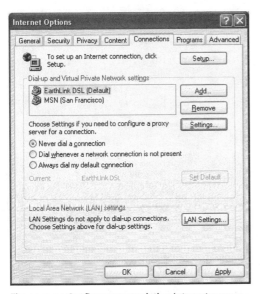

Figure 13.24 Configure your existing Internet connections or create a new one on this page.

Internet connections. To display and manage your Internet connections (Chapter 12), choose Tools > Internet Options > Connections tab (**Figure 13.24**).

Set the default browser. A newly installed browser may hijack default-browser status. To reinstate IE, choose Tools > Internet Options > Programs tab; then check Internet Explorer Should Check to See Whether It Is the Default Browser. You also can use the this tab to specify the default programs for other Internet services, such as email.

Downloading files. When you click a link to a file that you can download to your PC, IE displays **Figure 13.25**. Click Save; specify a download location on your hard drive; then click Save to start the download. After the download completes (**Figure 13.26**), you can move, double-click, or rename the new file.

View HTML. Web pages are formatted with a script called *HTML* (Hypertext Markup Language). To view a page's source HTML, choose View > Source.

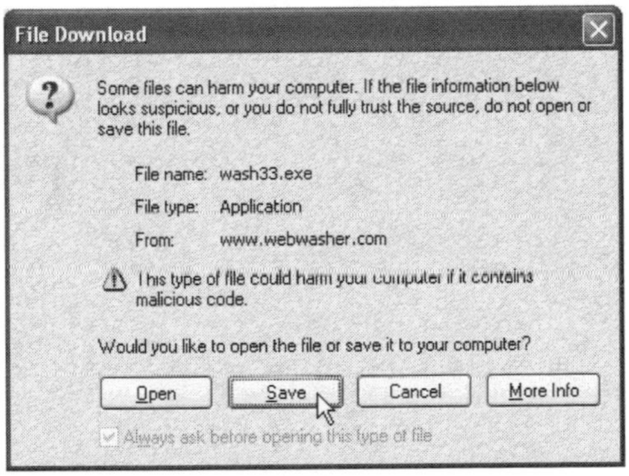

Figure 13.25 To bypass this dialog box, right-click a link; then choose Save Target As.

Figure 13.26 When the download completes, click Open Folder to open a window containing the downloaded file.

Plug-ins. For Web pages with video, sounds, and animation, you need free add-on software called *plug-ins*. The most popular plug-ins are QuickTime (movies), Flash and Shockwave (animations), Acrobat Reader (documents), and RealPlayer (music). IE may prompt you automatically to download needed plug-ins; or you can visit www.plugins.com to download them yourself.

Java. The *Java Virtual Machine* is a useful plug-in that may be missing from IE, depending on your version of XP and IE, as well as the status of the lawsuit between Microsoft and Sun Microsystems (Java's creator). The Java VM runs many stock tickers, games, and other complex Web programs, called *applets*. Windows XP Service Pack 1 (SP1) includes the Java VM, and IE should prompt you to download it the first time it encounters an applet. If you're having Java trouble, visit www.microsoft.com/java/xp.htm.

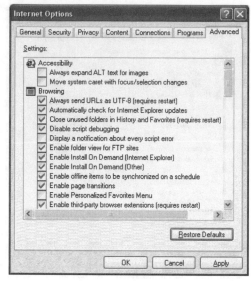

Figure 13.27 Dozens of settings are available to make browsing faster, stop annoying animations, strengthen security, and so on.

Media bar. IE's Media bar lets you play music, video, and multimedia files, as well as listen to Internet radio stations. Click Media on the toolbar to show the Media bar, which is a stripped-down version of Media Player (Chapter 10).

Other options. IE has a slew of other options that you can change to suit your preferences; choose Tools > Internet Options > Advanced tab (**Figure 13.27**).

Cut/Copy/Paste. You can copy (but not cut, of course) selected text and images from Web pages and paste them into other programs by using the usual Edit-menu commands.

MSN Explorer. If MSN is your ISP (see Chapter 12), your default browser may be *MSN Explorer*, a "friendlier" all-in-one program that integrates browsing, email, chat, and so on. Most experienced users forgo MSN Explorer for IE, Outlook or Outlook Express, Windows Messenger, and so on.

BROWSING TIPS

OUTLOOK EXPRESS— EMAIL AND NEWS

Email is a fast, convenient, and cheap way to exchange written messages and files over the Internet. Windows XP includes Outlook Express to let you send and receive email, as well as read newsgroups (Internet discussion forums). You can communicate with anyone who has an email account. Your recipient doesn't have to have Outlook Express to read and reply to your messages; any email program can talk to any other one.

Outlook Express works with the Internet standards that traditional ISPs use to transmit email. These aren't the same standards that online services use, so you can't use Outlook Express with, for example, America Online, CompuServe, or Prodigy. These services build an email client into the one-size-fits-all software they give you, and you have to use that.

You *can* use Outlook Express for Hotmail and MSN, both of which are Web-based and belong to Microsoft.

✔ Tips

- You can find other (better) email programs. I like Eudora; it's free at www. eudora.com. Trying a particular application doesn't lock you into it—email programs can import each other's mailboxes.

- Don't confuse Outlook Express with Outlook, its bigger brother in the Microsoft Office suite. Outlook is a complex application that manages your email, schedule, meetings, contacts, and more.

Getting Started with Outlook Express

Figure 14.1 shows Outlook Express's main panes and controls. If your copy of Outlook Express doesn't look like the pictured one, it's configured differently; choose View > Layout to show, hide, customize, or rearrange the panes. To resize panes, drag the gray horizontal or vertical lines that separate them.

To start Outlook Express:

◆ Choose Start > Outlook Express (or Start > All Programs > Outlook Express).

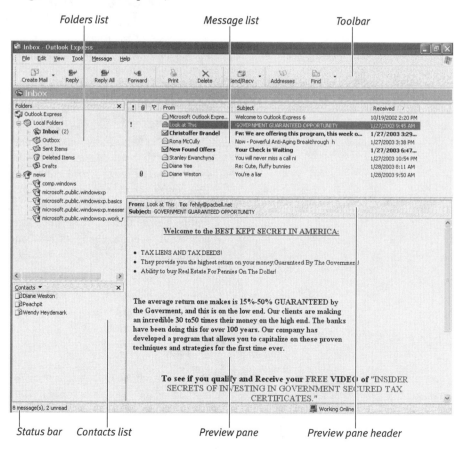

Figure 14.1 The parts of Outlook Express. Click a message name in the Message list to make the message itself appear in the Preview pane. (Most of my email is spam.)

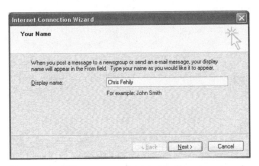

Figure 14.2 This name appears in the From header of email that you send. Don't type something cute or clever; people may mistake your messages for junk mail.

Figure 14.3 A email address has two parts. To the left of the @ is the *alias*, which you choose. To the right is the *domain*, which depends on your ISP.

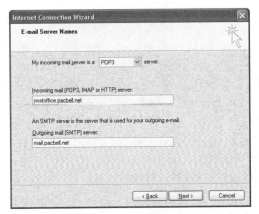

Figure 14.4 Your ISP provides server names, which usually look like this. For Hotmail accounts, choose HTTP from the mail-server drop-down list.

Setting up an Email Account

Before you set up an email account, you must connect to the Internet (see Chapter 12). If you used the New Connection Wizard, your email settings may be in place already, and you can skip this section. Otherwise, the Internet Connection Wizard appears the first time that you start Outlook Express. The wizard helps you enter the addresses (provided by your ISP) that let Outlook Express find your electronic mailbox.

To set up an email account:

1. Type your display name (**Figure 14.2**); then click Next.

2. Type the email address that you chose when you signed up with your ISP (**Figure 14.3**); then click Next.

3. Type the information that your ISP provided about its mail servers (see the sidebar) (**Figure 14.4**); then click Next.

(continues on next page)

4. Type your logon name and password; check Remember Password to avoid being prompted for it each time you check your mail (**Figure 14.5**); then click Next.

5. Click Finish to create the account.

Now you should be able to send and receive email.

✔ Tips

■ If you have multiple email accounts, choose Tools > Accounts > Add > Mail. The Internet Connection Wizard reappears, ready to accept another account.

■ If your users have Windows user accounts (see Chapter 16), each user should create an email account when logged on.

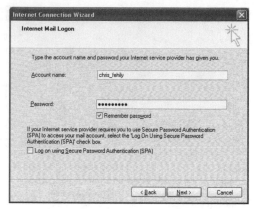

Figure 14.5 Check Log on Using Secure Password Authentication (SPA) only if your ISP tells you to.

Email Protocols

Mail servers are networked computers that manage your mailbox. ISP server administrators limit the number and size of messages that you can send or receive, as well as how much space is available in your mailbox. A server handles *incoming* messages by using one of three standards, or *protocols*. (Your ISP can tell you which protocol it uses.)

A *POP3* server (the most common type) transfers your messages to your hard drive before you read them and then deletes its server copies. You save, manage, delete, and back up messages yourself.

An *IMAP4* server lets you read, delete, and search your messages while they're still on the server. Then you can choose which messages to download to your hard drive. If your server mailbox reaches its capacity, incoming messages bounce back to their senders.

An *HTTP* server, such as Yahoo or Hotmail, lets you send, receive, and manage your email with any Web browser. Messages remain on the server. If your server mailbox reaches its capacity, you're nagged to subscribe to premium service, and incoming messages are thrown away.

SMTP servers handle *outgoing* messages.

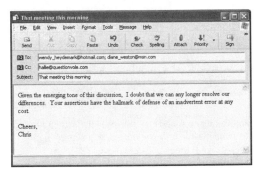

Figure 14.6 The two sections of a message are the headers (top), which contains information about the message, and body (bottom), which contains the message itself. Each message window contains its own menu bar and toolbar.

Sending Email

After you've set up your email account, you can compose a message and send it.

To compose and send a message:

1. Choose Message > New Message (Ctrl+N).

   or

    Click Create Mail on the toolbar.

   A new message window appears (**Figure 14.6**).

2. Type the recipient's email address in the To box.

   To send the message to more than one person, separate the addresses with semicolons (;).

   As you type, Outlook Express autocompletes each address (or plain-English name) with an entry from your address book. If autocomplete guesses wrong, keep typing; if it guesses right, press Tab to jump to the Cc box, or press the semicolon to stay in the To box and type another address.

3. To send a copy of the message to other recipients, type additional email addresses in the Cc box, pressing Tab when you're finished.

   Each address auto-completes as before.

   Cc (carbon-copy) recipients receive the same message as To recipients, but Cc lets them know that you sent them the message as a courtesy and that you're not expecting them to reply.

4. Type the message's topic in the Subject box; then press Tab.

   Recipients appreciate a descriptive subject rather than, say, "Hi," which makes your mail look like junk.

(continues on next page)

5. Type the text of your message.

You can use Cut, Copy, Paste, and all the standard editing techniques.

6. [Send] Click Send on the toolbar (Alt+S). Your PC sends the message over the Internet, connecting to it if necessary.

✔ Tips

■ [Attach] To attach a file to a message, click Attach on the toolbar; locate the file; then click Attach. Alternatively, drag files from Windows Explorer to the message window (**Figure 14.7**). ISPs usually limit attached-file sizes to a few megabytes; compress large files before sending them (see "Compressing Files and Folders" in Chapter 5).

■ [Addresses] Names that you add to your address book (press Ctrl+Shift+B or click Addresses on the toolbar) appear in your Contacts list (**Figure 14.8**) and let Outlook Express autocomplete email addresses. To add the sender of a message to your address book quickly, right-click the message in the Message list; then choose Add Sender to Address Book.

■ [Spelling] If Microsoft Word is installed on your PC, click Spelling on the toolbar (F7) to spell-check your message.

■ A *signature* is a distinctive bit of text— usually, your choice of contact information, a Bartlett's quotation, or something flippant—added at the bottom of outgoing messages. To create signatures, choose Tools > Options > Signatures tab > New; then type a signature in the Edit Signature box. Click New again if you want to create multiple signatures. You can add a signature to *all* messages by checking Add Signatures to All Outgoing Messages in this dialog box; or to individual messages by choosing Insert > Signature in the New Message window.

Figure 14.7 Attached files appear in the Attach header. To remove a file from the outgoing message, right-click its icon; then choose Remove.

Figure 14.8 To scroll quickly to a contact name, type its first few letters. Right-click a name to send email, edit it, or delete it. Double-clicking a name opens a new, blank message window addressed to the contact.

- The Bcc (blind carbon copy) header is hidden by default. To show it, choose View > All Headers. Bcc recipients receive the same message as To and Cc recipients, but *secretly*, without the other recipients knowing. If you send, say, a joke to many recipients, it's polite to put them *all* in the Bcc list; then no one has to scroll through the long list of To or Cc names that appears at the top of the message, and individual email addresses aren't revealed to the entire list.

- To save a draft of a message in the Drafts folder, choose File > Save, and finish composing it later.

- If you've defined multiple email accounts and want to send from an account other than the current one, click the From box; then click the account that you want to use.

Plain Text or HTML?

You can format your message body as plain text or HTML. Plain-text messages contain only unadorned text without italics, boldface, colors, custom font sizes, and so on. HTML—the language used to format Web pages—permits fancy formatting. In general, use plain text because:

◆ Some email programs (especially on Unix) can't read HTML formatting.

◆ Amateurish HTML formatting irritates recipients.

◆ Most junk email (spam) uses HTML formatting. *Your* HTML messages may be caught by filtering software and routed—unread—to the recipient's trash folder.

To change the *default* format for all new messages, choose Tools > Options > Send tab > Mail Sending Format section; select HTML or Plain Text; then click OK (refer to Figure 14.20).

No matter what the default format, you can switch it for individual messages: In the New Message window, choose Format > Plain Text or Format > Rich Text (HTML). Choosing HTML activates the HTML toolbar, with buttons for styles, formatting, hyperlinks, and so on. Choosing Plain Text brings up a warning that certain embellishments, such as images, won't be possible.

SENDING EMAIL

Reading Email

When you open Outlook Express, it retrieves (downloads) your messages automatically from your ISP's mail server. If you keep Outlook Express running, it checks for new mail every 30 minutes, but you can change the interval or check on demand.

To check immediately for new messages:

◆  Click Send/Recv on the toolbar (Ctrl+M).

✔ Tips

■ The preceding method receives messages *and* sends any messages in your Outbox. To *receive* only, choose Tools > Send and Receive > Receive All, or click the small arrow on the Send/Recv button and choose Receive All (**Figure 14.9**).

■ If you've defined several email accounts, you don't have to check them *all*. To disable an account, choose Tools > Accounts > Mail tab; double-click the account's name; then uncheck Include This Account When Receiving Mail or Synchronizing. To check a disabled account occasionally, choose its name from the Send/Recv menu (refer to Figure 14.9).

■ To change the mail-retrieval interval, choose Tools > Options > General tab; then change the time period in the Check for New Messages Every __ Minutes box.

Figure 14.9 Click the Send/Recv button's small arrow to reveal a drop-down list, where you can choose to send messages, receive them, or both. To check an individual email account (rather than all of them), click its name at the bottom of the list.

Organizing Your Messages

Use the Folders list (refer to Figure 14.1) to organize your messages. It contains the following folders initially (but you can create new ones):

Inbox holds mail that you've received.

Outbox holds mail that you've written but haven't sent.

Sent Items holds copies of messages that you've sent.

Deleted Items holds mail that you've deleted.

Drafts holds mail that you're working on but aren't ready to send.

The Folders list acts like a normal Windows Explorer tree. Click a folder to see what's in it. Choose File > New > Folder (Ctrl+Shift+E) to create a new folder. Right-click a folder that you've created to rename or delete it. To file a message, drag it from the Message list to a folder icon, or right-click it and choose Move to Folder or Copy to Folder. To save a message in a Windows Explorer folder, choose File > Save As.

Figure 14.10 The names of new (unread) messages appear in bold in the Message list (on the right). Folders (on the left) containing new messages appear in bold, too, along with the number of unread messages.

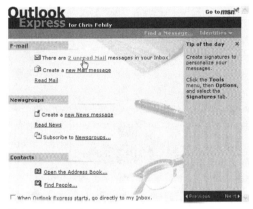

Figure 14.11 Outlook Express' opening screen shows your Inbox status and provides links to common tasks.

- To hide read messages, choose View > Current View > Hide Read Messages.

- The Message list behaves like Windows Explorer in Details view. Choose View > Columns to choose which columns to display. To resize a column, drag its heading's right edge left or right (or double-click the right edge to autosize the column). To rearrange columns, drag the headings horizontally. To sort by a column, click its heading; click again to reverse sort order.

- Outlook Express comes with a "very special" message, *Welcome to Outlook Express 6,* from Microsoft. This message didn't arrive via the Internet; read and delete it.

Newly arrived messages land in your Inbox (**Figure 14.10**) unless they're redirected by rules (see the next section). Arrivals display a notification-area icon near the taskbar clock and play a sound.

When you open Outlook Express, you may see **Figure 14.11** instead of the Message list and Preview pane. Click the Unread Mail link to display the Inbox. To display the Inbox at startup, check When Outlook Express Starts, Go Directly to My Inbox at the bottom of Figure 14.11, or check the similar box in Tools > Options > General tab.

To read messages:

1. Click Inbox (or another folder) in the Folders list.

2. To view a message in the Preview pane, click the message in the Message list.

   or

   To view a message in a separate window, double-click the message in the Message list.

3. To move back or forward through messages, press Ctrl+<, Ctrl+>, or (in preview mode) the up- or down-arrow key.

   or

   To view the next *unread* message, press Ctrl+U.

✔ Tips

- To view all of a message's information, right-click it; then choose Properties.

- To switch a message's read/unread status manually, right-click the message; then choose Mark as Unread or Mark as Read.

- To read and delete (but not reply to) messages from any browser, anywhere, visit a POP3-access Web site such as www.mail2web.com.

READING EMAIL

After you've read a message, you can print it, delete it, reply to it, forward it (that is, pass it on to a third person), or file it in a folder (see the sidebar). You can process a message that's displayed in the Preview pane or one that's open in a separate window.

To print, delete, forward, or file multiple messages simultaneously, Ctrl-click each message to select it. (Ctrl-clicking again deselects it.) To select a group of contiguous messages, click the first message; then Shift-click the last.

To print a message:

◆   **Print**   Select a message and click Print on the toolbar (Ctrl+P).

To delete a message:

1.   **Delete**   Select a message; then click Delete on the toolbar (or press Delete).

   Deleted messages aren't erased but are placed in the Deleted Items folder.

2. To remove *all* deleted messages permanently, choose Edit > Empty Deleted Items Folder.

   or

   To remove a specific deleted message permanently, select it in the Deleted Items folder; then press Delete.

   or

   To delete messages automatically, choose Tools > Options > Maintenance tab > check Empty Messages from Deleted Items Folder on Exit.

3. To rescue a deleted message, drag it from Deleted Items to another folder.

Stopping Spam

You can't, really. *Spam*—unsolicited commercial email—will clog your Inbox eventually. Practicing safe email (posting disguised addresses in newsgroups, for example) only delays it. Spammers scour the Web for email addresses, and nothing stops ISPs (yours or your recipients') from selling your address. Eventually, you'll end up on a spammer's list—and soon thereafter, on hundreds of them.

Short of getting a new email address, the only effective way avoid spam is to use filters to redirect it to the trash. Applying individual message rules (described next) isn't effective, because the rules are hard to maintain, miss too much spam, and discard too much legitimate email identified as spam. *Bayesian filtering*, an effective statistical spam-reduction technique, is new and not yet common in email programs, but it's making its way to the mainstream. See www.paulgraham.com/antispam.html for a start; then search with Google. See also spam.abuse.net.

READING EMAIL

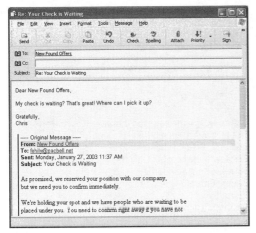

Figure 14.12 A preaddressed reply opens with *Re* (regarding) added to the subject line and the original message's text (which you can edit, cut, or commingle with your own comments) in the body. To turn off the original-text feature, choose Tools > Options > Send tab > uncheck Include Message in Reply.

To reply to a message:

1. To reply to only the sender, select a message; then click Reply on the toolbar (Ctrl+R) (**Figure 14.12**).

or

To reply to everyone in the To and Cc lines (for group discussions), select a message; then click Reply All on the toolbar (Ctrl+Shift+R).

2. Type a response to the message.

3. Click Send on the toolbar (Alt+S).

To forward a message:

1. Select a message; then click Forward on the toolbar (Ctrl+F). A new message opens, containing the original message's text.

2. Type the email addresses of the recipients (see "Sending Email" earlier in this chapter).

3. Edit the subject line or original message, or add your own comments, if you want.

4. Click Send on the toolbar (Alt+S).

READING EMAIL

If someone has sent a you a file, a paper-clip icon appears next to the message name in the Message list (refer to Figure 14.10). Outlook Express stores an attachment with its message in a single, specially encoded mail file. You can open an attachment from the mail file or save it separately as a normal file on your hard drive. (To *send* attachments, see "Sending Email" earlier in this chapter.)

To open an attachment:

◆ In the Preview pane, click the paper-clip icon in the header; then choose the file name (**Figure 14.13**).

   or

   At the top of the message window, double-click the file icon in the Attach header (refer to Figure 14.7).

To save an attachment:

1. In the Preview pane, click the paper-clip icon in the header, then choose Save Attachments (refer to Figure 14.13).

   or

   Select the message; then choose File > Save Attachments.

2. Select a folder for the file; then click Save (**Figure 14.14**).

✔ Tips

■ Delete attached .exe, .scr, and .vbs files immediately—even those from friends, because the (forged) name of the sender may have been picked out of your own address book. Such files often contain viruses or worms. If you don't have a virus scanner, get one; if you do, make sure that it's set to check your incoming and outgoing mail.

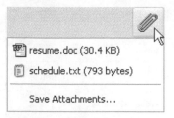

Figure 14.13 If the selected message has files attached, a paper-clip icon appears on the right side of the Preview pane header. Click the icon for a shortcut menu; then choose the name of the attached file to open (in Word, Excel, or whatever), or choose Save Attachments to save it to disk.

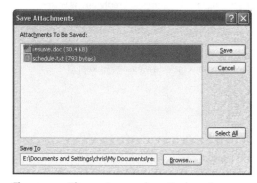

Figure 14.14 After you've saved an attachment on your hard drive, you can delete the message it came with.

■ When you receive an important message, you can *flag* it for later reference. Select a message and choose Message > Flag Message, or click the flag column next to the message. A small red flag appears (refer to Figure 14.10). You can click a flag icon to remove it, or click the flag-column header to sort flagged messages together.

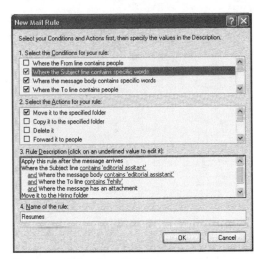

Figure 14.15 This rule, named Resumes, moves a message to my Hiring folder if the message is addressed to *fehily* directly, contains *editorial assistant* in the Subject line or message body, and has an attachment (presumably, a résumé).

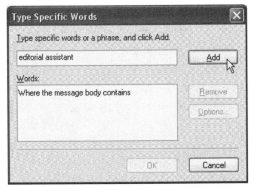

Figure 14.16 Enter the values to watch for in the dialog box that appears when you click an underlined phrase.

Applying Message Rules

Outlook Express lets you define *message rules* that answer, redirect, or delete incoming messages automatically, based on subject, sender, message text, size, or other criteria.

To set up message rules:

1. Choose Tools > Message Rules > Mail (**Figure 14.15**).

2. In the top box, specify selection criteria for messages.

   To look for messages from a certain person, for example, check Where the From Line Contains People.

3. In the second box, specify what happens to messages that meet the selection criteria.

   You can define complex rule systems that move, copy, delete, reply to, forward, flag, ignore, or highlight messages automatically.

4. In the third box, click underlined phrases to specify which people, words, or values the message rules apply to (**Figure 14.16**).

(continues on next page)

5. In the bottom text box, type the rule's name; then click OK.

The Message Rules dialog box appears (**Figure 14.17**).

✔ Tips

- Don't expect to get all your rules right the first time. Outlook Express applies the rules in the Message Rules dialog box from top to bottom. You may find that an earlier rule contradicts a later one or that legitimate messages are deleted inadvertently. After creating a new rule, watch how it's applied as new mail arrives.

- To create a rule based on a selected message, choose Message > Create Rule from Message.

- Message rules apply to all defined accounts.

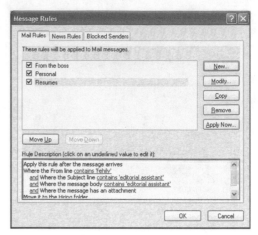

Figure 14.17 All the rules that you've created appear in this dialog box. Select a rule to see what it does, or double-click it to edit it. Use the Move Up and Move Down buttons to change the order in which rules run.

Figure 14.18 For dial-up connections, use the drop-down list to tell Outlook Express how, or whether, to connect to check for new mail.

Figure 14.19 Uncheck the first box to stop Outlook Express from marking your messages as read automatically.

Configuring Outlook Express

Rather than explain each of Outlook Express' scores of options, I'll describe the 10 tabs in the Tools > Options dialog box. (Most tabs have buttons that open *more* dialog boxes.) Many options are self-explanatory, but you can right-click an option for a "What's This?" pop-up tip.

General options control what happens when Outlook Express starts and when messages are sent and received (**Figure 14.18**).

Read options control how Inbox messages are treated, and let you change their font and font size (**Figure 14.19**).

Receipts adds a *return receipt* to your outgoing messages, letting you know when your message has been read (*if* the recipient agrees to return it). Return receipts generally annoy recipients, and not all email programs support them.

Send options control how outgoing messages are treated and let you change the default sending format (**Figure 14.20**).

Compose lets you specify the font for outgoing messages, add fancy *stationery* to HTML messages (don't bother), and include electronic business cards with outgoing messages so that your recipients can add you to their address books.

Signatures is described in the tips in "Sending Email" earlier in this chapter.

Spelling configures the spell-check feature, which works only if Microsoft Word is installed.

Security has options for virus protection and sending secure email, as well as using encryption and digital IDs.

Connection controls dial-up options and your Internet connection (see Chapter 12), which Outlook Express shares with Internet Explorer.

Maintenance has housekeeping features for cleaning up old messages and downloads.

Figure 14.20 For dial-up connections, uncheck Send Messages Immediately to stop Outlook Express from dialing every time you click the Send button. When you're ready to send a batch of messages (from your Outbox), press Ctrl+M.

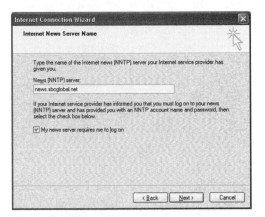

Figure 14.21 Get your user name, password, and (NNTP) news-server address from your ISP. If your ISP doesn't provide newsgroup access, try www.newsguy. com or www.easynews.com.

Figure 14.22 A newsgroup name is a series of dot-separated words that indicates the newsgroup's topic in increasingly narrow categories, such as microsoft. public.windowsxp.help_and_support.

Using Newsgroups

The Internet's uncensored anarchy is evident in the tens of thousands of online forums, called *newsgroups* (or *Usenet*), that cover almost every conceivable interest. A newsgroup consists of messages and follow-up posts, which are (supposed to be) related to the original message's subject line. A message and its follow-ups are called a *thread*. To view and post messages to newsgroups, use Outlook Express as a *newsreader*. Setting up a news account is similar to setting up an email account, described earlier in this chapter.

To set up and use a news account:

1. Choose Tools > Accounts > Add > News.

2. Follow the onscreen instructions, clicking Finish when you're done (**Figure 14.21**).

3. Click Yes when you're prompted to download newsgroups.

   You may have to wait a few minutes, but it's a one-time process.

4. In the Newsgroup Subscriptions dialog box that appears, type a term of interest in the text box. As you type, newsgroups that *don't* match that text are hidden (**Figure 14.22**).

   To summon Newsgroup Subscriptions at any time, choose Tools > Newsgroups (Ctrl+W).

5. When you find an interesting newsgroup, select it; then click Subscribe.

   An icon appears near the newsgroup name.

6. When you finish subscribing to newsgroups, click OK.

   The new newsgroups appear in the Folders list, below the news-server name.

7. In the Folders list, click a newsgroup name to download its recent threads (**Figure 14.23**).

8. Click (or double-click) a header in the Message list to read the message.

Reply to or post newsgroup messages as you would normal email. Note the Reply (to individuals) and Reply Group (for public posts) toolbar buttons.

✔ Tips

■ Usenet, home of newsgroups, is one of the oldest parts of the Internet and is encrusted with etiquette and rules, some of which may seem silly. They're not. Usenet is as pragmatic and ruthless as anyplace else on the Internet, and it suffers fools reluctantly at best. Before you post extensively in a newsgroup, hang out in it silently (*lurk*) for a few days, and test the climate.

■ Learn the ropes by joining and reading `news.answers` and `news.announce.newusers`. Find out what *crossposting* is and how not to do it.

■ Usenet, like chat, will gobble your life if you dive into it headlong. Don't plan on joining more than three or four newsgroups, but if you do, make yourself cut back to what really interests you.

■ If you join a newsgroup, find and read its FAQ (frequently asked questions), which may answer a lot of *your* questions before you take up the group's time asking them again.

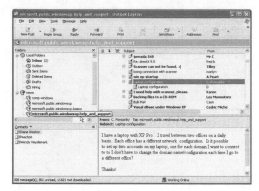

Figure 14.23 *Lurk* on a newsgroup before participating. Asking recently answered (or dumb) questions irritates people. Use Google's Groups tab to search newsgroups.

CHATTING ONLINE WITH WINDOWS MESSENGER 15

Windows Messenger (formerly MSN Messenger) is instant gratification for those of us impatient with email's delays. Messenger lets you *chat* privately with other people on the Internet—one or several at a time—by typing live comments in a small window. This communications channel, called *instant messaging*, is also the idea behind AOL Instant Messenger (AIM), Yahoo Messenger, and ICQ. Unfortunately, whoever you want to chat with must use the same messaging system that you do, so if you chat with a lot of friends, it's not unusual to have two or three of these programs on your computer. In fact, the shareware program Trillian (www.ceruleanstudios.com) exists solely to help you run several of these at the same time.

Like Internet Explorer, Messenger is closely tied to Windows, so it's powerful and versatile. Besides chatting (or even while you're chatting), you can monitor your email, send files, have a teleconference, make free voice calls, or work collaboratively with a whiteboard program.

Connection Requirements

To use Windows Messenger, you need an Internet connection (see Chapter 12). High-speed DSL or cable connections are ideal, but chatting on 28 Kbps or 56 Kbps dial-up connection is adequate.

If your connection goes directly to a cable or jack without passing through a router, you can enable Internet Connection Firewall to protect your network, and Internet Connection Sharing to distribute your connection, and still use all Messenger's features. Otherwise, to use features other than text messaging, you need a router that supports *Universal Plug and Play* (UPnP). Routers made before late 2001 probably *don't* support UPnP and won't let you make Internet voice and video calls.

Getting a .NET Passport

Along with your Internet connection, you need a Microsoft *.NET Passport* to run Messenger, even to chat within your local area network. Your Passport is Microsoft's way of identifying you uniquely on the Internet. It's free and requires only an email address.

If you've already obtained a Passport and linked it to your user account, you can skip this section. Windows sometimes nags you to set up a Passport (**Figure 15.1**), or if you open Messenger, the .NET Passport Wizard appears when you try to sign in. You also can launch the wizard yourself.

To get a .NET Passport:

1. In Control Panel, choose User Accounts; click your user-account icon; then click Set Up My Account to Use a .NET Passport. The .NET Passport Wizard appears (**Figure 15.2**).

2. Click Next to skip the first screen.

3. Specify whether to use your existing email address or sign up for a new, free one with MSN.com (**Figure 15.3**); then click Next.

4. Follow the onscreen instructions, and click Finish when you're done.

    Along the way, you're asked for your name, location, and other personal information. (Your Passport password doesn't have to be the same as your Windows password.)

    When the wizard finishes, Windows starts Messenger and signs you in automatically.

✔ Tips

- After you sign up, Microsoft sends a message to your Passport email address. Reply to this message to make your Passport official. Until then, other Messenger users see you as "E-mail Address Not Verified."

Figure 15.1 This pop-up balloon appears periodically in the notification area.

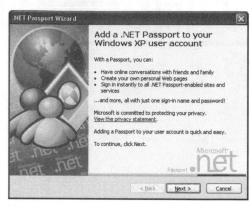

Figure 15.2 Microsoft implies otherwise, but .NET Passport is required for Messenger only, not for other Windows programs or features.

Figure 15.3 Any (nonbogus) email address works; previous Passport versions required a Hotmail or MSN address.

- Go to memberservices.passport.com to edit your Passport profile, change your password, or recover a forgotten password.

Figure 15.4 The Messenger icon appears whether or not you're online and signed in. The left icon indicates that you're offline; the right one means you're online and signed in.

Figure 15.5 Your sign-in screen will be more elaborate than this one if you've signed in before.

Signing in to Messenger

If Messenger doesn't sign you in automatically when you go online, you must do so manually. When you're finished using Messenger, sign out.

To open Messenger and sign in:

1. Choose Start > All Programs > Windows Messenger.

   or

   Double-click Messenger's notification-area icon on the taskbar (**Figure 15.4**).

2. Click the link titled Click Here to Sign In (**Figure 15.5**).

3. Type your Passport email address and password.

(continues on next page)

4. If you don't want to type your password every time you sign in, check Sign Me In Automatically (**Figure 15.6**).

Don't check this box on public PCs or a PC where your user account is shared.

5. Click OK to go online (**Figure 15.7**).

To sign out:

◆ Choose File > Sign Out.

Signing out doesn't log you off the Internet or close Messenger. When you sign out, you'll appear offline to others, but you'll still be online.

✔ Tips

■ To stop Messenger from starting automatically, choose Tools > Options > Preferences tab > uncheck Run This Program When Windows Starts. You can start Messenger manually from the Start menu.

■ After you sign in the first time, Messenger's sign-in screen will show your email address. To sign in with a different Passport, click To Sign in With a Different Account, Click Here.

Figure 15.6 Passwords are case-sensitive.

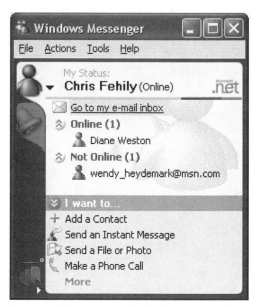

Figure 15.7 Messenger's main window appears after you sign in.

Figure 15.8 The wizard checks whether this person has a Passport and, if so, adds the name to your contact list.

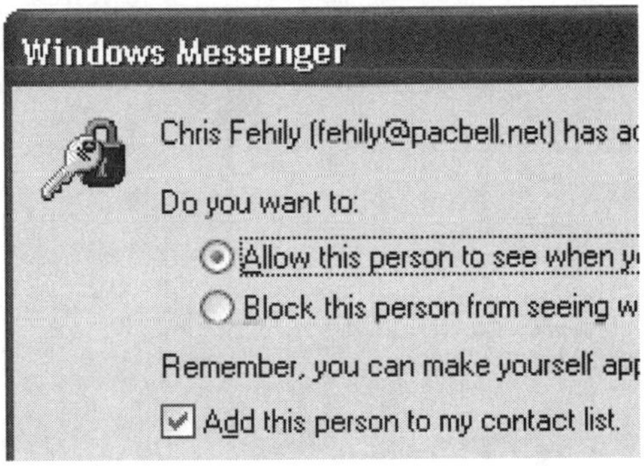

Figure 15.9 When someone adds *you* to her contact list, you can choose whether to allow the contact or block it. Check the box to add that person to *your* contact list. To see everyone who's added you, choose Tools > Options > Privacy tab > View button.

■ To add a contact from in Outlook Express, right-click the person's name in the Contacts list (see Figure 14.1 in Chapter 14); then choose New Online Contact.

Creating a Contact List

To send instant messages, you need a list of contacts who have Passport accounts and Windows Messenger (or MSN Messenger) installed. The best way to add a contact is to specify an email address, as described here. You can search a directory for contacts, but these searches tend to be ineffective. Messenger scans only your Outlook Express address book and Microsoft's Hotmail Member Directory, which people often decline to be listed in.

To add a contact:

1. Choose File > Add a Contact.

2. Select By E-mail Address or Sign-in Name; then click Next.

3. Enter the person's email address (**Figure 15.8**); then click Next.

4. Click Next to add another contact or click Finish to quit the wizard.

   Contact names appear in the main window.

✔ Tips

■ As a privacy precaution, Messenger displays the dialog box shown in **Figure 15.9** on a new contact's screen.

■ To allow others to add you without seeking your approval, choose Tools > Options > Privacy tab > uncheck Alert Me When Other Users Add Me to Their Contact Lists.

■ If the person whose email address you specified doesn't have a Passport, the wizard offers to send that person an email message (from you) with instructions on how to get one.

■ To remove a contact, choose Tools > Manage Contacts > Delete a Contact; then double-click the contact to delete.

CREATING A CONTACT LIST

Chatting Online

After you've created a contact list, you're ready to chat with anyone who's running Messenger in the background. All parties to the conversation must be connected to the Internet.

✔ Tip

■ Before starting your first chat, you may want to change your Messenger display name. Choose Tools > Options > Personal tab; in the text box, type your name as you want other users to see it (**Figure 15.10**). (Unlike AIM, Windows Messenger doesn't demand that your screen name be unique.)

To send an instant message:

1. In your contact list, double-click the name of someone who's online (refer to Figure 15.7).

   The conversation window opens.

2. Type your message in the box at the bottom of the window; then click Send (or press Enter) (**Figure 15.11**).

   Your message appears in the top box.

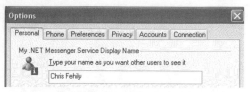

Figure 15.10 By default, Messenger displays your email address. Instead, you can use your real name (or a nickname, to protect your anonymity).

Figure 15.11 To start a new line while typing, press Shift+Enter. Each instant message can contain up to 400 characters.

Figure 15.12 The other person hears a chime and sees this pop-up invitation, which she can click to open a conversation window. The Messenger taskbar button, shown here, changes color and blinks to get her attention.

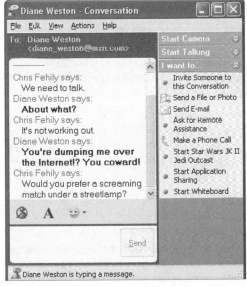

Figure 15.13 You can see when the other person is typing by looking at the bottom of the window. The date and time of the last message you received appear here as well.

3. The other person receives an onscreen invitation to chat (**Figure 15.12**) and (presumably) replies.

4. Type your reply in the bottom box; then click Send (or press Enter).

Now you're chatting. You can use Cut, Copy, Paste, and all the standard editing techniques. The conversation's transcript rolls down the top box, identifying each message's speaker (**Figure 15.13**).

5. Close the conversation window when you're done chatting, or leave it open to continue the conversation later.

You remain signed in to Messenger when you close a conversation window.

CHATTING ONLINE

Chatting Tips

This section contains tips on chatting and using Windows Messenger's features.

Choose commands quickly. A conversation window's toolbar and right sidebar contain links to common tasks (refer to Figure 15.13). To show or hide the toolbar or sidebar, choose View > Show Toolbar, or View > Show Sidebar.

Change fonts. Change the font or color of your messages to distinguish them from the other person's messages. In the main window, choose Tools > Options > Personal tab > Change Font; or, in a conversation window, choose Edit > Change Font. Both of you will see the change (assuming that you have similar fonts installed). You can't change the other person's font in your window, but you can change text size with the View > Text Size submenu.

Add other chatters. To add more people to a chat, in a conversation window, choose Actions > Invite Someone to This Conversation; then double-click the name of an online contact.

Cold-shoulder someone. To block somebody from chatting with you:

◆ In a conversation window with the person that you want to block, choose Actions > Block, or click Block on the toolbar.

   or

   In the main window, right-click a contact's name; then choose Block.

   or

   In the main window, choose Tools > Options > Privacy tab; click the victim's name; then click Block.

If a dialog box explaining your action's consequences appears, click OK. To unblock someone, repeat the Block command. (Block toggles to Unblock.)

Ignore people. If you step away from your computer or don't want to be bothered, broadcast your status by using the File > My Status submenu in the main window (choose Busy, Be Right Back, On the Phone, and so on).

Express your feelings. On the toolbar near the bottom of a conversation window is a drop-down list of smiley-face icons. You can insert these *emoticons* into your messages to indicate how the message should be interpreted (that is, your mood—embarrassment, anger, surprise, delight, whatever). Emoticons may be annoying, but they help prevent misunderstandings if your correspondent has no sense of irony. Messenger converts common text emoticons to graphic ones automatically; type :) to make a smiley face, for example. To turn off autoconversion, choose Tools > Options > Personal tab > uncheck Show Graphics (Emoticons) in Instant Messages.

Save conversations. To save a transcript of your chat as plain text on your hard drive, in a conversation window, choose File > Save As. If you'd rather preserve the transcript's colors and fonts, click in the transcript pane; choose Edit > Select All to highlight all the text; then copy and paste the text into WordPad or Word.

Keep Messenger in sight. To make Messenger remain in front of all other windows unless minimized, in the main window, choose Tools > Always On Top; or, in a conversation window, choose View > Always On Top.

Configure Messenger. The Tools > Options dialog box contains six tabs for setting personal preferences, Messenger settings, and privacy options. "What's This?" pop-up help doesn't work here; click Help instead.

Add features. Microsoft adds new features quietly to Messenger over time, and some of the built-in features won't work unless you download appropriate modules from

Microsoft's Add-In Web page. In the main window, choose Tools > Add-In Web Site. Your browser opens to the site, which lists available add-ins. Click the link titled Click Here to Download This Add-In; then click Open to install it.

Get help from a friend. To start a Remote Assistance session from Messenger, see Chapter 3.

Exchange files. To send a file to your chat partner, drag a file icon from Explorer or your desktop to the chat window. Or Click Send a File or Photo in the right sidebar; then, in the Send a File dialog box that appears, locate and double-click the file.

Messenger asks the other person to Accept (Alt+T) or Decline (Alt+D) the file. Or *you* can Cancel (Alt+Q) the file transfer. If the recipient accepts the file, Messenger displays a dire virus warning, followed by a download-progress readout. Use this feature to circumvent ISP-imposed file-size limits on email attachments.

Add voice to a conversation. Free long distance! If you and your chat partner have USB headsets or microphones and speakers, attached to your PCs, you can have a live, not-quite-phone-quality conversation. To do so, in the main window, right-click an online contact and choose Start a Voice Conversation; or, in a conversation window, click Start Talking in the right sidebar. If you haven't set up your audio equipment, Messenger runs Audio and Video Tuning Wizard; otherwise, speaker and microphone controls appear in the right pane. Start talking when your chat partner accepts the call. To hang up, click Stop Talking.

Add video to a conversation. If you or your chat partner have a digital video camera or webcam hooked up to your PC, you can add grainy, jerky video to your voice conversation. To do so, in a conversation

window, click Start Camera in the right sidebar. When your contact accepts, a video picture appears in the right pane. Below the picture is an Options menu that lets you see your picture inset in your contact's picture or stop sending *your* image to the contact. To end the conversation, click Stop Talking or Stop Camera. If your contact doesn't have a camera, and you do, she'll see you, but you won't see her.

Make a phone call. Messenger also lets you make computer-to-*phone* calls to an actual phone number. It's not free: you have to sign up and pay a third-party voice-service provider. To do so, choose Actions > Make a Phone Call.

Send a pager message. To send a text message to a cell phone or pager, in the main window, right-click a contact name, and choose Send a Message to a Mobile Device. To receive a message, a person must have mobile information set up (Tools > Options > Phone tab).

Share applications. Application Sharing lets your chat partner use any program on *your* PC—Word, Excel, and so on—even if it's not installed on *her* PC. Only open programs can be shared; you can open them before or after you send the invitation. (Don't block the view of the shared program with other windows.) To share a program, in the main window, right-click an online contact, and choose Start Application Sharing; or, in a conversation window, click Start Application Sharing in the right sidebar. After the invitation is accepted, select the program in the Sharing dialog box; click Share; then click Allow Control. To take control of the program, the chat partner clicks Request Control. In response, you click Accept. To retake control, press Esc.

CHATTING TIPS

Use a whiteboard. Whiteboard is a graphics window that allows you to work with someone else simultaneously. Anything that you draw, type, or paste in this window appears on your chat partner's screen (and vice versa). To start Whiteboard, in the main window, right-click an online contact, and choose Start Whiteboard; or, in a conversation window, click Start Whiteboard in the right sidebar.

Check your email. In the main window, right-click a contact; then choose Send E-Mail to open your email program with a preaddressed message to the contact. To check your email, click Go to My E-Mail Inbox near the top of the window. If you have a Hotmail or MSN account, this link indicates how many new messages await you.

Chat without Messenger. Microsoft Chat is an older no-Passport-required program for chatting with someone connected to your network (LAN). To open Chat, choose Start > Run; type winchat; then press Enter. To have a videoconference without Messenger, use Microsoft NetMeeting: Choose Start > Run; type conf; then press Enter.

✔ Tips

■ Among veteran chatters, blocking is a mild to significant insult, depending on circumstances. If you're trying to remain open to some people while avoiding others, Messenger doesn't give you many options; the best is probably to set yourself as Away or Busy and continue your chats of choice while letting others think you're not at the keyboard.

■ For the same purpose, you can use the Appear Offline setting, but that's of less use than it might be. You can see who's online and they can't see you, but you also can't send a message without changing your visibility setting first. (ICQ's Invisible setting gives you much more flexibility.)

■ Messenger's size limit for a single message is 400 characters, and if you try to exceed it, your typing stops as though you'd hit a wall. If you must continue one thought over two messages, it's polite to back up a bit and end the first message with [more] or >>.

■ If you want to save the transcript, you must do so explicitly (in Word or Notepad) before you close your session. Otherwise, the traffic is discarded when you exit Messenger.

■ Unlike some other chat clients, and unlike email, Messenger doesn't stamp its saved messages with the date and time. The only such record you have is the creation date and time of the saved file.

■ Microsoft will send you periodic pop-up notifications that a new version of Messenger is available. I suggest that you skip a new version until its paint dries.

CHATTING TIPS

MANAGING USER ACCOUNTS

Windows XP is a true multiple-user OS that lets several people use one PC without intruding on—or even viewing—one another's files, settings, and tastes. To start a Windows session, you log on to your *user account*, which gives you personalized access to the system. Each user has his or her own desktop, Start menu, My Documents folder, Control Panel settings, email account, Internet details (Favorites, History, cookies, and cached Web pages), application settings, permissions, and other odds and ends. A user's private files, folders, and preferences are stored in C:\Documents and Settings\ *<user name>*, which enables Windows to personalize the desktop each time the user logs on.

In this chapter, you'll learn to create, edit, and delete user accounts as an administrator. If you're an end user who's not called on to administer, you still need to know (and will learn) how to maintain your *own* account.

Workgroup vs. Domain

The type of network (Chapter 17) you're on determines how you administer accounts.

A *workgroup* is a simple home or small-business network whose computers each maintain separate user accounts and security settings. These informal networks exist primarily to help users share printers, folders, and other resources. User accounts don't float around the network; you need a separate account on each networked PC to access its files.

PRO A *domain* is a large, business-oriented, centrally administered network. Files may reside on local hard disks or on a network *server* that distributes files across the network. Centralized user accounts let you log on to any domain computer. XP Home supports only workgroups; Pro supports both workgroups and domains.

Setting up User Accounts

Use Control Panel's User Accounts applet to set up user accounts on a workgroup PC or a stand-alone (non-networked) PC. If you're an XP Pro user on a domain, skip to the tips later in this section.

Your computer will have at least one account: yours. It may have other accounts if you upgraded from an earlier Windows version. If your PC is new, its manufacturer may have created a predefined account named *Owner*. See "Logging on and Logging off Windows XP" in Chapter 1.

To see existing accounts:

◆ Choose Start > Control Panel > User Accounts (**Figure 16.1**).

User Accounts offers straightforward controls to create, change, and delete accounts.

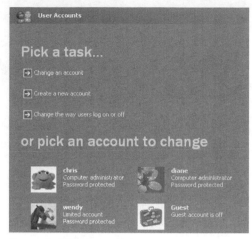

Figure 16.1 This window lists everyone who has a user account.

Account Types

An *account type* defines a user's *privileges*—rights to perform specific tasks. The account type appears below each user's name.

A *computer administrator* has sweeping systemwide rights to create, change, and delete user accounts and passwords; access *all* files (including other users' files); and install programs and hardware. Many of the settings described in this book require administrative privileges, which you should grant to few users besides yourself. XP must have at least one administrator, and if you installed Windows or maintain it, this is *your* account type.

If you're not an administrator, you're an everyday *Limited* user who can change your own password, picture, .NET Passport, desktop theme, and Start menu; change *some* Control Panel settings (you can't change the system time, for example); access files in your My Documents folder (everyone else's files are off limits); and view files in the Shared Documents "community" folder (see "Saving Documents" in Chapter 6).

Windows also comes with a no-password *Guest* account that has the same privileges as a limited account. This account, intended for visitors, is disabled by default and should stay that way.

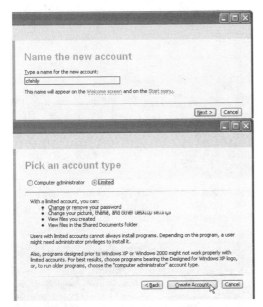

Figure 16.2 Best practice: Don't use spaces in a user name, as they may cause problems with some applications and command-line tools. Capitalization doesn't matter, but favor only lowercase letters. Most punctuation is forbidden.

Figure 16.3 Administrators have full access to all accounts. Some options are available for only your account; other options, for only others' accounts. Limited users see fewer options; they can't change their name or account type, nor can they modify other users' accounts.

To create an account:

1. In User Accounts, click Create a New Account.

2. Type a user name for the account; then click Next.

   Use this name to log on to domains and to computers without the Welcome screen.

3. Select an account type (see the "Account Types" sidebar) (**Figure 16.2**); then click Create Account.

   The new account will appear in the User Accounts window.

After creating a user account, you edit it to set up its other information. You can change a user account's details, such as its password and picture, at any time after creating it.

To edit an account:

1. In User Accounts, click the name or icon of the account that you want to change.

   Don't bother with the extra click of the Change an Account link.

2. In the window that appears (**Figure 16.3**), choose among these options:

   Name. Type a new user name, which appears in the Welcome screen, Start menu, and User Accounts window.

   (continues on next page)

Password. Type (and retype) a password and optional logon hint to remind you of a forgotten password (**Figures 16.4** and **16.5**). If the account already is password-protected, you can change or remove the existing password. Capitalization counts. See the "Passwords" sidebar for password tips.

Picture. Change the picture associated with you in the Welcome screen, Start menu, and User Accounts window. (The picture doesn't appear if you're a domain member or if you use the classic Start menu.) Double-click your Start-menu picture to open this dialog box quickly (**Figure 16.6**).

Account type. Change an Administrator account into a Limited account, or vice versa. See the "Account Types" sidebar and Figure 16.2.

.NET Passport. Set up a new .NET Passport or change one that's linked to your account; this option appears for only your account. See "Getting a .NET Passport" in Chapter 15.

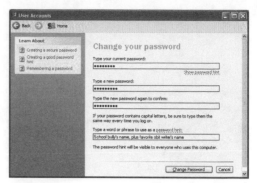

Figure 16.4 If you provide a password hint, use one that's meaningful to only you, because...

Figure 16.5 ...everyone who uses your PC can see it. Click the ? icon on the Welcome screen to reveal your password hint.

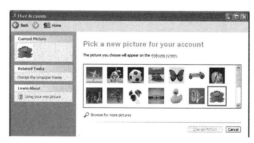

Figure 16.6 Click Browse for More Pictures to post your own picture, automatically scaled to fit. If a camera is connected to your PC, you'll see Get a Picture from a Camera or Scanner.

Figure 16.7 You can have only one password reset disk for each account. If you make a new one, the old one becomes unusable.

If you're worried that you'll forget your password and draw a blank on your password hint, create a *password reset disk* to recover it. You must create it now, before you actually need it. Keep the disk safe; anyone can use it to change your password. (An administrator always can reset your forgotten password, but a reset wipes your secondary passwords; see the "Passwords" sidebar.)

To create a password reset disk:

1. In User Accounts, click your account's name or icon.

2. In the task pane at the left, click Prevent a Forgotten Password.

   The Forgotten Password Wizard opens (**Figure 16.7**).

   (continues on next page)

Passwords

The first time you create a password for your own account, XP asks you whether you want to make your files and folders private (*if* you have an NTFS-formatted hard drive; see Appendix A). Click Yes, Make Private to deny others access to your C:\Documents and Settings\<*your name*> folder. (An unethical administrator still can inspect your files by changing your password.) See also "Sharing Files" in Chapter 17.

The secondary passwords stored in your account for certain Web sites, network files and folders, encrypted files, your .NET Passport, and so on *are lost* if an administrator changes your password (but not if *you* change it), thus preventing someone unscrupulous from, say, cleaning out your bank account courtesy of a password memorized by your browser.

If you upgraded from Windows 9x with user accounts, XP set the imported accounts to Administrator and *erased* their passwords. XP forbids passwordless network logons, but passersby can log on. To plug this security hole, assign passwords and downgrade account types to Limited.

In most situations, it's imperative to password-protect every account. The Web has good advice on how to choose (and not choose) passwords; search for *choosing a password* on Google. For starters, see www.cs.umd.edu/faq/Passwords.shtml.

3. Follow the onscreen instructions.

You'll need a formatted floppy disk.

If you mistype a password in future logons, Windows displays a Use Your Password Reset Disk link (if you're using the Welcome screen) or a Reset button (if you're not). Click the link or button to launch the Password Reset Wizard, and follow the onscreen instructions. You don't need to make a new password reset disk after you're logged on; reuse the old one.

Figure 16.8 Windows saves only documents, not the user's email, Favorites, or settings.

You, an administrator, can delete any account that's not logged on. (Press Ctrl+Shift+Esc and click the Users tab to see who's connected.) You *can't* delete the account that you're logged on to or the last administrator account. A deleted account is gone forever, along with its settings and secondary passwords, as described in the "Passwords" sidebar. If you create a new account with the same name and password, Windows considers it to be a different account.

To delete an account:

1. In User Accounts, click the name or icon of the account that you want to delete.

2. Click Delete This Account.

3. Click Keep Files to save the user's desktop and My Documents files on your desktop in a folder named after the deleted user (**Figure 16.8**).

   or

   Click Delete Files to erase the user's files.

4. Click Delete Account.

✔ Tips

■ For information about sharing files and folders with other users, see "Sharing Files" in Chapter 17.

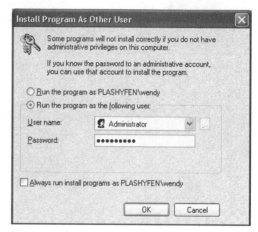

Figure 16.9 If this dialog box doesn't appear automatically, right-click the program's .exe icon (not its shortcut); then choose Run As.

■ Manage accounts through only User Accounts. If you tinker with accounts in the Documents and Settings folder, you'll create a confusing array of duplicate folders with the computer name appended (diane and diane.NILE, for example).

■ For security reasons, many pros use a limited account for frequent logons and an administrator account for special occasions. If you're logged on as a limited user and try to install a program—which requires administrator privileges—**Figure 16.9** appears to let you install it as an administrator.

SETTING UP USER ACCOUNTS

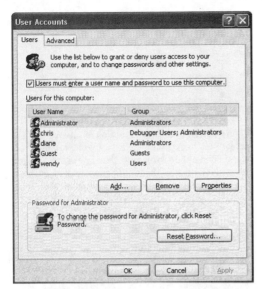

Figure 16.10 This dialog box is more powerful and direct than Control Panel's User Accounts. You can create, edit, and delete accounts without slogging through wizard screens. Click the Advanced tab for more options.

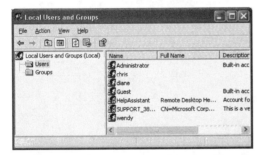

Figure 16.11 Despite its austere appearance, this tool offers power and flexibility. Double-click an account name to set advanced options, for example.

■ XP has a built-in, hidden administrative account named Administrator, which has no password. You can use this account for emergencies: when you start your PC in Safe mode (see "Recovering After a Crash" in Chapter 19) or when no other administrative accounts exist, for example. To manage this account, use the dialog box described in the next tip.

■ Power users prefer the Windows 2000-style User Accounts dialog box to manage user accounts. It's hidden in XP. To reveal it, choose Start > Run, type `control userpasswords2`; then press Enter (**Figure 16.10**).

■ **PRO** If you're a domain member, choose Start > Control Panel > User Accounts to create and manage accounts. The dialog box that appears is almost identical to Figure 16.10, except that the users list has an extra column named Domain. The ideas described earlier in this section apply here, with a few extras. Accounts created here are *local* accounts stored on your PC, not on the domain server. You'll want a local—not domain—administrator account to update drivers, for example. You also can assign people to groups, as described in the next tip.

■ Upon graduation to advanced user management, you'll use the Local Users and Groups console. Choose Start > Run; type `lusrmgr.msc`; then press Enter (**Figure 16.11**). With this console, you can create and manage users and groups. *Groups* are named collections of users that transcend the standard Administrator/Limited account types and give you great flexibility in fine-tuning file and folder permissions.

SETTING UP USER ACCOUNTS

Controlling the Logon Process

As described in "Logging on and Logging off Windows XP" in Chapter 1, Windows gives you two ways to log on (if you're not on a domain):

◆ The *Welcome screen* (refer to Figure 1.1) is the easiest and fastest way to log on. You simply click your name and type your password (if you have one).

◆ The *classic logon prompt* (refer to Figure 16.14) is a more secure, less convenient method. You must type your user name and, if necessary, your password.

You can enable Fast User Switching (described in Chapter 1) if:

◆ The Welcome screen is turned on.

◆ **PRO** You're not on a domain.

◆ **PRO** The offline-files feature is disabled. See "Making Network Files and Folders Available Offline" in Chapter 5.

To control how users log on:

1. Choose Start > Control Panel > User Accounts.

2. Click Change the Way Users Log On or Off (refer to Figure 16.1).

3. Select the logon options; then click Apply Options (**Figure 16.12**).

✔ Tip

■ For added security, force users to press Ctrl+Alt+Delete to prevent user-name and password theft by programs that mimic the logon screen. Choose Start > Run; type control userpasswords2; then press Enter. The old-style User Accounts dialog box appears (refer to Figure 16.10). Click the Advanced tab; check Require Users to Press Ctrl+Alt+Delete; then click OK. From now on, users are greeted with **Figure 16.13**.

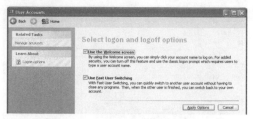

Figure 16.12 Check the first option for the Welcome screen; uncheck it for the classic logon prompt. Check the second option to let more than one user be logged on at the same time. These options are related; unchecking the first turns off the second automatically.

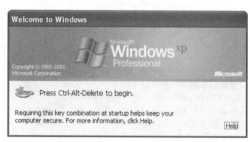

Figure 16.13 Pressing Ctrl+Alt+Delete temporarily halts any other programs running on your PC, guaranteeing an authentic logon prompt. (For this to work, the Welcome screen must be turned off in Figure 16.12.)

Figure 16.14 The classic logon prompt usually displays the name of the previous user who logged on.

Figure 16.15 Sometimes, you must pass through this extra security checkpoint to reach the logon prompt.

Logging on to a Domain

If you've turned off the Welcome screen, or if you're joined to an XP Pro network domain, you'll log on via the classic logon prompt (**Figure 16.14**). Domain logon is like standard logon but requires an extra bit of information: a domain name.

To log on to a workgroup or stand-alone computer:

1. If the dialog box in **Figure 16.15** appears, press Ctrl+Alt+Delete to display the classic logon prompt.

2. Type your user name in the User Name box.

3. If your account is password-protected, type your password in the Password box.

4. Press Enter or click OK.

PRO To log on to a domain:

1. Follow steps 1 to 3 in "To log on to a workgroup or stand-alone computer."

2. If the Log on To box doesn't appear, click Options to expand the dialog box.

3. Click the down arrow to the right of the Log on To box; then choose the correct domain name from the drop-down list.

4. Click OK to log on to Windows XP and your network domain.

✔ Tips

- See also "Joining a Domain" in Chapter 17.

- If you're at the Welcome screen, you can press Ctrl+Alt+Delete to make the classic logon prompt appear. If you have difficulty with this keyboard shortcut, hold down Ctrl and Alt; then press Delete twice.

LOGGING ON TO A DOMAIN

Managing User Profiles

A *user profile* contains an account's personal settings that Windows uses to configure the desktop each time a user logs on. Each user's desktop settings, network connections, and application settings are saved in C:\Documents and Settings\<*user name*> (which also contains the user's My Documents folder). Windows also maintains the *All Users* profile to store things common to everybody. You saw in "Installing Programs" in Chapter 6, for example, that you can copy icons to the Programs folder in the All Users profile to make applications available to everyone. All Users contains folders similar to those in individual user profiles (**Figure 16.16**).

When you create a new account, Windows determines the new user's desktop look by using the Default User profile (a hidden folder in Documents and Settings). To change this starting point, change the desktop, Start menu, Favorites menu, and theme of a normal account (your own, perhaps) to what you want the new default to be; then complete the following steps.

To change the Default User profile:

1. In Windows Explorer, choose Tools > Folder Options > View tab; select Show Hidden Files and Folders; then click OK.

2. Choose Start > Control Panel > Performance and Maintenance > System > User Profiles section > Settings (**Figure 16.17**).

3. Select the account whose settings you want to copy; then click Copy To.

4. Click Browse, and navigate to C:\Documents and Settings\Default User.

5. Click OK in each of the dialog boxes that Windows opened along the way.

6. In Explorer, re-hide hidden files.

Figure 16.16 What you see on your desktop—the Favorites menu, Send To menu, Start menu, and so on—is a combination of what's in your user profile and what's in the All Users profile.

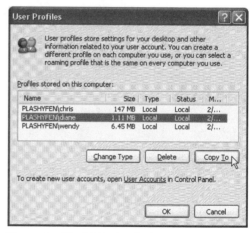

Figure 16.17 The (hidden) Default User profile determines what a newly created user sees on the desktop. Use the User Profiles dialog box to change the default appearance by copying other profile settings to the Default User profile.

✔ Tip

- **PRO** A *roaming user profile*, which your system administrator creates, is available every time you log on to any domain computer.

Managing User Profiles

SETTING UP A SMALL NETWORK

You create a *network* when you connect two or more computers to exchange data or share equipment. Cheap hardware and simpler configurations have made networks common in homes and small businesses. Setup is no longer the frustrating, complex experience it used to be, thanks to XP's Network Setup Wizard (but the hassle of buying and installing network hardware remains). Networks let you:

◆ **Share files.** No more straying floppies and duplicate files. You can designate disks, folders, and files as shared network resources.

◆ **Share printers and devices.** Any computer on the network can use a printer connected to another network computer. Ditto for backup devices, scanners, and other devices.

◆ **Share an Internet connection.** You can set up an Internet connection on one computer and let every computer on the network share that connection.

✔ Tips

■ You must be an administrator to perform many of the tasks in this chapter. See "Setting up User Accounts" in Chapter 16.

■ A geographically limited network that spans a small area (typically, a building or two) is called a *local area network* (*LAN*).

■ **PRO** This chapter describes how to set up a simple *workgroup* network (also called a *peer-to-peer* network), appropriate for 10 or fewer computers, on XP Home and Pro editions. XP Pro (but not Home) also supports *domain* networks for large organizations. A full-time geek sets up and administers a domain, which can have thousands of users. In this chapter, I don't cover domain setup, but I do describe how to join an existing domain. Ordinary users can set up and administer their own workgroup, but not a domain.

Understanding Network Types

Before you can set up XP's network software, you must install and configure network hardware. Your choice of network depends on your budget, the proximity of the computers to be networked, and your inclination to lay cable.

Ethernet

The most popular network standard, *Ethernet*, is cheap, fast, and reliable, and it imposes few limits on where the networked PCs are placed in your home or office. To create an Ethernet network, you'll need three components along with your PCs (**Figure 17.1**):

◆ **Network adapter.** Each computer must have a *network adapter* (about $25 U.S.) that provides a physical connection to the network. An adapter has an *RJ-45 jack* that you connect an Ethernet cable to. If your PC didn't come with an Ethernet jack, you can buy a *network interface card,* or *NIC* (a PCI expansion card that you open your computer to install), or an external network adapter that plugs into a USB port. For laptops, plug in a PC Card (about $80) that provides an Ethernet jack. All newer NICs are Plug and Play. For installation tips, see "Connecting Devices to Your Computer" in Chapter 8.

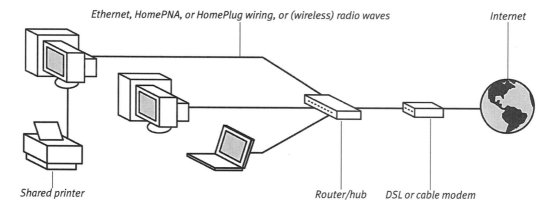

Ethernet, HomePNA, or HomePlug wiring, or (wireless) radio waves   *Internet*

Shared printer   *Router/hub*   *DSL or cable modem*

Figure 17.1 A typical network in which three computers share a printer and a high-speed Internet connection.

◆ **Ethernet cables.** The cables used in Ethernet networks are a little thicker than telephone cables, and the *RJ-45 connectors* at each end are wider than ordinary phone (RJ-11) connectors. You can buy Ethernet cables, called *10BaseT, 100BaseT, CAT5, CAT5e,* or *twisted-pair* cables, with preattached connectors ($5 to $50, depending on length). For custom lengths, you (or someone at the store) can cut the cable off a spool and attach the connectors. Each cable's length shouldn't exceed 100 meters (328 feet). If you're drilling through walls to lay cable, consider hiring a professional cable installer (or use a wireless network).

◆ **Hub.** On an Ethernet network, you connect each cable from a PC's network adapter to a central connection point called a *hub* (about $30)—a small box with a row of five to eight or more jacks (called *ports*) that accept RJ-45 connectors. Small green lights on the hub glow or flicker to signal an active connection. Computers communicate through the hub, so there's no direct connection between any two PCs. One port, labeled *Uplink,* connects to a router, broadband modem, or another hub to expand the network. The other ports usually are numbered, and it doesn't matter which port you plug which cable into. You can also connect shared peripherals, such as printers, to the hub.

If you have an Internet connection, consider using a *router/hub* instead of an ordinary hub to share the connection, as described in the next section.

Wireless

Wireless, or *Wi-Fi* (for *wireless fidelity*), networks have become popular because they're versatile, don't require cables, and have dropped in price. Most wireless network equipment uses the *802.11b* standard, known by Mac users as *AirPort.* A wireless network adapter (about $70) has a small antenna to transmit radio waves over a range of about 150 feet (through walls) but is subject to interference from pipes, weather, microwave ovens, and 2.4 GHz cordless phones. To share a high-speed Internet connection, you need a *base station* or *access point* (about $100). Turn on the *Wireless Equivalent Privacy* (WEP) security option to stop neighbors or passersby from stealing your Internet bandwidth and eavesdropping. For more information, see www.wi-fi.org.

Newer, pricier *802.11a* wireless equipment is faster than 802.11b gear (54 Mbps vs. 11Mbps) and doesn't get interference from cordless phones, but its range is shorter (60 feet vs. 150 feet). Wireless *a* and *b* devices aren't compatible—but mass-market routers and adapters often are *dual band,* meaning that they handle both.

Telephone wires

Network equipment certified by the *Home Phoneline Networking Alliance,* or *HomePNA,* uses your existing phone wires to connect computers. HomePNA networks don't interfere with other wire communications. You can use standard telephones, dial-up modems, DSL or cable modems, faxes, and answering machines simultaneously with HomePNA, because even though the devices use the same telephone wires, they occupy different frequency bands. These networks don't require a hub; instead, you plug your HomePNA network adapter (about $70) into the nearest phone jack. For more information, see www.homepna.org.

Electrical wires

Network equipment certified by the *Home-Plug Powerline Alliance* uses the existing electrical wiring in your home to connect computers. Unlike phone jacks, power outlets are available in almost every room, ready to pull double-duty as a power source and a network port. HomePlug networks are easy to set up; you plug your HomePlug network adapter (about $100) into the nearest power outlet. The network range is about 1000 feet, including the length that the wires travel in your walls. For more information, see www.homeplug.org.

✔ Tips

- If your network has only two computers that are close together, you can connect them with a *crossover cable* (about $10), which runs directly between the two PCs' Ethernet jacks. This no-hassle network saves you the cost of a hub and works exactly like a "real" Ethernet network. (If you expand the network to three computers, you must buy a hub.)

- Network speeds are measured in *megabits per second* (*Mbps*). 10 Mbps, called *10BaseT* or *Ethernet*, is adequate for most homes and small businesses. Most new hubs and adapters handle both 10BaseT and *100BaseT* or *Fast Ethernet* (100 Mbps) on the same network; look for the label *10/100* or *dual speed*. Pricier *Gigabit Ethernet* (1000 Mbps) equipment also is available. Wireless, HomePNA, and HomePlug speeds are comparable to 10BaseT. (Network speed doesn't affect Internet-connection speed; DSL and cable modems are 10 to 20 times slower than 10BaseT.)

- Check Microsoft's Hardware Compatibility List before you buy network equipment; see "Installing Plug and Play Devices" in Chapter 8. Manufacturers include 3Com, Belkin, D-Link, Linksys, Microsoft, Netgear, and SMC. No-name hardware is cheaper, but the few dollars extra that you pay for a name brand get you phone and Web support, as well as regularly updated drivers.

Sharing an Internet Connection

To share one Internet connection with every computer on a network, you have two options:

Install a router. A *router*—called a *residential gateway* by Microsoft but by no one else on the planet—is a small box that has one jack that connects to a hub and another jack that connects to a DSL, cable, or dial-up modem. A *router/hub* (about $70) doubles as a hub, sharing the modem's bandwidth among multiple Ethernet ports that the network PCs connect to. A slightly more expensive *router/switch* gives the modem's full bandwidth to multiple computers simultaneously. In most cases, you're better off with a router than dealing with ICS's limits, described next. Routers are easy to install and configure, use little power, let any PC go online at any time, and have built-in firewalls. To the outside world, a router appears to be a computer, but one without programs and hard drives to attack or infect. Buy a *Universal Plug and Play* (UPnP) router, which allows programs such as Windows Messenger and Remote Desktop to work.

Use Internet Connection Sharing (ICS). ICS is a built-in Windows feature that acts like a router in software. It's free but difficult to configure. You must designate one computer as the *host*, or *gateway*, PC through which all Internet traffic passes. For high-speed (broadband) Internet connections, the host PC must have *two* Ethernet adapters: one that connects to the DSL or cable modem and the other that connects to a hub. If the host PC is turned off, the other PCs—called *clients*—can't go online. See the sidebar for more information. Like a router, ICS works best with a high-speed Internet connection, but a dial-up modem works acceptably.

ICS Checklist

Some setup and troubleshooting tips for Internet Connection Sharing:

♦ Make sure that the host PC can go online *before* you run the Network Setup Wizard.

♦ The host PC must have Windows XP installed; the other PCs can be running earlier Windows versions (except Windows 95/3.*x*).

♦ Turn on the host PC *before* turning on the client PCs.

♦ If your DSL service has multiple static IP addresses, you can share a connection without designating a single PC as host.

♦ If you're using the Internet Connection Firewall, turn it on for all PCs *except* the host PC. See "Setting up an Existing Internet Account" in Chapter 12.

♦ For dial-up connections, if the host PC tries to maintain a continuous Internet connection by dialing repeatedly, choose (on the host) Control Panel > Network and Internet Connections > Network Connections; right-click your ISP's icon; choose Properties > Options tab; then uncheck Redial If Line Is Dropped.

♦ For dial-up connections, a client PC's browser or email program may report a "server/page unavailable" error before the host PC gets a chance to dial and go online. Wait a moment; then try again (that is, click Refresh or Send/Receive).

Running the Network Setup Wizard

When you've installed your network hardware according to the manufacturer's instructions, and everything's working properly, you're ready to run the Network Setup Wizard on *every* computer on the network. Windows 98/Me/2000/NT PCs can coexist peacefully with XP on the same network. If you're using Internet Connection Sharing, run the wizard on the *host* computer first.

Even if your network seems to be operating properly, play by the rules: Run the wizard to set workgroup names and IP addresses, configure file-sharing permissions, enable or disable the Internet Connection Firewall, and modify the registry. After the wizard finishes, you can tweak network settings manually.

To run the Network Setup Wizard:

1. In Control Panel, choose Network and Internet Connections > Network Connections; then click Set Up a Home Or Small Office Network in the task pane at left.

   or

   Choose Start > All Programs > Accessories > Communications > Network Setup Wizard.

   The wizard appears.

2. Click Next to skip the Welcome page.

3. On the Before You Continue page, click Checklist for Creating a Network for a list of the preparatory setup steps (many of which are described earlier in this chapter); then close the checklist window and click Next.

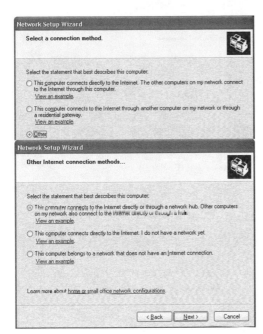

Figure 17.2 Select the option that best describes this computer's Internet connection. Click View an Example for a pop-up illustration of a particular configuration.

4. On the Select a Connection Method page, specify how to this computer connects to the Internet; then click Next.

Choose one of five following options. (To select one of the latter three options, select Other; then click Next) (**Figure 17.2**).

If you're using Internet Connection Sharing (ICS) and this computer is the *host* PC, select This Computer Connects Directly to the Internet; The Other Computers on My Network Connect to the Internet Through This Computer.

or

If you've installed a router (residential gateway), and you're not using ICS, select This Computer Connects to the Internet Through Another Computer or Through a Residential Gateway.

(If you're using ICS, and this computer is a *client* PC, you shouldn't see this page; you should see Figure 17.6, described later.)

or

If each PC connects to the Internet directly and independently, with no connection sharing, select This Computer Connects to The Internet Directly or Through a Network Hub; Other Computers on My Network Also Connect to the Internet Directly or Through a Hub.

or

If you have only one computer, select This Computer Connects Directly to the Internet; I Do Not Have a Network Yet.

or

If you don't plan to use the Internet, select This Computer Belongs to a Network That Does Not Have an Internet Connection.

(continues on next page)

5. If this computer has more than one Internet connection, select the one that you want to use and click Next (**Figure 17.3, top**); otherwise, skip to the next step.

6. Edit this computer's description and name, if necessary; then click Next (**Figure 17.3, middle**).

The name must be unique on the network; can be up to 15 characters long with no spaces or punctuation (except hyphens and apostrophes); and can't be the same as any user-account name.

7. If you don't want to use the default workgroup (network) name, *MSHOME,* change it here; then click Next (**Figure 17.3, bottom**).

Every PC on the network must have the same workgroup name.

8. Review your settings; then click Next (**Figure 17.4**).

The wizard displays an animation while it configures this computer.

9. On the wizard's final page (**Figure 17.5**), choose one of the following options, depending on the OS of the *next* network PC that you're going to run the wizard on.

If the next PC is running XP, select Just Finish the Wizard; I Don't Need to Run the Wizard on Other Computers. After that, click Next; then click Finish.

or

If the next PC is running an earlier Windows version, select Create a Network Setup Disk; click Next; and follow the onscreen instructions.

You'll need a blank, formatted floppy disk for the wizard to transfer a copy of itself to.

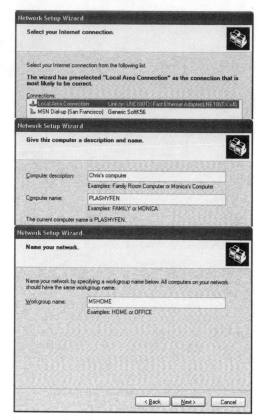

Figure 17.3 Top: Chapter 12 describes how these connections appeared on this list. Middle: Windows remembers the name given this computer during XP installation. Bottom: If you change the default workgroup name on one PC, you must change it on *all* network PCs. Don't just click Next to blow through this page when you run the wizard on the other PCs.

RUNNING THE NETWORK SETUP WIZARD

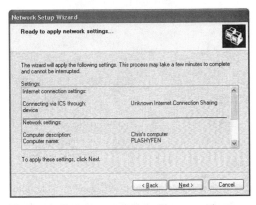

Figure 17.4 If you're unsatisfied with your settings, click Back to change them.

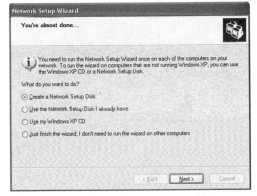

Figure 17.5 Your choice here depends on the Windows version that other network PCs are running.

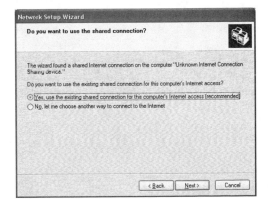

Figure 17.6 ICS users see this page when connecting to a network as a *client* PC. Select the first option for a simplified trip through the wizard.

10. After running the wizard on the first PC, repeat the process on the other network PCs.

If a PC has XP, start with step 1.

or

If a PC has an earlier Windows version, insert the network setup disk into the floppy drive; choose Start > My Computer; double-click 3½ Floppy (A:); then double-click netsetup.exe to start the wizard.

In either case, the preceding steps are the same, except that **Figure 17.6** appears instead of Figure 17.2 if you're using Internet Connection Sharing. (Also, don't create another network setup disk in step 9.)

After you restart the computer as instructed, the PC becomes part of the network.

✔ Tips

- Test the network: Choose Start > My Network Places to see the shared folders and disks that your PC can detect on other computers on the network (**Figure 17.7**). If you're running an earlier Windows version, the icon may be called Network Neighborhood. See also "Navigating the Network" later in this chapter.

- If you're unable to see icons for other computers in My Network Places (or in Network Neighborhood), make sure that your hub or router is plugged in and turned on; also make sure that all network adapters are firmly seated and cables are firmly connected to their jacks and ports. Also, use Device Manager to make sure that each network adapter is working properly; see "Managing Device Drivers" in Chapter 8.

- To change the computer name or description quickly, choose Control Panel > Performance and Maintenance > System > Computer Name tab (**Figure 17.8**). Don't rename your computer (or workgroup) when you're disconnected from the network; if you do, duplicate names might appear.

- If one of the network PCs has Windows Me, *don't* run that OS's Home Networking Wizard. Use the XP network setup disk to join the network.

- If you search Help Center for *net services commands,* you'll find some useful, geeky network commands. Type `net view` at a command prompt for a list of computers on your network, for example. `ping`, `tracert`, `ipconfig`, and `netstat` also are handy.

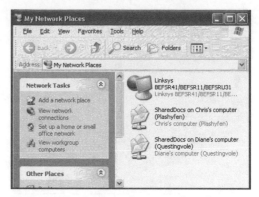

Figure 17.7 There's not much to see at first. The top icon shows this network's router. The other icons show the shared folders on this network's two computers. (This window starts out in Details view; Tiles view appears here.)

Figure 17.8 Click Change to change the computer name without slogging through the Network Setup Wizard.

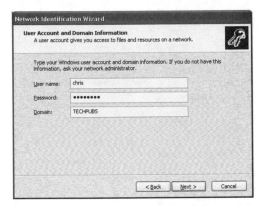

Figure 17.9 You can join a network domain during XP Pro installation or at any time afterward.

Joining a Domain

PRO If you're part of an organization that's large enough to have a domain, your network administrator probably added your PC to the domain for you. But you can join one yourself if the need arises. (See also "Logging on to a Domain" in Chapter16.)

To join a domain:

1. In Control Panel, choose Performance and Maintenance > System > Computer Name tab > Network ID button.
   The Network Identification Wizard appears.

2. Click Next to skip the Welcome page.

3. Select This Computer Is Part of a Business Network; then click Next.

4. Select My Company Uses a Network Domain; then click Next.

5. Click Next to skip the Network Information page.
   This page tells you what information you'll need to know in advance to join the domain.

6. Type the user name, password, and domain name supplied by your network administrator; then click Next (**Figure 17.9**).

7. If the Active Directory domain doesn't recognize your PC, the Computer Domain page appears; consult your network administrator and click Next.

8. Select Do Not Add a User at This Time; click Next; then click Finish.

9. Restart your computer to join the domain.

JOINING A DOMAIN

Navigating the Network

After the network is running, you can explore the contents of other people's *shared* disks, folders, and files on the network. (You'll learn how to share your own items in the next section.)

To explore the network:

1. Choose Start > My Network Places (**Figure 17.10**).

2. To see icons for each network computer, click View Workgroup Computers in the task pane at left (**Figure 17.11**).

3. Double-click shared items to open them, just as though you were working in your My Computer folder (**Figure 17.12**).

✔ Tips

■ In My Network Places (or Network Neighborhood), you can choose View > Arrange Icons By to sort icons by computer or network location.

■ It's easy to use Windows Explorer to move and copy items between network computers (**Figure 17.13**). See "Exploring Your Computer" in Chapter 5.

Figure 17.10 My Network Places shows shared disks and folders, including the ones on your own PC.

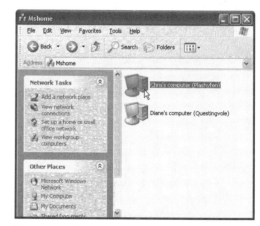

Figure 17.11 This view is great for crowded networks. Each network computer—instead of each shared resource—appears in this window.

NAVIGATING THE NETWORK

Figure 17.12 If you're looking for a shared item on a specific PC, double-click that computer's icon in Figure 17.11. That PC's shared resources aren't intermingled with those of other computers, as in Figure 17.10.

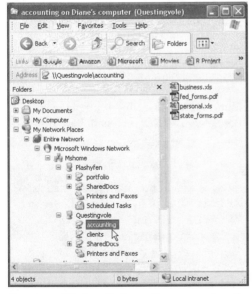

Figure 17.13 Windows Explorer offers an overview of the entire network.

■ In Explorer and on the desktop, you can rename, delete, select, and manipulate shared network items just as you would items on your local drive. See Chapter 5. (Beware: If you delete a shared item on another computer, the item bypasses the Recycle Bin and disappears forever.)

■ To use Search Companion to find shared network items, choose Start > Search (or press Ctrl+E in Explorer); choose Browse from the Look In drop-down list; click My Network Places; then click OK. For details, see "Searching for Files and Folders" in Chapter 5.

■ In applications, shared files are available via the standard File > Open and File > Save As dialog boxes. Click My Network Places in the left-side panel or choose it from the Look In drop-down list. File > Save saves a file in its original network location; to save a local copy on your hard disk, choose File > Save As.

(continues on next page)

NAVIGATING THE NETWORK

- You can *map* (assign) a shared disk or folder to a drive letter so that you can access the item via My Computer or the Open or Save As dialog boxes. To do so, in Explorer or My Network Places, choose Tools > Map Network Drive (**Figure 17.14**); select a drive letter; browse for an item or type its UNC name; check Reconnect at Logon; then click Finish. The new "drive" appears on your Explorer tree. To kill the mapping, choose Tools > Disconnect Network Drive.

- To treat an online storage space—such as an FTP site, intranet folder, or Web-based backup-service drive—as though it were connected to your network, click Add a Network Place on the task pane in My Network Places; then follow the onscreen instructions in the Add Network Place Wizard. Or if you're at a storage site in Internet Explorer, simply drag its icon from the Address bar to a local folder (typically, to My Network Places).

- **PRO** If you see a list of domains instead of a list of network computers, double-click the domain you want. You may have to type your password to gain access.

Figure 17.14 Mapping a shared network item lets you refer to it by a drive letter, the same way you refer to your local A or C drive.

UNC Names

The *Uniform Naming Convention* (*UNC*) is a system of naming network files, folders, and other shared resources so that an item's address identifies it uniquely on the network. UNC uses the following format:

`\\server\resource_pathname`

server is a computer name (assigned at XP installation or in the Network Setup Wizard) or an IP address; *resource_pathname* is a standard pathname (see "Exploring Your Computer" in Chapter 5). Some example UNCs for a folder, file, and printer are:

`\\amazon\budget\2003\qtr2`

`\\nile\books\mynovel\chap1.doc`

`\\yangtze\HPcolor`

To view a shared item quickly, type its UNC name in Explorer's Address bar or in the Start > Run dialog box.

Sharing Files

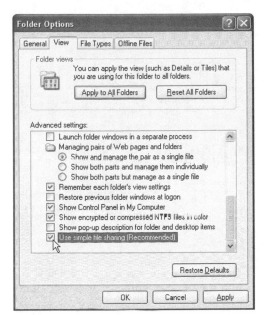

Figure 17.15 Oddly, this check box appears even if you're joined to a domain. No matter—checking it still won't activate Simple file sharing.

Just as networked computers can share a single Internet connection (as described earlier in this chapter) or network printer (see Chapter 7), they can share disks, folders, files, and devices—specific documents, MP3s, videos, CDs, or DVDs—from any networked PC, including yours. You in turn can access them if you're logged on to a network computer other than your usual one. File sharing abolishes "sneakernet"—transferring files by carrying floppies or CDs from one machine to another.

Windows XP offers two types of sharing: easy-to-use, slightly risky *Simple file sharing* and complex, secure *Classic file sharing*, inherited from Windows 2000. XP Home edition users have no choice: they must use Simple file sharing. Pro edition users can use either Simple or Classic file sharing unless they're joined to a domain, which *always* uses Classic file sharing.

PRO To switch between Simple and Classic file sharing:

1. In Windows Explorer, choose Tools > Folder Options > View tab.

2. Scroll to the bottom of the Advanced Settings list; then check Use Simple File Sharing (Recommended) to use Simple file sharing or uncheck it to use Classic file sharing (**Figure 17.15**).

3. Click OK (or Apply).

✔ Tip

■ If you're not on a network, you can use the techniques described here to share files with other users on the *same* PC. If they try to open a private folder or file, they see an "Access is denied" error message.

Simple file sharing

Simple file sharing is appropriate for a home or a small office, where you trust *all* the other people on the network. Configuration is easy; you can share a disk or folder by checking a box. Unfortunately, it's not very safe. *Every* network user can view your shared items and, if you're collaborating, edit and delete them, too. (Remember, files deleted across a network disappear instantly, bypassing the Recycle Bin.)

To share a disk or folder:

1. In Windows Explorer or My Computer, locate the disk or folder to share.

   You can share only disks and folders, not individual files. Sharing a disk or folder shares all its files, folders, and nested folders. Folder sharing is safer than disk sharing and doesn't make other users search your entire drive for a relevant folder.

2. Right-click the icon; then choose Sharing and Security (or choose Properties > Sharing tab).

   If you're sharing a disk, you'll see a warning; click If You Understand the Risk But Still Want to Share the Root of This Drive, Click Here.

3. In the Network Sharing and Security section, check Share This Folder on the Network (**Figure 17.16**).

4. In the Share Name box, type a name for the shared item.

   Other users see this name in their My Network Places windows, so use a short, descriptive name. (This network name won't change the item's name on *your* computer.)

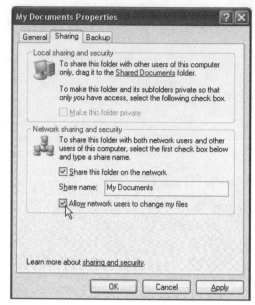

Figure 17.16 The sharing check boxes are available only if you ran the Network Setup Wizard on this computer and unchecked Make This Folder Private.

SHARING FILES

Figure 17.17 A hand cradles a shared item's icon.

5. To allow *all* users to change the files in the shared folder, check Allow Network Users to Change My Files.

Unchecking this box creates a *read-only* disk or folder. Other users can open what's inside it, but they can't edit, delete, or rename anything; neither can they add new files. They can, however, copy items *out* of the folder to their own disks.

6. Click OK.

The shared item's icon changes (**Figure 17.17**).

✔ Tips

- In step 5, you can't determine *which* users have full access to your files; either all do, or none does. Classic file sharing remedies this problem.

- You can't share Documents and Settings, Program Files, and Windows system folders. If you're not an administrator, you can't share folders in other users' profiles.

- Turning on a folder's sharing check boxes (refer to Figure 17.16) doesn't turn on the same check boxes for its nested folders, but those nested folders *are* shared, no matter what their check boxes say.

- To make a nested folder in a shared folder private, right-click the nested folder; choose Properties > Sharing tab; then check Make This Folder Private (refer to Figure 17.16).

- If you append a $ character to a share name in step 4 (GamblingDebts$, for example), that item is shared but *hidden*; it won't appear in anyone's My Network Places window. You and anyone else entrusted with the name can connect to the item by typing its UNC name—including the $—any place network paths are accepted, such as an Address bar or the Map Network Drive dialog box.

PRO Classic file sharing

Classic file sharing is more secure and flexible than Simple file sharing, at the cost of added complexity. You can set share permissions for individual users and groups to, say, grant some people full access, others read-only access, and others no access. (To turn on Classic file sharing, see "To switch between Simple and Classic file sharing" earlier in this section.)

Classic file sharing, roughly speaking, adds a permissions step to Simple file sharing. Unfortunately, the subtleties lurking behind that step—such as group policies, inherited permissions, and interactions with NTFS permissions—are quite complicated. I cover only the basics here. To appreciate this sharing model and use it competently, consult a book on Windows XP or 2000 network administration.

To share a disk or folder:

1. In Windows Explorer or My Computer, locate the disk or folder to share.

2. Right-click the icon; then choose Sharing and Security (or choose Properties > Sharing tab).

3. Select Share This Folder (**Figure 17.18**).

4. Accept or edit the proposed share name.

5. To avoid slowing your PC or to moderate network traffic, select Allow This Number of Users, and type the maximum number of people who can use the share at the same time.

   (If you click OK now, everyone on the network gets full access.)

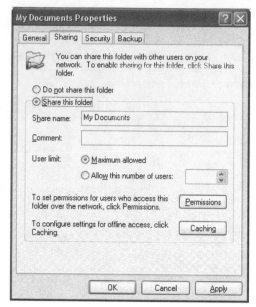

Figure 17.18 If you've ever used Simple file sharing, this dialog box is Classic file sharing's more complicated version of Figure 7.16.

SHARING FILES

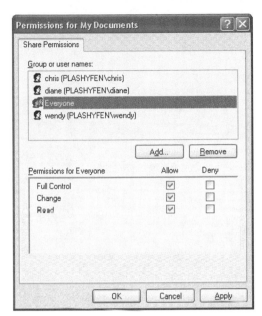

Figure 17.19 The top half of this dialog box lists users or groups that you've granted or denied access permissions. The bottom shows the access levels of the selected user or group.

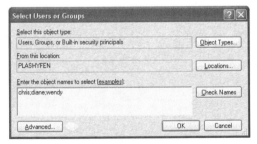

Figure 17.20 Spelling counts. Click Check Names to validate your "object" names before you add them.

6. Click Permissions (**Figure 17.19**).

   The first time that you share a folder, the Permissions dialog box contains only Everyone in the Group or User Names list.

7. To add users or groups, click Add; type one or more user or group names separated by semicolons; then click OK (**Figure 17.20**).

8. Click the name of a person or group.

9. Select Allow, Deny, or neither for each access-control entry.

   Full Control allows users to read, edit, delete, rename, and create files. In addition, users can change permissions and take file ownership (possibly locking you out of your own documents).

   Change allows users to read, edit, delete, and rename files but not create new files.

   Read allows users to read files but not edit, delete, or rename them.

10. Click OK in each of the open dialog boxes.

    The shared item's icon changes (refer to Figure 17.17).

WORKING REMOTELY

Remote Connections

Windows' remote-access features come in two flavors: remote networking (direct dialing and VPN) and remote control (Remote Desktop).

Remote networking lets your local PC access remote-PC or network resources over a modem link. If you double-click a Word file that resides on the remote PC, for example, the file is transmitted to your local PC and opens in your *local* copy of Word. If you have no copy of Word on your local PC, Word is transmitted, too—which would take days over dial-up. The moral: Avoid running programs that reside only on the remote PC, especially for slow connections.

Remote control doesn't have this problem; *all* work is done on the remote PC. If you double-click that same Word file, the remote PC's copy of Word opens. Only keystrokes, mouse gestures, and desktop images are transmitted between the two PCs. Unfortunately, refresh of a fully graphical screen over a dial-up connection is glacial.

Windows XP gives you several ways to connect to a computer remotely. If you're a business traveler on the road or a late sleeper working from home, for example, you can dial in from your laptop or home PC (the *local computer*) to the unattended, distant machine (the *remote computer* or *host computer*) in your office to access its files and resources. In this chapter, you'll learn three preferred remote-access techniques:

- Traditional **direct dialing** connects to a faraway PC via phone lines, probably racking up monstrous toll charges.

- **Virtual private networking (VPN)** lets you connect to a PC or network via the Internet, thus avoiding long-distance charges.

- **Remote Desktop** lets you control an XP-Pro-using remote computer, whose desktop appears on your local PC's screen just as though you were sitting at the remote PC's keyboard.

Dialing Direct

A direct (modem-to-modem) connection requires the remote computer to have a phone line that only it answers. (If a modem answers a voice call, the human caller gets an earful of squeal.) Before making your first call, you must set up both PCs.

To set up the remote computer:

1. Choose Start > Control Panel > Network and Internet Connections > Network Connections.

2. In the task pane at left, click Create a New Connection.

   The New Connection Wizard appears.

3. Click Next to skip the Welcome page.

4. Select Set up an Advanced Connection; then click Next.

5. Select Accept Incoming Connections; then click Next.

6. Check the box for your modem; then click Next (**Figure 18.1**).

7. Select Do Not Allow Virtual Private Connections; then click Next.

8. Check the boxes of the people who should be allowed to dial in to the remote PC; then click Next (**Figure 18.2**).

9. Confirm that all the networking software boxes are checked; then click Next.

10. Click Finish (**Figure 18.3**).

    Now the remote PC's modem answers incoming calls.

✔ Tip

■ In step 8, you can click Properties to turn on the *callback* security feature. This feature makes the remote PC hang up and call you back after you dial in, thwarting impersonators and reducing phone bills. For details, search for *callback* in Help Center.

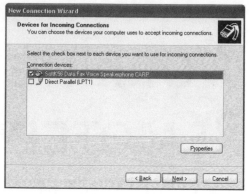

Figure 18.1 You can click Properties and check Disconnect a Call If Idle for More Than __ Mins to make the remote PC hang up automatically after an inactive period.

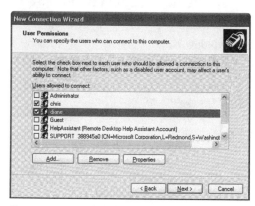

Figure 18.2 Don't check Guest; you'd create a security hole.

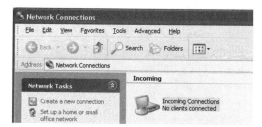

Figure 18.3 A new Incoming Connections icon appears in Network Connections when you finish the wizard. To change settings manually, right-click the icon; then choose Properties.

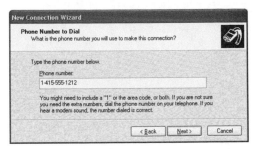

Figure 18.4 If you're a laptop user, you can add dialing codes when you make the call (in Figure 18.6), depending on what city you're in.

Figure 18.5 A new Dial-Up icon appears in Network Connections when you finish the wizard. To change settings manually, right-click the icon; then choose Properties.

Figure 18.6 Type your name and password exactly as you would if you were logging on to the remote PC in person.

To set up the local computer:

1. Choose Start > Control Panel > Network and Internet Connections > Network Connections.

2. In the task pane at left, click Create a New Connection.

   The New Connection Wizard appears.

3. Click Next to skip the Welcome page.

4. Select Connect to a Network at My Workplace; then click Next.

5. Select Dial-Up Connection; then click Next.

6. Type a connection name (such as *Work computer*); then click Next.

7. Type the phone number of the remote PC; then click Next (**Figure 18.4**).

8. Specify whether you want to add a connection shortcut to your desktop; then click Finish (**Figure 18.5**).

   Windows opens a Connect dialog box to call the remote PC; see the next task.

To make a call:

1. Double-click the desktop shortcut that you created in step 8 of the preceding task.

   or

   Double-click the Dial-Up icon in Network Connections (refer to Figure 18.5).

2. Type your name and password, and verify the phone number (**Figure 18.6**).

3. Click Dial to call the remote PC.

   A notification-area icon and pop-up balloon appear upon connection.

   You can check email, browse the Web, open shared folders, print documents, transfer files to the local PC, and so on.

4. To hang up, right-click the notification-area icon; then choose Disconnect.

DIALING DIRECT

Connecting to a Virtual Private Network Server

A *virtual private network* (*VPN*) lets you connect from one PC to another securely and privately by using the Internet as a conduit. Think of a VPN connection as a small steel pipe, carrying encrypted data, that links two PCs and tunnels *inside* the larger transparent pipe of the Internet.

By using an Internet connection (Chapter 12), you can travel worldwide and dial your ISP's *local* access number to connect to your far-off PC or network (a good reason for laptop owners to sign up with a national or international ISP). If your remote PC is rooted in place or doesn't move much, a high-speed (DSL or cable) Internet connection lets you communicate faster than any dial-up modem call. Together, high-speed lines and VPNs overcome direct dialing's twin evils: slow speeds and high costs.

Setting up a local PC to connect to a VPN server is easy. Setting up a remote PC to act as a VPN server can be another story, especially if it's part of a network. (Most people use VPNs to connect to an administered network at their workplace, rather than to their home PCs.) A VPN server needs an always-on Internet connection (DSL or cable) and a static IP address (see the sidebar). The local PC doesn't need these things.

To set up the remote computer as a VPN server:

1. Choose Start > Control Panel > Network and Internet Connections > Network Connections.

2. In the task pane at left, click Create a New Connection.
   The New Connection Wizard appears.

3. Click Next to skip the Welcome page.

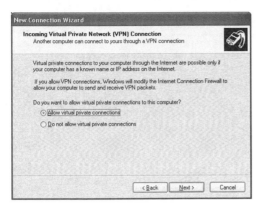

Figure 18.7 If you're using Internet Connection Firewall, Windows changes its settings behind the scenes to allow VPN connections.

4. Select Set up an Advanced Connection; then click Next.

5. Select Accept Incoming Connections; then click Next.

6. If the Devices for Incoming Connections page appears (refer to Figure 18.1), click Next.

   These settings don't apply to VPN servers.

7. Select Allow Virtual Private Connections; then click Next (**Figure 18.7**).

8. Check the boxes of the people who should be allowed to dial in to the remote PC; then click Next (refer to Figure 18.2).

(continues on next page)

IP Addresses and Remote Access

An *IP address* identifies your computer uniquely on the Internet for the purposes of communication. A *static* (or *fixed*) IP address is the same every time you connect; a *dynamic* IP address changes each time. An IP address is expressed as four numbers separated by dots: 127.160.0.1, for example.

Most Internet connections use dynamic IP addresses. (See the "Why Dynamic IP Addresses?" sidebar in Chapter 12.) That's unfortunate, because remote PCs (but not local PCs) require static IP addresses to work with VPN and Remote Desktop. Furthermore, connecting a private network to the Internet requires a *registered* IP address to prevent duplicates. Your ISP or network administrator can give you this information, or you can check yourself: Choose Start > All Programs > Accessories > Command Prompt; type ipconfig; then press Enter. Your IP address is *not* registered if it's in these ranges: 10.*x.x.x*, 169.254.*x.x*, 172.16.*x.x*–172.31.*x.x*, and 192.168.*x.x*.

If you don't have a registered, static IP address, your ISP may offer one for an extra fee. Otherwise, you can get a free (or cheap) unchanging alias for a dynamic IP address from a *dynamic DNS service* such as www.dyndns.org or www.easydns.com. Your chosen DNS name (*yourname*.dyndns.org, for example) is translated automatically into a numerical IP address, which communications software uses.

Another snag: VPN and Remote Desktop work fine with Windows' built-in Internet Connection Firewall and Internet Connection Sharing, but you'll have trouble if you've installed your own firewall (software or hardware) or router (see "Sharing an Internet Connection" in Chapter 17). All in all, setting up a VPN server or Remote Desktop may require consultation with a bonafide geek or your router manufacturer.

CONNECTING TO A VPN SERVER

9. Confirm that all the networking software boxes are checked; then click Next.

10. Click Finish (refer to Figure 18.3).

Now the remote PC listens to the Internet for incoming VPN connection requests.

To set up the local computer:

1. Choose Start > Control Panel > Network and Internet Connections > Network Connections.

2. In the task pane at left, click Create a New Connection.

The New Connection Wizard appears.

3. Click Next to skip the Welcome page.

4. Select Connect to a Network at My Workplace; then click Next.

5. Select Virtual Private Network Connection; then click Next.

6. Type a connection name (such as *Work VPN* or the VPN server name); then click Next.

The Public Network page may appear depending on your Network Connections setup.

7. If you have a dial-up Internet connection, select Automatically Dial This Initial Connection; choose the dial-up connection from the drop-down list; then click Next.

or

If you have an always-on Internet connection (DSL or cable), select Do Not Dial the Initial Connection; then click Next.

8. On the VPN Server Selection page, type the host name or static IP address of the computer that you want to connect to; then click Next (**Figure 18.8**).

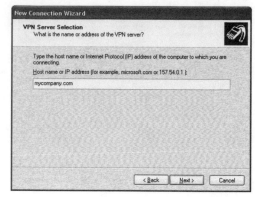

Figure 18.8 If you're connecting to a workplace network, type the host name or the IP address that your network administrator gave you. Or, if you signed up for a dynamic DNS service (see the sidebar), type the host's registered DNS name.

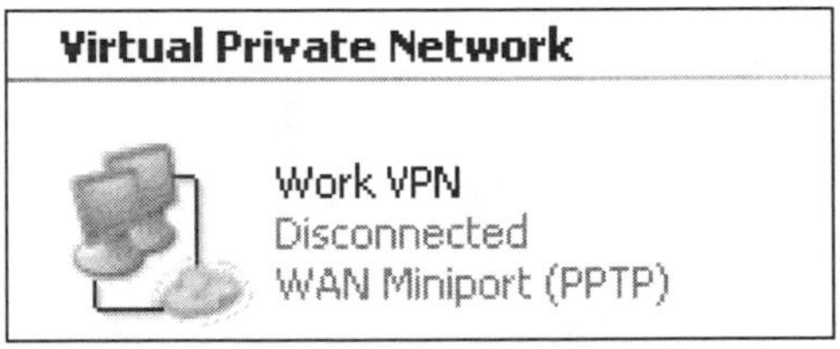

Virtual Private Network

Work VPN
Disconnected
WAN Miniport (PPTP)

Figure 18.9 A new Virtual Private Network icon appears in Network Connections when you finish the wizard. To change settings manually, right-click the icon; then choose Properties.

Figure 18.10 If you don't already have an Internet connection open, Windows offers to connect.

9. Specify whether you want to add a connection shortcut to your desktop; then click Finish (**Figure 18.9**).

   Windows opens a Connect dialog box to connect to the VPN server; see the next task.

To connect to a VPN server:

1. Double-click the desktop shortcut that you created in step 9 of the preceding task.

   or

   Double-click the Virtual Private Network icon in Network Connections (refer to Figure 18.9).

2. Type your name and password (**Figure 18.10**).

3. Click Connect to connect to the VPN server.

   A notification-area icon and pop-up balloon appear upon connection.

   You can check email, browse the Web, open shared folders, print documents, transfer files to the local PC, and so on.

4. To hang up, right-click the notification-area icon; then choose Disconnect.

Controlling a Computer with Remote Desktop

Remote Desktop lets you connect to a remote XP Pro computer and use it as though you were sitting in front of it. Much more than a simple direct-dial or VPN connection, Remote Desktop lets you control the remote PC's full desktop, with its Start menu, taskbar, icons, documents, and programs. Programs run on the remote computer, and only the keyboard input, mouse input, and display output are transmitted over the connection. The *remote computer* is the PC that you want to control from afar. The *local,* or *client, computer* is the one that you'll be sitting at, driving the remote PC. The requirements are:

◆ **PRO** **Remote computer.** An XP Pro PC with an Internet or network connection, or a dial-up modem that's configured to answer incoming calls automatically. If you're connecting over the Internet, a registered, static IP address is required (see the sidebar in the preceding section).

◆ **Local computer.** A PC running any version of Windows since Windows 95 can control the remote PC. This PC must have access to the remote PC via a network, Internet, VPN, or dial-up connection.

✔ Tips

■ Remote Desktop replaces Windows 2000's Terminal Services.

■ You can use Remote Desktop to let someone connect to *your* PC to give you technical help, much like Remote Assistance (Chapter 3), except that you don't have to be present at your PC to accept the connection.

■ Commercial alternatives to Remote Desktop include Carbon Copy, CoSession, LapLink, and pcAnywhere. Read reviews first; these programs vary in price, ease of setup, connection options, and response time. Unlike Remote Desktop, they can control PCs running all modern Windows versions, not only XP Pro. Or try VNC, a *free* alternative that works with Unix and Mac too; see www.uk.research.att.com/vnc/.

Figure 18.11 Check the bottom check box to let other users control this computer remotely.

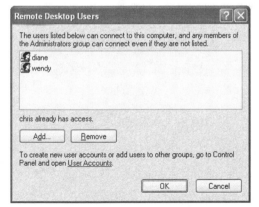

Figure 18.12 Don't add anybody you don't trust to this list. For security reasons, only users with password-protected accounts can make a Remote Desktop connection.

Your local PC running Windows XP (Home or Pro edition) won't need additional software to control the remote computer. If you use Windows 95, 98, Me, NT 4, or 2000 on the local computer, you must install Remote Desktop Connection client software from the Windows XP Pro CD.

To set up a non-XP local computer:

1. Insert the Windows XP Professional CD into the local PC's drive.

2. When the Welcome to Microsoft Windows XP window appears, click Perform Additional Tasks.

   If this window doesn't appear, open the CD in Windows Explorer, and double-click setup.exe in the topmost (root) folder.

3. Click Set up Remote Desktop Connection. The InstallShield Wizard for Remote Desktop Connection appears.

4. Follow the onscreen instructions.

To set up the remote computer:

1. Choose Start > Control Panel > Performance and Maintenance > System (or press Windows logo key + Break); then click the Remote tab.

2. In the Remote Desktop section, check Allow Users to Connect Remotely to This Computer (**Figure 18.11**).

3. Click Select Remote Users to change which users can connect remotely (**Figure 18.12**).

   Initially, the logged-on user and all users with Administrator accounts can connect (see "Setting up User Accounts" in Chapter 16). To add users, click Add; then type one or more user names, separated by semicolons.

(continues on next page)

4. Click OK in each of the open dialog boxes.
   Now the remote computer listens for
   incoming Remote Desktop connection
   requests.

✔ Tip

■ If you're connecting over an Internet
   connection protected by XP's Internet
   Connection Firewall, take this extra step:
   Choose Start > Control Panel > Network
   and Internet Connections > Network Connections; right-click the Internet connection; choose Properties > Advanced tab >
   Settings button > Services tab; then check
   Remote Desktop.

To connect to a remote desktop:

1. Connect to the Internet normally.
   Skip this step if the remote PC is on your
   local area network.

2. Choose Start > All Programs >
   Accessories > Communications >
   Remote Desktop Connection.
   The Remote Desktop dialog box appears.

3. Click Options to expand the dialog box,
   if necessary; then fill in the Logon
   Settings section (**Figure 18.13**).

Figure 18.13 In the Computer box, type the remote
computer's network name, IP address, or registered
DNS name. Type your name and password (and
domain, if necessary) exactly as you would if you
were logging on the remote PC in person.

4. Click Connect.

Your screen goes black momentarily; then the remote PC's desktop fills the screen, hiding *your* desktop and taskbar (**Figure 18.14**).

Now you can operate the distant PC as though you were sitting in front of it. All your actions—running programs, printing, sending email, whatever—happen on the remote PC.

Anyone looking at the remote PC in person sees a Welcome screen or an Unlock Computer dialog box; that person can't see what you're doing.

Restore—Displays the remote desktop in a floating, resizable window on your own desktop

Minimize—Reduces the remote desktop to a taskbar button on your own desktop

Pushpin—Locks this title bar in place or makes it hide automatically

Close—Disconnects the remote PC but doesn't log off

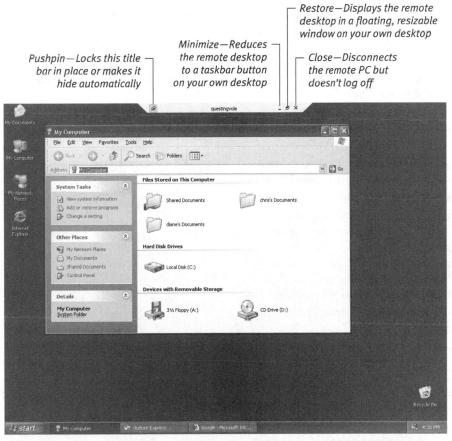

Figure 18.14 A full-screen remote desktop shows a title bar at the screen's top edge, letting you switch between your own desktop and the remote desktop. The title bar retracts from view unless you lock it or move your pointer to the top edge.

✔ Tips

- Clicking Restore (refer to Figure 18.14) puts the remote desktop in a floating, resizable window on your *local* desktop (**Figure 18.15**).

- You can use standard Cut, Copy, and Paste to transfer text, graphics, and files between the two PCs. If both desktops are visible (as in Figure 18.15), you can drag between local and remote windows.

- Clicking Close (refer to Figure 18.14) disconnects the remote PC but doesn't log it off; it leaves your documents open and programs running, as though you had used Fast User Switching (see "Logging on and Logging off Windows XP" in Chapter 1). To pick up where you left off, reconnect via Remote Desktop or log on in person at the remote PC. To log off the remote PC, choose Log Off from *its* Start menu, not yours.

- To shut down the remote PC, choose Start > Windows Security remotely; then use Task Manager's Shut Down menu to shut down, restart, disconnect, and so on. (The Windows Security command appears only when you're connected remotely.)

- If someone else is already logged on the remote PC that you're connecting to, Windows warns you that you're about to bump that person off. The message that you see depends on whether Fast User Switching is enabled on the remote PC (see "Controlling the Logon Process" in Chapter 16):

Fast User Switching is turned on. You'll see **Figure 18.16** when you try to connect. If you click Yes, the other user sees **Figure 18.17** and must respond within seconds or be disconnected without ceremony. Fortunately, that user remains logged on, loses no work, and can resume her session later as she left it, just as in Fast User Switching.

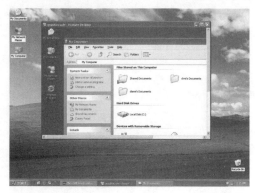

Figure 18.15 Click Restore to show your own desktop. To return to full-screen view, click Maximize in the remote window's title bar.

Figure 18.16 If someone else is logged on the remote PC, you're given a chance to cancel your connection request.

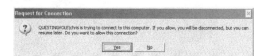

Figure 18.17 The logged-on user can reject your attempted intrusion.

Figure 18.18 Clicking Yes here won't make you any friends. The other user is logged off instantly and loses all unsaved work.

Figure 18.19 This vaguely puzzling message means that someone else has logged on to the remote PC in person and disconnected your session. You don't lose your unsaved work.

Table 18.1

Keyboard Shortcuts

LOCAL DESKTOP SHORTCUT	REMOTE DESKTOP SHORTCUT	DESCRIPTION
Alt+Tab	Alt+Page Up	Switches between programs
Alt+Shift+Tab	Alt+Page Down	Switches between programs in reverse order
Alt+Esc	Alt+Insert	Cycles through programs in the order in which they were started
Ctrl+Esc	Alt+Home	Opens the Start menu
Ctrl+Alt+Del	Ctrl+Alt+End	Displays Task Manager or, for domains, the Windows Security dialog box
N/A	Ctrl+Alt+Break	Switches the remote desktop between a window and full screen
N/A	Alt+Delete	Displays the active window's Control menu

Fast User Switching is turned off. You'll see **Figure 18.18** when you try to connect. If you click Yes, the other user is logged off without warning and loses all unsaved work.

■ If someone logs on to the remote PC in person while *you're* connected, the situation is opposite: *Your* remote session gets bumped off. If Fast User Switching is enabled on the remote PC, you'll see **Figure 18.19**, remain logged on, and lose no unsaved work; you can reconnect after the other party logs off. If Fast User Switching is turned off, you're logged off instantly, losing all unsaved work.

■ If the Remote Desktop window is maximized (refer to Figure 18.14), the standard Windows keyboard shortcuts apply to the *remote* computer. Alt+Tab, for example, switches between programs on the distant PC, not your local one. But if the Remote Desktop window is active and floating on your desktop (refer to Figure 18.15), those same shortcuts apply to the *local* PC. (Alt+Tab will switch between locally running programs.) Fortunately, keyboard junkies can use the standard shortcuts in the first column of **Table 18.1** to control the *local* desktop and the second-column shortcuts to perform the equivalent function on an active, floating Remote Desktop window.

■ *Before* you connect, you can configure the way Remote Desktop works by using the tabs in the Remote Desktop Connection dialog box. You may want to try a remote session or two before adjusting the default settings.

(continues on next page)

The **General** tab (refer to Figure 18.13) lets you enter or change logon or connection settings. You can have Windows save your password or all your current settings to speed future connections, which is useful if you connect to multiple PCs.

The **Display** tab (**Figure 18.20**) controls the remote desktop's size (screen resolution) and color depth.

The **Local Resources** tab (**Figure 18.21**) controls sound, keyboard, and local devices.

The **Programs** tab controls which, if any, programs run automatically upon connection.

The **Experience** tab (**Figure 18.22**) lets you tell Windows your connection speed so that it can turn off eye candy to improve performance. When you first used Remote Desktop, for example, you may have noticed that the remote desktop didn't display a background. This time-waster is disabled by default in this tab.

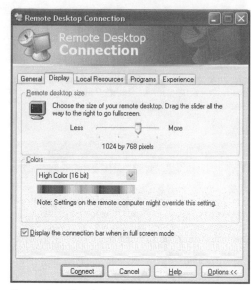

Figure 18.20 The size option is useful if the local and remote screen sizes differ.

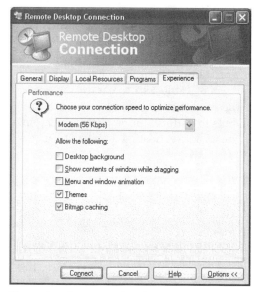

Figure 18.22 Remote Desktop has a default collection of settings for each connection speed, but you can use your own settings.

Figure 18.21 Use this tab to specify where sounds should play, which PC responds to keyboard shortcuts, and which local devices to display on the remote desktop.

MAINTENANCE AND TROUBLESHOOTING

New drivers learn to change the oil in their cars, and new computer users grapple with proper care and feeding of their PCs. Periodic checkups and routine maintenance tame temperamental machinery and keep your system running smoothly. In this chapter, you'll learn how to use Windows tools to monitor your PC's health and:

- Update Windows XP with the latest bug fixes from Microsoft

- Restore your PC to a previous working condition

- Keep your hard drives purring

- Back up your data

- Schedule tasks

- Recover from a crash

- View or edit the Registry

✔ Tip

- Type **troubleshooting** in the Help Center index to see a list of XP's troubleshooting wizards and other tools designed to identify and resolve hardware, software, and networking problems.

Updating Windows XP

Over time, Microsoft publishes patches, bug fixes, and other improvements on its Web site. These changes include minor additions to the Windows feature set, upgrades to the freebie programs, and driver updates. The most important changes are those designated *critical updates* or *hotfixes,* which plug security holes or fix stability problems. Periodically, Microsoft combines many of these fixes into a package called a *Service Pack.* (As I write this chapter, Service Pack 1a—SP1a—is the current release.) Installing a Service Pack is equivalent to, and much less trouble than, installing its constituent fixes piecemeal. But you shouldn't wait for an SP to install critical updates, which appear with alarming regularity.

Use Automatic Update to choose how and when updates are installed on your PC. When you first install Windows, notification-area pop-up messages remind you to set up this feature, but you can adjust its options at any time.

If you don't want your PC to contact the mother ship without your permission, you can turn off the Keep My Computer up to Date option (described next) and use Windows Update to visit the Microsoft Update Web site, `http://windowsupdate.microsoft.com`.

To set up automatic updating:

1. In Control Panel, choose Performance and Maintenance > System (or press Windows logo key+Break); then click the Automatic Update tab (**Figure 19.1**).

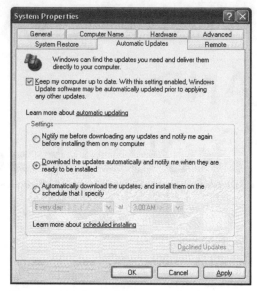

Figure 19.1 The first option is appropriate for dial-up connections; the second, for always-on connections (DSL or cable); and the third, for workplace PCs that get updates from a central network location.

Figure 19.2 After the download completes, a notification-area icon appears with a message that the updates are ready to install.

Figure 19.3 When you click the icon or message in Figure 19.2, a description of the updates appears. Review the list; uncheck specific updates (if you like); then click Install to proceed.

Figure 19.4 Windows compares Microsoft's list of all available updates against the updates that you've already installed.

2. Check the Keep My Computer up to Date box to turn on automatic updates.
   Uncheck this box if you want to update Windows manually (described next).

3. In the Settings section, specify whether you want to be notified *before* the update is downloaded (top option) or *after* it has been downloaded and is ready to install (middle option); you can also make Windows download and install updates on a regular schedule that you specify (third option).

4. Click OK (or Apply).
   From now on, whenever Windows finds an update, it displays an icon in the notification area, which you can click to begin installation (**Figures 19.2** and **19.3**).

To update Windows manually:

1. Choose Start > All Programs > Windows Update.
   or
   In Internet Explorer, choose Tools > Windows Update.

2. If a Security Warning dialog box appears, click Yes to install the latest version of Windows Update Control; then restart your PC and begin again.

3. On the Windows Update home page, click Scan for Updates (**Figure 19.4**).

(continues on next page)

UPDATING WINDOWS XP

4. Click a category to see its updates (**Figure 19.5**); then choose to install or decline each update, using its Add or Remove button.

5. Click Review and Install Updates (**Figure 19.6**).

6. Click Install Now (**Figure 19.7**).

Follow the onscreen instructions. You may have to accept a license agreement and restart your PC.

✔ Tips

■ Downloads occur in the background, letting you continue working uninterrupted.

■ Typically, you can install a critical update only by itself, separately from noncritical ones. Run Windows Update again to install the noncritical updates.

■ To have Windows remind you about pending updates, click Remind Me Later in Figure 19.3; then specify the amount of time Windows should wait before reminding you.

■ If you choose not to install a specific update that's been downloaded, Windows deletes it from your PC. If you change your mind later, click Declined Updates in Figure 19.1 to download it again.

■ The Update Web site has a privacy statement describing the information that Windows Update sends to Microsoft.

■ To uninstall an update, see "Removing Programs" in Chapter 6.

■ Windows Update works with only Internet Explorer.

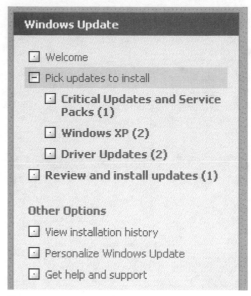

Figure 19.5 Any new updates are listed in the left pane in three categories.

Figure 19.6 Each update has Add and Remove buttons.

Figure 19.7 Click Install Now to start the download and installation process. If you install a Service Pack or major updates to Internet Explorer, don't expect it to be quick.

- If you've used Windows Update before, click View Installation History (refer to Figure 19.4 or 19.5) to see a list of previously installed updates.

- The General tab of the System Properties dialog box will tell you the edition, version, and Service Pack of your Windows XP copy.

- Numerous updates are time-consuming to download. If you have a slow connection and several PCs to update, you can download update files and install them manually on each PC (or burn them on a CD). To do so, in Windows Update (refer to Figure 19.4), click Personalize Windows Update; check the Display the Link to the Windows Update Catalog Under See Also box (yes, that really is its name); click Save Settings; click the newly appeared Windows Update Catalog link in the left pane; then follow the onscreen instructions to see a list of downloadable updates.

Updating Device Drivers

Windows Update can provide new device drivers for your PC's hardware; click the Driver Updates category in Figure 19.5 for a list of recommendations. Unlike the other categories, this one should be approached skeptically, because Windows Update has a habit of recommending the *wrong* drivers for some hardware.

I recommend that you install Microsoft drivers for only Microsoft hardware, such as mice, keyboards, and game controllers. For other products, download drivers from the manufacturers' Web sites directly. And don't be surprised if they *don't* offer an updated driver; it means only that Windows Update guessed wrong about your equipment. For details, see "Installing a New Device" in Chapter 8.

Getting System Information

System Information compiles and reports information about your PC's hardware, drivers, system resources, and Internet settings. This overview saves you from visiting scores of Control Panel dialog boxes to see how your PC is configured. You can find information quickly to give to a techie who's troubleshooting your system.

To display system data:

1. Choose Start > All Programs > Accessories > System Tools > System Information.

2. Use the Explorerlike tree to display information in the various categories (**Figure 19.8**):

   Hardware Resources displays hardware settings, such as IRQs and memory addresses. The Conflicts/Sharing view identifies devices that are sharing resources or are in conflict.

   Components displays Windows configuration information for device drivers, as well as networking and multimedia software.

   Software Environment displays a snapshot of the software loaded into computer memory. Use this information to see whether a process is still running or to check version information.

   Internet Settings displays browser-related security, connection, and version data.

✔ Tips

■ To get system information for a different computer on your network, choose View > Remote Computer.

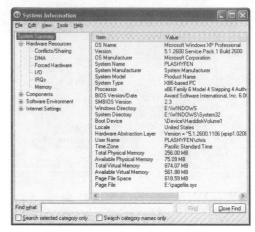

Figure 19.8 To find system data, type a search phrase in the Find What box at the bottom of the window; check the appropriate search-option boxes; then click Find.

■ To save system data in a System Information file—which you can archive or email to a techie to open in his copy of System Information—choose File > Save. To save system data in a text file, choose File > Export.

■ File > Print produces a 50-page printout. I recommend exporting the data to a text file and printing your choice of sections in Notepad.

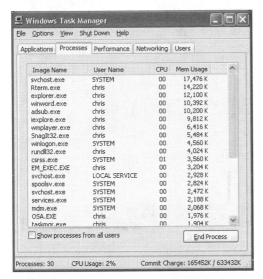

Figure 19.9 This tab shows all programs (including background tasks) running on your PC. Click a column header to sort by that column; this display is sorted by memory use.

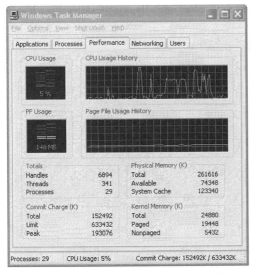

Figure 19.10 This tab shows real-time graphs of the load on your CPU and virtual memory, expressed as a percentage of capacity.

Managing Tasks

Task Manager is one of the most useful tools in Windows. It displays running programs, background processes, performance statistics, network activity, and user information. It also can shut misbehaving programs.

To start Task Manager:

1. Right-click a blank space on the taskbar; then choose Task Manager (or press Ctrl+Shift+Esc).

2. Click any of the following tabs:

   Applications for a list of foreground applications and the status of each one. See also "Killing Unresponsive Programs" in Chapter 6.

   Processes for a list of every program running on your computer, including background programs and those shown in the Applications tab (**Figure 19.9**).

   Performance for real-time graphs and statistics that show your system's performance (**Figure 19.10**).

   Networking is similar to the Performance tab, except that it shows real-time graphs of network traffic.

   Users displays logged-on users and the status of each one. See "Logging on and Logging off Windows XP" in Chapter 1.

✔ Tips

- Use the Options and View menus to select preferences. These menus' commands change depending on the selected tab.

- Turn on Options > Always on Top to make Task Manager remain in front of all other windows unless it's minimized.

- You can right-click an entry in the Applications, Processes, or Users tab for a shortcut menu.

- The Processes tab lists filenames, not application names. Internet Explorer appears as `iexplore.exe`, for example.

MANAGING TASKS

413

Restoring Your System

If your system stops running correctly or becomes persistently unstable—thanks to an incompatible program, faulty driver, or bad system setting, or for no apparent reason—use System Restore to return your computer's configuration to its previous, working state without risk to personal documents, email, cookies, and Favorites.

System Restore protects only Windows *system* files and settings; use Backup (described later in this chapter) to protect your personal data files and documents. Neither can you rely on System Restore to protect you from viruses. By the time you discover the infection, it may have spread to other files that System Restore doesn't touch, in which case rolling back does you no good. Use an antivirus program instead.

System Restore runs invisibly in the background, monitoring and taking snapshots of critical system files and Registry entries. These snapshots, called *restore points,* are created the first time that you boot XP and daily thereafter; every time that you install a program through Windows Installer or InstallShield; or whenever Windows Update or Automatic Update runs. Before you make a major change to your system or its settings, you can create a restore point manually.

To create a restore point manually:

1. Choose Start > All Programs > Accessories > System Tools > System Restore (**Figure 19.11**).

2. Select Create a Restore Point; then click Next.

3. Type a name for the restore point; then click Create (**Figure 19.12**). Windows creates a restore point and adds the date and time to its description.

4. Click Close.

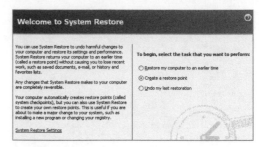

Figure 19.11 Create a restore point before you install an iffy driver or program, or change the Registry.

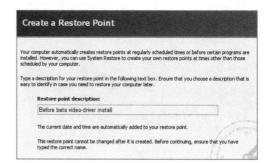

Figure 19.12 Give the restore point a meaningful name.

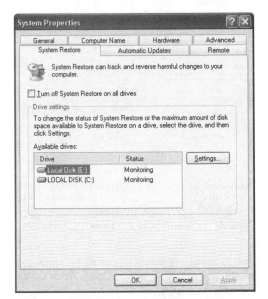

Figure 19.13 By default, System Restore monitors changes to every drive on your system and reserves 12 percent of each drive to archive restore points.

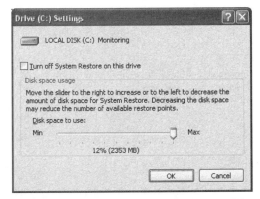

Figure 19.14 Drag the slider to the left to reclaim disk space from System Restore (but reduce the number of saved restore points). In general, don't set this value below five percent.

- On each drive, Windows stores backup configurations in the hidden/system folder System Volume Information, which you can unhide but not move, rename, or delete.

By default, System Restore is turned on, using up to a hefty 12 percent of each hard drive to store copies of your system configuration. That's almost 5 GB of a 40 GB drive. You can allocate less space or turn off System Restore.

To configure System Restore:

1. In Control Panel, choose Performance and Maintenance > System > System Restore tab (**Figure 19.13**).

2. Adjust any of the following settings:

   To disable System Restore, check Turn off System Restore on All Drives.

   To change the disk space allocated to restore points, click a drive in the Available Drives list; click Settings; drag the Disk Space to Use slider to change the allocation; then click OK (**Figure 19.14**).

   To disable System Restore on a specific drives, check Turn off System Restore on This Drive in Figure 19.14. You can turn off System Restore safely for nonsystem drives that store only documents or backup files.

3. Click OK (or Apply).

✔ Tips

- Turning off System Restore, even for an instant, erases existing restore points.

- System Restore deletes restore points older than 90 days automatically.

- System Restore requires at least 200 MB of free disk space. When a drive runs low on space, System Restore turns itself off automatically and silently, losing all that drive's restore points. If you receive a "low disk space" warning for a drive, check that drive's status in Figure 19.13 to see whether it's listed as Suspended. System Restore turns itself back on when you free enough space.

RESTORING YOUR SYSTEM

When your PC behaves badly, you can return Windows to one of the restore points that System Restore, or you, created. But do so only as a last resort. Remember, if a driver upgrade doesn't work out, you can roll back *just* the driver rather than your entire system. See "Managing Device Drivers" in Chapter 8.

To restore your system:

1. Choose Start > Help and Support.

2. In the Pick a Task section, click Undo Changes to Your Computer With System Restore.

3. Select Restore My Computer to an Earlier Time; then click Next (refer to Figure 19.11).

4. On the calendar, click the boldface date on which your computer last worked properly.

5. Click one of the restore points listed to the right of the calendar; then click Next (**Figure 19.15**).

6. Heed the warning to save your changes and close any open programs; then click Next.

   System Restore rewinds your system and restarts Windows automatically.

7. Click OK in the Restoration Complete window that appears after you log on (**Figure 19.16**).

✔ Tips

■ If restoring the system didn't fix your problem (or made it worse), you can repeat the process and choose a restore point farther back in the past. Or you can undo the restoration: Select Undo My Last Restoration in step 2 (refer to Figure 19.11); then follow the onscreen instructions.

■ If you have a severe startup problem, run System Restore in safe mode. See "Recovering After a Crash" later in this chapter.

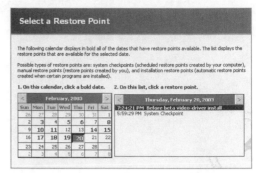

Figure 19.15 System Restore stores several weeks of restore points, depending on how much space you've allocated to it. Boldface days indicate restore points. Click the < and > buttons to move through the months.

Figure 19.16 Success. Now check your system to see whether it's running correctly.

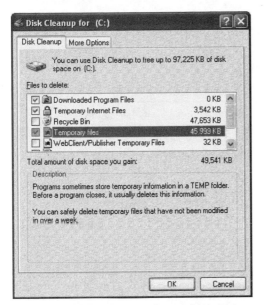

Figure 19.17 Disk Cleanup searches your drive and then shows you temporary files, Internet cache files, and unnecessary program files that you can delete safely.

Cleaning up a Disk

Over time, your hard disk will accumulate temporary files, stale components, recycled junk, and space-wasters that you can remove safely. Use Disk Cleanup to reclaim disk space if you're running out of room.

To remove unneeded files:

1. Choose Start > All Programs > Accessories > System Tools > Disk Cleanup; select a drive (if you have more than one); then click OK.

   or

   Right-click a drive icon in My Computer; then choose Properties > General tab > Disk Cleanup.

   or

   Choose Start > Run; type cleanmgr; press Enter; select a drive; then click OK.

2. In the Disk Cleanup dialog box, check the boxes of the files that you want to delete (**Figure 19.17**).

   The right column shows how much space you can make available. The text below the list box describes the selected option.

3. Click OK.

✔ Tips

- The More Options tab contains three other cleanup tools that let you remove optional Windows components, installed programs, and all but your most recent System Restore restore point.

- Avoid deleting Downloaded Program Files, which are often useful add-ins.

- The Temporary Files option deletes only temporary files more than one week old, so the right column may show 0 KB even if your temporary folder contains many files. To clean out this folder manually, close all programs; choose Start > Run; type %temp%; press Enter; then delete the files in the folder window that appears.

Defragmenting a Disk

When a file grows, it won't fit back into its original disk location and becomes physically fragmented into noncontiguous pieces on the disk. As more files become fragmented, Windows has to retrieve the chopped-up pieces and reassemble them, impairing the disk's performance and reliability. Disk Defragmenter consolidates fragmented files, making both files and free space contiguous. Large blocks of available space make it less likely that new files will be fragmented.

To defragment a disk:

1. Exit all programs; disable antivirus software; then run Disk Cleanup.

2. Choose Start > All Programs > Accessories > System Tools > Disk Defragmenter.

   or

   Right-click a drive icon in My Computer; then choose Properties > Tools tab > Defragment Now.

   or

   Choose Start > Run; type `dfrg.msc`; then press Enter.

3. Click a drive to defragment.

4. Click Analyze.

   The program analyzes the disk and makes a recommendation (**Figures 19.18** and **19.19**).

5. Click Defragment to start defragmentation (**Figure 19.20**).

   Colored graphs and the status bar display defragmentation progress.

6. Click Close in the dialog box that appears when defragmentation completes.

7. Choose File > Exit, or defragment other disks as necessary.

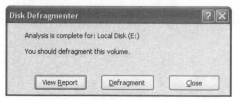

Figure 19.18 Defragmentation is a time-consuming process; don't bother for drives that are only slightly fragmented. To see the extent of the fragmentation, click View Report for a...

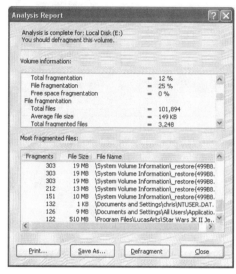

Figure 19.19 ...list of fragmented files and the number of pieces they're in.

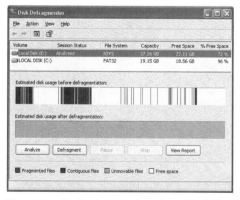

Figure 19.20 For best results, do nothing else during the delicate defragmentation process. If you *must* do something, click Pause.

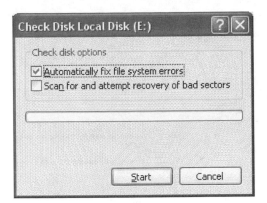

Figure 19.21 The two options of the Check Disk utility are better suited to NTFS-formatted drives than to FAT32-formatted drives. For a comparative discussion of Windows XP file systems, see "Getting Ready to Install Windows XP" in Appendix A.

Figure 19.22 This message appears if the disk is in use. Check Disk runs the next time you restart your system. The disk won't be available for other tasks during the check.

✔ Tip

■ The best protection against disk dings from power fluctuation is an Uninterruptible Power Supply (UPS). See "Conserving Power" in Chapter 4.

Checking for Disk Errors

Improper Windows shutdowns—usually caused by power outages, mechanical problems, or system crashes (blue screens)—may create defects on disk surfaces. These errors can cause numerous problems, such as random crashes, data corruption, or the inability to save or open files. Check Disk, a more powerful upgrade to the Windows 9*x* ScanDisk utility, scans the disk surface for errors and fixes any that it finds.

To detect and repair disk errors:

1. Exit all programs.

2. Right-click a drive icon in My Computer; then choose Properties > Tools tab > Check Now (**Figure 19.21**).

3. Check or uncheck the following boxes:

   Automatically Fix File System Errors. Check this box to make Windows repair any errors it finds; if it's unchecked, errors are merely *reported,* not fixed. If the disk is in use, or if you're checking the system disk (the one with Windows on it), you'll see **Figure 19.22**; click Yes to defer the scan until the next time you restart your PC.

   Scan for and Attempt Recovery of Bad Sectors. Check this box to make Windows recover readable files and folders it finds in the disk's defective sections, and move them elsewhere on the disk. This option fixes errors as well, even if the other option is unchecked. Unrepairable sections are locked out of available storage.

4. Click Start to begin the checking process.

   The progress bar indicates the phase Check Disk is in. When all phases complete, a dialog box tells you how things turned out.

Managing Disks

Disk Management is a system utility that lets you inspect and manage hard disks. You can use it to initialize a disk, create partitions, and format partitions with FAT, FAT32, or NTFS file systems on *new* hardware. Otherwise, use Disk Management to assess a disk's health, assign drive letters, format, and perform related tasks.

To open Disk Management:

1. In Control Panel, choose Performance and Maintenance > Administrative Tools > Computer Management; then click Disk Management in the left pane (**Figure 19.23**).

   or

   In the Start menu, right-click My Computer; choose Manage; then click Disk Management in the left pane.

   or

   Choose Start > Run; type `diskmgmt.msc`; then press Enter.

2. Right-click any disk or partition for a list of commands, or use the View menu to specify how disks are displayed.

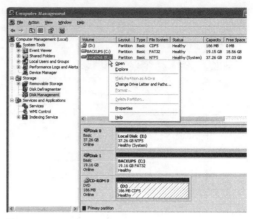

Figure 19.23 Drive Management is a cog in the larger machine named Computer Management, which groups many tools described elsewhere in this book. Click a tool in the left pane's console tree to open it.

Floppy Disks

If your PC is connected to a network or the Internet, you probably have little use for floppy disks. They remain useful for backing up or transporting small files, however. Most floppies come preformatted and ready for use, but you can format one manually (or erase an already-formatted one):

1. Insert a floppy into its drive.

2. In Windows Explorer or My Computer, right-click the drive's icon (3½ Floppy (A:)); then choose Format.

3. Choose a size from the Capacity list (usually, 1.44 MB).

4. Click Start.

To copy a floppy disk, follow the preceding steps, but choose Copy Disk from the shortcut menu in step 2; then choose where you want the copy to be made.

Backing up Your Files

The love that you shower on your hard drive isn't requited. Eventually, it will betray you and fail catastrophically, taking your data with it. Forestall the heartbreak by making regular backup copies of your work. Backups also protect you against accidental deletions and let you archive finished projects for remote storage.

XP's Backup program lets you back up an entire hard disk or specified files and folders periodically. You *can* back up to a tape drive, but most people choose to back up to a second local drive, a shared network folder, or a high-capacity storage device such as an external USB drive. Never back up to a different partition on the same physical hard drive, because if the drive fails, all partitions go with it. The Backup or Restore Wizard walks you through the process of backing up your files or restoring backed-up files when disaster strikes.

✔ Tips

- If you store your files on a network server at work, you don't have to back up your work. Your network administrator does it for you.

- Backup won't write directly to CD recorders, but you can create a backup file and burn it on a CD.

- If you have a high-speed Internet connection (DSL or cable), consider a Web-based backup service such as www.backup.com.

Backup is installed by default on XP Pro edition PCs but not on Home edition PCs.

To install Backup on a Windows XP Home edition computer:

1. Insert the Windows XP Home CD.

2. When the Welcome screen appears, click Exit.

What's a Partition?

A *partition,* or *volume,* is a portion of a physical disk that functions as though it were a separate disk. After you create a partition, you must format it and assign it a drive letter before you can store data on it.

Every hard disk has one partition, but you can create several on one disk, mainly to:

- ◆ Separate files and folders from the operating system, keeping your personal documents safe if an OS upgrade turns ugly.

- ◆ Create dual boot systems with multiple OSes. See "Performing a Clean Install or a Dual-Boot Install" in Appendix A.

Unfortunately, Disk Management is lazy and *erases* a hard disk before partitioning it, which makes it suitable—in real terms—for blank or new disks only. If you want to create or resize partitions without erasing everything, buy PartitionMagic (www.powerquest.com).

3. Choose Start > My Computer.

4. In the My Computer window, right-click the CD drive icon; then choose Explorer.

5. In the Explorer window, navigate to the folder \VALUEADD\MSFT\NTBACKUP; then double-click NTBACKUP.MSI (**Figure 19.24**).

6. Click Finish when the wizard completes the installation.

To back up files:

1. Exit all programs (because Backup can't back up open files).

2. Choose Start > All Programs > Accessories > System Tools > Backup.
   The Backup or Restore Wizard starts.

3. Click Next to skip the Welcome page.

4. Select Back up Files and Settings; then click Next (**Figure 19.25**).

5. Specify the items to back up; then click Next.

   My Documents and Settings. Backs up your entire user profile (see "Managing User Profiles" in Chapter 16), including your My Documents folder and your desktop contents and settings.

   Everyone's Documents and Settings. Backs up everyone's user profile—in other words, the entire Documents and Settings folder.

   All Information on This Computer. Creates a monster backup of every file on the PC—including Windows XP itself, which is largely pointless for system disks, because you have those files on the Windows CD.

   Let Me Choose What to Back Up. Displays **Figure 19.26** when you click Next, letting you pick specific folders and files to back up.

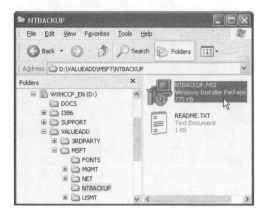

Figure 19.24 Windows XP Home users must install Backup manually.

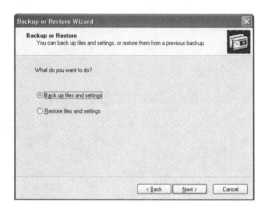

Figure 19.25 Backup lets you back up or restore your files.

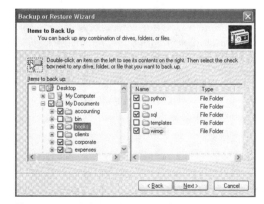

Figure 19.26 Click the plus sign in the tree to expand the list of drives and folders. Turn on the check box of each item to back up. You can drag the vertical separator bar to resize the panels.

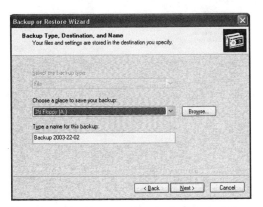

Figure 19.27 Backing up to floppies is absurd, given today's hard-disk sizes. If you have a Zip drive connected, choose it from the drop-down list; otherwise, click Browse and specify a local or network drive.

6. Specify a location and name for the backup; then click Next (**Figure 19.27**). Unless you have an XP-compatible tape drive, the Backup Type option is File; you have no other choices.

7. Click Finish to begin the backup immediately (skip to step 11), or click Advanced to choose the additional options.

8. If you clicked Advanced in the preceding step, select one of the backup types listed in **Table 19.1**; then click Next.

9. Work your way through the rest of the wizard, selecting the desired options (described in each window).

10. On the last page, review your settings; then click Finish to start the backup.

   The process takes minutes or hours, depending its size and type.

11. Click Close in the Backup Progress dialog box when the backup completes.

   Backup creates a .bkf file, using the name and location you specified in step 6.

Table 19.1

Advanced Backup Types

Type	Description
Normal	Backs up all the selected files and marks them as backed up, letting subsequent Incremental and Differential backups copy only those files that have changed since their Normal backup.
Copy	Backs up all the selected files but doesn't mark them as backed up.
Incremental	Backs up only files that have changed since the last Normal backup and marks them as backed up. Incremental backups are very fast to perform but very slow to restore; you must restore your last Normal backup and *each* succeeding Incremental backup.
Differential	Backs up the same files as an Incremental backup but *doesn't* mark them as backed up. Differential backups are moderately fast to perform and to restore; you must restore your last Normal backup and only *the most recent* Differential backup.
Daily	Backs up files that you created or changed today but doesn't mark them as backed up. This setting is handy for copying a day's work without interfering with your regular backup schedule.

BACKING UP YOUR FILES

✔ Tips

- In Figure 19.26, expand My Computer and click System State to back up your boot files, Registry, and other system components, letting you restore the *exact* state of your PC at the time you did the backup.

- If an error message appears, click Report in the Backup Progress dialog box for a record of what went wrong.

- If you choose to run the backup at a later time (by using the advanced options in step 9), Windows can create a scheduled task that you can edit manually. See "Scheduling Tasks" later in this chapter.

To restore backed-up files:

1. Choose Start > All Programs > Accessories > System Tools > Backup.
   The Backup or Restore Wizard starts.

2. Click Next to skip the Welcome page.

3. Select Restore Files and Settings; then click Next (refer to Figure 19.25).

4. Select the files and folders that you want to restore; then click Next (**Figure 19.28**).

5. Click Finish to begin the restore immediately (skip to step 9), or click Advanced to choose additional options.

6. If you clicked Advanced in the preceding step, specify where to restore your backed-up files and folders; then click Next.

   Select **Original Location** if you're restoring damaged or lost files.

   Select **Alternate Location** and specify a location if you need some old files but don't want to overwrite any of the current files or folders on your disk.

   Select **Single Folder** and specify a folder if you're searching for a file and don't know its location. (This option doesn't retain the structure of the backed-up folders and files.)

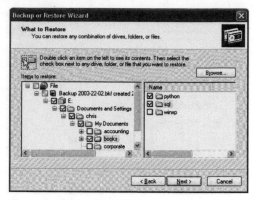

Figure 19.28 If you have a Zip or tape drive, select it in the left panel. Use the tree view to select the backed-up files and folders to restore, exactly as you did in Figure 19.26.

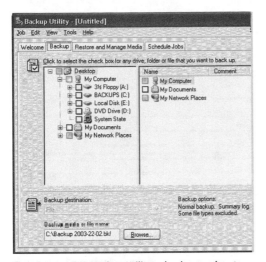

Figure 19.29 Use Backup Utility to back up and restore files without slogging through the Backup or Restore Wizard.

7. Specify whether you want Backup to overwrite existing files; then click Next.

   Leave Existing Files (Recommended), the safest method, won't overwrite files already on your hard disk.

   Replace Existing Files If They Are Older Than the Backup File ensures that you won't lose any changes that you've made to files since you last backed up your data.

   Replace Existing Files restores *every* backed-up file on your hard drive. You'll lose any changes made to those files since your last backup.

8. Accept the default settings in the next screen (the options are quite technical); then click Next.

9. On the last page, review your settings; then click Finish to start the restore.

10. Click Close in the Restore Progress dialog box when the restore completes.

✔ Tips

- To back up and restore without the Backup and Restore Wizard, click Advanced Mode in the wizard's opening page to make **Figure 19.29** appear.

- If an error message appears, click Report in the Restore Progress dialog box for a record of what went wrong.

- It's wise to restore backups regularly to a test folder to confirm that they're working properly.

Scheduling Tasks

Periodic maintenance and backups aren't useful unless they're actually periodic—and human memory is notoriously poor here. Scheduled Tasks, which starts and runs each time you start Windows XP, can schedule programs to run according to a schedule that you specify.

Now things become more technical. It does you no good simply to *open* a program on schedule; you must specify the command name and command-line options that make it run to completion without your intervention. A *command name* is a program's file-name as typed at a command prompt (choose Start > All Programs > Accessories > Command Prompt). Disk Defragmenter's command name is defrag, and Backup's is ntbackup, for example. *Command-line options,* or *switches,* are space-separated parameters—prefixed by a - or / character—that follow the command name and control that command's behavior. Search for *command-line reference* in Help Center to find commands, their switches, and examples (**Figure 19.30**).

To schedule a new task:

1. Choose Start > All Programs > Accessories > System Tools > Scheduled Tasks.

2. Right-click an empty area in the Scheduled tasks window; then choose New > Scheduled Task (**Figure 19.31**).

3. Type a name for the task; then press Enter.

4. Double-click the new task.

5. On the Task tab (**Figure 19.32**), in the Run box, type the command to run as the scheduled task.

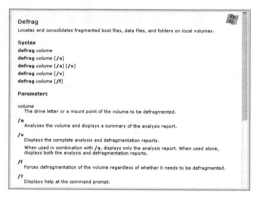

Figure 19.30 Help Center's description of the defrag command and its command-line options. The command defrag C: /f defragments your C drive, for example.

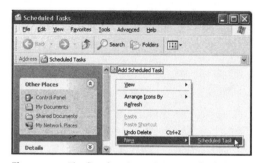

Figure 19.31 The first few times that you schedule a new task, you may want to double-click Add Scheduled Task for a wizard to walk you through the process.

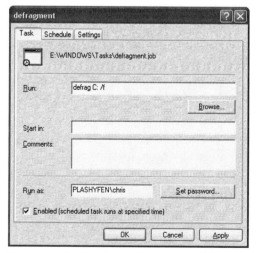

Figure 19.32 In this tab, specify the program that you want to run on a schedule.

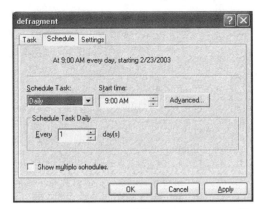

Figure 19.33 Click Advanced if you want to set a task's start and end date or make it run repeatedly at specified intervals.

Figure 19.34 Don't just accept some of the nonsensical factory settings on this tab; you should stop a task if it runs for 4 or 5 hours (not 72, as Microsoft suggests). The bottom section is for laptop users.

- At the command prompt, type a command followed by -? (or /?) to see its command-line options. Type defrag -?, for example.

- Command-prompt junkies can use the at command instead of Scheduled Tasks.

If necessary, include command-line options and a pathname (see "Exploring Your Computer" in Chapter 5). If the pathname includes spaces, type double quotation marks (") around the entire command.

If the command requires an administrator to run, and you're not one, type an administrator's user name in the Run As box; then click Set Password. (Blank passwords are forbidden.) If you're on an XP Pro domain, type *domain_name\user_name*.

6. On the Schedule tab (**Figure 19.33**), specify when and how often to run the task.

7. On the Settings tab (**Figure 19.34**), set the conditions under which the task will run.

8. Click OK (or Apply).

   Now the task will run according to schedule, even if somebody else (or nobody) is logged on.

✔ Tips

- Choose View > Details to see schedule information for all tasks, including the earlier and next run times. A 0 or 0x0 in the Last Result column means that a task ran successfully; any other value represents an error.

- The Advanced menu offers some not-very-advanced commands. Use it to pause all scheduled tasks, shut down Task Scheduler, or notify you of missed tasks.

- To run a task on demand, right-click it; then choose Run.

- You can place multiple commands in a text file with a .bat extension and run this *batch file* as a single task instead of running each command individually.

- Double-click the taskbar clock to confirm that the system date and time on your computer are accurate. Scheduled Tasks relies on this information.

SCHEDULING TASKS

Recovering After a Crash

If you've installed a criminally faulty driver or program, and Windows XP won't boot—perhaps greeting you with a black screen (symbolizing thick smoke) instead of the Windows logo—you can invoke XP's *startup menu* to recover from catastrophe. This menu takes a little fancy fingerwork to bring up.

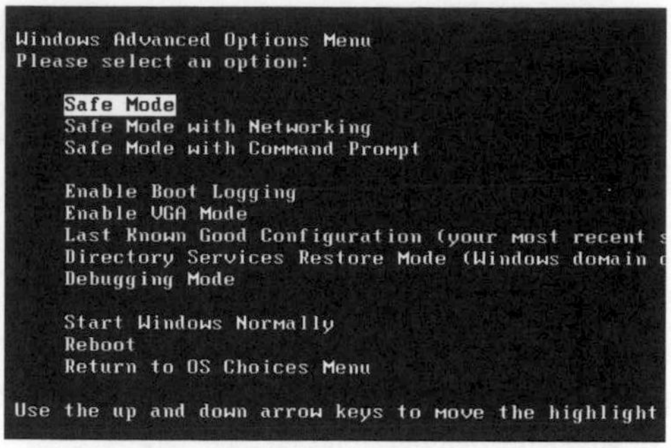

To use the startup menu:

1. Restart your computer.

2. When the BIOS startup messages (DOS-like text against a black screen) finish, tap the F8 key repeatedly until the Windows Advanced Options menu appears (**Figure 19.35**).

   If you have a dual-boot system, use the arrow keys to select the OS that you need; then press Enter.

3. Use the arrow keys to select a startup option; then press Enter.

   Table 19.2 lists the most appropriate options.

Figure 19.35 If Windows won't boot, this screen gives you an excellent chance of recovering .

Table 19.2

Startup Menu Options

OPTION	DESCRIPTION
Safe Mode	Starts Windows with only its fundamental files, drivers, and components. Only your mouse, keyboard, monitor, and disk drives will work. A generic video driver makes everything appear in jaggy 640x480 screen resolution. Safe mode lets you run most essential configuration and troubleshooting tools, including Device Manager, System Restore, Registry Editor, Backup, Services, and Help and Support. You can uninstall a program or driver that you suspect is causing the problems.
Safe Mode with Networking	Offers the same functions as safe mode, plus access to your network connections. Use this mode if you need files or drivers from another PC on the network. This mode won't work for laptops that connect via a PC Card network adapter; PC Card drivers are disabled in safe mode.
Safe Mode with Command Prompt	Loads the same set of services as safe mode but displays only the command prompt instead of the Windows graphical interface. This mode is for command-line geeks only.
Enable VGA Mode	Starts the PC with the safe-mode VGA driver but doesn't invoke any *other* part of safe mode. Use this option to boot past a bogus video driver.
Last Known Good Configuration	Starts the PC by using the Registry information and drivers that were in effect that last time your PC was working, effectively undoing the changes that caused the problems. (This is the old Windows 2000 system rollback option; System Restore is preferable, because it restores OS system files too.)
Start Windows Normally	Starts Windows in the usual way.
Reboot	Restarts the computer.
Return to OS Choices Menu	Backs up to the screen that lets you choose the operating system. Most people have only one choice: Windows XP.

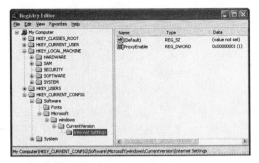

Figure 19.36 Windows stores its configuration information in a database (the Registry). Registry Editor organizes the data in tree format.

Editing the Registry

Windows stores its configuration information in a large database called the *Registry,* containing all user profiles and information about system hardware, installed programs, and property settings. Windows references this information and updates it continually. That's why Help Center tells us sternly: "Incorrectly editing the Registry may severely damage your system. Before making changes to the Registry, you should back up any valued data on your computer."

Lots of books, magazines, Web sites, and geeks, however, offer useful tips that involve Registry changes. Although you shouldn't edit the Registry arbitrarily, it's safe to modify it if you follow precise instructions.

To edit the Registry:

1. Choose Start > Run; type regedit; then press Enter.

2. In the left pane, use the Explorerlike tree to navigate to the desired folder; then double-click an entry (called a *key*) in the right pane to edit its value (**Figure 19.36**).

✔ Tips

- Caution: Changing key values in the Registry can alter any and every aspect of the way your computer behaves. Editing Registry keys gives you unrivaled control of tweaks; but *some of its values must never be changed,* and I advise you to learn enough about the Registry to know—at least—which ones those are.

- Visit www.winguides.com/registry and www.annoyances.org for Registry tricks and tweaks that enhance Windows.

EDITING THE REGISTRY

INSTALLING WINDOWS XP

If your PC came with Windows XP installed, you may be able to use it for the life of the machine without ever referring to this appendix. But if you're upgrading to XP from Windows 98, Me, 2000, or NT, this appendix will show you how to install your new operating system. Tinkerers and hobbyists will find useful information here too; many users consider a clean Windows installation to be the last word in restoring the speed of a computer that has grown slow with accumulated software glitches and other baggage. Read on to learn the particulars of the Windows Setup program.

Getting Ready to Install Windows XP

Before you stick that Windows XP CD into your drive, you'll need to do some planning and make a few decisions. This section describes the steps to take and information to gather before installation. (You'll need a pen to write things down.) Some steps are only for those of you upgrading from a previous Windows version.

Check system requirements

The Windows XP box lists these minimal hardware requirements:

- PC with 300 megahertz (MHz) or higher processor clock speed recommended, 233-MHz minimum required; Intel Pentium/Celeron family, AMD K6/Athlon/Duron family, or compatible processor recommended

- 64 megabytes (MB) of RAM "supported," 128 MB or higher recommended

- 1.5 gigabytes (GB) of available hard disk space

- Super VGA (800x600) or higher-resolution video adapter and monitor

- CD-ROM or DVD drive

- Keyboard and Microsoft Mouse or compatible pointing device

These requirements are a tasteless joke by Microsoft's marketing department. Such a minimal machine might "run" XP, but opening the Start menu probably would take minutes. For a tolerable XPerience, your PC should have at least a 1 GHz processor and 256 MB of RAM. If you're upgrading a PC to run XP, don't skimp on (now cheap) RAM. Lots of memory and a fast hard disk can compensate for a slowish processor. Always check Microsoft's Hardware Compatibility List (www.microsoft.com/hcl) before you buy equipment; see "Installing Plug and Play Devices" in Chapter 8.

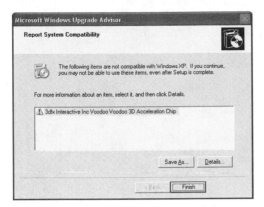

Figure A.1 The Upgrade Advisor report can help you decide whether to upgrade your computer to Windows XP.

Check system compatibility

Run Upgrade Advisor to get information about potential problems that your computer may have if you upgrade to Windows XP, especially if you're using software designed for Windows 95/98/Me or older hardware. Upgrade Advisor checks the system peripherals and programs, and generates a list of items that may not work correctly with XP.

Windows Setup runs Upgrade Advisor automatically when you upgrade from a previous Windows version, but you're wise to run it manually before beginning installation.

To check system compatibility:

1. Insert the Windows XP CD.

   The Welcome window appears. (If it doesn't: Open Windows Explorer; navigate to the CD drive; then double-click `setup.exe`.)

2. Click Check System Compatibility.

3. Click Check My System Automatically.

4. If you have an Internet connection, download the updated Setup files; then click Next.

   Update Advisor displays a list of potential problems, if any (**Figure A.1**).

5. For a full problem description and advice, click a problem in the list; then click Details.

6. To save the compatibility information in a text file, click Save As.

7. Click Finish.

✔ Tips

- To check system compatibility *before* you buy XP, download Upgrade Advisor from www.microsoft.com/windowsxp/home/howtobuy/upgrading/advisor.asp (Home edition) or www.microsoft.com/windowsxp/pro/howtobuy/upgrading/advisor.asp (Pro edition).

(continues on next page)

GETTING READY TO INSTALL WINDOWS XP

- *Before* installation, download updated XP-compatible drivers—particularly for graphics, audio, and multimedia devices—from manufacturers' Web sites. Driver sites such as www.driverguide.com and www.windrivers.com may be helpful too.

- If you feel like being really organized, make a folder on your hard disk called Drivers and a subfolder for the driver for each component or peripheral. (Each driver will need its own folder, because one of its files will be called setup.exe or setup.inf.) You'll be glad to have these drivers while you're installing XP, and even more later, when your computer is a couple of years old and the drivers vanish from the Web sites.

- On an ancient (pre-2001) PC, confirm that the *BIOS*—low-level startup software embedded in a chip on the motherboard—is compatible with XP. If you have any doubt, go to your PC manufacturer's Web site, and poke around for a file called "flash BIOS" or "BIOS utility," or maybe one of each. There will be instructions on how to use this software; follow them *exactly*, because you're performing the rough equivalent of open-heart surgery.

  If your computer's BIOS is too old for XP, and no update is available, you may have to contact the manufacturer and request a newer chip.

- Never try to run obsolete system utilities on XP. Upgrade to the latest version of your virus scanner, backup program, hard-disk partitioning tool, or CD burner. (Look for the Designed for Windows XP logo.)

- If your Windows 95/98/Me disk has been compressed with the DoubleSpace or DriveSpace utility, uncompress it before installation.

Figure A.2 The dual-boot menu that appears when you turn on your PC offers you a choice of operating system. If you don't choose within 30 seconds, the computer chooses for you.

- To learn more about dual-boot setups, visit www.microsoft.com/windows/multiboot.asp.

- For more information about partitions, see "Managing Disks" in Chapter 19.

Choose an installation type

If your PC is running an older version of Windows, you must choose one of three installation types (**Table A.1**). If your target PC has a blank drive, your only choice is a clean install.

✔ Tips

- The Upgrade version of Windows XP is cheaper than the Full version, but if you ever need to install the Upgrade version on a clean drive, you must first install an older (but qualifying) Windows version and *then* install XP on top of it. (This is one reason to take good care of your obsolete Windows CDs, the other one being that you *might* need a copy of an old DLL…)

- See also "Transferring Existing Files and Settings" later in this chapter.

Table A.1

Windows XP Installation Types	
INSTALLATION	**DESCRIPTION**
Clean install	Installs a fresh copy of XP on your hard drive, replacing any existing operating system and erasing all files on the drive. During a clean install, you reformat or repartition your hard drive, wiping out all its accumulated crud, including outdated drivers, fragmented files, incompatible programs, and stale Registry entries. Windows veterans will tell you that a clean install has a restorative effect on a PC that's grown sluggish over time.
Upgrade	First, check Table i.2 in the introduction to see whether your current Windows version qualifies for the upgrade to XP; if not, you must perform a clean install. Upgrading to XP preserves your existing settings, installed programs, and data files, including your personal desktop elements, Favorites list, and everything in your My Documents folder. Windows Setup also attempts to upgrade device drivers to XP-compatible versions. Upgrading saves you from laborious rebuilding of preferred settings but doesn't invigorate your PC the way a clean install does. Following the upgrade, you may find that some programs run poorly on XP and need to be removed and reinstalled, possibly after being updated with a patch from the software publisher's Web site.
Dual boot	If you want to preserve your existing copy of Windows *and* run XP, you can set up your PC to maintain both of them side by side. Each time you turn on your PC, it asks you which operating system to run (**Figure A.2**). Dual booting is useful if you have a critical piece of hardware or software that runs only on the older OS.
	Crucial advice: *Never install both OSes on the same hard-drive partition*. It would be a disaster—and Microsoft Support doesn't even answer questions about such setups. Instead, take one of the following paths:
	◆ Buy a second hard drive, and use it for one of the two OSes.
	◆ *Partition* your existing disk—that is, divide it so that each portion functions as though it were a separate disk, with its own icon and drive letter in My Computer. Windows Setup offers a disk tool that erases as it partitions, but you may prefer to buy PartitionMagic (www.powerquest.com), a friendlier, more flexible utility that creates and manages partitions without wiping out their data.

Choose a file system

Within an operating system, a *file system* is the overall structure in which files are named, stored, and organized. Windows XP offers you two choices: *FAT32* and *NTFS* (**Table A.2**).

Unfortunately, Windows 95/98/Me doesn't recognize NTFS drives. Choose FAT32 over NTFS only if you're sharing files and folders with a Windows 95/98/Me user.

If you're unsure which file system to choose, use FAT. You can always convert a FAT drive to NTFS, but not vice versa.

To convert a FAT drive to NTFS:

1. Choose Start > All Programs > Accessories > Command Prompt.

2. Type convert C: /FS:NTFS; then press Enter.

   (Replace *C:* with the letter of the drive that you're converting.)

   If you're converting the drive with Windows XP on it, the conversion happens when you restart your PC.

✔ Tips

- If you plan to dual-boot between Windows 95/98/Me and Windows XP, the startup drive or partition must be FAT.

- You can't boot an NTFS drive off a DOS floppy disk. Boot off the XP CD instead.

- If your upgrade involves converting your system drive from FAT to FAT32, be *sure* to defragment the disk immediately after the conversion. Your computer will be faster.

- Some computers with an older BIOS (see "Check system compatibility" earlier in this chapter) and drives upgraded to FAT32 won't be able to use XP's Hibernate feature, because they can't read the Hibernate file. The cure is a BIOS upgrade.

Table A.2

Windows XP File Systems	
FILE SYSTEM	DESCRIPTION
FAT32	FAT32 (file allocation table) descends from the ancient DOS file system and still is used in Windows 98/Me systems.
NTFS	NTFS (NT file system), inherited from Windows 2000/NT, is a robust, secure file system that's far more reliable than FAT. NTFS also manages big hard disks more efficiently than FAT; Microsoft recommends NTFS for all 32 GB-plus drives. Some advanced features—such as automatic file compression, encryption, and file permissions—are available on NTFS but not on FAT32.

Back up your data files

No matter what type of installation you choose, back up all your data files just before installation by using your usual backup medium (such as an external hard drive, CD burner, Zip drive, tape backup drive, second PC, or Web-based backup service).

Plug in and switch on devices

Make sure that peripheral devices, such as your printer or scanner, are attached to your computer and powered up, so that Windows Setup can detect them during installation.

✔ Tip

- Some older non-Plug and Play devices may cause problems for Windows Setup. Disconnect them, then reconnect them after Setup completes.

Get Internet settings

If you plan to connect to the Internet (see Chapter 12) during installation, gather your connection settings beforehand. (You can configure your settings during setup or postpone this step until afterward.) Your ISP's Web site will have necessary information, such as IP addresses and access phone numbers; Customer Service has a record of your account user name and password, if you've mislaid them. While you're at it, you may want to write down your user names and passwords for Web sites that you visit regularly.

Get network settings

If you plan to connect to a network (see
Chapter 17) during installation, gather your
connection settings beforehand. (You can configure your settings during setup or postpone
this step until afterward.) You will need:

- The name of your computer

- The name of the workgroup or domain

- **PRO** If your computer is a domain
member, your domain user name
and password

- **PRO** IP address, if your network doesn't
have a DHCP or WINS server

Your Ethernet adapter and other network
hardware should be connected and working
properly before installation.

Turn off background programs

If you're upgrading, turn off your virus
checker, lest it interpret Windows XP as
a harmful infestation (ha ha). Also, turn
off Web ad blockers, non-Microsoft firewall
software such as ZoneAlarm, and other
utilities that load automatically.

Figure A.3 This window is the starting point for installing Windows XP. Installation will take at least an hour.

Figure A.4 Use this drop-down list to choose an upgrade or clean installation.

Upgrading to Windows XP

Here's how to upgrade an older Windows version to Windows XP. If you're doing a clean install, skip to the next section.

To upgrade to Windows XP:

1. Start your computer; then insert the Windows XP CD into its drive.

   The Welcome window appears (**Figure A.3**). (If it doesn't, open Windows Explorer; navigate to the CD drive; then double-click setup.exe.)

2. Click Install Windows XP.

   The Windows Setup wizard appears.

3. Choose Upgrade from the Installation Type drop-down list (**Figure A.4**); then click Next.

4. Review the End-User License Agreement (EULA); be mildly outraged by its terms; select I Accept This Agreement; then click Next.

5. Type the 25-character product key that appears on the back of the Windows XP folder; then click Next.

6. If you're online, select Yes to download updated Setup files; otherwise, select No to bypass this option; then click Next.

   Setup examines your system for XP potential problems and displays the Report System Compatibility page (refer to Figure A.1)—which you should have run manually before installation, as described in the preceding section.

7. Click Finish.

   Read a book while Setup copies files to your hard drive and reboots your PC. When it's done, you'll see the Welcome to Microsoft Windows screen. Proceed to "Using the Setup Wizard" later in this chapter.

Performing a Clean Install or a Dual-Boot Install

Here's how to install a clean copy of Windows on an empty disk or partition—or a non-empty disk or partition that you want to reformat and overwrite.

These instructions describe the installation of Windows XP Pro edition, which is a super-set of Home edition. For Home edition, the process is the same, except that some screens either don't appear or are missing some options. (Domain settings don't pertain to Home edition, for example.) Simply ignore the steps and settings that aren't required for your installation.

To perform a clean install or a dual-boot install:

1. Start your computer from the Windows XP CD.

   Most PCs can boot up from a CD rather than a hard drive. Look for onscreen instructions when the BIOS messages appear. You may have to press a particular key (or any key). No luck? Read the PC's manual, or ask the manufacturer. Still no luck? See the tips later in this section.

2. When the Welcome to Setup screen appears, press Enter.

   The first few screens are DOS-like text on a solid background.

3. Review the End-User License Agreement (EULA); then press F8.

4. If Setup finds a previous Windows XP installation, it asks whether you want to repair it or install a fresh (clean) copy; press Esc to install a fresh copy.

5. Press the up- or down-arrow key to select the hard-drive partition on which you want to install XP; then press Enter.

   Unless you've partitioned your drive for a dual-boot system, you probably have only one partition. For more about partitions, see "Getting Ready to Install Windows XP" earlier in this chapter.

6. If the selected partition already contains a copy of XP, Setup asks you to confirm your decision; press C to continue.

7. Press the up- or down-arrow key to select a file system (NTFS or FAT); then press Enter.

   For file-system details, see "Getting Ready to Install Windows XP" earlier in this chapter.

8. If the selected partition already contains files, Setup asks you to confirm your decision to wipe out the files; press F to format and continue.

   Setup formats the partition, copies files to it, and restarts the PC. The next few screens look like Windows, not DOS.

9. On the Regional and Language Options screen, click Next if Setup has guessed your language and country correctly; otherwise, click Customize, and choose the appropriate options.

10. On the Personalize Your Software screen, type your name and (optionally) the name of your organization; then click Next.

11. On the Your Product Key screen, type the 25-character product key that appears on the back of the Windows XP folder; then click Next.

    If your computer came with Windows XP installed, the product key may be on a sticker on the side of your PC.

12. On the Computer Name and Administrator Password screen, type a punctuation-free name for your computer; type (and retype) a password for the Administrator account; then click Next.

You can always change the computer name later; see "Running the Network Setup Wizard" in Chapter 17. For password tips, see "Setting up User Accounts" in Chapter 16.

13. If the Modem Dialing Information screen appears, specify your country, phone-system type (tone or pulse dialing), area code, and the number to dial (if any); then click Next.

14. On the Date and Time Settings screen, set the date, time, and time zone; then click Next.

If you have a network card installed, Setup detects it and displays the Network Settings screen; otherwise, skip to step 18.

15. On the Network Settings screen, select Typical Settings; then click Next.

16. On the Workgroup or Computer Domain screen, specify whether your computer is part of a workgroup or a domain; type the workgroup or domain name; then click Next.

If you're a domain member, ask your network administrator for this information.

These concepts are described in detail in Chapters 16 and 17.

17. **PRO** If you're a domain member, but your network administrator hasn't added your computer to the domain, Setup gives you the opportunity to join the domain later; click Yes to continue.

(Discuss this omission with your administrator later.)

18. When Setup restarts your PC and greets you with the Welcome to Microsoft Windows screen, proceed to "Using the Setup Wizard" later in this chapter.

✔ Tips

■ If your PC can't boot from the CD in step 1, visit http://support.microsoft.com, and search for Knowledge Base article 310994, "Obtaining Windows XP Setup Boot Disks." From there, you can download the Setup program onto six floppy disks. These disks contain the files and drivers that are required to access the CD drive and begin the Setup process.

■ If you're installing a dual-boot system, step 5 of Setup gives you the chance to delete a partition and create a new one.

PERFORMING A CLEAN OR A DUAL-BOOT INSTALL

Using the Setup Wizard

All XP installations eventually converge at the Setup Wizard, which starts with the Welcome to Microsoft Windows screen and its animated question-mark icon, which you can click for help along the way. This wizard guides you through:

◆ Identifying and configuring your dial-up, high-speed (DSL or cable), or network Internet connection. See Chapter 12.

◆ Entering IP and DNS addresses for your network connection. See Chapter 17.

◆ Activating your copy of Windows. See the next section.

◆ Registering Windows. Registration is not the same thing as Activation and is optional, so click No unless you want junk email.

◆ Setting up the first five user accounts (but not their passwords), if they aren't already set up.

   If you upgraded from Windows 98/Me, XP imported existing accounts as Administrators and erased their passwords.

   To plug these security holes, add passwords immediately after you finish the wizard. See "Setting up User Accounts" in Chapter 16.

When you're done, Windows greets you with the desktop and Welcome screen. Windows XP is ready to use.

✔ Tips

■ The Setup Wizard's steps vary depending on your installed hardware, your configuration, and whether you're running Home or Pro edition.

■ You can skip many of the steps and perform them later without the Setup Wizard.

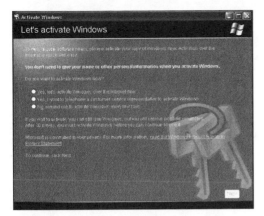

Figure A.5 You can activate Windows XP over your Internet connection or over the phone. If you don't activate it within 30 days, XP stops working.

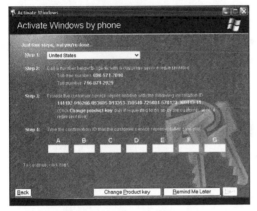

Figure A.6 If you don't have an Internet connection, you can activate XP via a tedious phone call.

Activating Windows XP

Windows XP has an undesirable new feature—copy protection—that prevents you from running the same copy of Windows on more than one computer. During installation, Windows Setup examines your PC; computes a Special Secret Identifier from the exact system time plus data about key internal parts (hard drive, video card, motherboard, memory, and so on); and sends this identifier, along with your 25-character product key, over the Internet to Microsoft, thereby *activating* Windows XP (**Figure A.5**).

If you don't have an Internet connection, you must call a toll-free number; enter a 50-digit installation ID number on the phone's dial pad; get a 42-digit confirmation ID code back from Microsoft; then type that code in the Activate Windows screen (**Figure A.6**).

Later, if you install the same copy of Windows on another PC without uninstalling the first one, Microsoft will discover your duplicity during activation and lock you out of Windows. Unless you activate XP on the second PC, lockout occurs automatically in 30 days.

✔ Tips

- Activation is anonymous and transfers no personal information to Microsoft.

- If you skip activation during Setup, reminders pop up occasionally on the taskbar (**Figure A.7**). Click a reminder or choose Start > All Programs > Activate Windows to start the activation process.

- Bulk-purchased corporate copies of Windows XP are exempt from activation, and many new PCs come with a preactivated copy. But new retail PCs are preactivated by a method that writes to the computer's BIOS, meaning that if you update the BIOS (see "Check system compatibility" earlier in this chapter) *after* installing XP, you may have to reactivate.

- If you replace four or more of your computer's 10 key internal parts in a four-month period, you'll have to reactivate XP.

- Windows stores its activation code in two small files, wpa.dbl and wpa.bak, in C:\Windows\System32. If you replace your system drive, copy these files to a floppy and then copy them back to the new drive to keep Windows Activation happy.

- wpa.dbl and wpa.bak are *not* included in the files backed up by System Restore when you set a restore point—meaning that after you roll back your system, depending on the depth of the damage you were trying to undo, you may have to reactivate. (I suggest, again, that if these files exist on your system, you keep a backup copy, because Microsoft isn't completely straightforward about how or why they might change.)

Figure A.7 Windows nags you to activate.

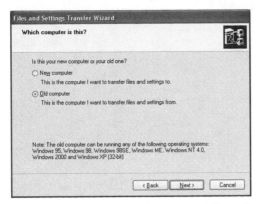

Figure A.8 Use the same wizard to save your files and settings on one computer (no matter what version of Windows it runs) and reinstate them on your Windows XP computer.

Transferring Existing Files and Settings

The Files and Settings Transfer Wizard will help you move settings from one computer to another, including your personal files and info for Internet Explorer, Outlook Express, Microsoft Office, and some third-party applications (Eudora, AOL Instant Messenger, WordPerfect, Quicken, Photoshop, and Acrobat Reader, for example), as well as desktop, display, and dial-up connection settings. The XP CD contains a version of the wizard that you can run on another Windows computer—even one that's not running XP.

If you have two computers, you can transfer files and settings from the old one to the new one via a network connection, direct cable connection, floppies, CD-R, or Zip disk. If you have only one computer, run the wizard before you install XP, and save the file and settings to disk or a second hard drive.

To collect the files and settings from the old computer:

1. Insert the Windows XP CD into the drive of the computer from which you want to transfer files and settings.

   The Welcome window appears (refer to Figure A.3). (If it doesn't, open Windows Explorer; navigate to the CD drive; then double-click setup.exe.)

2. Click Perform Additional Tasks.

3. Click Transfer Files and Settings.

   The Files and Settings Transfer Wizard appears.

4. Click Next to skip the Welcome screen.

5. Select Old Computer (**Figure A.8**); then click Next.

   (continues on next page)

6. Select the transfer method that you want to use (**Figure A.9**); then click Next.

7. If you selected Direct Cable in the preceding step, follow the instructions on the Set up Your Serial Connection page that appears; then click Next.

8. Select the information that you want to transfer to the new PC (**Figure A.10**); then click Next.

9. If you checked Let Me Select a Custom List of Files and Settings When I Click Next in the preceding step, build a custom list on the Select Custom Files and Settings page that appears; then click Next.

10. The Install Programs on Your New Computer page tells you which programs are associated with the settings you've chosen; click Next.

Install these programs on your new computer *before* you transfer the settings. The wizard displays its progress as it collects your files and settings.

11. If you selected Floppy Drive or Other Removable Media in step 6, Windows prompts you to insert the media (such as a floppy disk).

12. Click Finish.

To transfer the files and settings to the new computer:

1. On the Windows XP computer, choose Start > All Programs > Accessories > System Tools > Files and Settings Transfer Wizard.

2. Click Next to skip the Welcome screen.

3. Select New Computer (refer to Figure A.8); then click Next.

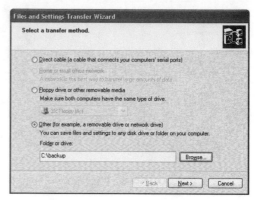

Figure A.9 If you back up to removable disks, keep track of the order in which you create them. You'll have to insert them into the new computer in that same order.

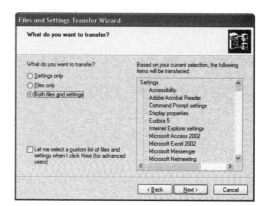

Figure A.10 You can transfer your settings, files, or both. Check the box if you want to create a list of *specific* files and settings to transfer.

4. Select I Don't Need the Wizard Disk; then click Next.

5. Specify the location of the saved files and settings on the old computer (that is, specify the same transfer method that you chose in Figure A.9); then click Next.

6. Follow the onscreen instructions, which vary by transfer method.

The wizard displays its transfer progress.

7. Click Finish.

You may have to log off or restart your computer for the settings to take effect.

✔ Tip

■ Some settings may not carry over to the new computer. The wizard won't transfer old-computer settings for devices that are not available on, or incompatible with, Windows XP. On completion, the wizard lists files or folders that it couldn't restore. In particular, the wizard won't transfer third-party driver files for devices that aren't installed on the new computer and for network printers unavailable on the new computer.

TRANSFERRING EXISTING FILES AND SETTINGS

Uninstalling Windows XP

If you're unhappy with Windows XP, you can trash it and roll back to your previous version of Windows—providing that it was Windows 98 or Me. Some restrictions apply. If you're sure that you *never* want to roll back to Windows 98/Me, you can delete your old copy and reclaim the hundreds of megabytes that it occupies on your hard drive.

You *can't* roll back if you upgraded from Windows 2000 or NT, converted from FAT to NTFS after upgrading, or repartitioned your drive since upgrading.

To reinstate Windows 98/Me:

1. Choose Start > Control Panel > Add or Remove Programs > Change or Remove Programs.

2. In the Currently Installed Programs list, click Windows XP Uninstall.

3. Click the Change/Remove button; then click Yes to confirm the removal.

   Windows XP uninstalls itself. Your PC restarts with your old copy of Windows 98/Me.

To delete Windows 98/Me's files:

1. Choose Start > All Programs > Accessories > System Tools > Disk Cleanup.

2. If necessary, select the system drive; then click OK.

3. In the Files to Delete list, check Windows 98/Me Installation Files.

4. Click OK.

INDEX

INDEX

W

X-Z

WWW.PEACHPIT.COM

Quality How-to Computer Books

Visit Peachpit Press on the Web at www.peachpit.com

- Check out new feature articles each Monday: excerpts, interviews, tips, and plenty of how-tos

- Find any Peachpit book by title, series, author, or topic on the Books page

- See what our authors are up to on the News page: signings, chats, appearances, and more

- Meet the Peachpit staff and authors in the About section: bios, profiles, and candid shots

- Use Resources to reach our academic, sales, customer service, and tech support areas and find out how to become a Peachpit author

About

News

Books

Features

Resources

Order

Find

Welcome!

Peachpit.com is also the place to:

- Chat with our authors online
- Take advantage of special Web-only offers
- Get the latest info on new books